PHILOSOPHER

PHILOSOPHER

A kind of life

Ted Honderich

London and New York

First published 2001
by Routledge
11 New Fetter Lane, London EC4P 4EE

Simultaneously published in the USA and Canada
by Routledge
29 West 35th Street, New York, NY 10001

Routledge is an imprint of the Taylor & Francis Group

Typeset in Times by
Keystroke, Jacaranda Lodge, Wolverhampton
Printed and bound in Great Britain by
TJ International Ltd, Padstow, Cornwall

British Library Cataloguing in Publication Data
A catalogue record for this book is available from the British Library

Library of Congress Cataloging in Publication Data
Honderich, Ted.
    Philosopher : a kind of life / Ted Honderich.
        p.   cm.
    Includes bibliographical references and index.
    1. Honderich, Ted. 2. Philosophers—England.—Biography. I. Title.

    B1646.H764 A3 2000
    192—dc21
    [B]   00–042213

ISBN 0–415–23697–5

TO INGRID COGGIN PURKISS

CONTENTS

CONTENTS

PLATES

ix

Stuart Hampshire, sitting apart on another hill retir'd
Bernard Williams also later on, but still on the wing

Third section, between pages 260 and 261

4 Keats Grove, main house and entrance, with The Studio on the left
At home

Helen Marshall, proud Scot
Janet Radcliffe Richards, sceptical feminist

1986 television: Ronald Dworkin, Paul Sieghart, Neil MacCormick
   and me
Farewell to my college eyrie

Jane O'Grady, looking for quotations

Fourth section, between pages 352 and 353

Ingrid Coggin Purkiss, ideal partner, en route to Cintra
W. V. Quine, me, and Alastair Hannay, in Oslo, seeing things
On Hampstead Heath
Peter Strawson, don of dons

Jerry Cohen, pilgrim of political progress
Hidé Ishiguro, both imaginative and technical
Myles Burnyeat, giver of good name to ancient philosophy
Michael Dummett, superior philosopher and anti-racist

Derek Parfit, meticulous and friendly
Anthony Kenny, philosopher of powers
Another of photographer Pyke's subjects in 1990
David Wiggins, Incompatibilist

With Ingrid, on departure from Keats Grove for Iran and its dress code
   for women
Last lecture, Grote's room

1

THIS GREEN SUMMER

This is now a place where I am alone, a small room of recesses and bays, bright at the window. It is made calm by the green palisade of trees against the sky at the bottom of the gardens, a backdrop waiting for the rest of the play. The room is freshly painted in its old colours, two light and just different blues on the walls, the whiter one above the picture rail under the white ceiling. In the room there are now the things of only my own life, and only one kind of life. It is an orderly study again. A table in the window without clutter, a brass clock on it that gets attention. Watercolours and paintings, two of them large and emotional impressions of trees, framed by me. In place of women's radio programmes, there is quiet Bach and Mozart, or silence except for the birds. In a recess, a framed announcement recalling my inaugural lecture, 'The Mind, Neuroscience, and Life-Hopes', not certain to escape the eye of a visitor rightly seated.

Up the few steps from the study and along the hallway, past the undetaining watercolours, past the empty space from which the too detaining still-life departed with Jane, is the drawing room. I learned to call it by that name, a little resolutely. It is large enough to have held a few dozen friends and acquaintances who trooped in once more to the Christmas drinks, perhaps some of them a little resolutely too.

Through three good windows, their slender glazing bars as well preserved as those of the study, the drawing room also looks out to the palisade of trees. This room is still brighter than the study, being somewhat higher in the house. It has six sides, in two light and just different greens, the nearly white one above. Wainscot rail reinstated in very living memory. Older urns and swales in relief on the fireplace. Odd pillars of books on the tables and on the carpet, next to the wicker settee and chairs and the brown Victorian sofa. Flowers and candles, and some small brass vessels, nicely worked frowa caskets, brought back from visits as external examiner to the university in Ghana. Eleven small portraits in a line around the room, some of eighteenth-century gents in ruffs, several of Russian lads, the latter in memory of the Soviet Union I was too sensible or respectable or timid to support.

I see again that the room is a bit contrived, perhaps a bit comic. Even worse in the report of a guest of sceptical sensibility or with an eye for social aspiration? This does not much touch my simple pleasure in it. In particular, I do not follow persons of more rigorous taste who would exchange its decorous ease for, say, one of those white cells of the Palais Wittgenstein, those stern products of functional necessity and geometry, dutifully visited in Vienna the other week. The philosopher-architect, after arriving at the dimensions for his white shoeboxes, took more aesthetic thought only to conceal the central heating and to determine the right height for the door handles. They look pretty high to me.

The third of my more easeful rooms is through two facing doors from the drawing room. It too is in accord with the principle of decoration already noticed, owed to departed Janet: two just different yellows here. A good table and ten chairs. This dining room is heavy with more pictures, some above others, a motley but all in accord with another principle, my own. It is that the main value of art must surely have to do with its being *true of something*, and so it is better when we are not left wondering what that thing might be. Hence the reproduction of a portrait of Hume, patron saint of philosophers of my inclination, and also, Victorian or later, the still-lifes, studies of women and landscapes, etchings on wood of lion, tiger and fox, profile of the Spanish lieutenant and so on, and portrait of the host. There are French doors to a pretty balcony. Some later Juliet could lean against that white balustrade. An older and wiser one might be best.

What remains to be noted in Flat B, this first-floor setting of my life, is a bedroom. One large window of sixteen panes, looking into the boughs of a great tree at the front of the house. A smaller room, two pinks, more pictures. In a section of the bookcase are the books I have written. Those once brave hopes, still not extinguished. They are somewhat revived now by the growing company of their translations. There is space left for another two or three vols, including the one that will do the trick, at last guarantee me a future. I made the solid bed too. It is in a new position now, against a different wall. For a time I avert my eyes from it.

Out of the window and down below, in the garden between the house and the street, in the shadow of the chestnut boughs, connected to the house by stained-glass porch and perambulator store, is something else. It is *The Studio*, as it says on its door, and as it is named, its definite article intact, in five hundred letters about rent arrears and damp and keys. An artist's studio of good size, added to the property, like the porch and pram store, by some Victorian. Good-enough brickwork, chimney, slate roof, broad skylight over a good working space and two galleries. In it is an adversary, the socialist landlord's problem, the occupant who seized her moment and would succeed the tenant. Does my life have an adversary in it more often than others? Do I just make more of my ordinary allotment of adversaries than others do? Let me look away from that for a time too.

The narrow street takes its short way down from St John's Church at the top, cream and upstanding, to the shops and Hampstead Heath at the bottom. The street is still quiet enough, save for the morning cars. Its cited charm has not been too much touched by garden designers and by the determination of new residents to floodlight their Regency stucco, for purposes of night security as they say. Once Albion Grove, it now has a name not writ in water, Keats's. In it, when it was a village path, he wrote and lived a part of his brief life, the best part and some of the rest. The nightingale in the garden, other odes, beauty and truth, love of Fanny, the drop of blood on the pillow, and the parting. I pedal past his house each morning to the other place of my life. Down the hill through Belsize Park, Chalk Farm, Primrose Hill, Camden Town and Euston, to Bloomsbury and my other room.

It too can seem closer to being my life than just a setting of it, closer to being the stuff of my life than just a principal location of it. Can there be some sense in this, some plain truth? Some actual philosophy, some English philosophy, not only fancy or feeling or French performance?

The room is one of pride and success, history, work, many lectures and papers, fewer pleasures, argument in good temper and bad, strategies and alliances, beginnings and endings of careers, hurt and sad drama. The main hurt and sad drama was also a stabbing, some say. It is of a size owed to the good opinion that was had, by himself and others, of an earlier and larger Grote Professor of the Philosophy of Mind and Logic at University College London. A. J. Ayer, Professor Sir Alfred, Freddie, known to me in all those roles, all attacked with practised panache. In the first, he wrote the book *Language, Truth and Logic*. It inspired my retorts to teachers of my late boyhood who tried to lead me into deep thinking. Along with the decency of the Welfare State, which lingers on far less well, and placenames, and the lure of a past, and not much susceptibility to the American way of life, the book brought me to England.

University College London, as resistant to the inclusion of a comma in its name as The Studio is to the loss of its definite article, stands as firmly and as godlessly in Gower Street as it did in 1828, when it first set out to awaken Oxford and Cambridge from their dogmatic slumbers. It was the original University of London. Its Corinthian portico and measured dome, partly paid for by the worthy Grote, welcomed atheists, Dissenters, Catholics, Utilitarians, Jews, women, and other lower orders. It was a breath of fresh air. It still is, despite being effectively a university itself, with some thousands of students and with a good sense of its achievements and of the worth of respectability. Such a breath was Jeremy Bentham himself, its presiding spirit and household god. The great Utilitarian also had self-regard, presumably even more than Freddie. His auto-icon, which is to say his mummified skeleton, remains with us in a college cloister, according to his instructions. The beadles unlock his box to tourists with moderate gravity.

My room is away from the portico and dome, on the other side of the college, in Gordon Square, where blue plaques recall the Bloomsbury past. In particular those Stracheys, Bells, Carringtons, Morrells and Woolfs, not quite immortal, officially committed to the pleasures of human intercourse and the enjoyment of beautiful objects. The room is large, L-shaped and suited to a worthy Victorian. It is all of the first floor of the house of the philosophers of the college, my colleagues, the Department of Philosophy. Six floors of Lecturers, Senior Lecturers and Readers, working their way down from the attic or up from the basement by patience and publications.

In the settled scheme of things, the room is both the Grote's own study and teaching room and also a place for other lectures, seminars and meetings. Thus it welcomes visiting philosophers, up from Oxford to do a turn on this metropolitan stage, or in from Berkeley to bring confident news of California and the future. The ring of soft armchairs and sofa, now green, has behind it rows of upright and serviceable chairs, 45 of them. Undergraduates or postgraduates hear about and may find themselves in only the company of only a philosophical subject-matter. Time and space, causation, possible worlds, the Redundancy Theory of Truth, modal logic, mind and brain, or Functionalism. Scepticism, Moral Realism, the values of art, the rationality of the free market, what it is like to be a bat, or, once in a long while, the proprietary doctrines of Aristotle, Kant and other greats of the past. No longer, I am pleased to say, Freud's theory of sexuality, which, after an extended appearance, slipped off the curriculum.

The rest of life just comes to a stop for a while as various propositions are laid out and turned over by me or by the visitors, or by my departmental colleagues when they book my room in the hope that their own smaller rooms will be insufficient for their audience. But the room has long had another part to play in our lives as well. Here we have had our departmental meetings. Occasions for the sharing out of labours, the gathering of opinions on undergraduates, and the massed interviewing of candidates for lectureships. Who is to join us and who not? *Very* serious matter. Here too the Headship of the department has been our unofficial or official subject. That was the hurt and the sad drama, maybe a stabbing.

In a distant corner, a personal computer and a steamer trunk. The computer delivers my thoughts of yesterday back to me for further revision, and also the e-mail, often from my daughter in Princeton. My son, not having an ocean between us, preserves his independence more sternly. The steamer trunk has past in it. A thousand dated notes, many of self-mortification or self-justification, an official complaint or two of injustice, histories of academic struggles and transactions, and also very many letters, some of them sweet letters of love, desire and marriage. Safer here than in Hampstead. A small archive of the struggle.

I admit to the usual amount of interest in myself and my thinking, but am reassured that this self-interest may issue in something more general. My aim, of course, is not another autobiography. Who in my authorial situation does not promise more? The first of my two aims is to open up *a kind of life*. It is to make plain *a kind* of life by a good means, quite possibly the very best means. That is getting into view and telling the truth about a suitable instance or example of the thing. My life, although notable in parts, is not much more than middle-sized. I do not have the satisfaction and misfortune of being a real individual, so impressively and uselessly different that to learn of me is to learn only of me.

The kind of life in question is that of a working, academic or university philosopher. Not real life, they say. Still, carried on quite as fully elsewhere as in studies, lecture rooms, common rooms and committee rooms. We do not leave our natures behind in leaving our places of work.

Of course this example of the full-time professional philosopher will be different from other examples of the kind, even greatly different, perhaps to their relief. But will it not be more enlightening as to the kind, nevertheless, than any general distillation, composite, constructed average member, survey, or group photo? Particularly if I really make use of my unique knowledge of the example from the inside, really try to tell the truth? Rousseau left a lot out in his confessions, and not just the bit about baring his bum in the street in the hope of a spanking. May I, in this more confessional age, be different from him not only in being middle-sized but by leaving less out?

My second aim is explanation. How do I and my kind get to places like this? What explains the rest of what else needs saying of me in this green summer – about my philosophical commitments and tendencies, my daily round, and my inner life? They say philosophy doesn't come from nowhere, summoned into being by pure reason and reading good books. Also, why did those non-philosophical things in the recent past happen as they did? Could it be that the philosophy and the habits in it explain more of the rest of my life than the rest of life explains them? Out of what prehistory did the philosophy and its habits and the rest of life come? But perhaps this aim of explanation is too brave – even before it turns to trying to explain itself.

I see from the philosophical quotations book of Jane and Freddie that it was Kierkegaard, gloomy sod that he was, who said that life must be understood backwards, but has to be lived forwards, and so it can never be understood at all. No moment can have the complete stillness needed for a real view backwards. Is it true? Or, before we get to that, there is that old reflex question. What does it actually mean that might be true? And if we have to be content with an answer about the *reach* of explanation, the extent to which a life and a kind of life can be explained, that in itself will be to find out something.

The philosophical furniture of my mind consists in fewer pieces than are in my rooms, heavier ones. Whatever their history, and whether they stand to love, beds, rent and adversaries as effects or causes or neither, they do not seem external to me, but internal. They are not goods for sale, for example, or means of getting on in the world, helpful though they have been. Do these pieces hang together themselves? They are certainly no three-piece suite. I have had a thought or two of adding and rearranging things, if not of getting rid of any. Well, maybe even getting rid of something.

One large item of my inner furniture is determinism, or rather one kind of thing that goes under that heavy name. I expound it to the first-year undergraduates who drift into my college room for their General Introduction to Philosophy, Mondays at 11, the more incredulous taking themselves to deserve the soft armchairs. We use the heavy name 'determinism' in a certain way, for theories that say nothing about freedom or responsibility or hopes, but leave all that to later.

What the theories do say, very roughly, is that each of the actions in our lives and also the choosing and willing of it is an *effect*. It is the effect of a sequence of events or states or properties, each of these also being an effect. The sequence starts further back than any first thought or feeling about the action, let alone the choosing or willing of it. Indeed the sequence goes back to events that are not thoughts or feelings at all. Each effect is what it sounds like, something that had to happen. There was no other possibility. It wasn't just probable, to any degree. If a story of this kind is clear enough to be true or false, and if it is true, then there is a sense in which everything is fixed or settled in advance, all choices and decisions and all actions, and thus a sense in which everything could have been predicted. All of it, if you subtract the mythology from the word, was fated.

I am the somewhat reluctant owner of such a theory, a philosophy of mind in itself, worked out in more detail than some of my fellow workers have valued. 644 pages of detail. Some people say it is clear enough, and many say that any such thing is false – falsified by the physics of Einstein *et al*. They say Quantum Theory settles the matter. Determinism is now history, quite a good piece of history since it has Spinoza, Hume, Newton and indeed Einstein himself and most of science in it, but still history. The fact of the matter is that we now know there are things that happen that are not effects. Ask any physicist.

This has been hard for me to believe, partly because the interpretation of Quantum Theory, the understanding of what it comes to in terms of the world, is allowed by most of its users to be a mess. Certainly it *is* a mess, and has remained so for too long. Sometimes verbiage and enthusiasm conceals this, but not very much. What is the mathematics or formalism of the theory *about*? Certainly not particles or waves of matter in any ordinary or plain senses of the words, as is readily admitted, even celebrated. The fundamental question of what the theory is about goes without a decent answer. So another question arises. Are the things in the theory that are said not to be effects in fact things which we determinists say *are* effects? We only say events are effects. There are certainly things that are irrelevant to determinism, these being non-events in general, starting with numbers, propositions and locations. We don't say 7 is an effect.

There is also some other trouble for the disprovers of determinism. Suppose, despite my sensible doubt, that we take up the common interpretation of Quantum Theory. Suppose there really are real events that are uncaused or random, truly unpredictable events, down where they are supposed to be, at the physicist's micro-level of reality. They are so small as to be way below the level of ordinary things and events, including the electrochemical events in a brain that seem to go with choices and decisions. There is a troublesome question.

Do any random events at the micro-level translate upwards into events at the level with which determinism is concerned, the level of the brain events, choices, actions and so on? It is good sense to doubt it, for an excellent reason. It is that we encounter no random events at all in the world we experience. No planet leaves its orbit without explanation. No bicycle tyre goes flat for no reason. No spoon ever levitates at breakfast.

But then it seems that determinism may be unaffected by Quantum Theory even if the theory is interpreted in the common way. The small events of Quantum Theory are irrelevant.

Still, I am somewhat happier in having a view about something separate from the determinism problem. This is the problem of the consequences of determinism. If determinism is clear enough and true, what follows from it? What is its consequence or import for our lives? In my view not the heavy proposition that we are unfree. A regiment of philosophers has said that – or rather that if determinism were true, which it isn't, we would be unfree. They have thought so on account of being convinced that freedom by definition consists in Free Will, daily miracles of true origination, mental events somehow under our control but uncaused. The regiment is wrong.

But it doesn't seem to me either that if determinism is true, we nevertheless can still be fully free – because determinism and freedom are wholly compatible propositions. Another regiment of philosophers has cheerily said that, being convinced that freedom consists just in being able to do what you want, which you can be even if everything is caused. It is a touch discomfiting that the blessed Hume is among them.

My own view is at least new. Professor Daniel Dennett of Tufts University, agreeably doughty though he is, did not endear himself to me when he let the readers of his review in *The Times Literary Supplement* suppose he had thought of it too. It is in part that freedom is not so simple as either regiment supposes, a matter of a right definition, but is about attitudes and feelings. If determinism is true, we lose some of what we want, but not everything. This, as you will hear later, is where the real problem of determinism starts. It is coming to terms with things, making the right response. Affirmation of a kind.

My second piece of philosophical furniture is a conviction about minds, which is to say mainly about consciousness. The two problems here are the nature of consciousness itself and the relation of this consciousness to the brain. My conviction is that conscious events, states or properties involve what it is easier to name than analyse, a fundamental *subjectivity*. That is their essential nature. They are not anything less. This conviction about subjectivity, much more so than determinism, has a fortifying history. It also has a majority of sympathizers among contemporary philosophers generally – albeit that some have been frightened into hiding by the brash public relations and clutter of technicalities on the other side.

The ideas on that other side derive partly from two things I share. One of these is a kind of naturalism. It is the outlook that the natural world, in some sense the physical world, is all that there is. Hence all there is can be studied by unmysterious methods, the main ones being science, cool philosophy, good sense, and an empirical kind of literature and art. The mind, then, whatever it is, must be natural or physical and open to such study. The second and more particular thing I share is our new realization of the closeness of mind and brain, of conscious and neural events. A demonstrated fact of psychoneural intimacy, as I was pleased to name it, is the gift of neuroscience to philosophy. A better gift, as it seems to me, than anything from muddled physics.

From such sources has come the brash idea, of no great history, that the mind is the brain, that they are one thing – where this ambiguity is not taken to mean something innocuous, but that the mind has only the properties of the brain. Or rather, that our human minds have only the properties of our brains, which is to say electrochemical properties. Putting aside computers and other unlikely possessors of consciousness, consciousness is cells, those particular cells that are neurons. This idea gives a solution to the problem of the nature of consciousness that is also a quick solution of the problem of the mind–brain relation. The idea is in accord with naturalism all right. And it could not be more in accord with the fact of psychoneural intimacy. Nothing could make mind and brain more intimate than this particular way of making them identical. It is also an idea for those who are too averse to mystery, too frightened of it, too hooked on the sweet drug of simple clarity.

This identity idea takes a number of forms. The simplest version is indeed that consciousness is cells – Eliminative Materialism. Except in Australia and Southern California, those places of strong sunlight where powers of belief are evidently greater, the pill is always sweetened. One sweetener is that despite what has just been reported, that our conscious events are just brain events, what they really are in their essences is something else. They are functional events, so-called. They are events that function in a certain way. That is to say nothing mysterious, indeed nothing more than that they are certain causes and certain effects. They come from input and they issue in output. This thought could have begun in, but gets out of sight of, certain truisms. One is that a good definition of a particular desire will include, but of course not only include, something about a thing perceived, say a glass of wine, and some resulting behaviour, say an arm-movement – input and output. The thought also owes a lot to computers, those mesmerizing converters of input into output.

This imperfectly consistent story of the mind, then, is that the essential nature of our conscious events is not that they are just neural or material, although they are, but that they are things in the right causal relations. This is Functionalism boiled down or rather decluttered, which it cries out to be. Or, as you can also say, computerized philosophy of mind or cognitive science with philosophical ambition. As it has seemed to me, the coating doesn't make the pill swallowable. I think of what I had a moment ago, an uneasy feeling about my past. The idea that it had only neural properties isn't made better by the addition that it had causes and effects, and these were of the essence. There was a lot more essence to the feeling, which was its fundamental subjectivity. That is something easy to say, but a lot harder to say something clear about.

To admit the great difficulty is not to give up the truth that consciousness is other than neural properties in bare causal relations. As surely all must know? Nor is it to give up the conviction that conscious events are in intimate relation with neural events. Psychoneural intimacy. My own ultimate working out of that is that they are in a kind of union, as a matter of necessity or law. Or, rather, two different kinds of properties of ourselves go together in this way. And I haven't given up naturalism. Conscious properties in their real subjectivity must also *somehow* be physical properties, despite not being neural ones. What else could they be? There aren't ghosts, and there aren't ghostly properties in the head either.

My daily round starts early. It begins almost every morning at five or six, not by alarm clock but by a habit of awakening and a little determination. There is always something in particular to be done. But the determination is also a general one, to make use of my time. I have sometimes half-wondered if it is owed to what also happens at some stage almost every day, including almost every cheerful day. That is the thought that my time will come to an end.

On reflection, though, my onward marching could be a lot more fundamental to my life than my anticipation of its dark end. It may well be that my active determination in the early morning and in the rest of my life is not owed to the thought of death at all. Isn't it relevant that this determination is often happy, or anyway contented enough? It may not have roots in any thought at all, but be in a way primitive. And it may do some explaining itself, be more of a cause than an effect. Maybe a cause of my thinking about death?

At five or six, after coffee and the first dose of nicotine from the chewing gum I should have given up some years back, what happens has very much to do with what happened the evening before. If resolution did not fail and thus I did not exceed my daily ration of three quarters of a bottle of white wine, the early morning passes in happy work. The rest of life can just stop for philosophy. Philosophy can be time out, time away from the rest of life that is happening, and seemingly unconnected with it. This morning was that way. With a bit of luck, I will satisfy the anonymous cavillers who advise the editor of *The American Philosophical Quarterly* what articles to admit to its pages. With a bit of luck they will take 'Consciousness, Neural Functionalism, Real Subjectivity' as fit to print. *I* thought on looking it over that it was better than that, say measured but magnificent. It is a feeling I and my kind have had before.

Writing on these summer days of good hope, now that the college teaching terms are over for the year and the students are gone, can go on to lunchtime. Writing makes my life better. What a blessing to have a life in which the necessary work is engrossing. Piling up truths in solitude, or anyway goodish guesses, or at least things not obviously false. Doing the thing, making a future, rising over the past, escaping the problem of The Studio, getting my due. Nicotine is good, but work is wonderful.

I have read hardly a word of Marx, having shared the orthodox condescension of my analytical colleagues for his lumbering metaphysics of history. All that stuff about the dominion of matter over spirit through the several historical eras, got by reversing the unspeakable Hegel. Not to mention the economics. But lately a core of moral perception and feeling in Marx, owing nothing to Hegel, has seemed so

12

true. I have been tempted towards his sinking ship, now abandoned not only by the rats but also by the theoreticians who used to be on the bridge. All market-Marxists now. One part of the moral core of Marx has to do with work. It is his proper accusation against the arrangers of bad lives for others, bad because these others are estranged from their work.

Lunch at University College comes in several varieties and places. All the world's in the Lower Refectory, all colours feeding at close quarters on fish and cannelloni. The Senior Common Room, with good pictures from our Slade School of Fine Art, brings together my college colleagues with an inclination to the genteel, or a desire to get away from students. Or an ongoing interest in the college committees and an ear for the Provost's new thinking on top-up fees, senior promotions, the decline of the library, and the outrageous idea of selling Bentham's manuscripts in order to finance the project of editing them. I had an interest in the committees for a while. This college is no cut-throat place, but it is a good idea for a Head of Department to keep in touch. Once an insane Bursar had a look over the Grote's room, and ventured thoughts about the fuller utilization of space by partitioning, so to have two or three philosophers thinking where one thought before.

My lunch, whether in Lower Refectory or Senior Common Room, is usually solitary, partly because we philosophers of University College do not usually congregate. Maybe we are less in need of reassuring company than the physicists stuck with their Quantum Theory. There are other reasons for my solitude. One is shyness. I have had practice in breaking out of it, often into badinage and knock-about, but practice hasn't made perfect.

My daily round in the college teaching terms, most of the year, cannot be just the writing. Monday has an hour given over to devising a decent sequence of propositions for the lecture at 11, the week's instalment of the General Introduction to Philosophy for undergraduates just come up from their schools. The lecture is not new-minted, not thought up just before or in the hour. Why quarrel with success, even moderate success? The subjects are mainly my main interests of the past, determinism and the mind and so on. They are new to my listeners, even provocations to them. I do not have to try hard to get audience-participation, to prompt the philosophizing from the soft armchairs.

My two other regular classes of the week are postgraduate seminars, also in my room. When I became Grote Professor, the Senior Seminar at 5 on Mondays was the focus of my teaching ambitions. I remembered it from my own postgraduate years, as Freddie used to give it, a weekly colosseum in which mortal challenge was offered. The Thesis Seminar, at 5 on Thursdays, is for postgraduates not only from University College but also from those other colleges of the University of London in which philosophy flourishes. The seminar is conducted by me and another professor or two, our dignity not wholly concealed by our *bonhomie*. They come from King's College down in the Strand, founded as a reproach to the godless college in Gower Street, where the philosophy of religion has since succumbed to the logical paradoxes and the philosophy of psychology, or from the London School of Economics, whose philosophers breathe easier now that they have escaped the long shadow of Karl Popper.

He who had no doubt that he had solved the problem of induction and discovered the nature of science, and appointed lecturers inclined to propagate these two truths, the first being, if you will let me speak with my customary force of conviction, such that nothing is falser. The problem of induction, you can say, is the problem of explaining how a limited amount of evidence somehow does give rational support to the unlimited conclusion that all ordinary hen's eggs break when hit by heavy hammers, without the evidence logically entailing the conclusion. Plainly there isn't such an entailment between the two things as between 'Kant was a bachelor' and 'Kant was unmarried' or '2+2 =' and '4'. The problem is not solved by some bumble including the idea that we do not really *believe* the unlimited conclusion. Half-believing it, saying it's tentatively corroborated, conjecturing it, even just guessing it's true, which science is supposed to do, is enough to make for the very same problem.

The Thesis Seminar is for a postgraduate's reading out of a part of his or her thesis, or, more often, work in the direction of a thesis. My professorial colleagues and I do not join battle among ourselves in the discussion, in order to preserve decorum and out of an apprehensive sense that knowledge is diversely distributed among us. I have no love for Formal Logic, and enjoy the certainty that it has not solved or advanced any philosophical problem, and so I have not learned a lot. I am not always restrained by my ignorance, but mostly take care to sit back when others depend on their knowledge. Students discover that a thesis chapter is not impregnable, and provide me with materials, noted down, for the letters of reference to be written to try to get them jobs. In these I am generous, rather than given to severe standards of assessment.

That is the story too at those annual gatherings of the philosophers of the University of London, the meetings to settle the classes of B.A. degrees to be awarded to undergraduates. There was one the other day. I argue that our massed judgement is not so acute that it is clear that this borderline candidate or that can confidently be sent down into the Upper Seconds or the Lower Seconds or the Thirds. The fact of the matter, not congenial to me in every way, is that I identify with those being judged. Certainly I am known for my want of academic principle, as others are known for the opposite. It is my university colleagues whose politics are Rightward who consistently are able to discern muddle and failure. I speculate that they themselves were disappointed in their examinations, and do not want too many Firsts around, but I do not check up.

To the Monday lecture and the two seminars are added other teaching duties more time-consuming but as tolerable. Unlike my philosophical colleagues at University College, and not in perfect accord with each of their senses of justice, I as Grote escape the weekly grind of giving undergraduate tutorials, on subjects fixed by curriculum. That is the repetitive labour, rightly named the tutorial load, which is also familiar to the Fellows of colleges in Oxford, and leads them to say in passing, but more than once, that they might think about moving to a London chair. On the evidence of recent migrations, they must also have thought, in passing, of Chapel Hill in North Carolina, Geneva, and Pittsburgh.

In place of undergraduate tutorials, I give postgraduate supervisions. These higher things have their name because, officially, they are more a matter of talking about and advising on work being carried forward independently. They are fortnightly meetings with my own students, aspiring to the M.A., the M.Phil. or the Ph.D. They are encouraged to come with some philosophy got down on paper, since it seems to me that one learns most by the discipline of writing. Sections of thesis are better than thoughts on the wing. Not all graduate students have been well prepared for our local ways by their undergraduate years in Athens, Toronto, or literary Cambridge. I work hard with them, but better on some days than others. I am compensated by being instructed, the receiver of goods rather than the imparter, by others of my fortnightly visitors, those who have done more reading than me. On the whole they are amiable about this reversal of roles. For my part, I own up easily. I am not so open or so perfectly composed when they are cleverer than I.

We all get on pretty well, or all of us who have a proper sense of our intellectual line of life. That is required for good temper. Philosophy is not any of linguistics, psychology, cognitive science or any other science. To its credit or discredit, there is hardly any Philosophy of Life in it, not much on the meaning of life, hardly any consolation. It is not the history of ideas, morality, religion, politics or political theory. It is not wisdom, the deep, classical scholarship, dead languages, literature, literary theory or feminism. If it is not logic in any narrow sense, certainly not formal logic, you can't read the stuff like a novel, drift through it. You have to think on the way.

As for ongoing philosophy's relation to its own past, to the history of philosophy well and charmingly laid out in the best-seller *Sophie's World*, that is complicated. There is complication, anyway, with respect to ongoing philosophy in the English language. It does not quite slough off its past as science does, become new in more than its skin. But, except in the piety of historically minded practitioners and of classicists, our ongoing philosophy does not take its past to be a proper part of itself either. The philosophical past, for almost all of us, is a source of strong expressions of inevitable and inevitably contested views that interest us. That in seeing a cup or any other perceiving, each of us is aware of only private data, not a public thing, or that society somehow rests on a contract that saves us from a state of nature, and so on. For most philosophers, these strong expressions of views are in fact teaching aids. The philosophers of the past are rarely discussed for themselves in the foremost journals.

My students and I do not reflect a lot on this or on what our line of life actually is. Rather, having seemed to wake up in it, we get on with it. It is, some others say, the line of life owed to a certain impulse. That is the impulse to reduce to clarity and thereby get a systematic and comprehensive hold on the nature of one or two of the fundamental parts of reality, including human reality. The various fundamental parts, of which you have already heard something, include physical objects, effects, time, propositions, minds, the sources of action, sense perception, reasoning, responsibility, justice, and art. Such parts, some say, come together into three broad categories, having to do with what things exist, knowing about them, and what things are good. It is added that given this impulse of philosophy, getting a clarified hold on a fundamental part or two of reality, it must necessarily ask general questions. There is no alternative to this if you are to be true to the impulse. Nothing large comes into focus close up.

But pause a bit. All of that raises a question or two. It seems to make philosophy in its first broad category of concerns, about what exists, more or less indistinguishable from science generally. And does not the second category, about the acquisition of knowledge, make philosophy at least something like part of psychology and a good deal else in mathematics and science? And the third, about value, much the same as morality, religion, and politics? It would be too arrogant to suppose that these various disciplines do not aspire to systematic and comprehensive holds on their subject-matters, and it would be mistaken to suppose they do not ask general questions in addition to particular ones. In any case, there is no want of particularity in philosophy, for all its generality. You can't see the wood for the trees in a lot of philosophy, some of it about determinism and subjectivity.

I suspect the truth is that our line of life is different in that it concentrates more on something. It concentrates more on good thinking about the facts as against getting or using the facts, and good thinking about methods of knowing as against getting or using the methods, and good thinking about convictions as to what is good rather than embracing them. Good thinking in getting a clear hold. That is the real impulse in philosophy. As I say, you can wake up in it one day.

To put the main point again, as the diligent lecturer will, there is a kind of division of labour between philosophy and its rivals. Philosophy's initial and its subsequent questions are peculiarly well-formed, only formed after presuppositions have been examined, and its answers aspire more to clarity, completeness, and above all consistency and other logical relations. In a very general sense of the word, *logic* is the core of it. Philosophy in comparison with morality, religion and politics is more committed to independence from desire and hope. Philosophy in comparison with science certainly does less grubbing of particular facts, but that is far from saying that it is unempirical if that means it rides over facts or is not about the world. It doesn't always ride over subjectivity.

These generalities may make you forgetful of something already implied in passing. Hardly any philosopher has as his line of life a concern with all of present philosophy, or even just one of the three broad categories, let alone this and all of its past. We're not in Sophie's world. The panoramic historians among working philosophers are odd exceptions, maybe even suspect. Are they bunking off? What we try to do in our kind of life is the good thinking about just one or two or a few of the fundamental parts of reality. The strength of our ambition restricts our fields of operation.

Seminar over or postgraduate despatched, I cycle off from Gordon Square, usually up the hill to Hampstead for the television news at 7 in the study and my daily wine. So begins, often enough, a solitary evening. That is now the story two or three evenings out of seven in this summer. If I am inclined to reduce the number to zero, and will do so if I run true to past form, this solitude is no pain to me, but near enough a pleasure. Company and talk, save for the intimate kind which seems nearly half of life itself, has always had two sides for me. One is everything good about it. The other is the obligation to perform, at least to measure up.

I try to keep the goods in mind. The happy flare of talk or the rollick, amiability or instruction of it. Also the consolation of it and the credit of being trusted. In anticipation of one or another of these, I am diligent about arranging dinners. Down the street to South End Green and the Tandoori Paradise with someone of my present or past. Almost always with a woman, sometimes Pauline, the mother of my children. The Tandoori Paradise is half-price, since it faces hard competition, and they treat me well there. I do not mind saving a pound or two, whatever the real need.

On other evenings I go elsewhere. To parties of friends and acquaintances, once recently to Cheyne Walk where Ken Follett of the novels flourishes, as sagely cocky now as in those past tutorials in the attic at 19 Gordon Square. Or I take myself to the Garrick Club, from which fortuitously I did not resign the other year when the membership rose up to deny the passage of time and affirm that women will still not be admitted to membership. The club was founded to be a resort of actors and writers, and remains something of that, despite the influx of judges and politicians and titled persons looking for better company.

The membership committee at the Garrick does not look so kindly on applicants as I look on candidates for the B.A. Why, if I am a member at all, am I not sharp and superior with the reactionary and misogynist novelist or the pushy peer? Instead I try to hold up my end companionably and amiably. In fact I have not looked too closely into the question of whether being in this exclusive and self-approving crew is consistent with my principles. I do remember a line from my undergraduate days. It was that the argument for revolution is in part not the superiority of common culture, the moral grandeur of the working class, but the awfulness of that culture and class. True or false, I would not deliver the line now.

On yet other evenings, a few, I give a dinner in Hampstead. A little Boswell-like, and hardened against the charge of snob, I have in admiration sought out several who come. One is Michael Foot from up the hill. He knows how to sing for his supper. Would that the working class had risen over its unspeakable newspapers and elected him Prime Minister. Our local beggar Alan Cook might not be on the bench outside the church, but have a job, and our library might be open oftener. My dinners in Keats Grove are not short on drink, and those who come are organized into general conversation. I am in practice from the seminars, and, comic or not, do not plan to give up. I would do otherwise to suit my son if he would come, but usually he won't.

Some of that brings to mind a third philosophical conviction of mine, the Principle of Equality. It is not one of your lawyer's or sensible philosopher's or closet Conservative's principles of justice. It is not hung with weights of respect for the world as it is. It is not a petty principle of no more than equal respect for persons, which comes to nothing much until turned into something else. Nor is it the famous principle about the distribution of primary goods owed to the goodly if doctrinally-burdened liberal of Harvard, Professor Rawls, a principle whose upshot is uncertain, and leaves politicians of any party able to add it to their talk.

The Principle of Equality, in brief, is that we should not be distracted or detained in any way from trying to make well-off in a certain sense all those who are badly-off. That is the solution to the problem of justice.

This third philosophical conviction of mine is also a moral conviction, and so cannot have the kind of support of the first two, about determinism and subjectivity – the support of fact. Perhaps that is why I have held on to it tenaciously. It has needed allies. It would be fine, of course, to be able to agree with a handful of philosophers who have lately become bored with the orthodoxy about the nature of moral judgements – that all moral convictions are personal feelings. They have revived the earlier piety that moral convictions can be *true*. True, they say, in roughly the same way that it is now true that the trees I am looking at are green. We human perceivers contribute something in both cases, by way of our particular perceptual or other personal equipment, but value is as much a fact of the world as colour. They call this Moral Realism. How estimable and how merely audacious the idea is. Too good to be true. So much stands in its way, beginning with the intractable fact that we agree about what is green but not about what is right.

The Principle of Equality, when spelled out, stipulates what it is to be well-off or badly-off – in terms of the satisfaction or frustration of fundamental human desires. These six desires are for a decent length of life, material goods that give a quality to life, freedom and power, respect and self-respect, closer and wider relationships with others, and the goods of culture. The ways in which we are not to be distracted or detained from making people well-off are many. We are not to be unnecessarily concerned with incentive-rewards for those who contribute something to economic progress. We are not to be unnecessarily concerned either with improving the lot of those who are already well-off, or with any of deserts, special liberties, rights and privileges, duties to be done despite bad consequences, truth to oneself, or ties of loyalty and blood.

You will notice, close reader, that according to the principle there is to be no *unnecessary* concern with those things, which is not to say no concern at all. You may suspect, suspicious reader, that the principle is really not so brave. Not so brave in intent as that deceptive but in fact pregnant sentence of the English Revolution uttered by Col. Rainborowe in the Army Debates at Putney. 'The poorest he that is in England hath a life to live as the greatest he.' Well, it is certainly true that the principle is not out of sight of all other morality. It does not require overturning the world to the extent that might be supposed. There is the point too that it has not yet reduced me myself to penury, that I remain in the class not of champagne socialists but certainly prosecco.

On the braveness of the principle, one thing to be said is that it would be irrational not to adopt the various means to its end when they are really necessary, including the means of certain incentive-rewards and the resulting inequality. But note also that these will be means to *its* end, the reduction of the number of the badly-off, rather than the end of some self-serving economic progress, say an increase in total economic goods in a society. Further, and very importantly, the principle is to be so understood as enjoining us to work at reducing the incentive-demands of contributors to the goal. I have not been so alarmed as the amiable Lord Quinton, reviewer of a book of mine in *The Times*, by the idea of the need for re-education of the profiting classes.

With respect to the prosecco socialism, I do confess that in the disposition of my salary, I have not been very true to the Principle of Equality. What follows about me from this failure? Quite a lot. I may turn out to have no justification for myself, but only a thing or two to say in mitigation. Is it not better to be a self-preserving or even self-advertising advocate of a human principle than a more consistent advocate of an inhuman one? Something else is more important. What follows about the worth of the principle from my failure to act on it as I ought? Not much, as it still seems to me easy to say. Is a principle put into question by a failure to live up to it? This would be embarrassing not for one morality, but for many, maybe for all things that can claim the name of moralities. 'Do as I say, not as I have done', whatever it tells you of the sayer, may be exactly the right instruction.

Another conviction in this particular philosopher's bundle, a fifth if you do not count the one against Moral Realism, is about the problem of political means-to-ends and in particular political violence. It is that there is something rightly called democratic violence, something that has enough of the recommendation of democracy itself to deserve the name. Does it have a moral justification? Well, certainly no more automatically than the result of a democratic election is automatically right. But let me put aside for a while this item and some others related to it. They need slower handling.

21

Another conviction has not been put on paper before now, and is less worked out. It is yet more relevant to what follows in this book. The question of personal identity as philosophers ordinarily understand it is the question of what makes a person at a later time numerically identical with a person at an earlier time. What makes you today one and the same person as some boy or girl of the past? One bad answer now put aside by philosophers is an enduring inner self of an extraordinary kind, a voyaging thing in a person, different from both a flow of experiences and the continuation of a body. One better answer *is* that the later and earlier persons involve one body, one continuing organism. Another better answer, in essence, is that you today remember experiences of the boy or girl. My own philosophical conviction is not that one of those two better answers is right. It is that we are missing what is most important in this neighbourhood if we ask the ordinary question of what makes a later person identical with an earlier.

What do we have personal and moral attitudes to? In the ordinary course of life, what is it that we admire or hold responsible when we admire a woman or hold her responsible for something? The answer appears to be *the person she is*. That is not something which is the same as or includes the girl she was. We admire or morally disapprove of something to which certain facts are integral, say style or intolerance, which facts may have been no part of the girl she was. To express the point in a philosopher's way, our fundamental attitudes to others are to person-stages. Our attitudes are to a stage in the existence of a person, this being importantly a matter of two connected things, dispositions and conduct. We may also have lesser and more passive attitudes to a past person-stage, of course, a person someone was.

The thought has to do not only with our attitudes to others, but with our attitudes to ourselves. I, in being concerned with myself, am concerned with a person-stage, the person I am or a person I was. Suppose the two are different, and in particular that I have become more honourable. There is a sense, obviously, in which I cannot hold myself responsible for the dishonourable past or be shamed by it. The person I am is not dishonourable. Certainly we sometimes feel this way about other people. To be *convinced* that a man is reformed, which is not easy, is necessarily not to hold responsible the person he is for what happened in the past.

This thought in the direction of exculpation is not the only thought there is in this neighbourhood. If it were, then if I really did know I was reformed, everything would be rosy. I could contemplate my past not only in a passive but in a detached or dispassionate way. But could I? That is another thought. Even if I knew I was reformed, surely I might remain troubled or even tormented about my past. How can this be? If I were to believe in an inner self sailing through all my person-stages, that would seem like the beginning of an explanation. But I don't believe in an inner self. Thus my fifth philosophical conviction, to describe it again, is that the crucial questions of personal identity do not have to do with identity over time but with the persons we are, the persons we have been, and the connections between them.

This survey of my convictions might now turn in the direction of the question of the nature of truth. It seems to me a real question. It did not go up in smoke when the Cambridge philosopher Ramsey noticed in the 1920s that 'It's true that it's raining' seems to come to no more than 'It's raining', and thereby had the idea that philosophical talk of truth is redundant. Despite rediscovery of Ramsey's discovery by my new and esteemed colleague Professor Horwich, there *is* a question of the nature of truth, of the general condition under which a factual statement is true, and the answer, somehow or other, still seems to be some kind of correspondence to things in the world. Or the survey might turn to the problem of the nature of sense perception – seeing and the like, mentioned in passing some way back. Here there is now more allegiance to the reassuring proposition that the objects of our experience, the things each of us is aware of, are not private to the person in question and fleeting, but public and more or less enduring. Not sense-data of trees, but trees.

Or we might turn to the analysis of desert, or of what it is to argue that a man deserves punishment in particular. Take the second. My persistent proposal has been that it is really to argue that punishing him will give satisfaction to people, satisfaction in exactly the distress or suffering of others. That is what talk of desert comes to with the institution of punishment. Many have disagreed. They think better of it, and of us. They want more moral tone in their solution to the problem of the justification of punishment.

Or, something might be said of the nature of time. Does it amount only to relations? To things being before other things, simultaneous with them, and after them? If so, what of the facts of past, present, and future? *Can* it be that saying something is present is just saying it is simultaneous with the saying? And that saying something is past is saying it is before the saying? And that saying it is future is saying that it is after the saying? Many who like neatness have thought so. But let me leave all of that, and end this tour with more political philosophy, near to politics.

More of my political convictions, like the Principle of Equality, have in them a feeling that issues in rant and insult and sometimes seems what it never turns out to be, ungovernable. It is the feeling, certainly not unique to me, of the awfulness of the conditions of existence of so many people. For a start, so many are deprived of what almost all of us want above all, a living-time of decent length. With the twenty-first century begun, what is to be said of any political tradition or party that does not embarrass itself by shame or rage about societies where humans exist as if they were a lower species? I have in mind societies of half-lives, where an average life-expectancy is not about 72 years, as in the societies we know better, but about 40. This grisly fact about lifetimes in other places has smaller replicas at home, still awful enough, about the bottom socio-economic classes in Britain, America, and the like.

The feeling of shame and rage, in so far as it issues in political convictions, issues first in convictions about our democracies – those systems about which some of us are so morally reassured by the fall of Communism. These democracies, which we now propose to teach to all the world, make a signal contribution to deprivations in living-time at home and abroad, and to other deprivations as terrible. Given this fact and some others, how are we to understand our democracies?

The annual Conway Memorial Lecture had been given 68 times before I got my turn some months ago. I was mightily pleased to get it, not least because Bertrand Russell was among the figures in the list of my predecessors. My title told all in advance. 'Hierarchic Democracy and the Necessity of Mass Civil Disobedience.' Given the kind of democracy we have, mass civil disobedience is a rational and necessary supplement to it. This advice, you may say, is utopian. Well, utopianism is a right of philosophy, a right which has served us all very well. And I am not sure the advice is utopian. It was easier to be sure about that before the fall of Communism, before the civil disobedience that precipitated that once-impossible thing.

Still, was my confidence in laying out the two convictions of my lecture reduced by something other than the fact that Conway Hall was less than full? That the audience, true to the venue, seemed to consist mainly in the good autodidactic atheists of London? I think so. The prospect of laying out my footnotes to Rainborowe, Rousseau, Tom Paine, R. H. Tawney, Russell, and I suppose Marx, was less than a happy one. And still I believe my footnotes, or so it seems.

My inner life, as you will have gathered from my daily round, is in one large part exertion. It is my trying to do some of that good thinking and arrive at some of those high-quality questions and answers, the stuff of philosophy. But in my case, as with many of my fellows, this is not so elevated an activity as might be supposed from an abstract description. Even if philosophy alternates with the rest of life, switches it off for a while, it is not what might be called the project of pure inquiry. The activity is directed towards truth, but also towards truth got down on paper or anyway into the external world. Would I understand more if I were higher-minded, less concerned with output? More Cambridge, as Cambridge once prissily conceived itself? I doubt it. I suspect I would understand less without the pressure of my own and other people's deadlines. As a result of them, I may go out of this fallen world knowing more.

There is another kind of inner life, perhaps inner life proper. I have a lot of it. It is reflection and feeling not aimed at expression and other action. Its owners may keep it to themselves, even forever. Since it is not shaped or coloured by the intention of speaking or acting, not so much constrained by convention, prudence or principle, it may have more truth in it. It may not conceal hurts or try to talk up a reputation. But there is another side to the coin. Since this reflection and feeling is also not constrained by the scrutiny and judgement of others, by public tests, it may have less truth in it. So if inner lives can have less hypocrisy and calculation, they can also have less sense and realism. I have reason to remind myself of both points.

Inner lives of this second kind can have various concerns. There is the long spiritual but more intellectual than religious tradition, to me glowing in its aspiration, of those taken up with what they take to be true reality. Something better behind the appearances. Ingrid, lately sent by Plato to remind me that naturalism is not the only possible human condition, and that atheism is not identical with rationality, contemplates the Form of the Good and related matters. She presses on me a sentence from Iris Murdoch – 'Good represents the reality of which God is the dream.'

Attracted as I am, partly because of that fact of being a little death-minded, I feel the impulse at moments to try to join the glowing tradition. I resist cavilling about whether Iris's sentence should not have 'is' in places of 'represents'. I wonder again if there could be a kind of hope that in some way is true. It would still be hope, since it could not possibly be ordinarily supported belief. But it would be hope somehow partaking of truth. My last mother-in-law liked me more for the idea. It doesn't really come into focus. So I do not succeed in the impulse to join the glowing tradition. There is too much metaphysical mist.

Some take the line, of course, that despite the mist, you can have some sense of something. Although it is disputed by his less damp admirers, Wittgenstein seems to have been inclined this way. 'Whereof one cannot speak, thereof one must be silent.' It was Ramsey who in this case made what has seemed the right reply. 'What you can't say, you can't say, and you can't whistle it either.' That is right, isn't it? As for religion itself, or more literal religion, including plain immortality, that is unthinkable. Surely the autodidacts in Conway Hall are right about that. For me to turn to religion would be cowardice. It would be to hide from truth. Sad or terrible truth, but truth. I go to concerts in churches, and not only for the music, but I do not believe or, really, want to believe. You can only *want* what there is some chance of having.

All I have been able to do along these lines is to affirm to myself that despite my failings I have a vicarious membership card in a moral struggle, a great struggle in politics that will certainly outlast me. It seems at moments to have outlasted the Labour Party that we used to have. It will last as long as there is desire and there is reason. Reason will always see through pomp and sham and nonsense to the need for real fairness in the satisfaction of desire. I can identify with the struggle sometimes, be reassured by the thought of it going on after me. I have once or twice succeeded in thinking of it as holy.

To those several feelings are to be added some that can flow from a theory of determinism. The theory is hard to believe, and what has seemed the right response to it is hard to sustain, since our culture runs against it. Mothers, those first agents of culture, set us against this response. Rae Laura Armstrong Honderich was good at that, in no need of support from John William Honderich.

From time to time, I have the consolation of personal success, the kind that matters most. That is personal success by one's own present test. I wanted to be a professor and then the Grote. It has sometimes been my story that academic ambition was at first pressed upon me, that the asp was put into my breast by others. In whatever way it happened, and that is something to look into, I came to have the desire. On some days its being fulfilled is still worth something. I see from the phone book that some of my fellow professors announce their standing in their entry and some do not. Professor Wiggins of course does, and Professor Papineau does not. I do. Maybe I should take it out, but I think I won't. My life has something in it I like, and am willing to advertise. But perhaps I should fill out the entry. 'No sage, not so clever as could be, too quick to declaim truth rather than argue for it, shrewd, sticks to subject, has got one or two things right, more than most competitors, does not always make enough distinctions to satisfy former teachers, has a good sense of unnecessary distinctions.'

Another of my consolations is the happy contemplation of other minds when they are on view, and other bodies. I am never long in that bleak mood where all humankind are a bore. Seeing a happy couple swinging along downhill is a fine thing that can cure the mood. So is seeing a kiss. Hampstead High Street does very nicely for the purposes of this respectable voyeurism. I recommend it, and am pleased on occasion to be part of the cure for others.

The pleasure of seeing happy couples has to do with something larger in both the contemplative part of my inner life and the part that issues in action. That is love or affection for a woman together with desire and its satisfaction. I have been a man of many women, if that uncertain description is taken to mean a man who has been for a longish time with each of many women, a succession of them. Here my life has been a bit more than middle-sized. I have been a libertine too, if one of those goes on being free from convention, and does not go in for much concealment of his freedom. Not often a womanizer, if one of those is deceitfully unfaithful in his relations.

My relationships, certainly, have not been with bodies – with someone in terms of more than their bodily attributes strictly speaking, presumably, but not enough of the rest. My relationships have been more ordinary. They have been with persons, and, to the extent that the distinction can be made, have had more to do with qualities that give rise to affection or love or maybe admiration than with qualities that give rise directly to desire. At the very least my connections have been friendships. Our lives have been connected.

It is perhaps prim to say so, and suggestive of more restraint with women than has been the case, but I have been with a prostitute only once. She knocked on the door of my room one afternoon, and was pretty and drunk. That was Regent Square, not far from college. I was not in my quiet state, thinking of truth and ambition. We bargained a bit, and I, not wanting to be lost, which I would have been by giving her money, said I had only cigarettes. She performed a lesser act, only later dignified by the American presidency. Sometimes I have drifted into thinking that it was only on that occasion that my activity was not made respectable to myself by at least an illusion of something else, some future. That is not true. But it is not far from true. I have not been among those who have seen, no doubt truly, that sex can be a thing that is good in itself.

The fact that I have been a man of many women sits in my mind as something about which I am a touch rueful but it is not a large fact or a stigma. I care about it, and keep quiet about the number of my lovers, and how far I am ahead of Russell and lag behind Freddie and some energetic lesser lights in our way of life. But I care less about having been a man of many women than about having not taken the philosophical world by storm. I would not subtract one connection from my past, and I feel or can summon a fondness at the very least for each of them. I feel some of that traditional pride, the pride of having done what many other men have wanted to do but not done. I have on a few occasions, encouraged by another's curiosity or prurience, in a way boasted of it.

For the most part in my relationships, or so it has seemed, I have not strayed far from truth for long. I have with an exception or two been faithful until near the ending of each settled relationship in which faithfulness was the policy. Almost all my relationships have indeed begun with a hope of futurity in them. I intended not to be one of Donne's dull, sublunary lovers. There was a time when I could say, and did, that I wanted only to go to bed with a woman whose company I would want in the end, in dying. I guess I say it still. I am a little tired of the long quest, a little worn out, but I have not abandoned that best of hopes.

Defending myself in passing against the charge of having been with too many women brings me to a last large part of my inner life. I remain more uncertain about my general moral standing than my defence in connection with women suggests. That defence is not confident, but argumentative or speculative, and it is put in partly for the reason that nobody ever found his way to truth about himself by collapsing. I need to hear both sides, one of which is mine. I have heard something of the other side before now. Jane took up that brief on behalf of the sisterhood. But hearing from myself and remembering my critics has not answered the question of my human standing. The uncertainty does not have to do only with women, but also with my son and daughter, and maybe my academic progress down from the attic in Gordon Square, and my politics seeming to be inconsistent with other things.

The nature of morality is no easy matter, but clearly one's standing is not in itself the question of whether a particular action or a kind of action or a habit was right. That is the question of whether it ought to have been done or engaged in, given the best judgement and knowledge at the time, maybe not one's own. Many have done right things by mistake or in ignorance or out of bad motives, and hence got no credit. Many have done wrong things out of innocent ignorance or misjudgement, and earned no condemnation. Nor is the question of standing just about the judgements, beliefs, feelings and motives of a person with respect to a particular action, kind of action or maybe habit – about the person's moral credit or moral responsibility for that particular thing.

The question of general human standing, rather, is about a person's general decency in a whole stage of a lifetime or maybe all of it. This general decency or want of it is something like the sum of one's good and bad records in the particular cases of this action and that – the pluses and minuses of moral credit and moral responsibility. This general standing is one thing to worry about, as I do. Another, to revert to actions, is about whether mine were right. Whatever my beliefs and motives and the rest, and however things turned out, did I act rightly? It is very possible to think differently later. That the matter is not merely historical or theoretical, but troubling, suggests some doubt about my separating right actions from the matter of standing. But it can hardly be that one counts as bad just because one did the wrong thing – there are honest mistakes and there is ignorance.

Whatever the truth of all that, the questions of my standing and of whether I did the right things seem always in the offing. They are so hard. Partly they are hard because of the problems mentioned earlier, having to do with the person I am and the persons I was. There is also the problem of self-deception in one's struggles to see one's standing and whether one did right. Nietzsche, one hopes, was not yet mad, but merely being provocative, in writing his lines to the effect that in such struggles self-deception will always carry the day. '"I have done that" says my memory. "I cannot have done that" says my pride. At last – memory yields.' It doesn't always. It doesn't with me. Memory may see to it that self-deception does not put a happy end to the struggle.

Conscious self-deception, to introduce some useful detail, presumably does not consist in what people often suppose – the paradoxical feat of consciously believing opposite things at the same time. It isn't one's ordinary self or consciousness being two, the first believing X but successfully deceiving the second into believing Y. By my lights conscious self-deception consists in one single self maintaining itself in uncertainty, keeping a question open, taking care not to look closely at what might turn out to be evidence against what it wants to believe.

That is something we *can* do. Self-deception is essentially having the desire to look away from possible evidence, and this desire's resisting the pull to truth. If we think this way about self-deception, Nietzsche's thought turns into the somewhat different thought that we will always succeed in not looking at what might be unhappy evidence. Surely it isn't true. Evidence can raise its head, arm the inclination to truth, unsettle the strategy. I fear there is some in the archive of my steamer trunk.

Person-stages and self-deception are not the only problems. Do I bring a general and distorting guilt to my reflections, a predisposition to judge against myself? There are some thoughts that give me reason to wonder. They have to do with the effect on me of the gentle righteousness or anyway virtuousness of Rae Laura Armstrong Honderich. Or, on the other hand, do I take a necessary arrogance too far? If I will not find my way to truth about myself or anything else by collapsing, there is also the real danger of being too tough-minded.

To remember my critics, of whom I have a sufficient number, what is to be said about something else, the fact of mixed motivation? It has not been paid much attention by moral philosophers, who have mainly been content to think of purer cases. Much of my life has come out of both respectable and not so respectable thoughts and feelings. Judgement cannot be quick in this neighbourhood. Sometimes it seems that it can't be slow either. An ex-colleague of whom you will hear comes to mind, and the alleged stabbing in the Grote's room, and the thought that true rage can have calculation in it or going with it.

Coming towards the end of this tour of the interior, I see that I have left out so large a fact, my moods. Like my feelings focussed on or directed at persons and other things, which include rage, my moods are strong. My good ones are close to exuberance, my darker ones on the way to despair. These all-encompassing things have sometimes seemed to me in a way not prompted by events in my outer life at all, not owed to successes or failures, good luck or bad, or the contributions of others. That cannot be right. But it does seem true that my state of body, that large inner fact, ordinarily has more to do with the cast of my world. Depression is tiredness, I used to say, and I still find some sense in that false proposition.

So much, not a lot, for my inner life as I think about it, but one thing remains. Some doctrinalists of the self and personality say my inner life as I am aware of it is only part of the story, the smaller part. In a way they are absolutely right. I have an unconscious mind. Being human, I must have. It has been said about all of us so often. '. . . the absence of a conscious perception is no proof of the absence of mental activity.' There are 'processes in the soul of which we are unaware. . . .' 'Our human souls are not always conscious of whatever they have in them. . . .' 'consciousness and unconsciousness are like warp and weft.' '. . . ideas and matters of fact . . . lie by for use, till some fortuitous circumstance makes the information dart into the mind. . . .' 'Consciousness only touches the surface. . . . The great basic activity is unconscious.'

The six sentences are not Sigmund Freud's, of course, but come from a small selection of his predecessors. Plotinus in the third century AD, Aquinas in the thirteenth, Cudworth in the nineteenth, and then Goethe,

Wollstonecraft, and Nietzsche. The total number of Freud's predecessors, I suppose, were all the reflective members of the human race before him. It is no surprise to me that through known history the truism has been recorded that our lives have in them ongoing mental facts of which we are conscious only sometimes. One of mine, although not breathtaking, is my belief that my name on my birth certificate is Edgar Dawn Ross Honderich.

Philosophers have long given these ongoing mental facts the name of being *dispositions*. Dispositional beliefs and dispositional desires mainly. They are, as I sensibly see it, not items that are conscious in a second sense, items in a dimly lit or even pitch-black level or part of the mind separate from the ordinary conscious mind. What they are is neural facts, standing causes that may or may not issue in the only consciousness there is. It is convenient to use the language of ordinary consciousness on them, to speak of them as beliefs and the like, as it is convenient to talk about the rest of the natural world and machines in terms of goals and the like. Missiles seek targets. But let us not turn convenience into mystery. We have enough levels of reality already.

Freudians are inclined to let the innocent suppose that the large fact of the unconscious was discovered a while ago in Vienna. They are inclined, too, to let the truism that it exists do some work in recommending something entirely different from it. I have an attitude to that different thing and to the stratagems used in its defence. My attitude, I confess, is such that while there was time in my itinerary in Vienna, after the Palais Wittgenstein, to see the university staircase where the student shot the Logical Positivist, there was not quite enough time to get to the house where Freud lived. The thing different from the fact of the unconscious is a special theory of it, a theory of what is in it. At bottom this is the colourful if now somewhat faded story that what each of us mainly has in our unconscious is sexual desires somehow left over from earlier on. Mine, in the theory, were for Rae Laura, tired and other-worldly as she was. Here my powers of belief are weak. Test the idea, if you want, or astrology, with the narrative that now begins.

Mother and Father, fallen to the telephone house from the big house, but in good heart

Myself at six, before the embarrassment of spectacles

The first little barn, and the fine apple tree, with its king underneath

Mary Jean Kathleen Honderich, always a gentle sister

Robert Wayne Honderich in Africa before 12 April 1944

Bee in Baden's main street with Ted, about 12, standing at attention

Rae Laura and John William, before leaving Baden in 1950

Loine Christian Honderich, his mission well begun

Ruth Laura Honderich, in the early 1950s, definitely of Toronto rather than Baden

Margaret Penman and myself, at our wedding in
Toronto, in 1958

Down a cave in Kentucky to enlighten readers of *The Star Weekly*

2

VILLAGE

The Anabaptists were the Left Wing of the Protestant Reformation. They shared the view, too reasonable for the sixteenth century and indeed for Luther, that true baptism into the church cannot be of infants, but needs to be a commitment by adults who know what they are doing. 'The Christian life is not child's play.' They added to this view a strong distinction between the unworldly and the worldly, an avowal of the necessity of separating church from state, an aversion to hierarchy, and a refusal to bear arms or swear oaths. Some were burned and others drowned for their heresy – at bottom, as seems to me likely, for standing up a little against the world's injustice by way of their religion.

Among the Anabaptists were the Mennonites. They were still unpopular and migratory at the beginning of the nineteenth century. Unlike some of their earlier brethren, they were not looking for a place in which to practise community of goods and women, but only for a less radical religious freedom and quiet lives in good farming country. Among them were Christian and Margaret Honderich, who emigrated from South Germany to Canada in 1825. They cleared virgin forest near what would afterwards be the villages of Baden and New Hamburg in a Germanic township of the province of Ontario. Their son, to be the Rev. John Honderich, was, as his tombstone says, 'the first male white child born in Wilmot Township'.

My ancestors in Canada on my mother's side of the family tree also came as pioneers. Those on her mother's side came in 1831, to what subsequently were predominantly English and Scottish townships. Here the villages were to be Kincardine, Kinloss, and Lucknow. The original ancestral pair were Richard William Haldenby and his wife Hannah, he of an unprosperous generation of an old and well-connected Yorkshire and East Anglia family. Thus our family genealogists have been happy to prove that we share a past with Lady Diana Spencer as she was, she who was to have been Queen of England.

To the Haldenby or English line, there was subsequently an admixture of Irish, no doubt useful. County Armagh. I have not yet informed myself about our first Canadian ancestors on my mother's father's side, the Scottish side, or their ancestors in the border country, although research by others is well forward. Still, I have been pleased enough to count myself as not only coming from German, English, and Irish stock, but also of the Armstrong clan. True to my Anabaptist forebears, I left it until coming to my maturity to elect a nationality. Born a sixth-generation Canadian, British I became, at any rate by passport.

The church of the Reformed Mennonites were more liberal than some, the women not being confined to bonnets nor the men to hooks and eyes in place of the ornament of buttons. They were not paradigms of toleration, however. Their doctrine did not allow them to hear other religion. My grandfather and father on an occasion took themselves to hear False Gospel in another church, although, as will transpire, the verb 'to hear' is not quite right. They would not recant their visit, and were formally excommunicated from the Reformed Mennonites. Thereafter, other members of their own family, on meeting them, could not shake hands, but were permitted a grasp of the shoulder as a sign of affection. A lesser martyrdom.

Rae Laura Armstrong was a school teacher, her father being an officer of the court in Bruce County, and her mother, so it was afterwards said, being a reader of books rather than a keeper of a house in punctilious good order. Rae Laura was finding Anglicanism and the like insufficient to her soul's impulses, and was yet more engaged in the spiritual search than my father. They met on a train to a religious gathering. Perhaps it was early on that my father undertook with her, as at some stage he did, to devote their lives to being missionaries. In any case it was a spiritual side to him which overcame what he also possessed, a distinct shortcoming. He was profoundly deaf, the victim of a childhood sickness. He had learned to lip-read, but, because he was not expert in this, she was to learn sign-language.

They married within a year, he 29 and she 25. It was she, it seems, who brought character and invention to the naming of several of their six children: Ruth Laura, Loine Christian, Beland Hugh, Robert Wayne, Mary Jean Kathleen, and Edgar Dawn Ross. I, last of the six, was born on 30 January 1933 in my grandfather's house, to which we had succeeded. My mother was several weeks short of being 45.

Much later, in England, my accent having been worn down and also somewhat improved, 'going to mass on Sundays' having been made indistinguishable from 'going to moss on Sundays', the curious sometimes touched delicately on the matter of my antecedents. I sometimes responded with a weak jocularity. It was that I was born in a filthy peasant village. One aim of the jocularity, which I have given up, was to get in first with some superiority. It also conveyed another fact, a vestige of resentment. Do I feel it still? Is there something to be said for my unkind description of this place that seemed to be my life?

Baden in 1933 and into the 1940s had a population of about 700, very many of them bearing German names. Basts, Gingerichs, Naumanns, Schwartzentrubers, Webers, and Zehrs. They supplemented the English language with a German dialect. The village looked beyond itself, in so far as it looked anywhere, only to the county town, ten miles away. This had been named Berlin until the First World War. Then soldiers of English descent made trouble, throwing the Kaiser's statue into a lake, and it was thought wise to rename the town. It became Kitchener, which it still is. Baden, having no soldiery and no statue, saved its name.

In its twelve unnamed streets were about 165 houses, township hall, churches for Mennonites, Lutherans and Presbyterians, two hotels, school, bank, butcher, baker, cobbler, post office and four other shops. Also two declining blacksmiths, three garages, a foundry, mills for flour, linseed oil, wood and cider, places for the waxing of turnips and the making of Limburger cheese and electric fences for cattle. Railway station, volunteer fire hall, undertaker *cum* seed-merchant, softball diamond and two tennis courts, a stream, two dams. And, remembered in fullest detail, a telephone exchange.

I enumerate these partly to indicate that the village of 700 was sufficient unto itself. Partly because of this, it was a community, something with a membership. From the start, I seemed to myself not a full member. There was not only the reason of my family's excommunication from a respectable and conscientious local tradition of religion. That was a first cause of another fact. An unspoken breach eventually opened between us and the farming Honderichs, who would otherwise have been my allies of blood. My cousins, to my mind, were on that other side. We did not speak much at the softball games. There were also larger things that stood in the way of my being a full member of my village.

My father was odd, first on account of his deafness. When I became aware of him, he had already gone into his private world of silence. Certainly he made affectionate excursions from it, which I loved, and occasionally raging ones, but mostly he was in that other place, in which he was not unhappy. It would be wrong to say that the village was such that many in it made mock of him for his affliction and his departure from local space and time. But a few did, or at any rate included it in the roster of his shortcomings.

Chief among these was his lack of the principal virtue. He was not a good provider for his family. He had inherited a large house on the death of my grandfather, but also a decent amount of capital, and had founded a number of newspapers, one being *The Baden Sun*. It is difficult to see these and similar endeavours as manifesting a commercial realism. Nor was there great evidence of such an attribute when, as you might say, we met our Waterloo, more particularly the Waterloo Trust Co. It threatened to foreclose on a mortgage he had taken out on the house. His response was to circulate a petition on our behalf among the villagers, against the iniquity of the Waterloo Trust. This did not greatly detain it. He took his family to lodgings and then to a lesser habitation at the edge of the village. He did not learn to make ends meet.

Rae Laura no doubt rejoiced, as certainly she did on other occasions later, when the Almighty worked in a mysterious way. The post of village telephone operator fell vacant. With it went a proper house, the telephone exchange. Thereafter there were considerable hours of paid work at home. It was she who was the principal and steady provider for those of the family who had not taken wing, quite soon only I. I did most of my growing up in the telephone house, aware that we had come down in the world.

The eight rooms behind its front verandah included one for the telephone switchboard and an adjacent bedroom for my mother, to whose

36

operating of the switchboard for much of the day was added night-duty. My father paid visits from his bedroom upstairs. These were never explicitly connected by me with a side of life about which neither he nor Mother ever uttered a word to me, save for a later and inexplicit aspiration, by Mother, that I would come as a Christian to my wife. The house was not inferior to some others, and neat in seven of its eight rooms, but various reflections were to reduce its desirability for me as a residence.

We did not own it, and our having it was dependent on my mother's labours. There was the further fact of the hand pump in the kitchen, which drew water from a well. This did not compare with the gleaming taps in the kitchen of our neighbours the Kuhns, financed by the making of electric fences. There was also the outhouse or privy, attached to the nearer of the two small wooden barns in the long back garden.

The eighth room of the house, the one that was not neat, was the inner domain of my father, a sweet place of my early memories. It contained, above all, his printing press. Out of its slow breathing when the flywheel was sustained by the foot treadle, breathing unheard by him but listened to by me, came his pamphlets. Several of them, as I was to know later, were arguments for religious toleration. They were, to say the least, not widely circulated, but no doubt copies found their way to the Reformed Mennonites.

That Father was a pamphleteer in a small way may suggest that the household was at a high level of reflective and cultural activity. Well, he was concerned with ideas and, as it seemed, turned them over in a somewhat leisurely fashion in the silent world, but he was not burdened with learning. Nor did the printing press produce only pamphlets. From it came labels for his products, the last of these being VIM, a patent soap of some fierceness.

Mother and Father discussed religion, and argued peacefully about it, sometimes a little enlivened by the strongest drink in the house, which was Pepsi-Cola. But she was not of a persistent intellectual bent. Although she never lacked her school teacher's resolution that I be educated, she did not take on the task herself. I think she was worn down, not only by the switchboard but also by life's not having gone according to its high plan. They were, as I have said, to be missionaries. On many days she glorified God to me, but she never visited a foreign field to do so to those less familiar with the experience. My parents could not now divert dollars to enlarging the household library. It was meagre, containing such items as a volume of Byron, Robert Louis Stevenson's *Kidnapped*, and *The Boy's Own Annual*, insufficient antidotes to the Bibles, hymnals and tracts. Still, the collection existed, and was read through by me several times.

Thus the uncertainty of my membership in my village, and the part the village played in this, were owed not only to the old fact of excommunication, the casting-off by cousins, the deafness, Father's lack of the principal virtue, and the telephone house. We were also unique in the reflective and cultural activity, such as it was, undramatic and mainly religious. The meaning of life was not much considered elsewhere in the village, or the difficulty of justifying God's ways to man. Moreover, this activity and in fact the whole of our family life were rightly perceived as English and Scottish in timbre rather than Germanic. Father had in a way defected to Mother's side, perhaps in a way been overcome by her. If I did not do so then, it is hard to resist assigning a philistinism to my village. Baden was unprepared for us. You will find no public library in my list of its utilities.

Still, you may wonder if there is room for a question. My brother Bee may wonder. Was the uncertainty of my membership only in my own small head? Herb Miller lounged against the window of his corner shop, within range of a five-year-old and his tricycle. When I passed, I and he alone at that bare corner, or I and he with his crony, a foot of his would find its way under one of my rear wheels. My five-year-old falls to the pavement must have pleased him. Perhaps as much as his name for the Edgar I was. It was *Ga-Ga*, whose mockery served him well until I went to school and was discovered to need spectacles, after which time *Four Eyes* served him well. He was not deranged or defective. While not the most highly estimated of the 700, he was not excluded by them or notorious. Others took up his usages, but it is he who would come to mind first now if I were to try to excuse my later epithet for my birthplace.

What else is to be remembered of it? At least once after having been deemed to have attained that first level of personal responsibility to which all are called, I did not hold to it by making my way to the privy behind the first small barn. Rather, I produced a small brown pile, still nicely formed in my mind's eye today, behind the stove in the shadowy kitchen.

The result was remonstration, and guilt. The guilt was deep. In that way of families, a place had been prepared for it. I was not punished, nor, so far as I can remember, ever punished thereafter by my parents, for anything whatever. It would be agreeable to say that the pain of guilt was really the pain of withdrawal of love. That, I think, was not so. It was not the felt nature of the thing. As philosophers say, that was not the phenomenology of the feeling. I did consistently have, as it seemed to me, what affection Mother could muster, and more from my untroubled father. But guilt was a weight in itself, not to be avoided on account of something else, not made greatly heavier by what accompanied it by way of the feelings of others. No doubt it was sin.

School began when I was 6, in 1939, the year of the Royal Train. I began my education more impressively than it went on thereafter. My Es for Excellence from the Misses Martinson and Taylor perhaps owed something to a want of academic principle like my own as an examiner later on, or to a comparison with the unbookishness of the Mennonites. In fact I did not shine. Nor have I often shone since. Clever I have wanted to be, but not often been. If I am sometimes quick enough in thought, often ahead of others, I have not regularly been adroit or dexterous. I am no nimble inventor of speculations, and am not often good at retorts or quick escapes. My intellectual virtues, fully awakened only later, have from the beginning been more in the way of an involuntary interest in the very facts of things, scepticism, some judgement, orderliness, and an unwillingness to give up a campaign towards truth because of a little local difficulty. I value these duller virtues, and can say, if slightly morosely, that I might have chosen them.

Florence Ferguson, I fancy, had some of the same virtues. She had arrived in the first class before me, and was deputed to teach me my numbers. Subsequently she sharply put me right about words I had read but not mastered. 'Antique' was not to be pronounced, she said, so as to rhyme with something that might have been part of billiards, the anti-cue. She did well in her instruction of me, and has my gratitude, but is remembered for herself. She was the first of the girls. Tall, fair, and of a proud family. Scots among the Mennonites.

A year or two later, she was succeeded in my contemplations by Marjorie Miller, dark ringlets and composure, whose books I carried silently out of the village and up the Baden Hill to her door. Her family always seemed to be calling her away. They were not, so far as I know, related to the impediment to my tricycle. But I was adding a walk of two or three miles to the obligatory mile or two to follow, these later ones being my round of delivering the village's copies of *The Kitchener Daily Record*. So they may have deemed me ardent. I had no words for this attachment, any more than for its predecessor, and would need to struggle to find some now. I thought first of Marjorie Miller some decades later, on first hearing a line from Goethe, no doubt mistranslated or misunderstood: Stay with me a while, you are so beautiful.

My contemplations of girls, whatever desire may have been under them in my nature, in fact had nothing much explicit in them that would have dismayed Rae Laura. In this, perhaps, they were ordinary. Their explicit content was pure enough, and had to do with good looks and with respectable events. Still, and rightly, the very existence of these contemplations would not have reassured my mother. She may have had intimations. To school, and to religious homilies at home, having to do exclusively with the spirit rather than the loins, she added Presbyterian Sunday School. Then Mennonite Bible School during several weeks of my summer vacations. I went unwillingly.

That I came early to my resistance to the promise of Eternal Life presumably had to do with Father. His amicable discussions of religion with Mother continued, but in my time he never darkened a church door. He had for a time a postal relationship with the Church of Unity, presumably an institution not stiff with doctrine. He was, I suspect, following that line of personal religious development familiar in the English nineteenth century and indeed since. Its culmination, while having piety and eloquence in it, is small religious belief indeed. Conway Hall might have suited him for his final inquiries.

By the time I was about 7, all my siblings had departed. Ruth in the direction of good causes, and in particular the publicizing of them. Loine to learn to preach, as he never after failed to do. Bee was beginning his ascent from reporter for the *Kitchener Daily Record*. Lovely handsome Bob, best of black sheep, was incomprehensibly a chef in a restaurant in Kitchener. Mary was following her mother in the religious quest, wife to another preacher. All would reappear for short visits, bearing their new credentials as knowers of a wider world.

Bob returned smoking Sweet Caporal cigarettes, and, in the back garden, painted metal signs in the shape of shields, and told me something about them. He proposed to go round inspecting the kitchens of restaurants and their menus. If they were up to scratch, the restaurants would be enrolled in his association, and get a shield to hang outside. It is an old idea now, but was not then, in Baden in 1940. Loine came back too, from the dead. *En route* to the Bible College in Springfield, Missouri, there had been an awful car crash. News came that of the four young men in the car, three were dead, Loine among them. Was there some uncertainty in the message? Mother would not believe it, had faith, and prayed. In a day or two another message came, followed in due course by my brother, scarred and without some fingers, but in no way deterred from his mission.

On one of his returns, Bee took a first and maybe a reasonable step in exerting a worldly authority over me. He was, later, to succeed my father. I had wheedled the purchase of a toy truck out of Mother. Very likely the money came from Bee's subsidy to us. The truck had to be returned to the shop, the money got back. More guilt, whatever its efficacy, and some beginning of insubordination.

There followed two other larger events of my earlier boyhood. I gathered the reality of the first when I was 8, in 1941. Loine, Bee and I made a car journey through snow to a reformatory. Bob was in it, aged 20, found guilty on account of the restaurant shields. I did not see him, as my brothers did, but helped to hide a roast chicken for him in a farm building attached to the institution. Was he a victim of a judicial system not ready for the age of guides to restaurants and their certification? Did some of the restaurants pay their fee for their inspection, and pass, and then not get their shields? Was it worse? The matter has not been researched. It has to be said for my peasant village that no one ever spoke to me of it. Somehow subject to morality, I did not defend my brother to myself, but loved him more, and thought of his audacity, and perhaps of following him in a safer audacity.

Nor has the matter of his release from the reformatory been researched. I wonder if it came early, on the understanding that he fight for the King and his Dominions, which he did. He was in the RCAF by February of 1942. I read of the war in the *Record* before delivering it, and studied the few letters that came back from his flying school in Quebec, and then from a base in England. He was rapidly promoted. I study now his log book. '1943, Aug 19, convoy escort west.' '1944, Jan 5, Cairo-Wadi.' '1944, Mar 13, Scram. Investigate A/O.' He was killed on active service in April of 1944, at age 22.

I cannot say I was devastated, as was my mother. It was not like losing a son. His death, despite my love, had not enough reality. Children, as evolution has ordained, are saved from being destroyed by some bad things. I marched around my paper round, and first looked at myself from outside, a boy with lowered eyes, and doubted myself for this show.

So far, I have not much gilded my boyhood, recalled it as an idyll. This too is necessary. Certainly I was not wholly taken up with not being a full member of my village, or with any other discomfort or darkness. I was a boy among boys, sometimes leader, never far behind. I learned the possibility of happiness, even the expectation of it, conceivably too great an expectation. Together with James Nesbit, Douglas Kuhn, Glen Schwartzentruber, the older Kenneth and Robert Knoll, I climbed by stages towards 14, not always primly.

Some, it seems, awaken in philosophy early. Such, it seems, was the good fortune of my later acquaintance in another world, Bryan Magee, Member of Parliament and of the Garrick, veteran of broadcasting. Author not only of such diverse works as *Go West Young Man*, *The Television Interviewer*, *To Live in Danger*, *Towards 2000* and *Aspects of Wagner*, but also of *Confessions of a Philosopher*. We learn from the latter work that each night as a boy of 5 he approached a thought about falling asleep that Wittgenstein himself had about dying, that by definition we cannot experience it. At 7 or 8 he was entranced by how willing such an action as bending a finger is possible, and well on his way to the falsehood of determinism and the truth of Free Will. Between 9 and 12 he came on his own to contemplate Zeno's paradox of the arrow – at any instant of its flight, is it moving or at rest? If you try to say the first, how can it possibly move at an instant? If you say the second, how can it ever be moving?

The young Bryan went further, to reflect on the problem of fatalism that whatever is going to happen tomorrow is of course true now, and therefore is settled already. He was also upset to realize, without the help of Hume, that he was aware only of his own sense impressions of the world, not the world in itself. Sense-data of trees, not trees. Since he also reflected on the antinomy that space must surely have an end but that there must also be space on the other side, he grew up no less than a natural Kantian, as he reports.

I was not so fully conscious, but I and my comrades did other things. We brought back wild flowers from the black loam in the woods, played Run Sheep Run on summer evenings, reflected again on the heat which had bent the iron stanchions in the two barns burned down on two nights by the jealous brother who left his footprints in the snow. We carved flat arrows from pine shingles and slung them for distance with stick and string, and bravely came within a few yards of Depression hoboes camping beside the railway track. We set booby traps for my deaf father in his small barn in the long back garden, frustrated the invisible trapper by springing his muskrat traps in the stream, and fished for carp in the dam where once Jews had been seen. I was not always cowed by 'Take off your glasses', but fought, except with the Knolls.

We rafted on Brubacher's dam, shot at one another with BB guns from the willows and the crow's nest in the tree, hoped to unsettle householders at 10 p.m. by the moaning that comes from the end of a long thread tacked to an outside window when the other end is rubbed with resin. We ate from the watermelon patch on the Baden Hill and then, two of us, stamped on a dozen or two, leaving in me the shame of having been a complicit witness. We got a better idea of death when Glen Schwartzentruber was not careful in driving a tractor over the railway track.

Alone enough too, I had a full if lethargic sense of myself and my world, this place of existence. I was king of the apple tree beside the first barn, got matches and lit small wooden pyres in the outhouse, wrote the initials EDRH in wet concrete, ruminated during the paper round from which Mother would never release me, lay in the grass having a half-idea about the reality of it. I was alone too in the crime of turning off the school's electricity by the outside switch on a winter Sunday, thereby cancelling Monday morning's classes, and in exploding a .22 cartridge with the lead removed at the last Halloween party, making an impression on the party and also the impression that remains on my knuckle. If being out of school was better, I took a little pride in being left by a teacher to read by myself in some classes, and got more entangled with language.

In one way I was precocious. Paragraphs of mine, news of Baden, were appearing in *The Kitchener Record* when I was 13. Mother had had this commission, and also Bee. I sang of car crashes and the burning down of the flour mill, and clipped out these unsigned threnodies. I was most impressed by my manner of bringing the news of a victory of our grown-up village softball team over another village. The Baden Pirates, I wrote, had won the trophy emblematic of championship of the league. It was the 'emblematic' that made me wonderfully proud. It was Homeric.

The *Record* supplied scorecards for softball games, and I became scorekeeper to the village team, as official a scorekeeper as it ever had, with a seat on the players' bench, and, necessarily, a place in the truck that transported the team to its games in other villages. The departure from outside Stiffelmeyer's Hotel was itself a ritual that drew an audience. If Glen Honderich of my farming cousins was a third baseman whose hand was quicker than the eye, my humbler role was a satisfaction to me, no doubt an evident satisfaction.

In a late inning of one of our home games, an uncertainty arose about the score. A Pirate or two took one view, favouring the Pirates. The adult scorekeeper on the visitors' side took another, favouring the visitors. I agreed with the other scorekeeper. Was I subject to truth rather than overawed? A fortnight passed without forewarning, and I presented myself outside Stiffelmeyer's Hotel. The great Lloyd Miller, first base and manager, barred my way onto the truck, wordlessly dismissing me from my humble role and summoning a more loyal scorekeeper. I am uncertain if he was a Miller related to the impediment to my tricycle, but I am certain the hurt was greater. At 13 one knows disgrace. I cried at home. Mother said I should not be bothered by the ignorant. I was not bothered, but bleeding.

In the summer of the year when I was 13, I went to join Father, who, having found VIM no money-spinner, and bee-keeping no better, would take himself off in the summers to pick peaches and cherries in what was called the fruit belt of our Province of Ontario. We lived contentedly in a hut, and laboured together in the trees happily, our peace ruffled only by the effect on the farmer of my remarking to him that I would pick cherries faster if I were getting the profit on them.

In another summer Father lived in a tent in the fruit belt, and may have offered a pamphlet of his to someone. It is my recollection, as I have remarked, that his works were not limited to the subject of religious toleration, and that at least one was of a more seditious character. More particularly, as I seem to recollect, it was devoted to the propositions that

Christianity is true Communism, and Communism true Christianity. Both propositions are needed, as logic will tell you, to secure a perfect equivalence. My recollection has some support from an undoubted fact, that Father and his tent were visited by the Royal Canadian Mounted Police for the purpose of looking over the literature. These Mounties were vigilant early, since the miasma of McCarthyism south of the border was still to come. They thought Father no immediate danger to the security of the State. Perhaps they discerned he had probably read no word of Marx.

In March of 1947, when I was 14, winter brought life to a halt. There was a great blizzard. After it, we gathered in the schoolyard at the railway fence to wait for the two engines and the immense plough. They had backed up two miles in order to gain momentum to clear snow 15 feet deep from the cutting. They succeeded mightily, and threw up a deluge over the fence. Finding myself under three feet of snow, with time left before losing consciousness, I prayed in earnest, for the first and last time. We were dug out and I set to work. It was gratifying to read the next day's *Record*. BOY TELLS HIS OWN STORY OF BEING BURIED IN SNOW. By EDGAR HONDERICH. Nor did I much mind the interview with Mother about this first piece of writing identified as mine. 'Mrs Honderich said this morning it took him three hours to write it – he was that sincere about doing a good job.' Count on Rae Laura to find in this early breast-baring some moral responsibility.

She was much concerned with a religious form of it, and is somehow to be credited with what she would have taken to be a particular achievement in this connection. My first contemplations of girls, as I have reported, were restricted to a kind of respectable content, perhaps with some slight addition no more definable today than then. Subsequently, more content was made available to me. The two destroyers of the watermelons on the Baden Hill were the informants of me and my comrades as to another side of life, and its intransitive and transitive verbs. They also went beyond language, to the very demonstration of reality.

They spoke of *jerking off*, thereby providing me both with a new verb and, so to speak, with my first piece of carnal knowledge. For our instruction, they had competitions in jerking off, in the sunlight at the edge of Brubacher's Dam. The white spurts out into the water were mesmerizing. They did more, with amazingly compliant girls, proud to help. As we watched closely, they *felt them up*, in the course of a kind of dancing in front of the ice-cream counter in Roth's Garage, and while lying down with them in snow-houses. My second verb and piece of carnal knowledge.

Look and learn is what we did, but in my case the knowledge remained inert. It remained so despite my audacity in other respects, and despite the warm and inspiriting feeling produced in me when the rim of the drinking fountain at school pressed against my flies. I appreciated the feeling, but I never put my first piece of carnal knowledge into action until university, and then only experimentally, and after I had acquired a third. That I should act on the second, touch a girl *there*, was beyond all conception, not something in any possible world. This paralysis on my part was that particular achievement of Rae Laura of which I spoke a moment ago. It presumably had to do with her expressed aspiration that I would come as a Christian to my wife. I seemed to myself unimpressed by it, as by her other yet more general exhortations to virtue. As it seems, their efficacy did not depend on my seeming impressed. Vague thoughts came to me, but issued in no actions.

I seemed still less impressed by the last of my religious experiences, and in this case it had none of its intended effect. Rae Laura, having exhausted the resources of the Anglicans and the Presbyterians, had found her way not to something more mystical but to something more substantial. Not for her the Church of Unity. In what I think were her sorrows, she became a fundamentalist, a Pentecostal, and was able to take with her two of my siblings, Loine and Mary. She succeeded in taking me to the Pentecostal Tabernacle in Kitchener a time or two.

There, on one Sunday, I was *saved*. This enrolment in the army of the Lord was worked on my 15-year-old soul by emotion and ululation, and perhaps by speaking in tongues, and by my being led from the tabernacle to a side room for the *coup de grace*. I gave in to some urgent adult, and loathed myself and him for it on the way back to Baden. My conversion did not take, and was the late stimulus to my atheism. It was soon to find its plainer tongue, and to separate me from my religious brother and sister for too long thereafter.

My formal and other education in Baden completed, I became a pupil of the Kitchener-Waterloo Collegiate Institute, the high school of

Kitchener and the adjacent town of Waterloo. Very few if any of my village classmates ascended to a secondary school. I had no great inclination. Although my boyhood had contained no exhortations to success, but only to goodness, and would not change in this respect, my parents arranged that Grey Coach Lines would take me the ten miles to Kitchener each morning. I was less a scholar than earlier, and more attracted to urban life than to Latin. I doubt whether my want of commitment had much to do with another fact of membership. Again I was not a full member. I was a village boy in Kitchener. Its boys had English names, doctors for mothers, fathers with Buicks, shoes and haircuts of an ordained mode, and played hardball. They went to summer cottages on islands, presumably were not told by a dentist that another filling was needed but they should not come back except with money in hand, and they could dance.

This second experience of being outside a world, not owed to any intention of those inside, was no distress. Perhaps, some time after coming to know disgrace, one starts on the way to learning that always and for ever there is something of which one is not a member. Would that I had learned the lesson better. In fact, I was in a way beckoned inside Kitchener. Girls liked me, perhaps for some independence, pride, and lazy intelligence. Helen Geiger was one, as comely as she was serious. It was not rejection that kept me from the Christmas Prom, but, despite those mentioned strengths of mine, a temporary lack of nerve.

My boyhood moved towards a certain ending in tranquillity, owed in part to something's being kept from me. School went on uneventfully and I achieved no great distinction and did not kiss girls. Nor did I distinguish myself in jobs each summer. I learned the dreariness of the life of a factory labourer, in a Kitchener textile mill, and did not learn to do well at minding the machines. Another job, at 16, was working on the railway, with men of Baden. Having learned to drive in spikes, I tired of the labour, but had not the face to show myself and announce my resignation in advance of the agreed time, at the beginning of the school term. Mother saw the foreman at my suggestion, and to my disgrace. If I censured her in my mind for not minding her appearance enough, and more particularly for not arranging to support her bosom, and resented her for these failures, I did not hesitate to make use of her unfailing resolution on my behalf.

It had to be told me in the end, when I was approaching 17, that she was not only tired and disappointed. Something else was wrong. She would go to Toronto, where Ruth and Bee now lived, to a nursing home. Father, for reasons not wholly clear to me, would go to friends in Kitchener. The telephone house was at a sudden end, as was Baden. I would go to Toronto too, to live first with my sister and then with my brother.

It is too early for me, and may be too early for you, really to set about explaining me. There seems to me insufficient reason for a certain orthodoxy. It is the giving of greatest weight, in understanding the later or mature part of a life, to what came first. As it seems to me, what forms the later part and the person in it may be more recent. Certainly the middle, the time of youth, cannot simply be left out. Life does not consist in (1) childhood followed by (2) nothing much followed by (3) what is to be explained. Later life is not a large and remarkable case of action at a distance. So I shall wait a bit to think about any serious explaining.

With an eye on that, though, a summary of my boyhood is worth trying. My sense of membership and standing was small, which fact, to add a further thought, may have made me in some ways less rule-governed. The rules were the rules of others. My tendency to self-doubt was large, and, if it now seems I was not fully awake, I was not lacking in some pride and boldness. Places were much to me. I had the affection of my parents, and in different ways returned it, but with insufficient generosity to the parent to whom I was closer, in fact my mother. I was aware of their taking a moral view of things before any other, and of their morality's being decent. It was not selfishness. But, affected in my feelings as I was, this morality did not paralyse me. Perhaps it only kept me from acting on my inclination to girls, by whom I was always taken. As against all this, I was often sweetly happy out of school, and at least content in school. I was no cradle philosopher. I never fell easily into belief, without great effort took things in, was never touched by religion, was kept at work so far as that was possible, and did not fail to learn to fight sometimes.

3

CITY, SCHOOL,
SATURDAYS, GIRLS

My departures at 17 from my village and from the Kitchener-Waterloo Collegiate Institute were taken without reluctance. I took some satisfaction in the idea of being seen as being called away to cosmopolitan life, as becoming a member, one of the million or so members, of the great city of my country. Such was Toronto in 1950, in more eyes than my own. Montreal, although it challenged this claim, had the misfortune of being populated by French Canadians. Being a minority bent on maintaining their identity, they were intrinsically suspect. Their standing was further reduced by a useful store of our English folk-truths, one being that their French could not be understood in Paris. It is good to be able to say that nothing in the store was virulent. For example, it did not include the name *Pepsi* for a French Canadian. This, as I learned much later, was in use among Montrealers of another notable ethnicity, and was derived from what ignorant or penniless parents were purported to give their children in place of milk.

Still, if the Toronto to which I came was our metropolis, it was not then the metropolis it is today. Now it is cosmopolitan in fact, and capable of all manner of achievement. Its baseball team has won the trophy emblematic of victory in the World Series. Then, it must be said, Toronto called up its share of epithets from visitors. 'Oh for half an hour of Europe after this sanctimonious icebox.' That from Wyndham Lewis, having had no experience of the summers fine enough to ripen the watermelons. Saki's view of Toronto can be inferred from his wider view. 'Canada is all right, really, though not for the whole weekend.'

Torontonians could enter into this disparagement. Their want of civic pride, let alone urban megalomania of the American kind, was a natural part of the remarkable diffidence of Canadians generally. Evidently this was partly owed to their being a smallish country in population, next to a very large one. It was more owed to a history both short and thin. No revolution or seizing of independence, one brief rebellion in a country lane, and, putting aside the early English struggle with the real French, one brief war. Or so I recall. The War of 1812 with the Americans presumably did not have only the effect of giving the White House its name, repainting having been made necessary, but that is the effect usually remembered. No *nation* of Canada was formed by the war. In fact no nation had been formed by the 1950s, whatever may have happened since. I have in mind a people possessed by a pride and spirit owed to their past and culture.

The fact was evidenced by a certain preoccupation of Canadian writers, journalists, academics and politicians in the 1950s. *MacLean's Magazine* was to the fore in this, no year's issues being complete without a solemn return to it. The preoccupation was usually called the quest for our Canadian identity. Something is clearer to me now, not because of my having read some Oxford doctrine by Freddie's adversary J. L. Austin about the hidden nature of our speech-acts, but because of the realism into which I have fallen. It is that the question in our quest was not, as it pretended to be, 'What is our identity as a people?' or indeed 'Who are we?'. We knew the answer to that, too well. Canadians. The question, rather, was a lot closer to 'What is our standing?' or 'What is our worth, if any, over the Americans?'. Sufficient, we should have said.

My city was not only diffident but was Toronto the Good, to some extent subject to blue laws, these being bits of local legislation of moralistic intent. Some of its leading citizens went further than the laws required. The two very large department stores downtown lowered the blinds of their blocks of display windows on Saturday night, in order to save passers-by from the impiety of window-shopping on the Sabbath. There was a conformity in deference to all the churches, including the tabernacles. Newspaper photographs of bosomy girls in low blouses were subjected, surely more than elsewhere, to spraying by airbrush before publication, the effect being a curious anatomical vagueness.

As for social class, Toronto was sometimes said to be subject to the influence of WASPs, these being, as in the United States, White Anglo-Saxon Protestants of old money and family history. WASPs presumably existed, but their influence was immeasurably greater in the social theory of our Ukrainian taxi-drivers. There was a fee-paying school, Upper Canada College, which conferred some small cachet on those who went to it. An exclusive gentleman's club or two existed, one being the Granite Club, and there were golf clubs which spoke of themselves as having a restricted intake. No Jews was what it meant, according to my later informant about the Pepsis, but I am unsure.

None of this came near to a class ascendancy of the English kind. There were no noticeable distinctions in accent, no titles, no landed estates or great houses, no Oxbridge colleges, no social pyramid brought to mind by the real existence of King or Queen. There was also the fact of immigration. To earlier waves was added a tide during my decade, seeking the better life of full refrigerators.

Have I drifted into anachronism in some of this? Indeed so. In 1950, if I was capable of reflection on it, I was not outside my Toronto of diffidence, rectitude and classlessness. I took a true pleasure to be in a large and storied place. It was about as good as Rome. Auras attached to it. Maple Leaf Gardens on Saturday night for the ice hockey, preferably the Leafs against the Boston Bruins. Massey Hall for the symphonies, even Mahler. Jarvis Street where actual sex was reported to have a tenuous existence, the phenomenon of old-world restaurants being set up by the influx of Displaced Persons. North Toronto, where the houses had larger gardens and their owners were the better sort of people, having among them very few DPs but no doubt some of the elusive WASPs.

It was to North Toronto that I came, to the house of my sister Ruth and her husband Elmar Victor Spielbergs. He had been born in Latvia, and, as he may not have been averse to conveying, if only by a certain definiteness in enunciating his origins, was of no other descent that might have been suggested by his family name. An amiable man of parts, he was no recent arrival, and had been to university in Montreal. He now conducted a metal-hardening business, and painted decently on the week-ends, in the style of Utrillo. He dealt well with me, a juvenile in-law already capable of some scepticism about his residual European worldliness, and incapable of admitting to learning something from it. Ruthie

51

was vigorously engaged in the promotion and publicity of good causes. They included the Toronto Symphony Orchestra, the Salvation Army, and the Christmas fund-raising for the needy.

My transition from the telephone house to this pleasant urban place, from the hand-pump to the gleaming taps, was effortless, or at any rate without notable incident. I was made at home, given pocket money, and guided into the ways of a different life, mainly by my sister. She was 20 years older, 37, and we were by way of being confidantes. She might say her affection had begun at my birth, to which she was called when the midwife did not appear. To her good nature were added a shrewdness, a diplomacy that did not keep her from fighting her corner when advisable, a determination to stay well ahead of the Kuhns, and also a determination that I should acquire what she described, not wholly ironically, as the social graces. Refinements were made to my table manners, my shirts did less heavy duty, and I was introduced to the cocktail party. I did not sparkle, but did start to learn that a Mennonite severity was not the only possible mode of relation to the Elspeths and Deirdres.

Mother was in the nursing home, afflicted with amytrophic lateral sclerosis, a terrible wasting of the nervous system. With hindsight, it seemed to have been coming on for some years, and I was grieved by my earlier judgements on her for her want of vivacity and her failure to cut a good figure. She was confined to a bed, under some sedation. Having had her hopes of faith-healing destroyed, she did not talk much of religion, and was not keen on visits by preachers. She did not abandon God, however, and this may have made things less bad for her. My visits to her were dutiful. She exhorted me to be good.

Lawrence Park Collegiate Institute, where I continued my studies, thought well of itself, in part because of being attended by a number of rich kids. There were good teachers, such as the senatorial Mr Breslove, whose knowledge of the Latin text-book had a perfection due to his having written it, and Mr Campbell, whose judgement in English Composition was severe and his cynicism about originality prompt. I wrote him a short story about boys on an expedition from their village, the little plumes of dust rising from their heels as they walked in file along the country road, and about the insides of their heads. It bore some relation to reality, he allowed, but it was not so good a theft as might have been managed. Better things might have been stolen. Had I looked into Twain? Burns? He may have been taken aback by my composure in the face of this charge. I knew who wrote the thing. It was all mine. Later in life I remembered my composure, and tried to duplicate it in slightly less simple issues of ownership of academic words and ideas, to some avail.

I worked a little at what took my attention and required no sustained effort, these being English Literature as well as Composition, and Geometry and History. My highest pleasure at school, not much reduced by my incomplete familiarity with my Breslove, was in the Latin poets. Nothing written has struck me so much since. As in my previous collegiate institute, I did not inspire a general admiration, or a general affection. Now, however, I was stronger in my resistance. Mr Charlesworth, in charge of Physical Education and also the cadet corps, took me not to have exerted myself in the hundred yard dash, and conveyed this was a failure in character. It was not so great a failure, however, as a later one with respect to the khaki shirt required of all cadets for a Saturday morning parade. I did try to find khaki, but had no good grip on the existence of outfitters. Also, I saw that I would reduce the uniformity of Mr Charlesworth's serried ranks by my second choice, dusky rose.

My brother Bee, having served an apprenticeship at *The Kitchener Record* and having been kept out of the army by his spectacles, had come to *The Toronto Star* in 1943 – to a temporary job as general reporter that would end when the boys came back from the war. Three years later he was Financial Editor, a rising man. He too lived in North Toronto, with his winsome wife Florence and their two children, mercifully named John and Mary. Earlier than this year of 1950, I was on the way to taking him to be the head of my family, and to be a kind of brother-father to me. Now, after my first spell of living at Ruthie's, possibly in danger of outstaying my welcome, I was transferred to Bee and Florence. 46 Haslemere Road was another agreeable home, and again my in-law did well by me. Her folk-truths were as good as any. She could be tolerant of delay in the completion of my household duties, and had opportunity to be.

My relation to my brother-father was more challenging to me. He was 32 years old and I was 17, and this was not forgotten. He was no lax examiner in our conversations at dinner. No evasion, least of all silence, was possible. He was as severe a man as I have ever met, taking perfection by his lights to be the only tolerable option. By this means he was to improve what out of his good principles he preserved, the newspaper of indubitably the greatest value to his country. His severity, as all have said since, was often extended to himself. That did not lighten the effect of his judgements on me, but instead removed a defence against them. The effect was heavy and persistent. The feelings between us, certainly mine, were not slight ones. If I did not collapse, I never gave as good as I got.

As for defences of himself, which he was not called upon to supply, several now come to mind. He worked so hard, maintained so relentless a momentum, that it was difficult for him to slow down into the leisure required for some passages of life with others. I have also thought, since learning to work myself, that he was often tired. It is not easy to be dog-tired and gentle, let alone harassed by oneself and gentle. Also, he was in a way shy and uncertain, not easy in his life, another condition of which I have experience myself. It is not always possible, having found one's tongue, also to find the best use of it. In his case, this went with something else, that often enough he showed to me brotherly love, which term I use literally. As for my love for him, he has sometimes delayed its expression, but never lost it.

In my summer vacation of 1950, when I was still 17, Bee arranged instead for me to work at *The Star* as a reporter, or at least to have a try at proving myself. This newspaper was the largest in Canada, and, among the known ones, the only disinterested one. Unlike the rest it did not have the typical character of a paper owned by a rich man or well-off shareholders. In place of that common character it had good impulses. It had been founded by striking printers at the end of the nineteenth century. Being pragmatic and a touch paternalistic, not theoretical or inclined to fly in the face of public opinion, it did not declare itself for democratic socialism, but that was near to being the sum of its impulses. It hoped for the best from Russia after the Revolution, for a while, and sent good hopers there to find it.

There were also other facts about *The Star* up to the later 1950s. It was never near to being gutter press of the English variety, never a trough of tripe and prurience, but it was, as all said, sensational. Despite the fates accorded by airbrush to the bosomy girls in low blouses, it was an awful lot livelier than its city. It was also a newspaper of which myths of journalism are made. Hemingway had worked there. Partly for these reasons, my summer of writing obituaries and headings did not increase my commitment to my studies on returning to Lawrence Park Collegiate Institute. Nor was my commitment increased by what began when I turned 18 in 1951. This was my working Saturdays at *The Star* as a general reporter. I did not attempt to join an elevated circle of scholars with the University of Toronto in their sights. The lazy idea was that in the fulness of time I would show them. The future place to which I was headed, in so far as it was defined, was a place in which somehow I would cut some figure or other. Perhaps I would 'write'.

I was bespectacled, could pass as bookish, and in my journalism was precocious. It pleases me more that I was still taking things in. One of these, as before, was girls. They were in their natures more girls than what in fact they also were, young women. I was exchanging occasional letters and a visit or two with Helen Geiger of the Kitchener-Waterloo Collegiate Institute, still as comely as she was serious. We contemplated one another and discovered a lack of resolution. I suspect she took me as having some abilities but still a chancey proposition, maybe worse, and she was proud and not forward. Very like Ingrid at the present moment.

Other good-looking girls came into view in my neighbourhood or at Lawrence Park. Two of them had reputations and therefore suitable names among the boys. No doubt the reputations and names were owed as much to our rising inclinations of a bodily kind as to their activities. In my case, at any rate, it was only a matter of exactly a rising inclination of a bodily kind. The description is as accurate and enlightening as it can be. I might as well have missed the illustrated instructions received from the two advanced lads in Baden and missed the inspiriting feeling produced by leaning against the drinking fountain. I was not prurient. In place of lewd thoughts or images, I had only the bodily inclination. Going steady with a girl, if that desirable state could be entered into, would primarily be a connection of loyalty, confidences, secrets, revealed hopes, a possible future, and, importantly, a resulting public standing. Into the connection would enter kissing and conceivably what was called petting, as secondary if worthwhile features.

Perhaps it was because I thought the two girls with reputations and names might be different, not prurient but somehow expectant, that I did little to act on my inclination towards them. *Hot-Pants* could be seen on household duty, shovelling snow off the front path, no doubt for character-building purposes. I could do no more than nod. I did date *Nympho*. We came back to 46 Haslemere Road to listen to Glenn Miller on the record-player. She alarmed Bee, perhaps putting him in mind of the airbrush. Alarmed myself, I did not have the courage to ask her out again.

Something else restrained my activities with girls in general for a while longer. I was not handsome. Bob had been handsome, but I wasn't. If it did not oppress me, it came to mind a lot. When it did so at crucial moments, it issued at best in a show of arrogance and at worst nearly in flight. I was too tall, getting near to the final 6'4", and maybe skinny, a beanpole. There were also the specs, those mortifying proofs not only of weak eyes but of weak manhood. Further, my head wasn't big enough for my height, and the hair not wiry enough for the crew-cut.

I have said that my innocence and this self-image restrained me with girls for a while. The same is to be said of something else. If I had left Baden behind, something large from that time remained with me, contrary to expectation. Whatever its exact origin in terms of my village or my parents or myself, and however it fits together with a good deal of boy's happiness, it was of course an uncertainty about membership. My world in 1951 in North Toronto, my world to me, like other worlds thereafter, included a doubt about my acceptance and general standing in it. That was partly but certainly not wholly the question of whether I was admired by others. It had in it, as an essential element, my own estimate of myself. To the two insecurities, about appearance and general standing, others were added. My scholarly achievements were not heartening. As for my journalism, it was not as if I had worked for a summer at exactly a great newspaper. And evidently my self-discipline was not Bee's.

But it is too simple always to regard such insecurities only as restraints, whether in the matter of pursuing girls or anything else. They may be materials which go into the formation of a will. What is called not enough self-esteem may also be a sufficient amount of frustration and obstacle. There are happy souls, evidently, who do few things in their lives exactly because they have never had the early spur of misfortune and shortcoming, and the practice of trying to deal with it. Certainly my own insecurities have not only been restraints but also benefits. I have as often raged as despaired over my estimate of my standing in the world, my marks, my long legs, and my drinking. I still do. Better to rage than despair, since to rage is to be on the way to doing something. Would that I always raged.

It seems a good guess that in the matter of girls in the spring of 1951, my insecurities did me a service. I acquired the regular but still innocent company of two girls, necessarily not alarming girls. Marjorie Rennie was sweet in her silence and had a Grecian turn that held my eye. Shirley Trott was tall and fair with an engaging touch of superiority, and, despite her respectability, possessed of a better sense than I of possible relations between the sexes. In a few months, when I had gathered some resolution in a special cause, the elements came to my aid. A lashing rainstorm stopped a walk. We sheltered under a garage door, in the dark, and I kissed a girl. How fine to be a member of the kissing classes.

What also happened in this summer when I was 18 was the earliest event which still causes me the pain of shame. Together with two other episodes it seemed to make me hesitate for a moment about going forward with this book. Having worked the previous summer at *The Star*, and on Saturdays since February, I was there again full-time during this summer, now blooded and getting by-lines. I was summoned by my editor and told that an old hand, a practised woman, had failed to collect a photo of a boy who had killed himself on his motorcycle, decapitated himself, and that I should go out there and succeed where she had failed. I did, by an unspeakable subterfuge. If I did not lie, which might have been less bad, I allowed a member of the family to believe that I was not a journalist at all, but somehow more official, and in fact concerned with preparations for the funeral. When the photo appeared in the paper, the family, now more distraught, telephoned that same editor. I was sent back by him, carrying a framed enlargement of the photo, to face them and apologise for what I had done. All that can be said of me, which is no defence, is that the fact hung over me thereafter, and did have some effect.

Mother's decline over two years in the nursing home, bed-ridden and increasingly suffering, was terrible. There was no hope. Our regular visits, if they were a help to her, could not have done much to raise her spirits. She maintained a composure, and would not rage, but would go quietly into that good night. On 3 December 1951 Bee and I were there. He read the 23rd Psalm to her. 'Yea, though I walk through the valley of the shadow of death, I will fear no evil: for thou art with me: thy rod and thy staff comfort me.' He could not wholly succeed in not weeping. I was overcome. It was the most awful experience of my life.

That my mother's death was so terrible to me speaks some large fact, but a fact that has no easy description. I have remarked that I was closer to her than to my father, and that I grew up aware of her as my best supporter, someone to be called upon always: she knew more about me, and her loyalty was complete and she was able to act on it. My feelings of closeness and support, however, had natures owed to what was also true, that in ways I felt let down by her and judged her.

My poor reasons were her seeming to be defeated in her own life, and her not keeping herself in better trim, and the embarrassment caused to me by her religion. In contrast, while my father's shortcomings were a public fact, and in this way affected me, they were not to the fore in my feelings for him, and I did not judge him. Is there no justice at all in love? It may be that my love for my mother would have been sweeter if she had been able to demonstrate more of the love she had for me. Her blue-eyed boy, I thought, despite Loine's religion and Bee's success, was Bob. If all of these darker reflections about my love for my mother are true, or have some chance of being true, they need to be contemplated in the light of my experience of her death. She has not been forgotten since, and 'Rae Laura' is a computer password I now use daily.

At 19, having the possibility of going steady, I was less inclined to it, having also fallen into a certain frame of mind and feeling with respect to girls and women. It had in it, if you will put up with my unfortunate tendency to enumerate, at least seven elements, the first being the insecurities mentioned above, having to do with size of head, membership and so on. A second, a better beginning, was the inclination of a bodily kind. Another was the fact that I liked women better than men. Among men I had but one friend, Don McKinnon of pleasant memory, with whom I went to the Colonial Tavern, drank little, but was taken by the jazz, or the idea of jazz. Muggsy Spanier personified it, and on occasion Louis Armstrong. Did I like women better than men because of being more pleased by feminine as against masculine natures? Well, they were more reassuring to me. Women were not competitors. Another element in my frame of mind and feeling was my becoming accustomed to success. If I had not progressed much beyond kisses, I was certainly not being left forlorn. Girls took to me. This had much to do with an independence due initially to the insecurities. Girls were more keen on me than on their wholly smitten admirers. There was also a fifth element, different from the enjoyment of success. This was a taste for more of it, not to be satisfied by giving up the quest and settling into a connection.

Further, and above all, there was the difficulty of choosing. I was not then overwhelmed by any girl, and have rarely been overwhelmed by a successor since. I was caught in comparisons. This was so not because of an inclination to indecision, but because there was no effective rule or method of comparison. A girl had to be a good-looker to my conventional eye, or close to that, and also something else, a second thing. The further recommendation might be intelligence, spirit, humanity, morality, style, estimable success, or a perceptive acceptance of me. There was an insuperable difficulty, akin to one of which I learned later. John Stuart Mill says that in choosing among possible actions we are to take into account the higher and lower pleasures to which they give rise, and count the lower for less. But he cannot say how much less. He fudges the question of whether a given amount of lower pleasure is worth, say, half of the same amount of a higher pleasure, or more or less than half. So with my contemplation of the recommendations of my possible girl-friends. I could not weigh up degrees of good looks with the other recommendations, or weigh up the other recommendations one against another.

The situation is common enough, and it could be that the extent to which I was reflective rather than impulsive is not rare. Perhaps, to come to a seventh and related element in my carry-on, it *is* rarer to follow a certain policy in the situation of uncertainty. That, alas, is the policy of not plumping, but waiting to see if something more decisive comes along, and maybe having a look for it. I see from *The Oxford Companion to Philosophy*, lately much on my mind, that to *satisfice* is to accept a satisfactory upshot rather than go on to try to secure an optimum or ideal one. There is much to be said for it. But I was no satisficer.

My relation to women is a large matter in this book, and what has now been said baldly does not come close to settling it. After this time, more was to be added to my frame of mind and feeling. Let me end here with a piece of self-defence and also a piece of self-doubt, at least self-doubt.

There is a kind of high-mindedness that deplores our taking other individuals as what philosophers call, a bit technically, collections of properties. To take this attitude, say the high-minded, is also to take other individuals as interchangeable or replaceable. The high-mindedness typically has some mystery-mongering in it, a gesturing at an elusive and metaphysical idea of inner persons or inner selves, surely an illusion. Persons in our experience of them *are* collections of properties, inevitably. There is no coldness or want of humanity in registering the fact, even the happy fact. There are no soul-to-soul or I–Thou relations that are not relations to particular facts of body, mind, character, and personality, properly and usually taken together. I did not offend in 1952 and have not offended since by not pursuing what contains an illusion. That is the self-defence.

To offer it, however, is not to say that one does not acquire obligations to an individual, obligations that obviously have no counterparts at all to any other individual of the same general properties. Hopes and expectations arise. Individuals are indeed not interchangeable. That can be true without the illusion's being true. Have I often failed in personal obligations, failed more often than those who are subject to the illusion in the high-mindedness? That is the self-doubt or worse than that.

I ploughed on at Lawrence Park, or anyway turned over some furrows, few of them at the weekend since Saturday was given over to my employment at *The Star*. I spent much of my reading-time not on homework but with plays and novels, and sometimes potted science and philosophy. The philosophy was very intriguing, but not so open or possible to me as other things. It was somehow to one side of reality. My family sought to settle my mind on a degree at the University of Toronto, and pressed me to apply for entrance. If I went, I would be the first of our known family, whatever might have been the case with our European antecedents, to darken an academic door. This, in Canada at the time, would not be at all remarkable.

But university was more school, and there was no great need to go. Bee hadn't gone, and he was getting on fine, and was superior about university economists. Journalism tempted me, as well as 'writing'. The first was conceived by me as a means to the second. 'Writing' was Hemingway, and it also included someone above Hemingway. This higher figure was Arthur Miller, whose *Death of a Salesman* could be my exemplar.

My school-leaving examinations were not quite as might have been expected, and as I expected. My degree of entry into Trigonometry and Statics was such that my First in Geometry could not save me from a Third in Mathematics as a whole. So with the Latin, and only a Second in French. What was unexpected, and owed something to the exasperated labours of Mr Campbell, was my doing well enough at English and History, getting Firsts there, to be awarded a university entrance scholarship. It was only the Morley Wickett Scholarship, for the sum of no more than $35, but a scholarship. Indeed it was not grand, and never tempted me to return to Lawrence Park to see my photo hung in the marble corridor along with those of superior scholars. But it decided things. I would pause a little before setting out on the main path after my two leaders, Arthur Miller in front.

4

FROM UNIVERSITY DISTRACTED, FIRST LOVE

The University of Toronto was stately, its campus green before the snow. It was in the middle of the city and had good Victorian buildings, and also such necessary pieces of tradition as a Philosopher's Walk, which led out towards an old village enclosed by the growth of Toronto. The village had not yet been smartened up, and only those academics so supremely rational as to want to walk to work lived in it. There were also boarding houses for students. It was to one of these I came in September 1952 when I left my brother's home at 19, to work my way through college.

The university was comfortable in taking itself as first and foremost among Canadian ones, and it was capable of sometimes stirring in the general diffidence that it shared with its city and country. If it was more given to scholarship and the plod of normal science than to revolutionary theory, such an explorer as Marshall McLuhan could dash back from the future to proclaim, whatever it meant, that the medium was the message. It had to do with the advent of television. My college was University College, the original college of the university and a secular one, a black edifice in Canadian Gothic style. My registration was in the common first year for the B.A. Honours courses in various Arts subjects.

I was most attracted to Northrop Frye's precise lectures on William Blake, despite his being of another college attached to the United Church, and I aspired to write essays of true perception and fearful symmetry myself. In fact, in my first year, one essay got written, on The Failure of the Reforms of Diocletian and Constantine to Halt the Decline of the Roman Empire in the West. It got an *A*, with compliments. But a half-dozen other essays failed to get written at all. That they did not had something to do with the number of things that did get written, for *The Toronto Star*, on matters of more immediate concern, these being hit-and-run drivers, press conferences at the Royal York Hotel, prayers for the souls of men being hanged, and DPs making good in their new city.

I was working full-time as a general reporter on the night shift, and sleeping through the next morning's lectures. It would be agreeable to say that my academic record in my first term at university, or rather the want of an academic record, was just owed to my needing sleep. That is not all of the story. The journalism had caught my attention and distracted me. The night shift was not always filled up with hit-and-run drivers and the like. In fact there was time for trying to keep up with the History, French, Oriental Literature and so on. I did not use much of it, but instead, adding another scene to my rake's progress, played cards with my fellow workers and invested in a uranium mine on the stock market. Despite at least an interest in England's Welfare State, noted in my diary, I was not political.

At the end of my first academic year, with the exams a fortnight away, reality somehow broke through: Economics a closed book, seven-eighths of the Political Science lectures unheard, preliminary exams not taken, a raft of essays undone, and the professor of English Literature vowing he would find a regulation to prohibit my sitting *his* exam. I gave up. I attempted no papers, not being able to face doing badly, and took my way up Philosopher's Walk with roughly the correct amount of official credit for my first academic year, which was none.

In the summer when I was 20, spent at *The Star*, there was another episode of impersonation in the picking up of photos, not so awful as the first but awful enough, and also a piece of deception by omission. I wrote about them in my diary, accused myself without sincerity, and reflected ignorantly on what I called my amorality. In this summer I succumbed as well to social aspiration, and became a member of a self-approving tennis club. It may have had a restricted membership of the kind alluded to earlier in this narrative, but this was unknown to me. I was not so forward as to meet any other single member, and so had no one to play with.

The B.A. General Course at the University of Toronto was begun by me in the autumn, again registered as a First Year student. I would be working less than full-time at *The Star*, usually no more than four and a half hours a day. The General Course would take three years, not the four for an Honours course. The idea was that I would not be too long detained before setting out into the real future. Very likely that would be in the footsteps of Miller and Hemingway. But now there was also another possibility, politics. This path was less clear, but if pressed, I would again have mentioned the Welfare State.

Early in September I went to Union Station, bearing gifts I could not afford, to see off my most settled girlfriend of the previous academic year, now leaving to become a teacher in an Ontario town. Enid McLatchie gave me my first experience of coquettish propriety. Our connection, like my previous ones and others afterwards, was one of affection and uncertainty. This consisted partly in my not being satisfactorily serious. I persisted in jocularity. Generally a girl had to have a name other than her name. Enid was Andy.

The uncertainty of my connections, in so far as it was owed to me, had among its causes some of those things lately itemized. These were my insecurities of several kinds, only the one about spectacles having been escaped by way of contact lenses. There were the various elements of my general frame of mind and feeling with respect to actual and possible partners, notably my comparing-and-grading problem and my dis-inclination to satisficing. But there were also new causes of uncertainty in my relationships, two of which were to be persistent, the other to be temporary.

A self-observation in my diary at the time, overstated but not absurdly so, was that it was on the way to true that I could not exist by myself. If I was not gregarious, I had a strong inclination to a reassuring kind of company, almost necessarily the company of a girl. The inclination went with a certain activism or efficiency. The prospect of an evening by myself was usually bleak enough to issue in telephone calls to avoid it. This persisted. When deprived for a time of the company of my most settled girlfriend by the end of a university term or by whatever else, I filled in, with old friends and new. If this was not always being unfaithful, since oaths had not been exchanged or only weakly renewed, it did nothing to reduce the uncertainty of my most settled connection.

The second new complication, a complication of the comparing-and-grading problem, had to do with something noted above, a rise in ambition and aspiration. I could put sentences together in a way satisfactory to at least *The Star*. In its employ, also, I had demonstrated to myself a spiritedness. I had come away from my first year at university with no marks but some idea of my being the possessor of an intellectual bent. Was not good writing good thinking or near enough to it? So I did not propose a humble life to myself. And, to come to the point, about uncertainty in my connections, a *suitable* consort was required for the life on which a small beginning was being made.

The third new complication with a candidate, bound to be transient but real enough for a time, was our not allowing ourselves actually to make love, which activity had now come roughly into focus. That was true of Andy and me. This self-denial stood in the way of commitment, and, since it was not firm, could produce confusion. My farewell from Andy on the train in Union Station, our long kisses, obscured from me the fact that the train was leaving. I was carried off with her 20 miles to the first stop. We parted again, and, despite our letters, never met again.

Soon after, living in a university men's residence, I was to the fore in arranging group-dates with the student nurses in their nearby residence, also proceeding to degrees. We went in clumps to films and moonlit wiener roasts on the beach of an island in the bay. We all quickly disentangled ourselves from these mass outings, in my case to take up with she who was to be, so to speak, the first woman in my life. I loved her tentatively and in some confusion, and might say, as of others, that I love her still.

A shudder is also attached to my thoughts of her, since she alone knows the awfulness of my immaturity when I was still 21 and she 20, and for a year or two thereafter. Did I, paradoxically, fall into an immaturity from which earlier I had somehow been saved? Now I was not only what I have so far described myself as being, but also *a wheel*. Being a wheel was rather more primitive than what would succeed it, being *cool*. A wheel was fast with women and could talk a good line, and yet might be a sombre intellectual underneath, reflecting in his diary on the tremendous questions inherent in existence, including the essence of good.

First Love, as she will be known in this narrative, came from a distant part of Ontario and was of an intelligence plainer than mine, and of clearer emotions. She could talk sense, and was enamoured of me and loyal. She was also good-looking, bringing to mind the adverts aimed at establishing that women's specs can be flattering. I was impressed by her at the island wiener roast in October, and we said, if not too unsurely, that we would go steady. She kept to this. I, despite having been struck by her, did not, and then confessed. In December, nevertheless, we were officially in love. Alas, she had to go home for the holiday. I rang people up, but in January we were reconciled again.

When I was 22, in April, we agreed to become lovers, and failed because of mutual alarm as well as an uncertainty on my part about what was where. I said in my diary that I wanted to write of this event but would not, since such a passage of life could only properly be the subject of a master, or 'at least a writer greater than I at this point'. We did succeed an evening or two later, and I did not write of this yet greater event at all. Certainly the carnality of it was under heavy emotional drapery. Officially anyway, it was essentially persons who were getting close, and only accidentally bodies. Having acted on my third piece of carnal knowledge, that love could be made between man and woman, my mind subsequently turned to my first, acquired seven years before, from the advanced lads in Baden. This, although the verb had perhaps never passed my lips, was the possibility of jerking off. I masturbated for the first time, in the bath, to know the nature of the thing.

This second year of mine at university, in fact my first real year, was half-respectable. I was distracted by my pursuit of by-lines and my wheelishness, and, despite these, also by something a bit better. This was being a university student, being in a carefree way of life that had a large history. Johnson had been a student of sorts, and Burke, and Darwin, and Marx. Miller and Hemingway too. Still, all my essays had got written, and all had got *A*s and compliments but one, on Thomas More, which was *B*. I sought out a second opinion on this injustice, and wondered if the professor had been unimpressed by my manner of concluding my essay, with '30', the reporter's mark for the end of a story. Another professor had inquired if I took my reflections on Thucydides, Herodotus and Plutarch to be news, thereby teaching me something more of chagrin.

Despite a thin record of attendance at lectures, my examination results at the end of the year were tolerable or better, except for Geography. I failed it with *élan*, since a certain amount of fluency cannot conceal being unable to tell a drumlin from an esker. I got a prize for English, with some useful cash, and also a prize for a short story, and was pleased with the official letter that came with them. Your College, wrote its rightly esteemed Principal, Dr F. C. A. Jeanneret, takes special pride in your achievement, which helps to signalize the first year of its Second Century.

Father wrote to me of his endeavours in Kitchener. 'I have been doing some very constructive thinking these last two days, and I am really expecting results.' We met when he visited Toronto to stay with my brother or sister, and I took him out to tea, and got the cakes he liked. On a Sunday afternoon in September 1954, we talked at 46 Haslemere Road for some hours, of Baden and the fruit belt, of First Love, and of the results he was expecting. That evening after I left, during his nap on the sofa after a good dinner, he took his departure from this world, without knowing he was doing so. Bee and Florence, watching television in the room, did not notice him going. With luck I will follow him in the manner of his going. Much to be said for naps.

It was of course partly the easiness of his decline and death that made it so much less awful than Mother's. But that was not the main thing. If Mother's had been easy, it would still have been so much darker than Father's. The difference was that her life as I knew it was sad, and his was something like happy. If he did not do great things, or indeed middle-sized things, he had the great blessing of living in hope. Is there a greater? The actual satisfaction of desire, success, may not be so sweet and does not last so long as hope. Mother did not have the blessing of it. So is death always bad because it is annihilation, the end of a world, but worse than that, terrible, if it settles forever that someone lived sadly? No doubt I will try to do some constructive thinking on that sometime, and maybe expect results.

It cannot be said that my intention to return to university for my third year was resolute. Admittedly, returning was more promising since the principal of my college, having been petitioned, had sanctioned another change of course. I could abandon the General Course and the uphill task of distinguishing drumlins from eskers, and instead do the second year of the Honours course in English Language and Literature. I could find out more about grace in Milton, and hear further argument as to whether tragedy lives on in the twentieth century in *Death of a Salesman*. But, as against that, might it not be better to set out on the main path directly, to set about my own true writing? I returned instead to the study of Milton and Miller, uncertainly, giving only my Saturdays to working at *The Star*.

This was not the only thing I was uncertain about. In this autumn of 1954, First Love and I were most of the time a happy pair, as we had been since the evening when we first achieved personal union. She often seemed to me a woman of paradigmatic sense and warmth, and indeed the possessor of all human virtues. But I, and sometimes we, deliberated sadly about whether we were right for one another. Was she a suitable consort? The rub was that she was not intellectual, at any rate not *an* intellectual. No Canadian or at any rate English Canadian could then admit openly to the charge of being the thing, but this did not much reduce the rub for me. If her intelligence was clear, she was not literary. She was a passive rather than an active consumer of Canadian culture. She was a nurse. She could not or would not join me in my pretensions.

Our affair was carried on, in my room in my boarding house or in my men's residence. No effective precaution against pregnancy was taken by us, in part because of my spiritual delicacy. I knew of the existence of 'safes', these being condoms, but they were unspeakable in two senses, the second being a literal one. The word would have choked me. Can that be true? Well, despite being or having been a wheel, I never spoke of a safe. The first experience of fear of pregnancy, which lasted nine days, was paralysing. The subject of marriage was touched on with Bee and Ruth to prepare them. The subject then receded until the second scare, and the third. I never thought that the obstetrics and gynaecology that was part of her nurse's training must be giving her a good awareness of all our reproductive natures.

While First Love was back home at Christmas, I was true to her in body, but took out another girl or two. One of these was Margaret Penman, also doing English Language and Literature. In a long letter she proposed to me that I carry on my carnal experiment elsewhere, but meet her for cups of coffee as well, and wait to discover the truth that because of our unique sensitivity we were fated for one another. I did not agree, but she will reappear in this narrative.

My diary sets all this out, sometimes with the intention of ruminating somewhat complacently on my failings. I was notorious to myself, and sometimes satisfied by the notoriety. There was satisfaction in riding over convention, being free from society and from Rae Laura. I stole a book from the university bookshop, and glanced at my notes when left alone in a professor's room to do an informal exam. Some dates were written on cigarette papers to take to another test, but not used. Recollecting these facts has also given me pause about going forward with this book, if less than the episode of the photograph of the dead boy.

In connection with them, my diary in effect separates questions of goodness and badness in personal or intimate relations from such questions in connection with people at a distance, their property, and certainly their regulations. The latter questions are considered with less feeling, never with alarm. But the conclusion is drawn that infractions of the rules are not worth it. Not too long after, I came to have a kind of horror of risks, but did not come to the attitude that the value of all morality is that it pays, and have not come to that attitude since. Evidently some does and some doesn't.

No principle can be discerned in what happened next. I was no longer caught up in the adventure of journalism. My Saturdays as a reporter did not stand out above the week's lectures. But the lectures, despite my admiration of the severe sensibility of Professor Endicott and his colleagues, were not compelling either. In January 1955 about a week before my 22nd birthday I left the university, without intending to return. Tchaikowsky's Fifth Symphony was what I listened to most often, and what most affected me in it was the Theme of Destiny. I seem to remember taking myself as submitting to my destiny. What was also true was that, captured by neither, I was taking the easier of two options.

My destiny and easy option turned out not to be *The Star*, still of good political impulses and sensational, but an associated magazine, *The Star Weekly*. This was a sheaf of diversions, some of them decently enlightening, which helped several million Canadians to get through the whole weekend. The heart of the thing, however, was two sections of feature articles and short stories. For it, in February, a month after leaving university, I flew to New York for the first time, Eisenhower America. My resulting article was on Canine College, a dog-training establishment whose graduates were awarded the C.S. or Canus Sapiens degree, for dogmatic knowledge. My piece was not sufficiently superior to save me from some embarrassment. It did not consist in *thought*.

In June I was in the Canadian West, in the province of Alberta, back among Anabaptists. These were Hutterites, akin to some of the Mennonites, but actually following the ideal of community of goods, other than women. They were governed, they said, by a text that surely had turned up in my father's pamphlet. 'And all who believed were together and had all things common.' Acts 2:44. They lived austerely in communes, each with no more than a bit of pocket money. They were not loved by all their neighbours, who said they did not mind Communists but were not keen on these ones. Their refusal to bear arms had allowed their communes to become well-off while neighbouring farmers were away in the army. To me they were saintly. My piece did them a good turn.

When I came away from staying with them, to my hotel in the provincial capital, there was a more dramatic telegram for me, from First Love. Our connection had now persisted for 22 months, sometimes sweetly, sometimes contentedly, usually uncertainly. The telegram said that yes, there definitely was a child on the way, and I should come home soon. At first we talked of marriage and where to live. It was not a happy prospect to me, and not a wholly happy one to her, partly because of her determination to finish her degree and start on more than the life of a mother. Through two or three weeks we talked, ever more sadly. She came to suggest the alternative to having the child, the word for which was hardly uttered between us. I did not resist her suggestion, and we acted on it, necessarily illegally. My part in this, as against securing the photo of the dead boy, and stealing the book and so on, has given me more pause about writing this book. It has been the piece of my past that weighed most on me.

As it seemed to me then, the best thing was done, this being the least bad of bad things. That seems more true now. But one heavy question is the extent to which the outcome was secured by me through manipulation, or at least without honestly conveying my reluctance to marry. Certainly, as remarked earlier in this connection, it seems possible to act so that the right thing is done, and still be indecent oneself in the action. Another heavier question has to do with my having previously gone on in such a way as to end up in the situation. That question of guilt is not about not marrying, but about having so acted that a bad thing was necessary. The bad thing in my view, if it needs adding, was certainly not a violation of a right of the unborn, but of the feelings of the born. What was done to First Love was not done by the person who writes these lines, the person I now am, but as yet I have no sense of exculpation.

In the late summer there were more visits to New York, and with them came more control over my personal share of the national inferiority complex of Canadians. In my diary, not only to establish that my journalism had not taken me away from all higher things, I spent some time in a kind of philosophical rumination. Once this was on Existentialism as the logic of life. The description 'the logic of life' had no clear sense, and it is satisfactory to note that I had a proper inkling of this.

In October I was in Hollywood, first passing a day with Jack Benny, who had by then wisecracked his way through 40 years of radio, and had had a loyal audience in Baden. He and his script-writers were an agreeable introduction to happy Jewishness, indeed even to Jews, since their counterparts in my own country had gone further in the policy of assimilation. I was not awed but felt somewhat alien, if that is the word, as often enough since. A couple of lunches were had, too, with him of the movie 'Public Enemy', seen by me in the Lyric when I should have been at the Kitchener-Waterloo Collegiate Institute. Jimmy Cagney was up to expectation, and charmed me absolutely.

Having been given a chance in journalism by Bee, I was now making some use of it, and, if still somehow asleep, being a success. That he was Editor-in-Chief of *The Star*, in effect the editor of the editorial or leader page, disposed people to me, but it was not much of the explanation of my progress. Still, my heart's hopes were not in it, maybe less than before. I was not on the way to being what I was still aspiring to be, a writer with serious intent. My diary says I was in journalism only to pay off the considerable debt incurred through my investment in uranium stocks. Other diary entries were with good reason increasingly judgemental about themselves as well as me. They were also about feelings about death, swinging moods, and the rest of my ongoing performance, notably my lack of an answer to the woman question and my wandering eye. A tin box with a lock was got for my archive.

First Love and I carried on in Toronto, a couple of evenings a week, in my pink and black room at Mrs Foster's boarding house in

Lowther Avenue. We carried on sweetly, worriedly, or doggedly. We also separated in sad resolution, and got back together. In New York, I proved the dangers of a high good humour by asking the innocent Burmese starlet, Win Min Than, in a roomful of watchful agents and public-relations men, if she thought, as a girl in Toronto did, that I looked a little like her leading man, Gregory Peck. No, she said sweetly, in a yet more silent room, not really. Still, I did meet a charmer on that trip whose additional recommendations were her being a New Yorker and embodying the mysterious humanity of Jewishness. Also, she was a kind of mistress of good prose, although confined to the service of *Popular Science Monthly*. We met amicably on several of my subsequent visits, and she was inordinately moved by my true perception of the prettiness of her ankles.

Back in Toronto around Christmas, when First Love was away, I again was in touch with Margaret Penman – she whose time had not yet come, and whose future might have in it more poetry and a Canadian novel of sensibility, our reply to Virginia Woolf. We spoke abstractly of love and marriage, but she did not take me seriously, rightly, and we did not become lovers. Things were otherwise with my New Yorker, and in March she rang up, calmly, to let me know she was pregnant. She did not count on my doing the honourable thing, and I sent the money she needed. It had been an affair of affection, begun in a little hope, and it ended with less recrimination than I had earned. We corresponded for a while but did not rediscover hope.

It all reached a kind of climax in May 1956 when I travelled for a while with Elvis Presley. He was 21 and I was 23. He became less than keen on me, for a good reason. In order to keep my end up with this hillbilly on his way to at least a brief immortality, I essayed a gravitas. Certainly I would step on his blue suede shoes. I did not defer to the fact that in Memphis the most forward of the shrieking girls handed him the tribute of their panties by way of the security guards in front of the footlights. I did not defer either to the fact that his Cadillac was powder-blue when we arrived at the auditorium in Houston and more or less pink when we came out, having been worshipped by kissing. I also pretended an intimate knowledge of Beethoven. He responded well, taking the line that this was unlikely in a Canadian.

During this trip, First Love had been using my room to study in for her final examinations. On my return, the tin box containing the hundreds of loose pages of my diary was unlocked. Had I left it that way? She had spent two evenings reading. Since my harsh truth-seeking about myself, if that is what it was, had been accompanied by stuff of the same character on others, and in particular on her, the reading of it was more than wounding. Also, there was the revelation of my connection in New York and my contemplation of Margaret Penman. She contented herself with a letter less of rage than anguish. She said that I would not defeat her love, and enclosed some of Shakespeare's bitter sonnets.

We went to New York for a cathartic holiday before her graduation, and said we would marry in a year. She then went to her first post as a nurse in a Red Cross hospital a long way from Toronto. In July we were exchanging sad letters of doubt, and then separating by letter. This did not preclude our meeting in August for several days of further confession by me and torment for both of us. Our three years ended in weeping by both of us, an agony not since forgotten by me. I was to see her once more, but only in the street, by chance, on 10 December 1956. We did not have the cup of coffee that I wanted to suggest. She said hardly anything, and I hardly more. She had had enough of me.

In the course of the summer of sad confusion, one thing had become clearer. It was necessary to abandon a readership of millions and go back to university. I would study not only English literature but also philosophy, a joint degree. It seems to me not hard to give parts of the explanation of this turn to the subject of philosophy – but at least hard to find enough of them to provide a full or sufficient explanation. One part, reaching out of the past, was my early encounter with religion and with scepticism about it, those civil disputes between Mother and Father enlivened by Pepsi-Cola. Another and recent part was a weakening in my sense of possibly being a writer, a real writer. Did my desire to be one also weaken? In any case, something was coming into focus. There was something that I might be able to do better, and might like doing more. This was getting things straight, really straight, a lot straighter than you had a chance to do in journalism.

There was another consideration that moved me, less reputable. It was my wanting a rank or standing having to do with thinking. Membership in a better club. I said in England much later in an interview or two that some people become poets because they want the name of being a poet, and then go on to get caught up in poetry and do it well – and that some become philosophers because they want the name of being a philosopher, and then are captured by the questions in the subject, and answer them well. The higher motivation comes out of the lower. Let us hope so.

'Is there such a thing as the good for man, and if so, do you agree with Aristotle's account of it in Book One of the *Nichomachean Ethics*?' Mr Gallop set the question, and I answered it in my first philosophy essay, in September 1956, content with my prospective readership of one. In my fifth year after first registering in the University of Toronto, and fully 23, I was no further ahead than the start of the second year of a four-year Honours course. Still, it seemed that the right thing was happening.

To my eye now, my essay was a tolerable attempt at close argument about Aristotle's doctrine. It is that the good for man is *eudaimonia*, an active and pleasing life in accordance with man's unique virtue, this being his faculty of reason. No doubt persuaded that I was now embarking on such a life, I had written my essay confidently. I dragged into the discussion what seemed inseparable from it, the matter of what is right as against what is good. Was that not greatly more important? But the essay was as much distinguished by a certain attitude, a scepticism about ancient philosophy. My attitude was that it consisted to a large extent in strange things and mysteries. Why allow piety about our first ancestors in good thinking, let alone the irrelevant investment of our classical scholars in the study of their language, to detain us from looking for more recent guides we can understand better, or indeed setting out on our own? It was not the last time I appointed myself to guard the true nature of philosophy against intrusion or dilution. Mr Gallop gave me an *A* and wished me well in my philistinism, probably sadly. At the end of the term I was awarded a prize, since his colleagues were as approving about other essays.

It seems to me that my journalism had done me some service. If in my high-mindedness it embarrassed me, it also strengthened my inclination to plain-seeing and plain-speaking, something bound up with a habit of scepticism and empiricism. That habit is pretty much the inclination of a certain kind of philosophy, the main line of philosophy in the English language. To those of a more literary or spiritual bent, or those who want the lift of Parisian speculation, or to remain in awe of the German deep, or to wonder at fierce idiosyncrasy in Cambridge, it may seem dull. Its theories have smaller wings. It is true enough to Francis Bacon's outrageous dictum that the good imagination is the imagination hung with weights. Still, this *is* the main line in philosophy in English, and it gets to some places.

What is also true is that my idea that my journalism did me a service is no longer the confident idea that it once was – that what my journalism strengthened me in is demonstrably the very greatest of philosophical bents. I am no longer so certain about the main line of philosophy in the English language. Rather, my idea now is that my journalism, in fortifying my inclination to plain-seeing and plain-speaking, fortified *my* largest capability, maybe my only relevant capability. Of course I still prefer this bent, unproductive of fans as it is. It seems to me likely to get closest to clear truth. But if I now set about imagining the best of all possible philosophical worlds, with more fans for me in it, I can resist a pleasing temptation to restrain the Sartre in it, and the Heidegger and the Wittgenstein, by assigning them an early term of duty at *The Toronto Star*.

Not long after the start of this academic year 1956–57, in order to escape the need to cook for myself, I moved out of my garret, after drawing a floor plan in order to preserve an exact memory of that place of my life, and moved into the Sir Daniel Wilson Residence for Men. This was my college's new pride, lately erected in another fitting architectural style, Canadian Georgian. I was not to be there long. University College wished to keep up the high quality of its annual intake of undergraduates, and so had the practice of inviting high school pupils to tour the college's cloisters, chapter house, junior common room, and residences. On a Sunday afternoon in February, a first unshepherded flock of them reached Loudon House in the Sir Daniel Wilson Residence.

Some members of that house took it into their heads to enliven the weekend by doing negative public relations. I joined in, one of three of us who were to the fore. In a common room littered with bottles, we made speeches to our visitors, purporting to introduce them to the reality of undergraduate life. That impressionistic crucifixion on the wall from the college art collection was to us 'Christ on a popsicle stick', the shower rooms down the hall were masturbation chambers, the medical students among us were abortionists, here we were drunk on Sunday afternoon smoking our cigarettes languidly, and so on. There was not a lot of *eudaimonia* in it.

We found ourselves up before the Dean of Men. I confessed my part fully, but the other two performers who had been to the fore did not. I alone was forthwith expelled from the residence. Some days later the Dean, the agreeable Ian Macdonald, having been persuaded to look further into the matter by the student council, summoned me to say he had been misled and precipitate. I could return to the residence next term if I wanted, and the two less frank performers would not be doing so. Sharper in my memory is that Dr Jeanneret, the Principal, when I visited him to make an apology, was in tears for his college.

I would not mind having this episode out of my past, but, putting aside those tears, it does not hang over me. Take me aback it does, since I was at the time several weeks past my 24th birthday, and not born an idiot. Why did I do it? Part of the answer was a competitive spirit lately still more released, and attracted to almost any competition. If I was to be in a joint enterprise, I would not be at the tail-end of it. Another part of the explanation was that despite some experience of life I evidently was not at all far-sighted. I didn't see a goodly man's tears in the offing.

There was also something else not transient, which by then was not only a rooted antipathy to conventionality but nearly a disposition to the *outré*. Conventions have often seemed to me not merely boring but also suppressive and manipulative, or at any rate such as to benefit their defenders. I have not been good at dealing with constraint, even the mild constraint of decorum, and in fact have been ready to see constraint where others see reasonableness.

As for my confession to the Dean of Men, that was in character and remains so. My conviction of the goodness and worth of truth, including truth about myself, had by this time somehow come to be stronger. It has not weakened since, or so it seems to me. That is not to say that I have on every occasion told the truth. But I have had, and continue to have, as it seems to me, an aversion to falsehood and a fear of it. It is elementary that this includes falsehood by omission and by not being straightfoward. The writing of this book could have no attraction for me at all, partly because it could have no chance of coming in sight of a general truth or two, as distinct from truths about me, if it suppressed anything of large importance about my own feelings and actions. Although it saves some others from hurt, it leaves out no event of my life that to me is as bad as what it includes. More particularly, the little that is left out has to do with a momentary adventure or two in love, if that is the word, and a consequence or two of the making of love. These would be yours to reflect on, reader, save for the need to avoid a danger or two to the other party.

In this fifth academic year since my first appearance among my teachers, I had worked enough to finish at the head of my class, but without much distinction. My essays continued to get approval, and I demonstrated a zeal for both Hume and John Donne, lovely Donne, but I did not buckle down to preparing for exams. In this year I saw most of Joan Evans, another nurse at the university. We got together after her engagement to marry someone else was broken off without reaching any consummation, and at the time when First Love and I were coming to an end. We said we were getting together on the rebound, implying by that much-used diagnosis that we might be doomed from the beginning. We frolicked, and learned to drink a bit. She too was about 24, and, to her credit, was not suited by nature to what she sometimes spoke of doing, and in truth was called upon by me to do. This was to be fashioned by me in my role as Pygmalion. Instead of being sculpted into a consort, upgraded from nurse, she in fact went on being a feminist before feminism.

At the end of the university year I returned for the summer to a changed newspaper. A few months before, Bee had risen further. He was now not only Editor-in-Chief, but one of five members of the Board of Directors. He was well to the fore in a new policy for the paper, against sensationalism. In subsequent years, as all said, it was he who secured that *The Star* did not distract attention from its decent politics by its manner of presenting them. He did indeed improve what out of his good principles he preserved, the newspaper of greatest value to his country.

Jo, like First Love before her, read my diary, in circumstances I cannot recall. It is possible that this happened at my suggestion, since the brave idea had certainly come to me before now that proper love could only be based on full truth. The whole smelly pile, which description I suspected it deserved, did indeed contain full truth, not only on work and my moral and human standing, but on my feelings for others and any career plans contemplated on their behalf. Jo survived the experience of reading the pile, with justification noting down a fact or two for later use, and we went off to New York. The official purpose was articles by me for *The Star Weekly*. As real a purpose was higher culture for both of us, including the great Picasso show. We survived a knock on the door at 2 a.m. of the first night, by hotel detectives interested not in our morality but in our having avoided a higher rate for the room by not having been brave enough to register as a couple. We were awakened again at dawn by a telephone call. *The Star* needed me on the next plane home to edit the coming Saturday's literary page.

Until then it had tended to have on it summaries of lighter books – celebrations of their dogs by Canadian humorists, imaginative reconstructions such as *The Day Christ Died*, and undemanding fiction. Over the summer, my editorship having been indefinitely extended after the first Saturday, I began a change, having in mind the first lot of my life's critics, those in and around the departments of Philosophy and English at University College. The page could now carry a celebration of *The Complete Works of Nathanael West* and in particular his short novel *Miss Lonelyhearts*. There were also prominent reviews of books by Huxley, Waugh, and the like. English novelists, seeming in general to be more reflective than American ones, got more space. Politics also did better, *The New Class* by Milovan Djilas being welcomed by me as more or less the truth about Communism, the awful truth.

I wrote the principal review each week, and soon saw fit, being in charge of the layout of the page as well, to enclose this review in a kind of frame at the top. My style was not as formal as in my university essays, but, since this was *literary* journalism, not as simple as in rough-and-tumble journalism. One instance will certainly do. 'A heartening number of things may be said in recommendation of *Remember Me To God* and not the least of these is that this is a novel that forages stolidly through many, many pages, sometimes awkwardly and sometimes magnificently, and commands of a reader that he stays to the end.' I suppose novels can look for fodder, and that they can command *of* readers. But the author of *Remember Me To God*, Myron Kaufmann, may not have feared strictures on his own style in what followed.

In September of 1957 I returned to university, and, by further invitation from the Dean of Men, to the Sir Daniel Wilson Residence. However, I did not leave my editorship of the book page. Although I would need some money to get through the remaining two years to my degree, it was not really necessary that I get it by this means, in effect a full-time job. Despite Bee's further ascent, to being one of the owners of *The Star* and therefore rich, was I disinclined to ask him for money? Did I think clearly about the matter at all? Not to the point of action. My diary records more dissatisfaction with my degree of self-discipline, but also some ebullient confidence. Now having been wonderfully inspirited by A. J. Ayer's *Language, Truth and Logic*, I would stand my ground with distinction against metaphysics and Professor Fackenheim. I would also have the distinction of setting an elevated standard of judgement and taste for the reading public on Saturdays.

Aiding me in my civilizing mission were new reviewers, some of them professors from the university. Others were fellow students. Among them was Margaret Penman, whom the attentive reader will recall as a kind of Christmas fairy. We had contemplated one another around Christmas 1954, when the result had been hardly more than one of her poems. We had done so again around Christmas 1955, again with only a literary result. We had had cups of coffee since.

She satisfied that first requirement, still persisting, of being a good-looker to my conventional eye. As for the necessary further recommendation, that was evident. Literary she was, and now proceeding to the M.A. in Eng. Lit. Her pieces were strong in their approval of sensibility, and were cautious works of sensibility themselves. Her optimism about her life had some grandeur in it. Her being full-bodied somehow consorted with the sense you could get of her bestowing herself upon the world. Still, she sometimes seemed about to be immersed in her soul, searching for a course that would lead to spiritual security or maybe transcendence. She favoured such characters in her reports on novels, and wrote of them understandingly. 'For her own protection, Nicola decided she must not take God too seriously.'

She was, I see from the files, indefinite in her politics. She reported without noticeable judgement that Ayn Rand in a novel seemed to be on the side of her character who took Robin Hood to be of all human symbols the most immoral and contemptible. That was because he did not rob the thieving poor to give back to the productive rich. Margaret's tolerance did not distinguish her much from me. The state of development of my own politics, despite my being attracted to the Welfare State and my affection for the Hutterites, did not lead me to think of securing a sharper judgement from my reviewer on the moral drivel about Robin Hood.

Jo and I having met our doom, without drama, and another brief and sweet connection of mine having suffered from mischance, Margaret and I began to keep company. We walked in the snow, disdaining the *nouveaux riches* who put lights on the trees outside their houses. We, or anyway I, regressed to the stage of petting on sofas. In delicacy or perhaps a kind of superiority, I did not ask, then or after, about how advanced in intimacy her previous long connection had been. Early in December 1957 I proposed marriage, and was readily accepted. Writing a month later of my proposal, in a spirit of commitment to the future, I said: 'I must admit that I did not go out that night with the idea of it in mind. Nor was it anything of a resolve for many minutes prior to the actual moment. It simply occurred, without its antecedents being very conscious.' I went on in my diary entry to ask if I was in love with her, and after some dissecting of the idea of love, which dissecting was said to be no evidence of uncertainty of feeling, I concluded forcefully that I was.

My sister Ruthie and others arranged gift-showers, and my prospective parents-in-law were persuaded out of the idea that the wedding reception should be so proper as not to include strong drink. Mr Penman, a lawyer of Scots descent, agreed to part with a sum of money for Canadian champagne. The Dean of Men said this marriage was an eminently sensible one and the lads in Jeanneret House gave us a splendid green Hudson Bay blanket, under which I sleep still. A flat was found in the old village near the university. Men from Elmar's factory delivered furniture from our families. We persisted in not going to bed together, but waited instead for a union made deeper, no doubt of greater sensibility, by having been somehow sanctified.

It was not too much sanctified. We were married in a university chapel in February, when I was 25, by a Unitarian minister of whom I may remember that he wished to be known as Fred. His relation to actual religious belief, to my satisfaction, was unclear. The reception at the

University Women's Club was without incident, the supply of champagne not being endless. We proceeded to a honeymoon at a winter resort in Northern Ontario. Since this was to be not merely the beginning of married life, but of a larger progress, I took along books to read for a programme on the Canadian Broadcasting Corporation. When we returned, union very unremarkably achieved, Margaret's mother had left two sets of keys to our flat, one with a blue ribbon, one with a pink.

Why did I marry? Certainly not with the aim of having a family, and evidently not for sex. Nor does there seem much point in speculating about an instinct to mate, where that is supposed to be something other than sexual desire, some disposition of a species about which no more can be said. For a start, not all of the species has it, and some of us do not persist in it. I do not take back my forceful conclusion that I was in love, which was understood mainly in terms of a heightened concern for the happiness of another person, protectiveness, and sexual desire. But clearly this love, if it was part of the story, could not be near to all of it. I had been at least as much in love before.

I was now a little tired of trying to choose, trying to weigh up the recommendations of candidates, now a little inclined to satisficing. Another part of the story, perhaps surprising, was my being a little tired of being outside the circle of respectably settled couples. Evidently, if my resistance to convention has not always been discriminating, it has not been complete either. In getting married, I sought the approval given to those who are in a way conventional, the acceptance reserved for the orderly. Something else that can perhaps be called convention, even deep convention, was also in the story. That was an impulse, not insignificant, to join the major history of men and women. In other ways, too, I have at times wanted to take up or to be reassured of membership in a human history, where that has nothing to do with particular success, with excelling or standing out in that history. I have felt it, for example, not only about politics but about being an intellectual and a writer of books. But this has moved me no more than the impulse to join the major history of men and women.

Such thoughts in answer to the question of why I first married cannot possibly do the trick for anyone reflective and inclined to the ideal of finding a full or sufficient condition for something, an explanation that is not partial but really complete. It is easy enough to see that I might have been in love, and in the two ways conventional, and yet not got married. What was also required, to make one addition, was anticipation of pride, the pride of being in a unique relation to a person of some standing. In my case, in brief, that was the standing of being literary. It has often seemed to me that in this way I married Margaret on *general* grounds, was moved by properties she shared with others. That seems to me neither unusual nor terrible, but evidently it may not turn out well. One can be distracted by too persistent a focus on anything short of a whole person. As all know, but not as all see at the right time, one can be misled by ambition, ambition with respect to women and ambition with respect to men. A suitable consort is not all of a person.

You may wonder about other possible elements of a good explanation. Was I just precipitate? My diary entry makes it hard to resist the idea. If so, it was not the first or the last of such departures from rationality. Ignorance comes to mind too, that great engine for the producing of lives. Neither of the two of us, for all our previous Christmases, knew what we were getting. But I now give up, at least for a time, this pursuit of something like a full explanation.

Through this year of 1957–58 the book page had got better, and one of my critics said it went from strength to strength. My self-doubt allowed me to agree tentatively. My leaning to England and English men of letters had yet more influence. Pepys and Johnson and the rest of the English literary past jostled with the Angry Young Men and Kingsley Amis. The ring of English place-names, so evocative to my ear, led me to drop them regularly, and to suggest more of a grip than I had on Swiss Cottage and West Hampstead. Bertrand Russell was cabled to do a review of a book on the moral and political history of the scientists who had made the atomic bomb. I was delighted by his presence on my page, and gave over the special frame at its top to him, demoting my own eulogy of *Arthur Miller's Collected Plays*.

My American travels had not led me to the same enthusiasm for all of Mr Miller's countrymen, or their defenders. The French Catholic philosopher Jacques Maritain was piqued by the irreligion of his native land, and was moved to the thought, in his *Reflections on America*, that the American people are the least materialistic among the modern peoples which have attained the industrial stage. This was my first engagement with a French thinker, perhaps the French imagination, perhaps just its wilful battiness. He and they were put right by me, but mildly, since I was still a Canadian.

Also partly because I was still a Canadian, I was in general no patriot about Canadian writing. In October 1958, at the start of yet another of my undergraduate years, the winner of The All-Canada Fiction Award was announced. At the time, the Royal Canadian Mounted Police were less concerned with inspecting such dangerous writings as those of my father, and momentarily concerned with keeping smutty books from America from crossing the border. Rising over my mildness, but in conformity with self-doubt, I proposed that the Mounties ought instead to strive to keep within our borders the book that won The All-Canada Fiction Award, thereby saving us from the judgement of the rest of the world. A paper in Vancouver thought my proposal worth reprinting.

You may predict another part of the story. Not many lectures were getting into my schedule. I did drop in on Professor Grube's about Plato's Forms, those absolutes or exemplars that are independent of their worldly instantiations or manifestations. In addition to the Form of the Good, was there a Form of Mud? For Plato, it seemed, the question was not easy. I did make an hour or two in my schedule to clarify further the minds of my teachers on the nature of metaphysics. From the philosopher Ayer I could indeed get help to clip the wings of the angel Fackenheim. But it was not easy to use the time set aside for studying. Large tracts of philosophy were known to me only by hearsay.

Another part of the story may be less predictable. While failing to act rationally on the attraction, I was now truly attracted to philosophy – on the way to being awakened by it. The book page was not only a source of satisfaction to me, being good of its kind, but also a source of embarrassment, being of a lesser kind. The lesser kinds of things included everything but philosophy. I recorded in my diary that all other endeavours of the mind were second-rate. Philosophy was the only tolerable future. More particularly, I aspired to that plain seeing and plain speaking of fundamental things, now described by me as 'philosophy by means of close analysis'. Was my motivation mixed? Was I drawn to more than clear truth? Very likely, as on a similar occasion mentioned earlier. If I wanted to find things out by getting them straight, I also wanted the standing of the professors about whose judgement on my book page I speculated.

Thus, coming up to my final examinations in May of 1959, it was decided by me that the next step would be a higher degree in philosophy. The decision was something new in my experience, more clear and settled, less of a lurch. Possibly it was so because it was more a matter of satisfaction with something, or at any rate the prospect of something, than of dissatisfaction with something else. Where to do the higher degree? Harvard? Oxford? Was A. J. Ayer in Oxford? Might they all think twice about the fact that I had not shown myself to be academically swift? I was proceeding to the B.A. *seven years* after first setting foot on Philosopher's Walk. Mr Gallop wrote a note on my behalf to Professor Ryle in Oxford, who did not reply encouragingly. Harvard did, and admitted me, and would give me money. It never saw me, since it stood hardly any chance against the brief note of acceptance from Professor Ayer of University College London.

In those simple days, wives followed husbands without negotiation, but the prospect of London was as agreeable to Margaret as to me. It was, more particularly, the prospect of Bloomsbury and the Reading Room of the British Museum, a proper setting for the completion of a thesis on Virginia Woolf. More than a year of marriage and fidelity suggested more of the same to come, more good order. I was about as happy about marriage as about life. If I now had experience of the constraints of the institution, I did not chafe too much, and we were getting on amiably in our rather stylish flat of books and Scandinavian furniture. Our existence was ruffled only by a page or two of my diary in which past connections were remembered with affection. That Margaret was the third of my intimates to read my diary does raise a question. It seems all too possible that at all times I wanted it read, which is not a happy thought. She was the last reader.

In my final examinations I allowed myself to be detained for ever by the first question I chose to answer. Did I have the innocent hope that the examiners would take it on trust that the other three questions might have been answered as magnificently if I had not run out of time? I was not entirely innocent, but rather among the examinees who know the necessity of not having time for more answers. The classification of degrees was a lesser thing in Toronto than in England. But I was mortified to slip down into the first place in Second Class Honours in Philosophy and English Literature. It did not console me that I got Firsts on at least some of my philosophy papers, and apparently would have got First Class Honours in my degree if judged on the philosophy alone. Nor did it console me that Professor F. H. Anderson, the formidable head of the Philosophy Department, conscripted me after the exams to do what he spoke of as just the tightening up of his manuscript on Bacon. It would not have consoled me either to know something of the rich history of the Second Class Degree, and of which of the most notable philosophers of England are in that history.

Still, I had become resilient, having in my early manhood had practice in recovering from a thing or two. My wife and I made a visit to Baden, where she was surveyed from their cars by the Knoll brothers, and probably given a good mark. We prepared to leave for England.

So much for my early manhood, my years between 17 and 26, my Toronto years. They can do with a retrospect.

I was helped along by my sister, and helped more and hurt a little by my brother. Neither they nor I could overcome my somewhat unsettled and wilful nature. Girls caught my eye, and I theirs. Despite at least embarrassing facts of student misconduct, some morality or other stayed with me, a dominant way of looking at myself and all things. The world was certainly not only a place in which to succeed. My talk of my amorality was only talk. But particularly with women, whose love or affection I had, I made some escape from conventional morality, from being honourable or principled in a conventional sense. I did more than sow wild oats. If First Love gave me some help in doing so, I did badly by her. The apprehensive question of whether she thereafter could have children remained with me. My feelings of insecurity became focussed on my intellectual strengths and moral standing rather than anything else. Helped by Elvis, and good books, I got a first distaste for common culture. My general attitude to women became settled as one of appraisal, and helped a lot to bring about my marriage. I was no longer pulled towards the path of Arthur Miller, and turned towards philosophy, more for good reasons than bad. Still, I failed again to become really single-minded, or to see the possibility of being so, and instead was distracted by my Saturday mission. My not triumphing in my final examinations also reduced my patriotism. If in 1959 I did not have anything like a determined resolve to abandon my homeland, my ties to it were not strong.

To speak more generally, I came of age in a country of diffidence, rectitude and classlessness, and I was not so content with it as others were. There was a brief time before my leaning towards England, even before my first visit to New York, as might have been confessed earlier, when I had a feeling uncommon among Canadians, of being unfortunate in not being an American. Was my not being entirely content with Canada partly owed to ambition and personal self-doubt? The ambition, if not fully awake, had become less dream-like, and it and the self-doubt fed one another. In my want of contentment, my being no patriot, was there also some individuality and audacity, often unthinking? Not being a full member of Baden had been uncomfortable. But I did not acquire from the experience what might have been expected, a determination to conform, to do what was necessary to become a full member either of Toronto or Canada.

Can we speculate more confidently that it was ambition and self-doubt, together with some individuality and audacity, that gave rise to my not being fully content with Canada and my proposing to come away? There is the difficulty that other people have been insecure, ambitious, individual and audacious, and yet more contented with their homeland. My brother has been, and in a way my sister. It is clear that my four traits are not at all a full explanation. Can we get to full explanations? Can we specify a full cause for a thing, a causal circumstance for it? Above all for attitudes and actions? Let me leave this for a while and revert to a question touched on earlier.

How much does my early manhood explain? If you are trying to understand me today, the person who writes this book, should you give less attention to my early manhood than to the Baden boyhood before it? That would surely be a mistake. Nor would it be sensible to hold absolutely to a general principle about everyone that childhood facts explain more than early manhood facts. Some characters and personalities can almost be said to have been brought into existence by episodes in the later period, including disasters in it. But nor is it the case with ordinary and uneventful lives that childhood needs to be given most attention. There is a particular reason for denying this. It is entangled in something else, a problem to which philosophers have attended.

You strike the match and it lights. We ordinarily say that what explains the lighting, the cause of it, was the striking. And we spell this out partly by saying that if you hadn't struck it, the match wouldn't have lit. Anyway in that situation, where it wasn't being put in the flame of another match and so on. So this and other facts of causal connection between events are at bottom conditional facts – if or since something did happen, then something else did, or if something had happened, something else would have. So far so good. But while it is true that if you hadn't struck the match it wouldn't have lit, there is another truth. If the match hadn't been dry, it wouldn't have lit either. And, further, the presence of oxygen was just as much a required condition for the lighting as the striking and the dryness.

So there is a problem. You can call it the problem of the praising of causes. Why do we dignify the striking, give that particular condition the name of *cause*, talk of it as what explains the effect? Why not the oxygen? What is our general principle in giving *one* required condition in a situation a priority or ascendancy over the others? Some used to say of this problem, but not for long, that our general principle of selection is just that we pick out, from the rest of the required conditions, the human action involved. That is refuted by other cases where there is no human action at all, and also by cases where there is one but it is not counted as the cause. In the latter connection, I used to talk in my tutorials of the explosive gas that unpredictably and by nobody's doing gets into the room where the smoker lights yet another match, as he has been doing safely for years. It wasn't his action that was really the cause of the explosion, was it?

The end of my tutorial reflections on the praising of causes was that we are driven to say that our general principle for picking out the cause is just this: we name as cause a thing or fact that for one reason or another *interests* us, perhaps because it serves our purposes to do so. What things or facts are required for the occurrence of something else is not up to us. That is decided by the world outside us. But the world outside us does not decide what the cause is. We do.

Consider now (1) the childhood experience of my having been embarrassed and resentful in connection with my mother's not minding her appearance enough, and in particular not arranging to support her bosom. Consider too (2) my coming to a kind of male confidence in early manhood, my falling into that settled attitude of appraisal with respect to women. Suppose that the childhood embarrassment had something to do with the early-manhood habit of appraisal, maybe a lot, and that both had something to do with (3) events of my later life of which you have yet to hear, or just the event of my marriage near the borderline between early manhood and later life.

Evidently, as has lately come to my mind, tardily, the same problem about our selecting causes arises with such a sequence *over time* as with such simultaneous facts as the striking of the match, its dryness and the oxygen. That is, the same question arises about the boyhood embarrassment and the early-manhood habit of appraisal. The question of what is to be taken as explaining the event of my marriage and the rest, the question of what is to have the name of cause, is not answered by the facts outside of us, but by us. In choosing my early embarrassment, or my later habit of appraisal, we choose what interests us.

If you are interested in my embarrassment rather than the habit of appraisal, or for that matter interested in some other required condition before the time of my embarrassment in my early history, why is that? You may have an answer. You will also have trouble defending it, since interests aren't easy to defend. They aren't facts. You will certainly not show that while all conditions of something were required, one was *more* required than others, or any like thing. To stick to the main point, you will not dissuade me from a conviction, strengthened by my having made my sometimes unhappy way through my early manhood again in remembering it. That conviction is indeed that there is no reason to give priority to my childhood over later stages in explaining my present. It is all of the past that can come into explanations of the present.

Not that that makes anything simple. Consider my philosophical commitments now, the philosophical furniture of my mind in the summer of the first chapter of this book. If these mature commitments had required conditions in my early manhood, was more than that true? Were the commitments, as you might say, prefigured there, already on view? My present political philosophy comes to mind. It does seem true enough to say my present certitudes and passions were something like prefigured in my approval of the Welfare State and in my giving a good press to the Hutterites in their prairie communes. But other things are also true.

One is that I did not have political passions then. My egalitarianism or the like was mild and perfunctory, as their religion is to some Anglicans. There was no hatred in it. My mild politics in my early manhood, however prefiguring, do not seem to give us much explanation of my passionate politics now. Something else must have happened thereafter. Nothing is more common than earlier politics being abandoned or moderated, and in particular early politics of the Left. Mine weren't. People grow up, they say, and calm down. They get sense. I grew older and got less calm, had less sense. I didn't start out a Trotskyite and end up a Conservative minister running down the Health Service.

As for my other philosophical commitments now, propositions on which I have spent more time, the story is yet less simple. Despite my attachment to Tchaikowsky's Theme of Destiny, determinism did not figure at all in my early manhood. The most that can be said is that the related matters of morality and a kind of personal freedom did, mainly a freedom from convention. Nor, if freighted with full consciousness of things and of myself, was I concerned with the true subjectivity that is the real nature of our conscious states, or with any other of my subsequent philosophical concerns. These were to come. I was no thinker already caught in the nets of a few specific problems. The impulse in my stirring, more general and less discriminating, was just to see something or other clearly, get something or other really right.

5

AWAKE IN ENGLAND

It was not only what my eyes perceived but also William Blake's line that gave content to my first sight of the country of most of my life. What I therefore saw was England's green and pleasant land. It was unlike any earlier first sight, say of New York before it began to seem just pushier than anywhere else, or any subsequent first sight, say of Venice from the lagoon, or the square of the winter palace in St Petersburg. My sight of England, from the deck of the liner *Italia*, as we came in along the coast to Portsmouth harbour in July 1959, was wonderfully affecting. The image remains with me.

That it was so affecting was not owed to my sharing the radical spirit Blake expresses in his lines about building Jerusalem in the green and pleasant land. As lately mentioned, my politics were mild. I knew about dark satanic mills, but had no sense of the need for bow, arrows, spear, and chariot of fire. Would that there was one in sight now, or at any rate that we were marching in the streets about social security, like the rational French. My first sight was affecting partly because it was the sight of a large present grown out of a noble past. That is how I had come to think of England, whatever more particular thought or poet's line might strike me. The large present had in it that moral achievement also lately mentioned, the National Health Service, and an unapologetic culture, including unapologetic philosophers stronger and bolder than their American counterparts. The noble past had something called liberty in it, secured and defended by a socially conscientious yeomanry.

What I came to in England was not only a large present grown out of a noble past, but two other things – the fountain of my own language and a tradition of living not well known to me, but now esteemed by me above all. The latter was an intellectual, enlightened and somehow empirical tradition, in which I might try to put myself up for membership. Was I not a natural candidate? It had Locke, Berkeley and Hume in it, certainly, and great counterparts in science and also the novel and verse. But there would be lesser counterparts in an ordinary life of colleges, sitting rooms, letters to the editor and maybe pubs and buses. *England*. I half-remember thinking, even before Margaret and I set foot on the quay to find the boat-train to London, of never leaving. Being capable of much in my private ruminations on myself, I may have gone further. I may have managed the thought of never leaving home.

Either on the train or soon after, we took in that great distinction of the English into two classes. Two classes of classes of course, but still two classes. The first is of those who make their private conversation in public places audible to all, and the second is of those who do not. It took no powers of social observation to discern that the former, some of whom knew that 'mass' was pronounced 'moss', were not so much oblivious of their surroundings as not caring that they were overheard or in fact intending to be. It was an assertiveness of confidence or determination. It was not then thought of by me as being connected, maybe in the minds of these public speakers, with their defence of more substantial rights and possessions, even academic ones. Nor did I imagine ever hearing from an academic aspirant to membership in the class, at his party in Regent's Park, that the poor are outside of history. It is not clear what I would have thought of the proposition and its implications.

The public speakers caused me a little trepidation, and tempted me, not for the last time, to replies in kind. Speaking up would not be all that hard, and I might be different in having something to say when I did. But I felt at least some kinship with them for a large reason. Did they not have at least more connection, however uncertain, with something other than common culture, indeed with the particular England caught sight of by both the eye and the mind's eye from the *Italia*? They formed decent sentences, accepted the need for some kind of fairness, had some distinguishing marks left on them by a university. They might know about Mahler and of course Blake, and did not wear T-shirts.

The ride in the taxi from Victoria Station was a progress through street-names, none too humble to be evocative, to the Coram House Hotel, a genteel bed-and-breakfast establishment five minutes from University College London. But it was also a progress through a city of which one could not avoid seeing that it was run-down, often hotch-potch, and close to grimy. It did not proclaim to the English, as Mr Macmillan had proclaimed to them a year or two before after becoming Prime Minister, that you've never had it so good. It seemed, too, on the ride from Victoria, that the city had never had grandeur, or much of it. It had not had much grandeur even before the war that had left behind it the cleared bomb-sites, the props supporting the adjacent houses, and the new grey concrete of reconstruction. It was not a city of imperial avenues and graceful palaces. Bloomsbury was Georgian, distinct from Canadian Georgian. But its facades had overflow pipes in them for more recent plumbing, and blank windows without their original glazing bars. The opportunity for free speech at Speakers' Corner in Hyde Park on Sunday morning was taken up mainly by such lesser revolutionaries as vegetarians.

It may be that I mislead you. None of this dismayed me. Nor did subsequent intrusions of reality over several months. It is true that my general idealism about noble past and large present began to fade somewhat. It gave way to a realism. But there was more than compensation. The subsequent England *was* real, itself a recommendation, and it still did approximate to the ideal. It was more complex, richer, and gave my enthusiasm something to work on.

Guided by a beadle of University College London wearing a top hat with gold braid, these facts being satisfactory to me, I made my way to 19 Gordon Square and the Philosophy Department. There I was apprehended looking over the noticeboard in the front hallway. The first departmental secretary of my acquaintance was as characterful as the rest in her loyalty or other tie to the Head of Department she served. She conveyed that since I had not met him, and was not yet formally registered for the degree of Master of Arts, my dwelling on details of lecture courses and seminars was a misdemeanour. Presumably to correct this tendency in me, she gave me a Biblical tract. It was not at all necessary to reveal my familiarity with such items of spiritual improvement. But getting one from the factotum of Professor Ayer, known for removing religion from the agenda of thinking persons, and second only to Bertrand Russell among official atheists of the realm, was unexpected, as I managed to remark. She countered well, with some news.

It was that Professor Ayer had departed University College London for the University of Oxford. He would be on hand for his Monday evening seminar in the coming term, but supervise no students, or at any rate no new students. It was a disappointment, but not a severe one. Although his *Language, Truth and Logic* had been both reassuring and invigorating, and helped to bring me to England, I had not actually come to sit at his feet. Discipleship was not among my shortcomings.

I did not entertain at all the possibility of riding on his coat-tails to Oxford – although my situation was not absolutely unlike that of a professor's graduate student already under instruction, who may move with the professor. The explanation of my not entertaining the coat-tails possibility was partly my being content just to be in England and a certain want of nerve despite a temptation to speak up. I was a colonial lad in Bloomsbury. It never occurred to me, I think, that Professor Ayer might have let me know he would not be on hand in the college to which he had invited me, and which I had therefore preferred to Harvard.

You may think the want of nerve odd for a particular reason. It is that I was of some experience in a line of life not noted for want of nerve. Moreover, I had not wanted nerve when compared with other journalists. The truth, as it still seems to me, is that I did not bring any audacity of my journalism into my new life, carry on with old habits. My new life would be different. It would be one of restraint, decorum and the slow pursuit of truth. This anticipation of mine in 1959 seemed later to have been more idealism. When I acquired both realism and a new audacity, this grew out of later situations, and academic life itself. It was not a reversion to an earlier bent or style. Do you ask, reader, if this is really true? Do you suspect it is self-serving? Well, it is the idea I have.

My new life began in October with Professor Ayer's seminar for postgraduates in the first-floor salon that was the Grote Professor's room. Mondays at 5. He and his colleagues would listen to the week's paper by a postgraduate, perhaps on a chapter of Mr Peter Strawson's new book of descriptive metaphysics, *Individuals*, about persons and all other things, and what is needed in general for us to tell one from another. They would then lead the assembly in the discussion of the paper, or, if it would not bear extended examination, the chapter itself. Should that fail, as it did not with *Individuals*, there was the general subject of the chapter. It could fail too, of course. Things could turn out to be non-subjects. There were a lot of them, perhaps sufficient to cover all of contemporary French and German philosophy.

Professor Ayer was about 49, small, on the way to sallow in complexion and with a nose, besuited but dapper in a gentleman's way. He added the assurance of Eton and Oxford to a seemingly inbred and certainly lively demand for respect. He was, to me, a member of another species. Evidently he took pride in forming sentences rapidly, often good ones. It was the speed of thought, he intimated, that enabled it to hit the mark. He gave and perhaps intended to give an impression of self-restraint, of being on his own leash and sometimes in danger of letting go of the other end. If he seemed fastidious, he also lived some kind of high life and had a marriage behind him.

He also struck me as a little detached from the proceedings of the seminar, possibly a little bored. Subsequently, when I was better informed, this seemed to me to have had to do with his having finished the job of giving to University College London a distinction in philosophy which it had never had before, and his return to Oxford. His election to a chair there, as is common enough in academic life, had been regarded as scandalous by some. There had been resignations from a committee. It also faced him with a challenge, in the person of Professor J. L. Austin. The latter figure had had original thoughts about categories of speech-acts. He was more formidable than might be suggested by his labours on the differences between the reports (a_1) He clumsily trod on the snail, (a_2) Clumsily he trod on the snail, (b_1) He trod clumsily on the snail, and (b_2) He trod on the snail clumsily. The prospect of Oxford was concentrating Professor Ayer's mind, more than the scene he was leaving behind.

Second to him in the seminar was his colleague, Dr John Watling. He was a Lecturer, about 35, with specs and a shock of sandy hair at the top of a spare and lively frame. No particular accent, and an ordinary rate of sentences. As I was soon to learn, he had been a pacifist in the war and was a vegetarian, something rarer then than now, and perhaps a freethinker. He had found his way to philosophy after starting physics in Manchester and then getting a First in psychology here at University College. Of no large views himself, he was a man for whom the name of analytic philosopher was made.

If Professor Ayer did not defer to him in the seminar, deference not being in his repertoire, he was one with the rest of us in seeing as exemplary Dr Watling's ability to seize on and perhaps expose an element in an argument, line of thought, or doctrine. Only a superficial acquaintance with him, perhaps limited to his sandals, anorak, familiarity with English folk-song, and his uniform if nervous geniality, could allow one to make the mistake of locating him among tender-minded as against tough-minded philosophers. He was properly exasperated by mystery, and was writing a book on the philosophy of science for the Penguin series edited by Professor Ayer. Some of these things I learned at the seminar, others in my first weekly meetings with him, its having been decided that he would be my supervisor for my first term.

The University of Toronto had not offered tutorials to its under-graduates, or encouraged audience-participation in lectures, and so I had rarely discussed philosophy. To use the verb then favoured in England, I had not *done* much philosophy. My experience had been more a matter of reading and considering the philosophical doings of others. In the seminar Professor Ayer was certainly not so detached from the proceedings as to have lost the intention of cutting through to clear truth, and of cutting a figure in doing so. If he remained civil to all, and affectionate to those he knew better, there was for a graduate student the risk of undeclared disgrace. To speak up here was infinitely more dangerous than with a mere social class whose private conversation was audible in public places. It was to step out on the high wire. Despite the decorum, there seemed to be no net.

To the challenge of professor and supervisor and their several colleagues was added the challenge of my fellow students. Some had achieved a good deal of composure. One was Timothy Sprigge, lately down from Cambridge and already the possessor of a good amount of articulate doctrine. Evidently he was a kind of gent, if less dapper and somehow more English than Freddie, being given to fawn jerseys. Another was Alastair Hannay, down from Edinburgh. As tall as me, and dark, he had stepped out of at least the pages of a better women's novel, or one for all of us by Walter Scott. He seemed secure in a dignity acquired from a line of severe Scots thinkers, and possibly well-heeled. There were also furtive but impressive visitors at the back of the seminar, one being the medical doctor Jonathan Miller, not yet an impresario but capable of impassivity. Others appeared to take their silent but superior style from a character in a novel about the department. Of him it was written that, having heard a certain argument in the seminar, he picked up his filthy macintosh and left.

My first encounters upstairs in his bare and functional room with Dr Watling that October caused me as much apprehension as the seminar. If they did not carry the awful possibility of public embarrassment, they did require that I have something to say. Having no clear idea as to a subject on which to write my M.A. thesis, I found myself asked to have something to say on the sense-data theory of perception. This, as you heard from me earlier, is the theory that when we speak of seeing an ordinary thing, what each of us is really aware of is a private or subjective phenomenon, a sense-datum. The idea was supported by the classical argument from illusion, to the effect that a person's actual experience is just the same between ordinary seeing and an hallucination, and hence that the ordinary seeing must also be awareness of a private object. Dr Watling exercised his destructive powers, amiably, on my stubborn reply to the argument from illusion, an argument uncongenial to a 26-year-old realist unwilling to have London dissolved into privacy so soon after arrival.

The first seminars and supervisions were not only alarming. It has seemed since that they did no less than awaken me. I awakened in philosophy. This, as it has seemed, was different from earlier stirrings, and changed and fixed the course of my life. There was also something else. It was the start of an ambition to get accepted in this higher company, the assertive practitioners of the subject among whom I found myself. Did my awakening and ambition start me off in something that has gone on ever since? This is onward marching, active determination, keeping at it, the sustaining of hope by work. If I had doubts of being able to light up a room by quicksilver intelligence, something I both envied and suspected, I was confident of having an ability to find my way to clear things of my own to say, some of which might produce a longer light. But what was definitely also needed in order to produce these goods was the onward marching.

Having been present for at least some undergraduate lectures in another place over a period of seven years, I now set about attending more in my new setting, more regularly. Formal logic had to be got hold of, the theories of probability made sense of, the nature of conditional or if-then statements comprehended, the basis of moral judgements discerned. A notebook was got just for Russell and his Theory of Descriptions. It was about the problem of meaning, and in particular such descriptions in sentences as 'the lectern over there' and 'the present king of France'. The second raised a problem by being meaningful despite there plainly being nothing for which it stood. The theory seemed to be that in fact no description is ever meaningful in virtue of an experienced thing to which it seems to be tied. In the case of 'The present king of France is bald', the initial description involves the bare existential statement that there *is* something or other, and our describing this by curious single terms that *do* stand for somehow experienced items – after which the thing is also said to be bald.

It wasn't easy. There was also the suspect doctrine of meaning, about what was called the sense and reference of descriptions, owed to the German logician Gottlob Frege. He said 'the Evening Star' and 'the Morning Star' had as their referent or were about the same heavenly body, as indeed is true. But they were different in their senses, which were things called the modes of presentation of the referent. Did this easy talk really boil down to Russell's idea about curious terms for properties, including the properties of appearing in the morning and appearing in the evening?

The policy of work, which itself gave contentment, and made time pass unnoticed, bought pleasing returns. I took courage and escaped the policy of security through silence in the seminar. My interventions were succinct, partly because I feared losing my way in elaborating them, and they had some force. There were no serious mishaps, and the high wire became somewhat lower. What was unclear to me in a paper, if I raised a question about it, could turn out to be unclear to others. My own first paper to the seminar, if no triumph, was no disgrace. Professor Ayer conveyed afterwards that it was good. He would say so in a letter to get me a scholarship from the Canada Council, implying to me that he expected them to do as they were told. Timothy Sprigge said in the Orange Tree pub after a seminar that I had *made a point*, and Alastair Hannay nodded once. I made it again, to make sure. Johnny Watling, as he had become, did not set about its destruction.

In November he had a suggestion. Might I not rather aim at something other than the M.A. degree? Might I not feel like thinking some more about Russell and Frege, and taking a few qualifying exams in order to be registered for the higher degree of Ph.D.? Professor Ayer, not yet Freddie Ayer, thought so too. Very invigorating it was. I might be on the way to something. The first thing I might be on the way to was 'Dr Honderich', which had a good stern ring to it. The bearer of such a certification might well find some things out.

Margaret and I had settled into a furnished flat in a house behind Swiss Cottage, down the hill from Hampstead. This may not have been wholly accidental. A book review of mine some years earlier had spoken not only of the mecca-city of London but of eternal and seedy expatriate flats in the places Swiss Cottage and Kensington. It was the eternality I liked. Our flat, if it had not always existed and presumably would not exist forever, was old enough to satisfy my Anglophilia and seemed structurally sound. Winchester Road, however, had neighbourhood shops on one side, and perhaps was closer to seedy and expatriate than highly desirable. This, if I recall rightly, was clearer to Margaret than to me. Such a feeling on her part would have been consonant with what was a fact, that she did not or could not follow me in plunging headlong into English life.

The Philosophy Department at University College was what someone who had gone ahead to prepare a place for me would have prepared, at least someone not too given to the public speaking or thinking only of my career. Margaret was sustained by no such institution in trying to get on with her thesis on Virginia Woolf for the University of Toronto. Her substitute for 19 Gordon Square was the thinner atmosphere of the North Library in the British Museum. There she had mainly the company of other Commonwealth students, mostly Canadian. Only postgraduate gossip was added to whatever invigoration was provided by the works of Virginia, not in itself excessive. For my part, I was already engaged in going native. I did not feel alien in England. My necessary visits to Canada House in Trafalgar Square were furtive.

At the end of 1959, we decamped to a more salubrious flat in a setting reminiscent of leafy North Toronto. It was in Old Park Avenue, in the southernmost part of Clapham, seemingly far south of the river, and reached only by a half-hour on the tube. This removal to what seemed a suburb did not much help with what was clear to both of us, that we were in a middling marriage at best. To Margaret's struggle to bring her M.A.

into explicit sentences was added a further difficulty. To supplement our savings, and also out of a determination to be doing something public, Margaret was to write pieces for *The Star*, as I myself did sometimes. We assumed that she would succeed in this without having served my journalistic apprenticeship, by means of her familiarity with the limpidities of *To the Lighthouse*. My diary records my not dealing well with her dependence on me in this and other ways. This was, I allowed, a failing in my character. 'I have insufficient discipline in the matter of submitting to the needs of others.'

Nevertheless my experience, as I recorded it, was of being terribly bound, terribly unfree. Having been married two years, we began to contemplate the horror of separation. It *was* a horror, and in place of it, I began to talk of 'a free marriage', meaning a marriage that countenanced infidelity. If we did not know of one of these, they were in the air, and certainly in the English past – the Romantic poets and Bloomsbury for a start. We came to agree on my proposal. I may actually have persuaded myself that my aim was not actually to engage in infidelity, but by the means of the agreement to escape the feeling of being bound and unfree. Simply possessing this right, never to be acted upon, would change the atmosphere.

Still, I had noticed and been noticed at college by an English girl about to get her History degree. She was pretty and had an intricate smile, was well-spoken and acted in college plays, and evidently was characterful. Margaret for her part reported that she had fallen in love with the psychiatrist or counsellor to whom her doctor had referred her. None of this was auspicious. Our prospects were not improved, either, by my concern with getting on in the seminars and supervisions in Bloomsbury as against residing in Clapham. 'My present intention, as before, is salvation through industry. I hope to work like a German. Would I were more of one.'

When the second term of my first academic year began, I found myself seeking my salvation through industry under a new supervisor, who had been away in the first term. Mr Richard Wollheim was 36, about the same age as Johnny, and of a striking face, with still and hooded eyes. He was somehow more continental than Jewish, and was conveying something by his sharply creased black trousers and pink socks. He had come into the department at about the same time as Johnny, but by way of

Westminster School and Balliol College in Oxford. He was as much an Oxford man as Professor Ayer, but, as it seemed to me, one who aspired to and achieved greater and more arcane sophistications. His attitudes were more consistently superior, and he was a stylist in more than his sentences. These were often arresting and only sometimes lacked the art that conceals art.

His interests were not only philosophical but extended to psycho-analysis, painting, and good causes of a liberal kind. Married to the ex-wife of the journalist and writer Philip Toynbee, he was an engaged member of The Homosexual Law Reform Society. As transpired, he had the credit of being a rescuer of gays and the like in academic difficulties and in need of jobs. He pronounced the 'p' and the 'sych' of 'psycho-analysis' as two syllables. He was, as it seemed, a connoisseur of much, and presumably a gourmand, given the reflection with which he brought together on a plate a dried fish, an apple and one segment of cheese for lunch in the college refectory. His room in the department was not bare and functional, but a small drawing room. It alone had double glazing to keep out what noise might intrude from Gordon Square. He chose how to stand, and where to put an arm when he sat.

Certainly he was clever, and moreover had got down to writing, and so had quickly risen to being a Reader rather than a Lecturer. His book, a Penguin in the series edited by Professor Ayer, was on F. H. Bradley, the Oxford metaphysician at the turn of the century who had persisted in the philosophical idealism of the Germans and particularly Hegel. For Bradley, therefore, what really existed was not a multiplicity of distinct things, as vulgarly supposed, say black trousers and pink socks, these being merely appearances or illusions, but Reality or the Absolute. This was a single and all-inclusive thing, rather under-described as being large, and of some spiritual kind. I got hold of Mr Wollheim's book, worked my way through it, and was struck by its elegant care in attending to Bradley's arguments. It was superior but probably very good.

The closing part of the book was also striking. It was unprecedented in more than my own philosophical experience. Bradley and his doctrine were opened or subjected, although somewhat guardedly, to psycho-analysis. '. . . there can fairly be said to be a powerful, indeed an irresistible, analogy between the metaphysical attachment to the idea of an undivided Reality and the desire to establish "whole objects" which is of such crucial importance in infantile development.' In the library I had a look at another book referred to, by Melanie Klein, and learned that the infant's development was thought to have to do with the good breast and the bad breast, but did not inquire further.

Richard, as he soon became despite the apprehension he caused me, was at least as encouraging a supervisor as Johnny. Our meetings introduced me to philosophical subtlety and to further discriminations. I aspired to his philosophical urbanity, indeed to all of his style, including where to put an arm when sitting. Margaret and I went to lunch at his house in South Kensington, which left no doubt in my mind that in his wife he had chosen a consort well. In one of our meetings at college, I read to him an essay on Russell's 'On Denoting', the baffling article in which the Theory of Descriptions was unveiled for philosophers. To my gratification, Richard said it could be improved into something for publication, an article in *Analysis*. He thought I was good and acted on the thought. He was not cautious on my behalf, not holding me back. We began well.

There was also progress or anyway development on other fronts. I asked Johnny, from the pillion of his scooter as we buzzed along the Euston Road, about his politics. Although marching under a black flag and knocking over policemen did not seem to be in his repertoire, he said something about anarchism. Professor Ayer had made speeches for the Labour Party in the election in which, nonetheless, Mr Macmillan increased his majority over Mr Gaitskell. Richard was also a supporter of the Labour Party, concerned in particular with politics and culture. Following these good examples, I became a little political. In April of 1960, answering the call of the Campaign for Nuclear Disarmament, I took myself off on the Aldermaston March, and was among those marchers so superior to the towns of the capital's environs as to make use of Betjeman's line. 'Come, friendly bombs, and fall on Slough!' In Trafalgar Square with 100,000 others, the speeches of Lord Russell and the Labour M.P. Michael Foot were serious music to me.

Margaret and I had times of affection in leafy Clapham, sometimes when she was advancing in her new role as foreign correspondent. But as often we were caught in sad confusion and apprehension. She made analyses of the problem of our marriage. These were owed to intro-spection of herself and her needs but also to reflection on my personality and its failings, not least the inferiority complex she discerned, not without some evidence. The analyses were hopeful. But despite them she was not only depressed but also burdened by a nervous condition involving aches and debility, these in our shared opinion possibly being psychosomatic. The question of whether I was causing them was in the air.

In June, although impeded by our difficulties in my preparation for the qualifying examinations that could make me a candidate for the Ph.D., I had filled up more notebooks on Russell, Frege, and such successors as Strawson. I had taken for my own the superior attitude of University College to Professor Popper down the road at the London School of Economics, which attitude was reinforced by the fact that he did not submit his students to the common philosophy examinations in the University of London but only to less impartial assessment. My own exams were in fact the main four of the University of London B.A. finals papers, but were to be marked according to some higher standard. After I had sat them, unconfidently, Margaret and I decamped to Ireland for rest and recuperation.

We knocked hopefully on the door of a rooming house presided over by Harry Bewick. She was at the centre of the free and enlightened circle to which Johnny would retreat each summer at the earliest moment permitted by his duties. Harry surveyed us, and sent us on our way. We were, as subsequently she would reveal to me, merely conventional. There was the consolation of Ireland itself, which did not fail to evoke in me, as in so many others, both affection and awe, the first for its people and the second for the audacity of its writers. At the *poste restante* counter of the General Post Office, there was another consolation. The happy postcard from Johnny said two of my four papers had been marked, and were Firsts.

Over the rest of the summer I got to work on proceeding towards being Dr Honderich, encouraged further by Johnny's passing on to me something he had been asked to do. That was a review for the journal *Philosophy* of Russell's collection of papers, *Logic and Knowledge*. To him it was avoidable writing. To me it was irresistible, a step forward. Did I try, too, to work at my marriage? That was the down-to-earth advice of Margaret's new psychiatrist or counsellor when we went to see him near Harley Street. He did not spend time on my personality, but said that marriage was about a mutual and ongoing supply of security, and could not accommodate other ideas.

Out of my desires, we removed ourselves from Clapham in September to a maisonette near the West End, in George Street not far from Baker Street. The flat was above the shop and workroom of a couturier, and it looked out in front not on trees but on London life. At the rear it looked across to the back of a house in the next street. Sometime later the English girl with whom I had become entangled, she of the intricate smile who acted in college plays, took a back room in that house. We had been true to the letter of my marriage vow and so it came as a surprise to me. It was a bit unsettling, but she said it was chance, and in part it may have been.

An assortment of philosophers, including several of the greatest, have said that knowledge of one kind or another increases or even is the same as freedom of one kind or another. That is the nature of freedom. Mundane empiricists among them have said that practical knowledge of obstacles enables us to avoid them and thereby satisfy our desires. Indeed it does. Very true of cycling. Other philosophers have had in mind religious or moral knowledge, and taken that as bound up with another freedom. This knowledge, they say, frees us from the captivity of sin, more particularly sinful desire. One of them, having begun by liking girls too much, worked at abstinence, and became St Augustine. Still other philosophers in the assortment, not so high-minded, have had in mind knowledge of necessity. If we see that all things happen necessarily, that determinism is true, we will stop desiring them to be otherwise than they are, or desire this less – and to escape from desire is to be free.

The seventeenth-century rationalist, Spinoza, in a way combined the religious and the determinist lines of thought. Having identified God with Nature, made them into one thing, he held out the possibility that our increasing knowledge of this necessary thing, *Deus sive Natura*, and its necessary workings, could issue in our highest possible state of mind. This would be perfect freedom, also known as the intellectual love of God. *The intellectual love of God*. Yes, reader, the greatest conceptions are in philosophy.

There was some new idea about knowledge and freedom, not mundanely empirical, not a matter of either abstinence or determinism, and not so ultimate as the intellectual love of God, in a book that arrived in my life at the beginning of my second postgraduate year. It was closely followed by its author, my third teacher at University College. The book was *Thought and Action*, and its author was Stuart Hampshire. A fellow of All Souls in Oxford before the war, and after it something in the Foreign Office, he had subsequently been enlisted by Professor Ayer as a lecturer in my college and stayed for some years. He had written a book on Spinoza in Professor Ayer's Penguin series and returned to Oxford. He was now returning to London, to succeed Professor Ayer in the Grote Chair.

He was tall and slim, the very figure of a public school boy, with the head of an eagle. Greyfriars made flesh and come into a maturity. Whatever his other antecedents, he struck some of us in the Monday seminar as possibly patrician and certainly effortless. He was easy in his English correctness and formality, and sometimes more inclined to magniloquence than laboriously explaining himself. We had a healthy interest in the gossip that he had taken up with Professor Ayer's wife, as he had. No doubt we formed a sentence or two of academic urbanity about chairs and beds. We were more impressed by his high style. When he had been sounded out by the college as to whether he would take up the Grote Chair if invited, he had replied that he preferred not to consider the matter until invited, for reasons of economy of thought.

Although a bit reminiscent of my father in his detachment, he was good at putting me at my ease. My meetings with him in the large room were amiable, and, despite the figure he languidly cut, were conducted by him as if between equals. He had some kind of intellect that I lacked, and certainly some style of engagement with problems that was more elevated than my own. It did not include grappling. By our meetings I was indeed put in mind of Milton and of paradise, and of those persons sitting apart on a hill retir'd, in thoughts more elevate, and reasoning high of Providence, Fate, free will, foreknowledge absolute, and finding no end, in wandring mazes lost. But I learned things from him in our unstrenuous conversations about the papers I wrote. What *was* decidedly strenuous was my own private engagement with *Thought and Action*.

I spent a month or two months on the book, trying to reduce it to order according to my lights. I was already severe in philosophical judgement, having had a tendency of this kind strengthened by Johnny Watling in particular. This severity, but also a desire to admire, and admiration itself, entered into my struggle. One of the secondary themes of the book was that Locke, Berkeley and Hume, and such subsequent empiricists as Professor Ayer, in their sense-datum theories of our perception of the world, fatally left something out, something perhaps attended to by the French. This was not just the world. It was our existence as active agents, our being people moving things around or knocking them over, as distinct from our existence as passive observers. I was moved to upper-case letters in my verdict in my notes. THIS IS STRONG, I THINK, AND THE FIRST REALLY GOOD THING IN THE BOOK. A NECESSARY REDIRECTION OF ENGLISH THOUGHT. Might lower-case have been sufficient?

Certainly my struggle failed to reach its principal goal. In fact my goal was to get beyond an entrenched dispute, three centuries old and still fervent, the main one in English philosophy about determinism and freedom. This dispute was between the two regiments of philosophers touched on in the account you had at the beginning of my later philosophical commitments. Both regiments took determinism to be clear enough, perhaps rashly. Both gave relatively little time to the second question, of its truth or falsity. What they disputed about was the third question, of what follows if determinism is clear and true, the problem of the consequences of determinism.

The first regiment said that determinism is really consistent with freedom, you can have both together, because freedom is just being able to act as you want, an absence of obstacles. It is, so to speak, a matter of your own causes being in operation rather than other causes. The second regiment said that determinism isn't at all consistent with freedom, because freedom consists in the originating or willing of choices in an uncaused way. My goal was somehow to settle and escape all this, by way of the new idea in the tradition of thought about knowledge with St Augustine and Spinoza and others in it.

But my labours on *Thought and Action* did not issue in any effective idea of a new connection between knowledge and freedom. What was said had to do with self-knowledge, but did not become clear to me. In my stubbornness, or maybe good sense, I could not escape the thought that I might become infinitely self-knowing and yet, if determinism were true, I might still not be free. But struggles can have large consequences independently of whether or not they reach their goals. This one did. It attached me to the general subject of determinism and freedom. My future would be concerned with settling or upstaging the dispute as to whether determinism was consistent or inconsistent with freedom.

Will you say that what you have already learned of me goes a good way to explaining this turn in my life, this beginning of a persistent attraction to a particular subject in philosophy? Will you say that my attraction to high thinking about freedom was owed in good part to my lively sense of being under constraint in my life? Maybe the constraint of rules about girls? Will you say differently that the attraction of determinism was the attraction of the clear and simple? Or the reassurance of an orderly rather than an uncertain universe, as is said so impertinently of my fellow determinist Einstein? Perhaps that the attraction of determinism was just its being unconventional? Or that it was a promise of a large excuse for myself in my life?

You may be more confident in those ideas than me. If Professor Hampshire had instead written a book about the democratic socialism he defended in a college speech, might I not have got entangled forever in only political philosophy? Life is not always owed more to your personality and bent than to whom you run into, and how the meeting goes. I ran into the stately Stuart, and liked him.

There was also work for the Monday seminar. In it, we proceeded in accordance with our professor's determination to avoid old cart-tracks in philosophy, and also the recent cart-tracks of his predecessor. We buckled down to *Causation in the Law*, not the most likely choice. This was a solid work of jurisprudence by H. L. A. Hart and A. M. Honoré. It concerned something touched on already in this narrative – the principles and rules by which it is supposed that something counts as the cause of something else, rather than as just another required condition, and thereby may make for someone's legal liability or guilt. Having begun my own thoughts on causation and the problem of the praising of causes in connection with determinism, I tried hard in my seminar paper to dent *Causation in the Law*. In the end I was less confident that I had done so than was Stuart, as he had become. He conveyed his own confidence in my efforts to Professor Hart, who wrote from Oxford for a copy of my paper, which I tried to strengthen, and did not hurry to send to him.

About my seminar paper on *Word and Object* by Professor Quine of Harvard I felt better. It was careful work on his idea that no words have definite meanings to be found out. My confidence had something to do with the fact that I had preferred University College London to Harvard, and this was turning out nicely. We in Gordon Square had reason for more pride than the L.S.E., sunk in local dogmatics of the philosophy of science, and the other London colleges in their anonymity, and also reason for more pride than Americans in general. Americans had no Locke, Berkeley and Hume, these figures having survived the diagnosis of *Thought and Action*, and Americans were short on patricians. As for Oxford and Cambridge, Oxford was all right, and presumably Cambridge, but they were a little infected by Wittgenstein, and in any case provincial.

As 1961 began, I went off to a conference house in Surrey to stand in for Johnny as the official Humanist contending in the discussions against the Anglicans. Smoking my Embassy cigarettes, I answered No to the question 'Is Christianity Worth Defending?', and Yes to 'Can Ethics be Godless?', and One Or The Other to 'Is Christianity False or Meaningless?' My three talks were written up in advance, and read out with good attention to punctuation. Rather old news was brought of Professor Ayer's Logical Positivism, in which was to be found the Verification Principle of Meaning. This was for separating what is meaningful from what is meaningless, or, to put it more precisely but less satisfyingly, for separating utterances that are either true or false from utterances that are neither. The latter category, including religious, metaphysical and moral utterances, and also commands, expressions of hope and so on, could still be meaningful enough in an ordinary sense – not that this was very reassuring to Christians and the like if the utterances could not be true. In fact it was not this Logical Positivism or any other philosophical tenet or argument, but rather a settled empiricism and naturalism, that made the question of the existence of God of no intellectual interest to me.

There was also another extramural activity. Lord Russell had lost hope that CND and the Aldermaston Marches would persuade Mr Macmillan and his government into unilateral nuclear disarmament, and had formed the Committee of 100 to take direct action to get the bomb banned. I did not have the honour of being one of the 100, but resolutely joined into the civil disobedience, a mass sit-down in Whitehall. Lord Russell was sitting a yard or two ahead of me, composed in his moral and intellectual confidence, on a velvet cushion.

Should I not make his acquaintance? If we were separated by our ages of 28 and 88, and by another fact or two, we evidently had things in common. Might it not be in order for two philosophers obstructing the roadway actually to meet before being lifted off it by the bobbies? In any case, had I not employed him as a book reviewer? Might I not edge forward a bit, introduce myself, and exchange a word or two on his Theory of Descriptions? Mention my article about it that *Analysis* would surely publish? I was sorely tempted, but had acquired some English decorum, or rather, had failed to acquire enough of the forwardness possessed by one of the two classes of the English.

I came away from Bow Street Magistrates Court in the morning proud of my conviction and grateful to our leader. The Ban-the-Bomb movement, as it seemed to me, was on the side of moral and political intelligence. That is not to say that I was confident that Britain ought to disarm unilaterally, that Russia posed no danger at all. The Cold War ideology and propaganda on our side had affected me. What seemed to me clear was that the Ban-the-Bomb movement could only have good effects. There was hardly a chance that a British government would succumb to the movement, or, if it did, proceed without caution. But there was a decent chance that the movement would change the atmosphere.

To glance back to the Christmas just past, Margaret and I had returned briefly to Canada. In my head was the idea of preparing my family for a disappointment and also preparing the way for what I might be needing – a defence of myself and my character. I let Bee and Ruth know that my marriage had not improved, and was in doubt. There was a new fact pertaining to it, of uncertain size. It was an idea of my teachers Richard and Johnny. It was that I should think about teaching philosophy in England. It was gratifying that Stuart had taken up their idea and was looking out for a job for me, writing letters that the departmental secretary said were unusual. My future could be in England. Margaret, however, was cool about this. Should we not go back to Canada, to our families?

We had not become happier by the means of pleasing me by removing ourselves from leafy Clapham and S.W.12 to the flat in George Street and W.1. George Street could not save Margaret and me. This had much less to do than might be supposed with the English girl of the intricate smile in the back room of the house in the next street – despite its being true that on my return from Canada she had properly ended our occasional but persistent fondlings by carrying out a seduction. If she could with reason be taken as the agent in this, it is equally a fact that I, the less deliberate party, also played my role. So ended three years of fidelity.

What followed, despite this being the progressive year that was the first year of The Pill, was not free marriage by agreement. In March 1961, I took my departure from George Street in tears and fear, the fear being of the guilt of causing distress. I went to see Margaret in the Reading Room of the British Museum, told her of my decision, and gave her letters full of sad reasoning to support it. We needed to part, at least for 21 days, in order to come to a final decision as to whether to separate permanently. We had had hardly any rows before, having put desolate conversations in their place. We had only such a conversation now, in tears on both sides.

In the week that followed I struggled to work at a paper for the seminar, drank sherry, slept in the afternoons to escape moods of hysteria, and kept the disgrace of the failure of my marriage from my fellow postgraduates and teachers. By the end of another week, I found myself lonely, and in tentative conversations with postgraduate ladies from the Commonwealth and forward girls from Boston. About them, my diary records an awful hauteur of a masculist, an intellectual and a freethinking kind. It can make you cringe. It was, I pray, in its first or masculist part, a false pose prompted by the intoxication of freedom. In its second and third parts it was a temporary taking-on of certain English ways, essentially an open superiority to ordinariness and to convention. There was no particular woman in my life. Despite what you have heard of my neighbour in George Street, my wife had certainly not been left for anyone. We two were quite sufficient for our unhappiness, without help from any third party.

In April, after the 21st day of reflecting, I wrote to Margaret that we loved one another but we could not go on. Her 30 small pages in reply rightly pointed out that this was absurd. While she too had concluded we should not get back together immediately, we should struggle towards that glorious future. Why should two people in love give up? What I needed, as she had said before, was psychoanalysis, which would liberate me from my unconscious anxieties, free me as she had been freed. With her, the air was stirring, and great wings were beating. She had been to Amsterdam, which was awash with bells. We could do anything, partly because her analyst had settled her mind on one point, by reporting that he could find in her no trace of a desire to have children.

The idea of my being psychoanalysed never got a moment's consideration from me. My own idea was that a more sceptical view of our situation, and of our kindnesses to one another in our words, issued in another prescription. Did they have something to do with my being awake in philosophy? Perhaps a lot? The sceptical view had in it that we had turned out to be unsuited to one another, our hopes were different, and our affections had been worn down. Our being together was a burden to us, we had spent a couple of years in recurrent despair. Sex had not been enlivening, and we did not have children. The view seemed to me not confused and contradictory, or in need of being improved by anyone's delving further inside my head. We should give up, accept that some promises and contracts are better broken, do no more damage to one another. If I might not be right about that, and not get moral credit for it, it was also in some way necessary.

Later in the summer, having written firm letters to the English girl of the smile, saying that she was lovely but that we did not have a future, I found myself in dalliances. One with the striking and quick-eyed Jennifer Dawson. She had written a novel, *The Ha-Ha*, which, if things went aright, would not be ephemeral. She was now doing philosophy at University College. As it seemed to me, we contemplated one another, as earlier Helen Geiger and I had done, but wanted resolution. Since our lunches were packed ones in a Bloomsbury graveyard, she may have wanted not only resolution but also inclination.

When her next novel came out, I took more pleasure than embarrassment from a certain fact. The man in it was recognizably inspired by me. But his sexual carry-on, which was notable, was modelled on somebody else, if anyone at all. A saturnine postgraduate with psychoanalytical ambitions came to mind. I had a taste left for notoriety, and did not battle against Johnny's mistaken and resolute assumption about the novel, that

I had been more of an inspiration to it than I was. In this summer, I also saw something, less innocently, of the English girl who has been mentioned before and will be again. My firmness about our not having a future was greater in my letters than elsewhere.

In the seminar at University College, I got slightly more ambitious, despite my confidence and style not being the equal of that of several of my fellows. I could see and make a good point, and then not have the courage to persist with it. I was not untroubled. Still, I got forward in developing what possibly was my *métier*. That was the getting of an argument or doctrine into clear and succinct form preparatory to passing judgement on it. Also taken forward was my habit of declaring as false something seen as false to other persons than me – persons who could also see the worth and interest of hunting around in order to understand why someone else had thought the thing true. The editor of *Philosophy* thought well of my review of the collection of Russell's papers, my first publication in my new life.

The respectability was well rewarded. Letters of reference by my three teachers on my philosophical future and estimable character resulted in my being offered three scholarships, one from the Canada Council, one from the Commonwealth, and one from some other body now forgotten. One had to be chosen, but should be enough to live on by itself for a year. In July, Johnny and I went off to Cambridge and the annual convention of British philosophers, the Joint Session of the Mind and the Aristotelian Society. There was Professor Hart, keen to have me show him the dent in his *Causation in the Law*. My view of my paper was somewhat qualified. My gratification at finding myself in the group photo in *The Observer* of the Meeting of Minds was less qualified.

6

BRACING LIFE,
ASSIGNED TO PUNISHMENT,
MARRIED AGAIN

The idea had come up of my going to Ireland with Johnny after the Joint Session. His girlfriend declined to accompany us, but, by the chance of a coffee-shop conversation, a friend of hers came along instead. She was an anthropology student, maybe keen on a field-trip. We went in Johnny's Minivan, by way of Scotland and the short ferry crossing, camping on roadsides in the rain, sustained by vegetarian staples, tea made by means of our volcano kettle, and the reciting of poetry and the singing of folksongs.

In Dublin an Irish actor of a literary bent, and of the enlightened circle of the same Harry Bewick who had judged Margaret and me on her doorstep, replied to an idle question of mine. Peter Murray said that yes, he was married, but marriage was but a social form. Having said goodnight to him and his girl-friend Nuala O'Faolain, we reached Cherry Tree Cottage, up a hill from Glendalough in Wicklow at about 1 in the morning. Pauline Murray, wife of Peter, and mother of the infant Kiaran, got up to make us tea.

Evidently she too had escaped some social forms, being well-spoken in the Anglo-Irish way but also barefooted. A dark good-looker with a strong face and strong views, she seemed as free as a breeze in the night, and was Ireland to me. She did not catch but commanded my eye. I did not lose all of my equanimity in being introduced to nude sunbathing the next day. I kept some as well during her spirited refutations of my thoughts on the bog-Irish, Trinity College Dublin from which she had just graduated in English and French, her plan to leave Ireland for the Continent, and the boundaries of the category most important in life.

This was *the natural*. That I did not lose all my equanimity had something to do with what became as evident as her spiritedness, that it was an overcoming of a restraint and shyness bound up with a sense of standing or worth. That in turn had something to do with being of a Protestant family in the south of Ireland, a family of what perhaps still had the name of being The Ascendancy.

I was reassured by being at least tolerated by Harry. She came up the road from her small gardener's greenhouse in a field, to which dwelling she had permanently retreated from the rooming house in Dublin for more sun. I now had no necktie, did have sandals, and did not exercise my Logical Positivism on her reports of the teachings of Krishnamurti. Pauline and I happily shared a bed that night.

All of us but Harry then motored on to remote County Kerry in the south-west, and an ocean strand that was remote in the county. There, the main project of the holiday was begun, this being the building of Johnny's cottage. We also evaluated novels, dived from the rocks into the frigid Gulf Stream, roasted potatoes in pits of embers, and played with pretty Kiaran. She was as vegetarian as her mother and with the distinction of never in her life having been otherwise. Pauline and I made more fine love in my tent and resolutely exchanged views. If she did not take to my ratiocination, she was well able to deal with it. I was 28 and she 24, and she was the first woman in my life to be properly fierce in her determination not to lose her identity to a man.

Certainly I was not ready for this first taste of the future. On the drive back to Glendalough after a fortnight, she did not lose her identity as one who knew the back roads and needed no map. She was rather military, I thought, in getting directions from the peat-cutters, and showed no great amount of *noblesse oblige* in her gratitude. We were a long time getting to Glendalough. We then fell out. In the middle of the night on the road outside Cherry Tree Cottage, if I had known the way to Dublin, I would have set out for it on foot. But we fell back in.

We said that we would certainly battle if we got together, shots having already been fired into as well as over bows, but we might give it a try. What went with the battle might make the whole thing worthwhile. It was I who raised the idea of her coming to London with Kiaran, who was then 18 months old. She replied that there could be no question of permanence or obligation, just an experiment in love. We exchanged a lot of letters after my departure to London and to my room in Regent Square with its view over rooftops to St Pancras Station. The letters had strong feeling in them but then also our mutual uncertainty. I flew to Ireland for a weekend, which encouraged us but did not resolve matters.

Each of us was saved from breaking any vow of fidelity only by the fact that none was made. For my part, there was the prostitute mentioned in the opening reflections of this book, and also a new friend of both charm and honour. There was also the English girl, who would not be discouraged by my declarations that we were not a match, and my explicitness about what was happening in the rest of my life. She had the excuse that I could not always resist the temptation of both her character and herself. In late September this time of promiscuity ended. Pauline and Kiaran arrived in London with Johnny. We were to begin the experiment.

With the beginning of my third year as a postgraduate, 1961–62, another experiment was also begun, this being another tutorial relationship. Professor Ayer's last contribution to building up the Philosophy Department, having already brought in Richard, Johnny and others, was to enlist Bernard Williams from New College in Oxford, to which he had progressed from All Souls and Balliol. Bernard, as he immediately became, was about 32, four years older than me. That fact was hardly caught sight of in the consternation he caused to me when he became my supervisor, Stuart's having gone off to America to test the water before emigrating to Princeton.

Bernard, according to a sentence of mine in *The New Statesman* 20 years later, was too clever by no more than an eighth. There was a little edge to the compliment, but not much. What I mainly meant about my fourth teacher was that he was indubitably wonderfully quick and inventive, and funny with it, but in fact not in the category to which lesser critics sometimes consigned him – too clever by half. Of his book *Moral Luck*, my next sentence was that 'singularly acute distinctions are its fundamental stuff, and it is written from within rather than without human experience'. In our meetings in the attic room at 19 Gordon Square in 1961, on whatever philosophical subject, it seemed he could usually do better on the wing than I could as a result of having crawled over the ground carefully in advance.

In the previous term I had laboriously put together the first 15 or 20 pages of a doctoral dissertation. But these were merely history of philosophy rather than philosophy itself, and hence of no satisfaction to me. When he asked to see my pages, I reported the truth, which also had something to do with him. In order to make sure they could not be retrieved from a wastepaper basket, I had burned them. He was kind about this madness, and not too funny. Indeed he was always as egalitarian and encouraging as was possible in the course of the amiable but starring performance naturally carried forward by him. He was smallish, pale and alert, and, in his unpretentious suits, could definitely evince a demand for respect. Might he not be a builder's son at all, as he said, but really Freddie's – as someone else named as Freddie's was known to be Stuart's? I take some small credit from the fact that I did not give up in my discussions with him, or take the step of inviting him to lunch to say that I was frightened of him and throw myself on his mercy. This strategy was subsequently used to some good effect by another.

I take no credit at all from one or two of my means, in addition to not giving up, of trying to deal with him. Once in the attic room he elaborated and decorated a line of argument which may have owed something to an article by someone else in the current number of a journal. Seeking to stay on my feet I only retorted, in gruff Canadian, 'I too read *Analysis*.' He had attempted no theft, and the memory of my sentence is mortifying. He taught me things, and exemplified more than anyone else a main kind of philosophical excellence.

There was also an occasion as memorable to me but not of an intellectual character. Johnny and I and his girl-friend were to go to lunch on Sunday with Bernard and his wife Shirley at their cottage in the New Forest. Shirley was then general secretary of the Fabian Society and a parliamentary candidate for the Labour Party. Perhaps delayed not so much by the heavy rain as by our shared reluctance to measure up at lunch, our Minivan was two hours late in reaching the crossroads rendezvous where Bernard waited stoically in his sodden M.G. No drink appeared while lunch was being made. I was gratified to be experiencing for the first time what was surely an English bluestocking household.

Not so Johnny's girlfriend. Very capable of expressing her passing ideas, no doubt encouraged by therapy, she volunteered to the company that Ted had a half-bottle of Irish whiskey in his bag. This was true. It was true by queer chance, since I was no drinker. Might I, she asked, not produce it? Might I, as the question sounded to me, not make good a palpable shortcoming of our host? She kept at it, the brute. In agony, exposed as too worldly by half, I produced the bottle. To my greater agony I heard Shirley decline her glass in the kitchen, not too merrily, on grounds of pregnancy. Not only had I failed to make enough distinctions quickly in the attic room, but I was an agent of social disaster in the New Forest. My new notoriety helped to tie my tongue on our afternoon walk.

Life was less bracing for a while in the flat in St John's Wood into which Johnny, and Pauline, Kiaran and I, had moved in October. Johnny was good-natured in his acuteness. It was also a kind of satisfaction to me to have come up in the world, to be living with an accredited academic. Pauline was as engaging a figure as in her Irish cottage. Kiaran was quick and pretty, and the role of father towards which I might be moving with her was more pleasing than daunting. The glorious lentil graced the table I made, and I got a taste for the meatless steak.

But neither my spirits nor those of Pauline were long subdued by domesticity. Nor was Johnny's, whose views on a mother's obligations to a two-year-old were clear. On that subject, more particularly on the bringing of casual Irish ways to London, tensions increased, with me in the middle. To her credit, Pauline defeated her own nature, which was not much attracted to compromise. This could not save us. Part of the remaining trouble, as with Margaret, was my work. My thesis did not exist. It was the thinking that was the problem, not the writing. This embarrassing failure was taken by me, mistakenly, to have to do with the demands of co-existence in Wadham Gardens. Also, being settled down was not so fulfilling for me as it might have been if I had not so recently emerged from just that state into something freer. Should I not be able to take up the invitation to Jennifer Dawson's dinner party?

Things happened quickly. At the beginning of January, Pauline and Kiaran took their departure from Wadham Gardens. The experience was not as awful for me as the unforgotten parting from the first woman in my life, First Love, and the ending with Margaret. Promises and hopes grow without being made and declared, but in this case there had only been some months for them to do so. Still, the parting was bad. One of the things called love was part of it, and also the sense that I had not been sufficiently loyal and intelligent in the tensions. There was only a month for me to reflect on these shortcomings and to listen to new music in the hope of achieving productive tranquillity. The knock on the door one evening was not by Pauline. Nor would her pride have allowed her any plain commissioning of an emissary. An informant there was, however, with the information that in seven months or so I would be a father.

I sought out Pauline, learned that there was in her mind no question of not having the child, proposed that we get back together, and heard her sharp retort that perhaps I was confusing myself with the Salvation Army, of whose services she had no need. Nor did she propose to bargain away her independence for whatever was on offer from me. I tried to deal with this clarity of mind by way of the truths that it was not charity that I was engaged in, and that all we needed to agree on was to continue the experiment. Marriage was not discussed, and not because of the fact that each of us was married to somebody else. We found another flat in which to conduct the further trial run. Belsize Avenue, down another hill from Hampstead, in which we waited for the future.

Indeed it was not an act of charity that I performed, since there was a real obligation on me, to do the only right thing. Nor did it feel like an act of charity, since I did feel the obligation. Also, charity typically is the doing of a little and a relatively ineffective thing, when an alternative would be effective but cost you more, say in taxes. In setting up again with Pauline I was, so to speak, paying decent taxes rather than letting myself off lightly. But my feeling of obligation and the bit of moral pride were not my only feelings. There was the prospect of a continuation of my pride in our attachment, having to do with her and her fine style. In my decision to set up again there was fear too – of the personal shame of the alternative. Fear, like pride, lacks the self-denial of morality. Above all that, best of all, there was love. Love too is not the self-denial of morality.

Is morality easier to reflect on than love? It seems to be for me. In doing the right thing I felt, more particularly, that I was doing the honourable thing. I might also, if pressed, have found some less embarrassing way of admitting that it felt as if I was acting out of a necessary virtue. In fact getting back together wasn't very hard, because it was so necessary. That was the phenomenology of it, the way it felt. But saying so is a long way from the proposition of those moral philosophers, my fourth teacher at their head, who in these shadows succumb to what has seemed to me an illusion.

In one simple form the illusion is that what actually makes an action right is the virtuous disposition out of which it comes. The agent makes the action right. How can that be? Surely what made mine right, if anything did, was that in fact it was likely to turn out better than anything else, taking everyone into consideration. However little I needed to reflect on it to see the fact, it seemed to have the only possible sort of justification that actions can have – the end would justify the means, the consequences would make the chosen conduct right. Pauline wouldn't be left holding the baby. There wouldn't be a long hurt. To those who resist what has got the name of *consequentialism*, and say instead that the ends can't justify the means, that the consequences can't justify the conduct, Russell had the right answer: What else could? I still have confidence in that.

During this period in which Pauline and I posed to one another the moral and other perils now surveyed, my academic life progressed despite the state of my thesis. My failure to think of something worth writing down was no bar to some success. My four teachers, Johnny, Richard, Stuart and Bernard, saw to it that there were opportunities for me to make use of what they took to be my abilities. I was attending not only the Monday seminar for postgraduates but also, by invitation, the Wednesday seminar of my four teachers and their colleagues. Timothy Sprigge from Cambridge, my senior by a year or two, and doing some teaching in the department, was the only other postgraduate in this bracing company. At moments he bravely tried out some of his early metaphysics, maybe the panpsychism. I sullenly dragged down Bernard's flights once or twice.

There was also my first lecturing, secured for me by the same Bernard, to the students of fashion design in the Royal College of Art. The lectures were in General Studies, and were aimed at broadening minds, diverting them for a while from cravats and hemlines. My thoughts on Logical Positivism, determinism and moral responsibility, and the liberating imagination of D. H. Lawrence, at that moment being found not obscene by the High Court, were delivered in a style approximate to that of Professor Ayer. I was tall for the part of caged lion of intellect, but performed it happily, smoking Gauloises.

Richard, along with Stuart, proposed to Professor Ryle in Oxford that a job should be found for me there or in some place nearly as salubrious.

His letter of recommendation, as I learned later, was extraordinary in its praise and its estimate of my future. But there was nothing on offer in Oxford. Through his and Stuart's efforts, however, in February 1962, I found myself being interviewed along with other candidates elsewhere – in what for a brief moment was taken to be the next best thing to Oxford. It had the name of being Balliol by the Sea. This was the new University of Sussex at Brighton. It was the first of seven new universities that were to be the solution to the crisis in higher education, and the one to which Princess Anne might come.

I took along to the interview part of what I had acquired at University College, not my additional insecurity but something close to an arrogance. If in fact I did not feel that I had excelled at University College, I was nevertheless *of it*, certified by it. It is good to be able to add that I also took along some philosophical views, as well as what had grown in me, a full and nearly passionate seriousness about philosophy. There was a touch of tall caged lion in the interview too, but the performance was true to the actor. I was trying hard in philosophy. Professor Patrick Corbett wrote to me the same day that the interview had been an interesting experience. My starting salary as a Lecturer would be generous.

Pauline said our child should not be born in a dirty noisy city full of townies. It should be born in touch with nature. I did not share her estimate of the value of one impulse from a vernal wood, but the idea had charm, and anyway needed to be respected. Also, it would save money, a good idea since we had both entered our connection without any financial resources at all. Nor had we been scrupulous in managing my year's scholarship and what came in from my occasional pieces for *The Star* and her occasional teaching. We were above budgets. In June an old Citroen 2CV was found, a car then rare in England, even comic, but useful to my self-image or at least my hope. If I had taken to England, and England to me, did I not also have a kinship with the continental intellectual?

This first of my cars took us, and the cradle made by me, to the arranged birthplace. It was a stone cottage down a long lane from what fell short of being a hamlet, Ruan Highlanes, not far from a coast in Cornwall. Kiarney was delighted by a fine pig in a sty, whose future Pauline touched on with the tenant farmer. There we passed a summer of plain living and high thinking,

Our son arrived on 11 September 1962, in accordance with the principles of natural childbirth, with me present. I remember Pauline's stoic struggle and the first sight of my son, which stays in my mind without aid of a line from Blake. The jolly midwife then said 'ten fingers, ten toes'. I was taken aback, even made a little faint, by the idea which had never occurred to me, that things might have been otherwise. It was one of two times of physical faintness in my life, both having to do with him. Pauline said he should have a name from his birthplace, and thus be Ruan. Was it not Cornish for a brook? That was all right, but it was my idea that he might also have a use for something plainer in the future. John Ruan he became.

In the history of universities in England, there was first the grey and yellow stone of Oxford and Cambridge, and after that the grey of University College London. Then the red brick, or so it is said, of Leeds, Liverpool, Swansea and the like, which provincial institutions and their young lecturers were brought into critical focus by Kingsley Amis in his novel *Lucky Jim*. Then there was the pink brick of the University of Sussex, accented, if that is the word, by a bare concrete and plate glass. It was to be the first of English universities with a landscaped campus, formed out of an estate of the Earls of Chichester in the countryside east of Brighton. Its architect was Sir Basil Spence, who had improved the spirits of the Church of England for a time by raising up Coventry Cathedral again after the bombs.

There was a glade at the centre of the campus as it was in October 1962, and in this glade Sir Basil proposed to carry on his mission by raising up a university chapel. In this he had the support of the Court of the university, drawn from the great and the good of all the southern counties, and set in authority over the academic ranks. The Court was mindful of its obligations both to Our Majesty Queen Elizabeth II, who had agreed to be the Visitor to the university, and to a local car dealer. He was a man of piety, donating more than his good name to our new experiment in higher education. From the drawings in advance, it was possible to think that the chapel would nestle in the glade. The reality, as it grew before the eyes of me and my colleagues, began to overwhelm the glade. Should our new experiment, alive to Marx and the Beatles, have so prominent a structure of superstition at its centre?

We young lecturers became restive. In a committee meeting the chaplain, sensing the way the wind was blowing, wondered if it might be ecumenical in the fullest sense if there were no pews in the chapel, just chairs. Also, he put an item on the agenda for the next meeting. '*BELL*: I would be grateful for more discussion on this subject.' Pews there were none, and bell there was none, and, as the committee papers reported, agreement without capitulation was also achieved on another subject. The chapel would be a University Meeting House, in which, constitutionally speaking, quiet meditation might be carried forward on all things, including the non-existence of God and what to do about it.

Such matters as the chapel did not distract me from something of greater concern – being a success in my first lectures and tutorials. My high thinking in Cornwall had been devoted to a large piece of English political philosophy, John Stuart Mill's essay *On Liberty*, one of the things called liberalism. It had been subjected by me to the kind of close examination previously reserved for *Thought and Action*. In my first lectures at Sussex I reflected on Mill's supposedly simple principle about what extent or sphere of liberty is to be left to the individual in a society.

Could it be, as many continued to report, that neither the law nor other members of the society should interfere in the life of an individual against his will so long as he did not harm others? And hence that his own physical or moral good was not a sufficient warrant? This would not do by itself, since evidently it required a definition of harm. Could the principle be, as some said, that an individual was to be left alone so long as he did not violate the moral rights of others? This wouldn't suffice either, in the absence of a specification of the moral rights. And anyway all talk of rights was obscure.

Could it be, as a political scientist or two said, that the principle was that an individual was to be left to himself so long as he did not violate the legally established interests or rights of others, the existing law? This piece of supposed realism, in fact a piece of conservatism alien to Mill, would give different answers to the question of liberty for societies with different bodies of law. In fact it was no general principle at all. Could it be that the individual was to be unhindered just in thinking up an opinion and in the expression of it, even if all of the rest of mankind were of the contrary opinion? This was good stuff, of which I tremendously approved. But it could not possibly be *all* of Mill's principle. Evidently the individual was to be unhindered in more than thought and expression. He could go for a walk, couldn't he?

The upshot of my lectures was like the upshot of my examination of *Thought and Action*. Mill's actual principle of individual liberty was as obscure as the new idea of freedom through self-knowledge. I did not mind saying so. You did not have to think that *On Liberty*, this large and renowned piece of political philosophy, would necessarily turn out to be a success when subjected to proper scrutiny. That was the news I brought to my lecture audience. It did not include Princess Anne, but did have such consolations as the twin if sleepy daughters of a Labour Party eminence. There were also a number of stout lads in the audience, of Trotskyite tendency. One wrote a sentence or two in the undergraduate magazine on my lordly lecturing style – and more particularly on my inclination to try to bring an hour's line of inquiry to an end in a dramatic revelation. 'And Ted said let there be light, and there was light.' It did not embarrass me enough, and I did put this first review into my archive.

Patrick Corbett, our Professor, was a large and genial man, rather like the Hollywood actor John Wayne. He had passed through the Royal Naval College at Dartmouth before becoming a Fellow of Balliol. There he tutored Bernard, and now he was philosophically above the battle, or maybe *hors de combat*. However, he had views about the nature of philosophy. One was that it ought to include Applied Philosophy, on which he made a start by supplying its name. It would be about social reality and its problems. Furthermore, there ought to be new books written, in a series called 'Philosophy at Work', and I should write the first one, on the problem of the justification of punishment. Thus, by chance, began my progress towards joining the philosophers of punishment, a membership that dismayed me even in prospect. But there was no publisher's contract on offer for a treatise on a higher subject. Onward marching would be in another direction for a while. Philosophy and the rest of life would alternate, switch one another off, but the philosophy would be different for a while.

My reading informed me that there were 'theories' of the justification of punishment. Theories, roughly speaking, are speculations as to the explanation of observed or known facts. Was the justification of punishment an observed or known fact? If that was the case with some punishments in particular, then which? It seemed a good idea to be more open-minded. It also seemed a good idea to be open-minded about Immanuel Kant of the eighteenth century, the greatest of German philosophers, who declaimed one of these theories. 'Even if a Civil Society resolved to dissolve itself with the consent of all its members – as might be supposed in the case of a People inhabiting an island resolving to separate and scatter themselves throughout the whole world – the last Murderer lying in the prison ought to be executed before the resolution was carried out. This ought to be done in order that every one may realize the desert of his deeds. . . .'

Such sentences, like my evening classes in Lewes Prison, did not make me happier about joining the ring of the philosophers of punishment. Kant's idea was that punishing people had nothing whatever to do with good social effects in the future, less crime and fewer victims in a society. Rather, according to his Retribution Theory, punishment was justified and obligatory *because it was deserved*. Neither he nor Retributivists after him slowed down long enough on the way to the execution, as it seemed to me, to ask what it means to say that someone *deserves* something. That wasn't clear at all.

Jeremy Bentham the great Utilitarian had less natural taste for punishment. He did not have much less resolution, having taken time out from philosophy to design the Panopticon, which, if it had been built, would have been a privately owned prison under his management. His theory of punishment did have the recommendation of clarity, and was derived directly from the Utilitarianism of which he was the founder. The theory was that punishment, like anything else, was right when it served what was misleadingly called the Greatest Happiness of the Greatest Number. More particularly it was justified and obligatory when, compared to any alternative course of action, it brought about a greater total of satisfaction on the part of all those affected, by discouraging offences in the future. There was a problem with this, as later philosophers pointed out in articles with titles like 'The Retributivist Hits Back'. It was that a greatest total of satisfaction might need to be brought about by awful means, say an act of lying deception by the authorities – imprisoning a wholly innocent man if that would do the trick.

Enter Professor Hart, he of the seminar book on causation in the law, not much dented by me. His idea was that the battle between Kant and the like and Bentham and the like was a prolonged muddle. We could now be led out of it by Oxford's new linguistic or ordinary-language philosophy. There wasn't one question about the justification of punishment, but three. (1) What is the General Justifying Aim of having an institution of punishment? (2) To whom may punishment be given? (3) How severely may we punish? Peace could now be made between Kant and Bentham *et al*. The answer to the first question was Bentham's. We have courts and jails because of their good effects. The answer to the second and third questions was Kant's. We are right to punish some and not others because they deserve it, and they get two years because they deserve that rather than any more or any less. Professor Hart said let there be light. Was there? It would take time to decide.

You may remember that I had a scholarship for the last one of my three years of postgraduate work at University College. One of the numerous conditions in the small print attached to the £1,500 from the Commonwealth had been my saying that 'I intend to return to my country at the end of the tenure of my scholarship'. Saying this, at the time, seemed not greatly more onerous than saying I would let the scholarship people in Ottawa know of any change of address. Part of the sad story of my carelessness is that I was saying it to Canada, and Canada was no longer the place most alive in my conscience, or the place where I thought of being called to account in the future. Is something else also sadly true? That I said to myself at the time that while the idea of my teaching in England had already come up, there could only be a good chance that a job would materialize? That although I wanted to stay, it was not yet logically possible to *intend* to stay, since you can only intend what you think will happen? Anything else is a wish or the like. If I said that to myself, I was choosing to overlook various things, one being that I intended to try to stay.

Subsequent self-deception had not been entirely successful. My sense of my implied undertaking had been such that when the Sussex job was offered to me, I wrote to Ottawa saying that I wanted to take it, and would pay back the £1,500 over a period of time. They replied only that they hoped I would come home after another year, and felt I should. Now, towards the end of that year, the academic year 1962–63, the question arose of my giving up the life that had taken shape in the green and pleasant land. It had also taken shape in the pink brick. Having thrown my energies into the new experiment in higher education, I was well to the fore in the company of young philosophers and also the university. It was agreeable to have enough standing in them to secure that my friend Timothy Sprigge would deservedly be joining our number in the next year.

If the question of leaving all of this for Canada did come up, it did not fill the sky. Nor is my having defaulted heavy on my heart now. Should it be? My brother Bee, not only because of having been embarrassed by the fact at a cocktail party in Ottawa, did not let me forget it. That is what keeps it present in my memory, not an image but a lump. I do plead guilty to giving the initial undertaking to return to Canada – more to giving the undertaking than to failing to carry it out. My failing to carry it out was a human one, say I. More human than several earlier failures, which weigh on me more. My committee of benefactors in Ottawa could rightly ask that I throw my life into reverse, but it was a lot to ask. Pauline, Kiaran and Rooney showed no signs of wanting to be transplanted. I was giving donnish tutorials on Free Will or the lack of it, and forming good questions to ask the Oxford professors Isaiah Berlin and R. M. Hare when they came to lecture to us. I had gone native.

Our university had a large concern for the well-being of under-graduates and their good discipline. In accordance with our motto, they should *Be Still And Know*. Their boarding houses in Brighton were vetted in advance, and the landladies were instructed in the truth that we of the faculty and they in their boarding houses were *in loco parentis* with respect to our undergraduate females in particular. One of these went missing for three nights. Her landlady reported this to the Proctors and the Senior Tutor, and it was discovered that the undergraduate had been preferring the bed of one of my fellow lecturers in philosophy.

Necessarily this heavy truth was conveyed to the Vice-Chancellor, Sir John Fulton. He forcefully proposed that my colleague should either resign forthwith or be sacked. If he took the first and honourable course, Sir John said, a place would be found for him in the colonies. Having gone native, I felt no slight on my origins. But the penalty proposed for our Abelard and Heloise did seem excessive. It seemed excessive too to the judicious and kindly Jack Lively, who taught Politics and was a principled liberal. We put round a petition saying so.

It was signed by a great many, possibly nearly all, of the lecturers in Arts and Social Studies. It was signed by hardly any, if any, of the lecturers in Science. I put their lack of solidarity down to a culpable lack of familiarity with social reality and its problems, partly owed to their not having read enough novels. Sir John paid attention to the way the wind was blowing in the humane part of his domain, and reconsidered. Our Abelard suffered no more than a formal carpeting and warning, which was nevertheless a blow to a spirited young man with an adequate sense of self-worth.

It is a mark of something, more than one thing, that with the scandal just past, I fell into two small affairs, one after another, with under-graduates. The affairs, despite having affection and trust in them, were small in that they involved irregular meetings, no avowals, no large hopes, and I think little hurt. Both young women had previously had some sexual and other experience, one being the winningly cocky daughter of a professor, the other sweet but hurt, having gone to a university psychiatrist, ended up in bed with him, and paid dearly in emotion. Both women, as I might then have said, were also sensible. They did not try to take me away from the family maisonette in Hove, a municipality attached to Brighton and with aspirations to decorum. Does my falling into these connections, over teacups in a flat on the seafront and half-pints of bitter in rural pubs, and my being the more active partner, indicate foolhardiness? Worse than that?

As it seems to me, the explanation of my carry-on is not in part that I was unusually sensual. The useful term *l'homme moyen sensuel* applied to me. My sexual desires were not strong. Certainly I was different from a handful of men I have known who have been greatly pulled to sex itself, and whose lives have been taken up with it, even in the grip of it. Ordinarily randy I may sometimes have been, but no more than that. Some may find it difficult to credit a certain fact about a man of 30. But it is a fact that two decades were yet to pass before I was led by a doctor's incredulous question to identify a certain uncomfortable state of feeling as being one of male sexual frustration, owed to something physical.

My desires, if not strong, were also not explicit. Women caught my eye, as they always have, but forward women had no success with me. I enjoyed no sexual imagery, was not taken up with private parts of bodies, and averted my eyes from them. Pornography was not only an oddity of which I knew nothing, but an oddity whose attraction was unknown to me. I was not a frequent maker of love. A couple of times a week comes to mind. I was decorous and wholly orthodox in the act itself, which, so far as possible, was not spoken of. I was a man of whom a lover might say, with reason, that I was prim about sex. It was submerged in a *relationship*.

Those paragraphs have been written in what is my dominant state of slightly hesitant belief about much of my past. But now, having written them, doubt creeps in. If the more particular claims of fact are true, can the main one, about being *l'homme moyen sensuel*, be so certain? Surely, you may say, a man living with a young and agreeable partner, if he also finds two other lovers, is a desirous man? Are his desires not strong and explicit if they get him into the activity in question?

Well, it must be possible that a clear view of my feelings was not had by me then, and is not now. It is possible that my feelings were more urgent than has been reported in my paragraphs, but that I averted my eyes from them, and conducted myself primly in accordance with this self-deception. It is possible, that is, that I was not sealed off from more urgent feelings, took care not to look closely at them and thus kept open a question about them, but acted, however primly, in accordance with them. Do I still? This speculation about self-deception is about having a question in mind about one's feelings and taking care not to get it answered. The speculation about my past, then, is about what went on in a way in my consciousness.

Do you also contemplate, differently, that there were also desirous dispositions in operation that were strong and explicit and of which I was not conscious but unconscious? This kind of idea, remarked on in the first chapter of this book, was part of enlightened reflection before Freud, and will with good reason persist when his doctrines do not. This kind of idea need have nothing in it about any genesis or development of the dispositions, in particular no colourful story of one's relation to one's mother and so on, and need not have anything to do with a funny kind of consciousness over and above, or rather underneath and below, the only kind of consciousness there is. But let us not get into the deep water of these dispositions now. There are other possible explanations of my carry-on.

127

In the year 1963–64, the permissive society was coming into being. Did the tenor of the times and the influence of the enlightened Irish circle, contribute to my two affairs? Very likely. Perhaps more was contributed by Pauline's official tolerance of freedom in marriage and in similar partnerships, but that tolerance was not so outright or *outré* that I kept her well-informed of my two connections. Nor did I speak of my subsequent occasional meetings with the English girl of the intricate smile, who kept in touch with me.

As it seems to me, however, the principal explanation of my affairs was that conventional sexual morality had ceased to have any hold on me. Along the way from Baden to Toronto to London to Sussex, it had fallen away. No doubt it was weakened by philosophy and its scepticism. This lightening of my load, or loss, also had more to it. I was being true to my greater inclination to the company of women than men, my liking the look of them and the restfulness of them. Also, to make love was to be of the very same fine spirit as someone else for a while, united in happiness. There was no room for insecurity in it. Further, the affection of women was accrediting, a certification. If it would not then occur to me to boast of my success, that success was valued.

So there were things to be gained, things of value, in escaping conventional sexual morality. What was to be said against my escape? To deal first with just the fact of getting into bed with others than Pauline, any others, it could not be overlooked that it would not make her happy. It would not help our own relationship. But was the relationship not a settled and persistent one? And had we not in some sense agreed on freedom? Had not Harry ordained it? By these considerations I sought to excuse myself to myself.

As for the fact of being a lecturer in bed with undergraduates in particular, there was no possibility of avoiding the charge that this was an abuse of my position. But it was not easy to make clear sense of the charge. It was not as if my partners were reluctant, which they were not. They were not seduced, or hardly more seduced than me. To use a term not then current, there was no harassment worth the name. Nor did they act from the promise or anticipation of academic favours, or fear of reprisal if they declined my casual invitations. If they were impressed by me in my position, which very likely they were, I did in fact possess the attributes in question. Being impressed was not in itself being a victim.

Evidently I was breaking a tacit undertaking to Sir John Fulton and to others of his mind. But was the conventional view of the weight of this obligation correct? Why was there no explicit rule? It did not escape me either that I was not alone in my ways. There were others than our Abelard who were not burdened by their tacit undertaking.

So I would have said in setting out to defend myself. In fact, in these buoyant times, I did not reflect a lot on my actions and my moral standing, or suffer guilt, partly because of the optimistic feeling that if I worked at a defence, a confident one might be constructed. I was never called on to provide one.

Also, other things were on my mind, one of them as a result of a visit by Bernard Williams to give a paper to the Sussex philosophers. After my having agreed to be one of them, two years before, Richard Wollheim had become Grote Professor at University College, succeeding Stuart Hampshire. Now, in June 1964, Bernard was leaving to ascend to his first chair, at another London college. We went for a walk through the pink brick landscape. He said someone was needed to replace him at University College, and it had been decided that I was the man. No doubt he had forgotten my tutorial and social indiscretions.

It was wonderfully gratifying. I was being invited, by those whose good opinion was most valued by me, back to the place of most renown in my life. It had greater reality than the pink brick. It had past and present. It was a place of settled distinction, not one hoping to gain distinction. In it, the philosophy was stiffer, at a higher level. It was being taught not to all undergraduates but only to those specialists who had elected to do it. They were trying out answers to particular hard questions like 'What is a law of nature?' or 'Does knowledge consist in justified true belief?' rather than engage with all of The Modern European Mind. It was agreeable to hear from Bernard, as well, that I might be able to ease a new tension in the department. It was between Johnny Watling and another senior figure on the one hand, and, on the other, two young Turks appointed the year before, wearing their new Oxford spurs. Not only would I join the elect, but I would make peace among them.

It was not easy to tell Timothy Sprigge of my defection, since, as you have heard, I had been instrumental in his coming to Sussex in this same academic year from his temporary teaching post at that same University College. It turned out to be less easy because our conversation gave me my first experience of a kind of academic theorizing. Had I perhaps helped him out of his temporary teaching at University College so as to make my own return there more likely? Had I foresightedly been getting a sitting tenant in the department out of the way? He was satisfied, I hope, that for more than one reason I had not deprived him of being Bernard's successor. The opening of the question caused me dismay and consternation, as any such question always would, whatever its worth, but it did not affect our friendship.

Another part of my future was also being settled. Margaret and I had hardly met since separating. After the birth of Rooney, she had set about getting a divorce, which had come through by August 1964. In that same month Pauline and I married at Hove Town Hall, happily if coolly, in the presence of Timothy and Giglia Sprigge and Jack and Penelope Lively. We did so without negotiating private conditions for our legal union, any departures from our existing understanding. We were in fact getting on, and happy as parents. Kiarney was on the way to 5 and Rooney to 2. Both were lovely. Kiarney danced through her nursery school, Rooney skipped across the lawns of the seafront. But the first of these children was less than a full member of the legal family. It was unsettling. The idea came up of my legally adopting her, which contentedly I did.

In place of a farewell dinner at the University of Sussex, which indeed had not been earned, my colleagues gave me a large history of modern painting, perhaps to remind me that there was more in life than logic-chopping. Sir John Fulton sent a brief note. 'I had not heard that you were leaving and of course I am very sorry about it. You have thrown yourself with great energy into our affairs, and we shall miss you.'

7

A DEPARTMENT JOINED, MORAL AND POLITICAL UTTERANCES

G. E. Moore has the credit of not having been a wilfully imaginative philosopher, and of not having aspired to the oracular. So he does not have the fame of his contemporary in Cambridge, beatified Wittgenstein. There is justice, however, in his not having the standing of his other contemporary, Russell, who did so much so victoriously. If Moore has neither the nimbus of Wittgenstein nor the garlands of Russell, he is nevertheless remembered. He resisted the doctrine that what we are aware of in seeing is sense-data. He resisted scepticism about the existence of ordinary things, and the philosophical Idealism that makes out that everything that exists is mental or spiritual. He is remembered in particular for his Proof of an External World. This he took himself to achieve by holding up his two hands and saying to the lecture audience 'Here is one hand, and here is another'. Some thought he had done well at proving the existence of hands, but not so well at proving them to be external, which is to say not in the mind or dependent on it.

He also took himself to have proved something in moral philosophy – that good is indefinable. The first stage of the proof was to point out that certain questions containing both a term and a correct definition of the term, say 'Is a puppy a young dog?', are not open questions, not matters that need thinking about. The second stage was considering a formally similar question, 'Is what maximizes happiness good?', and all variants that come to mind, such as 'Is what is most evolved good?' These *are* open questions, and therefore they do not contain a definition of good. What also follows, Moore said, is that there is no definition of good. Moral utterances about good actions and the like are utterances

131

about an *indefinable* quality of them. We know this quality, but cannot say what it is.

The thought that our moral utterances are such items became an official concern of mine on my arrival in the Department of Philosophy at University College in autumn 1964. In fact, my interest in Moore's Proof of an External World was greater than my interest in his proof of the indefinability of good, and there was my book on punishment to write, but lectures in moral philosophy were needed by our undergraduates. My colleagues were no more keen to give them than I, and new arrivals in a department can't be choosers. I could choose nearly to chain-smoke my way through them in the style of several of my mentors, giving the impression of intellect in need of calming, indeed intellect under a head of steam produced by logical combustion. The impression was not wholly false. My lecturing caused me apprehension, more than it had in my previous place of employment, and did not come easily to me. I tried hard.

Moore's view of the nature of moral utterances was not the only one. Professor Ayer's, shared with others who had learned their Logical Positivism from the Vienna Circle, was different. By the Verification Principle of Meaning, the only true or false utterances were ones that are so as a result either of logical necessity, like 'All bachelors are unmarried', or by being verifiable in sense experience. Thus moral utterances, as you have heard, far from being true or false of indefinable properties, were not true or false at all. To this it was added that they were no more than expressions and evocations of emotion, more elaborate than exclamations and groans but like them.

Moore, Professor Ayer and others were engaged in meta-ethics. This is the study of the common nature of moral judgements. Thus it is something different from ethics, understood as the business of arriving at and embracing and defending some moral judgements as against others, including general ones which are moral principles. I could sympathize somewhat, of course, with the desire to retreat from ethics to meta-ethics. There was a better chance of actually proving something there. But the fact was that the retreat was away from the fundamental problems of ethics. Of the objections made in my lectures, the one I liked best was within meta-ethics but also suggested some ethics. It was my own, a thought-experiment laid out in graphic detail.

Suppose there is something like a telephone booth, but with just two buttons in it. If button S is pressed, suffering of a terrible kind will be caused to many people. If button H is pressed, happiness will be the result for many people. But the still more unusual thing about the situation is that someone able to choose between S and H knows only those two effects. He knows nothing more – say that the many people affected by the S button are war criminals, or that those affected by the H button are members of the working class – or that there is any particular effect on the button-presser himself of the choice he makes. He knows only that S gives rise to suffering and H to happiness.

Suppose in this circumstance a man says he ought to press S, and is serious. Will we say no more than that his judgement is an expression and evocation of emotion? Just an emotion we do not share? Will we say with Professor Hare that his judgement is a command that likely he would not make if he were on the receiving end? No, we will say that he is *less than human*, something like *mad*. Will we not also say something of this useful category, by the way, in connection with a telephone booth where the two buttons are E for equal shares for people of a very good or very bad thing and U for unequal shares, and where the chooser knows nothing more than that? In these thought-experiments there was a small start towards something different from Moore's account, but sharing some of the respectability of it. Not Moral Realism fortunately, but not any developed account or a sufficiently contentful *dénouement* for my lectures either. Not bad, though.

There was also another source of my coolness about meta-ethics, different from my professional resistance to its giving up on fundamental problems. Not being conventionally moral about the beds did not make me less of a moralized and a moralizing personality. Admittedly I was not *overcome* by moral concerns. If I had been, I would have been doing something more immediately useful than philosophy. I might have been a policeman, which unlikely thought sometimes drifted through my mind. Still, when moral concerns did come to my attention, they were urgent. Rae Laura had laid a good foundation for this personality of mine, and my brother Bee had then laboured a bit on it. There had been religion in a first stage of it, and then a firmness somehow owed to my superiority to religion. Now five years of England had done some more. My perception of England had enlivened my sense of the way things ought to be, given more political content to this sense. My joining England fortified it.

Canada had seemed to me a tolerable society but also without *resolution*. My first compatriots had carried no large moral intention into reality in their society. They had not constructed or allowed others to construct a Welfare State. My second compatriots had. It existed, and it worked. The term 'Welfare State' has become worn over the years, but for me in 1964 it had what it has continued to have, a unique ring of decency. Unlike 'freedom', it cannot be mouthed to any purpose, however foul. It makes no false sound, like 'the enterprise society', no uncertain sound, like 'democracy', and no dread sound, like 'revolution'. It seemed to me possible that societies should progress further than this state, possible that strong measures should be taken in order to go further. Very likely one should at least sit down in the street regularly.

Something else was not merely very likely, but a clear certainty. It was morally imperative that a society should take all ordinary democratic means to secure lives of decency for all its members by social organization. England had done this, made the Welfare State. It had not occurred to me, for good reason, that Mr Macmillan of the Conservatives would think of threatening what I might well have spoken of as this temple. Now Mr Wilson of the Labour Party was Prime Minister. He would preserve and add something to it. It would stand as long as England, true to the character of the nation itself. I had my small share in this national pride, perhaps less small for having been freely chosen rather than inherited. The moral cast of my outlook on life was strengthened by this membership.

Pauline, Kiaran, Rooney and I had transferred ourselves from Hove to North Finchley, a part of London which had the definable quality of being suburban. It lay beyond Golders Green and was near enough to Barnet, where Margaret Thatcher was M.P., contemplating her future and ours. These easy times for getting mortgages, and my salary having improved noticeably, we were able to borrow every penny for the buying of 107 Nether Street, N.12. My book on punishment went forward in the nether world, and, if we did not have the fullest of social lives in it, colleagues and friends to an occasional party.

The colleagues included Richard, perhaps least familiar with the outer postal districts, and Johnny, of whom you also know. Peter Downing was another, a Cambridge man who had got bored with being a solicitor and succumbed to the thrill of studying backward-looking subjunctive conditional statements – if Jim had been rude to Jack this morning, Jack would have hurt Jim's feelings yesterday. Myles Burnyeat, also Cambridge, did ancient philosophy with engaging zeal and knew its value to our later philosophical lives. Jerry Cohen was our departmental Marxist and the provider of insights into the homeland in which we had both grown up. Having thereafter been an Oxford postgraduate, his imitation of Isaiah Berlin in spate was excellent. Hans Sluga, Oxford via Munich, formal logician, appreciator of his countryman Gottlob Frege, was sweetly genial except under prolonged experience of hearing about backward-looking subjunctive conditionals. Hidé Ishiguro was a spirited and engaging Japanese. She was a Leibniz scholar and so much more, and like me had just come to teach in University College, in her case via Tokyo, Oxford, Paris and Leeds. Of these staging posts, she seemed to owe most to Oxford.

We were a pretty happy crew. Jerry Cohen and I, despite his Marxism and my lack of it, shared some politics. We delivered its truths to undergraduates not only in lectures but in the espresso bar. We went on demonstrations against the American bombing of Vietnam. The names of Cohen and Honderich, along with those of Ayer, Williams, Wollheim and Herbert Hart, appeared among hundreds at the end of the public statement in *The Guardian* in June 1965 urging Her Majesty's Labour Government to disassociate itself from the American aggression. Johnny and Peter Downing and I had lunches at Bertorelli's and Schmidt's in Charlotte Street, and, less often in the Vega, the dining room of senior vegetarians and humanists in Leicester Square, a kind of anteroom to the life not to come.

At college, in addition to my weekly lecture on moral philosophy and one on analytical political philosophy, and two seminars with colleagues, there was my round of undergraduate tutorials, in the attic room inherited from Bernard along with his three-piece suite. The room was a pleasing eyrie. It had a table rather than a desk at the window that looked out to the Post Office Tower, and a collapsible camp bed for naps. I was a successful tutor, or anyway sought-after. Shy young men from Derbyshire, knowing young men from Essex whose reefers gave fragrance and tone to the departmental parties, stunningly dim lads from Eton, leggy young women in mini-skirts not inclined to my being *in loco parentis* to them, their more decorous sisters from Rhode Island in twin sets and pearls – it was important to me that all of them got things straight, or anyway had got an idea that they hadn't.

The time given to these various departmental endeavours, along with reading in advance for them and writing out my lectures in full, came to 20 or 25 hours a week. This left time for *The International Library of Philosophy and Scientific Method*, an ongoing series of philosophy books published by Routledge & Kegan Paul. A distinction of the series was that one of the early volumes in it had been Wittgenstein's *Tractatus Logico-Philosophicus* – that march of mystic propositions whose numbers were so inscribed in the minds of its devotees.

Professor Ayer had been the general editor of the series of books in question, and in it he had commissioned some not very lively antidotes to the *Tractatus*. When he had tired of this unonerous task, he had arranged for Bernard to be his successor. Bernard had tired as quickly, principally under the burden put on his lively conscience by the regular rediscovery in his room of unsolicited manuscripts whose authors had not yet heard his opinion. I had found myself at lunch with the publisher in the Garrick Club in Garrick Street, pleased to be there, and pleased at being appointed Assistant Editor of the series, at Bernard's suggestion. Some months later, we were back in the club with Routledge reviewing progress. It had not been great. Philosophers and publishers did not see eye to eye as to why. Bernard rose above being huffy, at which he was always good, to taking a high line, at which he was better. He resigned forthwith as Editor, but at my request would continue his connection with the series in the elevated role of Consultant Editor. I would be Editor, at a tolerable fee of £450 per annum, firmly negotiated on my behalf by him.

At the start of the next academic year, 1965–66, I acquired another such post. It was not exactly inherited from my predecessor. The philosophy series published in paperback by Penguin Books had also had as its general editor Professor Ayer, as he still was to me. This series had more recent salience than the Routledge series. It had in it the general editor's own *The Problem of Knowledge*. Also Stuart's *Spinoza*, and Richard's *F. H. Bradley*. The series would have in it Johnny's philosophy of science, if that got written, and Bernard's *Descartes: The Project of Pure Inquiry*.

Such Penguins as Sir Allen Lane had lately defeated the old guard by publishing D. H. Lawrence's *Lady Chatterley's Lover* and not going to jail for the alleged obscenity of it. They were capable of going against the say-so of their general editor in philosophy. They could decline to publish sizeable works by genial persons met at international conferences. As I subsequently learned, they did so decline, and Professor Ayer renounced his office in dudgeon. Very likely at the suggestion of his natural successor, Bernard, I instead of he became general editor of Penguin philosophy.

Johnny Watling alerted me to the fact that Professor Ayer was saving some dudgeon for me in connection with editorships. He would bring it along from Oxford with his special lecture for us. The charge against me was not clear. It could be disloyalty, but I had not been aware of the circumstances of his resignation from Penguins. No doubt the fact of the matter was that he was annoyed by a plain truth, that I was not of such a stature that both of his editorial mantles should fall on me. Little remains in my mind of our hot exchanges in the Senior Common Room under the Stanley Spencer picture of a graveyard. Is it a pleasure to recall that I did not choose to restrain myself and defer to him with an eye to the future? Not act on a sense that standing up for myself could cost me something? The pleasure is reduced by the various thoughts that maybe I felt that penitence would not work, and that I have a temper which has sometimes left good sense behind, and that I have rarely been adept at judging when to fight and when to conciliate.

So began my editing of series of philosophy books, which soon came to have in it various elements of bad conscience and imperfect rationality. It was a satisfaction to see my name as editor on the jacket of the first Routledge book. But I had not written the book, and it had taken some time or anyway energy away from my ongoing reflections on the supposed justifications of punishment. Were philosophers not supposed to be doing their own thinking, engaged in their own personal projects of pure inquiry? And was that not their way forward in the world? Also, the word 'editing' covers a multitude of things, some of them sins. I did not spend half a week on a manuscript, producing a list of necessary revisions. Sometimes not every proposition was studied, sometimes not every page. My practice was true to the attitude, whether or not it was owed to it, that it was the author's job to write the book, and mine to decide whether to publish it, more or less as it stood.

137

There was one other academic role that sometimes distracted me from my own project of pure inquiry. A few of our undergraduates did not get their maintenance cheques on time from their local councils. A few had well-heeled but mean fathers, not making the required parental contribution to their upkeep. A few succeeded in finding the elastic limits of the rules of the department, difficult to do without the aid of mental disturbance. To help them or to exercise what discipline was thought to be needed in the Age of the Beatles, Richard took us to need a Departmental Tutor, also known as Moral Tutor. He took me as the man for the job. Would he have disapproved of something I added to it? It had not become easy for undergraduates who got pregnant to choose instead to continue with their degrees. The law still made it difficult. As Moral Tutor I came to have a telephone number or two for enlightened doctors. A good thing too.

Being the Tutor also involved the interviewing of applicants for our places in Philosophy and Economics, this being a joint honours degree. Admission to the single honours degree, Philosophy pure and un-adulterated, remained the duty and perquisite of Richard. Certainly I followed the principle that if two candidates for admission seemed more or less on a par, and one was from Eton or the like, the other candidate was to have the place. The argument was of course that the candidate from the lesser school, having been less well taught, was of greater ability. On occasion I went beyond this principle, in anticipation of the policy of Reverse Discrimination, and chose the slightly less advanced candidate in the striped jersey as against the more advanced one in the blue blazer.

As you will gather, six years in England had given me a more internal awareness of social class, and of the fact that more went with it than different degrees of readiness to make one's private conversation audible in public places. What could go with good family and school was that great thing *confidence*, a prize in life and a means to more prizes. Its possessors put it to good use. The largest fact was not that it resulted in interviews and jobs and being a member of the Garrick. It could on occasion result in *thinking* that was better. Confidence could sometimes make for better philosophy. There was this real fact about the class system. Further, it was a fact not only of the confident person's achievement, but also something with an effect on others. The system's beneficiaries used and defended their confidence, and thereby reduced

138

that of others. They did not do so unknowingly, in a dream. Here was something like injustice. The Welfare State had not overturned the world.

The annual conference of British philosophers of which you have heard, the Joint Session of the Mind Assocation and the Aristotelian Society, is held in a different university each year. It consists in a weekend of performances by chosen philosophers. They make up a list of rising or risen figures, somewhat diluted by worthies being done a favour by the organizing committee, or members of the organizing committee themselves. After summarizing their papers, these having been printed and circulated in a bound volume beforehand, the speakers defend themselves against objections from the floor. Also leading questions, speeches, and insinuations of serious oversight. In these contributions from the floor, sometimes by younger members of the profession, reputations come into being or do not, wax or wane. There are thrills and spills, enough of them to deter the faint-hearted from participation.

I did not want to be among the faint-hearted, reduced to the well-known form of *l'esprit d'escalier* which is hauteur in the bar afterwards. Quite regularly, maybe too regularly, I was not among the faint-hearted. Refutation was my aim, and often I seemed to do well. Perhaps it was this, and my elevation to editor, that got me early invitations to read papers to those other small institutions in my line of life, the under-graduate philosophy societies of the English, Scottish and Welsh universities. Towards the end of 1965, an invitation came from Oxford.

The prospect was pleasing. This was partly for the little honour of it, and partly because of the connected fact that I had from a distance succumbed to the standing and the charm of Oxford. The card listing the term's meetings of the Voltaire Society, when it arrived through the post, did not reduce my sense of self-worth, since all the other speakers for the term were dons from within the circle of the dreaming spires. Nor did the card reduce the charm. The list of officers of the society included the Iconographer, Iris Murdoch, and the Corresponding Humanist, E. M. Forster.

As for the standing of Oxford, you may remember that in my days as a postgraduate my sense of it was imperfect. Now it was evident that something needed to be added to my jocularity about its being provincial. If it was provincial, it was doing well at governing parts of the capital, such as University College London. The three Grote Professors of my experience had come one after another from its colleges. So had Bernard, who had then promptly been elected to the chair in philosophy at another London college, Bedford, and now, after the minimum tour of duty, was *en route* to another chair, in Cambridge.

Evidently the governors sent out from Oxford included many who were able or exceptional. It would have taken great faith in a certain conspiracy theory to resist a certain proposition – that Oxford and also Cambridge graduates contained, along with all the noodles, a somewhat higher proportion of the able or exceptional than the graduates of other institutions. There was more to the story, of course, connected with the fact of social class lately noted. Oxford men and women, whatever their abilities, had the easy habit of taking themselves as contenders for whatever was going. Also of thinking of other Oxford men and women as contenders, thereby often saving the latter group from the indignity of putting themselves forward. What it all added up to was indeed a fact of standing, but also a challenge to those from outside the circle of dreaming spires.

The subject of my paper to the Voltaire Society was the problem of the nature of Truth, partly because the problem of Punishment was embarrassing. More particularly I had come along to adjudicate the dispute about truth between two of my Oxonian betters. These were Mr Strawson, don of dons and author of *Individuals*, and Professor Austin, he of the snails. My adjudication was tardy, coming after the second protagonist had died and the first had turned his attention elsewhere. But it seemed to me none the worse for that. Professor Austin, whatever his other enthusiasms, had purified from metaphor the ancient view that a statement is true when it corresponds to the facts. This he had done more delicately than is suggested by a quick summary of his purification – that a statement is true when what it refers to is as it is described to be by the statement. Correspondence is a matter of language-rules, not something deeper. Less of Mr Strawson's elaboration of a more recent view, owed originally to Ramsey in Cambridge and already mentioned to you, is lost in another quick summary. To say a statement is true is mainly just to make the statement in question, if also to do something like convey agreement with an earlier maker of the statement.

In my adjudication, neither protagonist got off unjudged. Mr Strawson had failed to see, about a question to which Professor Austin gave the

Correspondence Theory as an answer, that it was the philosophically fundamental question about truth. If Professor Austin was more in the right, he had failed to see, in connection with a true statement, that the thing referred to and described is never a *fact*, since facts are not satisfactorily in the world or parts of it. Something's being the case – that something is the case – is not in the world or a part of it. What is referred to by a statement is at bottom a perfectly ordinary thing, say a spire or the Iconographer or the Corresponding Humanist. There was a lot more along these lines. I think much the same today, despite being in what may be a minority among my fellow workers. In my stubbornness, though, I am one with most philosophers, who for the most part are impervious to argument. There is a truth about philosophy in this. At the bottom of philosophy are things underdescribed as commitments. They are better described as grips that the world gets on us, early.

This academic year also had something else in it. I and to a lesser extent Pauline were carrying forward what had become settled, a free or open marriage. The terms might be used faintly defensively in the wider world, but with respect and self-respect in more advanced circles. Was it not clear that people could not be owned? Who could fail to see that imprisonment in marriage destroyed love? Were communes not the conditions of living to which we should all have aspired? You have heard several times of the characterful English girl of the smile. She and I met rather rarely over five years. Now I went for a walk along the Thames with her and learned of freedom's penalty, to be heavier for others than for me.

Some time ago, she said, she had come to her own decision, to act on her love and to have a child by me. It was absolutely no accident. She had timed her visits to London well, and was now too advanced in pregnancy for there to be the ordinary question of not going forward with it. In any case, she was in no doubt about the project. It was entirely hers, never spoken of to me, and, she said, she asked nothing from me. Morally, materially, psychologically and legally, the child was her sole responsibility. Despite her guilt, she was profoundly content. All of those words she also put into a letter. My shock was followed by some bitterness. I thought and perhaps said that this was no act of relationship between two people, and that I now had an idea of what it might be to offend against the vague principle of Kant's moral philosophy mentioned some way back, that we are to treat each other person never as only a means but always as an end. Another letter arrived in due course. It said that I now had what for a long time thereafter I called a biological son.

Along with my bitterness went a new guilt. Putting the best face on it, I had allowed affection and desire, along with an unwillingness to hurt and weakness, to lead me into prolonging a connection that should have been ended. I had made possible what was not just a mess. Good thinking in philosophy had done no good service in a part of the rest of my life. I had been more pursued than pursuing, and had sent my declarations about there being no future, and acted on them at least by entering into and staying in a marriage. This did not greatly help. I was part of the story, and could not write myself out of it. For me there was not whatever exculpation is provided by a grand passion. There could be no simple assignment of personal responsibility to the other party in the story. As for the ideology of liberation, let alone its language, it was of no service at all in the face of this human fact.

What I would do within myself would be to try to keep the fact out of mind as much as possible. It carried some threat to my family, but this could be reduced by my maintaining a distance from the other mother and child. In any case, was help for them not beyond my capabilities? Did I not lack not only the desire and the will to become involved with them, but also the strength? So it seemed, no doubt falsely. I would tell Pauline of the fact, and in due course the two others in my family. If the shadow remained, it could become less definite, smaller. Perhaps it began to do so when we went to Ireland in the summer of 1966, in our Morris Traveller, the estate car framed in varnished wood and so favoured by sensible young families.

In October 1966 my brother Bee wrote with the news that a boardroom struggle at *The Star* had gone the right way. He would rise from being a director and Editor-in-Chief to being President and Publisher. So ended ascendancy in the newspaper by one family and so began, conceivably, ascendancy in it by another. Bee and I, 48 and 33, were about as close as was allowed by his having been an elder brother *in loco parentis*, one who preferred economics to philosophy, our having the Atlantic Ocean between us, and our two judgemental natures. By this time, I had one of those natures too. What are they? No doubt all humans judge, all find shortcomings in others. Were the two of us unusual, rather, not just in having high standards, but in the feeling which gave an edge to our judgements, even sometimes on our children? An unhappy desire and determination to find the fault in someone of taking things easy in the way of John William Honderich? Sin by another name?

Ruthie was flourishing in the promotion of her good causes and charities. Loine, free of politics but spontaneous in his Christianity of good works, was running foul of a judge in Miami. He had gone against the zoning by-laws and set up hostels for Cuban refugees in a good residential area of the city. His sentence was some hours each day in jail, to teach him the difference between religious and community values. Mary, gentle Mary, who should have written better things, was engaged instead in writing her hard-pressed husband's sermons, and sending witty if faintly hopeful letters to me about my atheism. Their true aim was evidently not to change my mind, but to show me love by way of concern, which they did clearly.

Despite my family ties, Canada and of course the United States were more than an ocean away. In England, as explained already, I had not merely gone native, but, so far as my view of myself was concerned, *was* a kind of native. My accent never occurred to me. I saw myself as no outsider. There was no pretence in my easiness in English life. This transfer of allegiance continued to be supported by what was happening around me, satisfactorily. Having no great burden of historical knowledge, I continued to see England as in its normal condition, which, after the great leap forward of the Welfare State, was again one of slow progress in decency. Mr Wilson of the Labour Party was now taking matters forward. Prescriptions for medicine on the National Health were now entirely free, and abortion would soon be legal. There was also the Rent Act. It gave greater security to tenants. In future they could not be got out easily by their landlords. An admirable piece of legislation. Long would it last.

All of that conceals some complexity, and may give some misleading impressions, one being that I had joined the democratic socialists of the Labour Party. The fact that this did not happen had something to do with my weekly lectures at college in analytical political philosophy, and in particular one large question in the area of the problem of justice. What was the fundamental principle of equality? What was at the bottom of the great tradition of egalitarianism?

Certainly it could not be the proposition that all men are in fact equal, say in basic natural endowments – despite the transparent attempt of critics to fasten this absurdity on egalitarianism. Nor could the fundamental principle be the ancient and boring injunction to treat like cases alike and different cases differently. That was a mere rule of consistency. It could be followed by treating whites alike and a lot better than blacks, even starving the blacks, so long as you did it to all of them. Nor did there seem to be a necessity with respect to how people ought to be compared for the purposes of equal or different treatment – say in terms of medical need rather than skin colour. Bernard had announced a piece of logic here, that necessarily help should go to those who needed it. He mainly got marks for good intentions. Against what he said, where was the *contradiction*, as distinct from the bad smell, in arranging for spectacles to go to short-sighted persons with money, as distinct from short-sighted persons?

Could the principle then simply be that we should give an equal respect to everyone? Take everyone, as perhaps Kant also said, as equal in the sight of God? That rule, at any rate in the minds of its main proponents, did not require that we do anything much to help out the poor, except maybe not condescend to them. Would we have to let them in out of the rain? There had to be something better. What about making everyone equal in income? But for a start that did not distinguish between making people equally poor and making them equally well-off. It certainly did not explain why the latter was preferable. Furthermore, might it not be better for us all to be unequally well-off as against equally badly-off? Whether or not this was actually the choice faced by societies, it was a good question. It remained such even if you doubted the social goodwill of the people who pressed it in these years, relatively few of them.

You will gather that my lectures did not reach a resounding conclusion about equality. But my failure to reach one did not do anything to weaken a conviction. If the world as it is can get grips on us early, so can the world as it ought to be. It *had* to be the case that a good and just society would realize some fundamental and formulable principle of equality.

Also, a good and just political party would be given over to that principle, really captured by it, even if the principle couldn't be got quite straight. You could tell when you were going in the right direction.

The Labour Party, while it had my respect and was making the slow progress towards decency, was not in the grip of my conviction, not sufficiently impassioned. I would not join it. As for the small schismatic parties of the Left, the Trotskyites and the like, my antipathy to Marx as a philosopher and also my inclination to what passed as political realism kept me out of them even though they were more given to my conviction.

You will infer, sagacious reader, that in addition to a fundamental principle of equality, something else seems to have been missing from my outlook, as indeed it was. How should we get going in the right direction, towards the end that might be recognizable when we got there, the society of equality? What political means-to-ends are rational and defensible? Is democracy as we know it the only one? I did not know. Nor did I struggle with the question – beyond confirming to myself that the good historian Eric Hobsbawn next door in Birkbeck College, and my colleague Jerry Cohen, were optimistic in declaring that proletarian revolution was inevitable. They were certainly more confident than me of the iron laws of historical necessity, the self-destructive nature of capitalism and all that. In place of reflection on my part, there was a bit of activity, prompted by the serenely grim secretary of Lord Russell, the American Ralph Schoenman.

In January 1967 almost a full page in *The Times* was given over to a statement of the need for Britain's Labour government to withdraw its support for the American bombing in Vietnam. It was signed by 1,600 teachers in British universities, 240 of them in the University of London. I had much to do with getting the 240 in line. Quite a few of us were at the demonstration at the American embassy in Grosvenor Square. No one had brought any marbles to throw under the hooves of the police horses. If I had had some, they would very likely have stayed in my pocket, maybe mistakenly. But in fact we university teachers did make contributions to a continuing campaign. And the campaign contributed more than voters had to the eventual ending in defeat and disgrace of a piece of barbarous aggression on behalf of free enterprise.

If my lectures in political philosophy were not properly conclusive, the ones in philosophical logic were happier and might lead to more. By persistence I had come to the truth about Truth, got by good sense and amending Professor Austin, and also the truth about meaning and the Theory of Descriptions, got by clarifying Lord Russell. In this second endeavour too, I was meeting objections by Mr Strawson. If the two subjects certainly interested me, there seems a possibility that I was also attracted or impelled by something else. This was to try to stand up to the man who was, not only in my eyes, the newly risen leader and flower of English philosophy, defer though he might himself to the older claims of Professor Ayer. I did not know him, but he was in my life – in my philosophical hours when they halted and replaced the other ones.

As you have heard, the problem to which Russell's theory was offered as a solution seemed clear. It had to do with a large class of terms in language including definite descriptions, the latter being terms like 'the lectern over there'. Did their meanings not consist in experienced things for which they stood, or rather, and a lot better, in rule-connections or conventions holding between them and the things – or anyway between them and some things or other? Surely that was the fundamental idea about meaning. But then what about the initial term in such a perfectly meaningful sentence as 'The present King of France is bald'? There was no thing in the world to which the initial term could be connected by a rule. That summed up the problem.

As my undergraduates heard, and as you have, Russell's theory when saved from the tedious encumbrance of formal logic was that 'The present King of France is bald' really comes to or is to be analysed into this: 'There is something that rules over France, and not more than one such thing, and that thing is bald'. In the analysis, there simply isn't a description or like term which lacks a thing or things in the world to give it its meaning. There you have the solution to the problem. More generally, language when rightly analysed remains in accord with the fundamental idea about meaning.

Mr Strawson saw the whole thing differently, and in particular said that the simple and harmless act of referring to something isn't an assertion that it exists. Maybe so, said I, but it didn't matter. The question wasn't about *using a term in order to refer*, but about *how it had got to be a term at all, how it had got to be meaningful*. Some residual confidence remains in me about that. It is not an embarrassment to me that my eventual article on the subject lingers on, if that is not too forceful a verb, in a dusty volume of the Proceedings of the Aristotelian Society.

This third year as a Lecturer at University College, 1966–67, was as satisfactory as the preceding ones, and I was pleased with my station and its duties. My colleagues were companionable, and our leader, Richard Wollheim, as before, was breathtaking in his aestheticism and his Freudianism. In these and all things he sought for style, and probably achieved it. Jerry Cohen and I remained political and departmental comrades and confidantes despite his zeal for Marx's theory of history. Pauline and I discussed my colleagues, Harry Bewick and the law of the lever at good vegetarian dinners with Johnny Watling and Jill Putt, the anthropology student who had come along with Johnny and me to Ireland five years before to build the cottage on the strand.

Despite the department's being so agreeable, and despite my proper sense of its standing and my good fortune in being in it, no arm-twisting was needed by Jack Lively when he rang up with an idea. It was that I should put in for a Fellowship in the Oxford college to which he had removed himself from the University of Sussex. St Peter's was not grand, not at all of the eminence of Balliol or Christ Church. But it was more or less Oxford. Nor was I restrained from applying by the fact that the department at University College and Richard in particular had nurtured me. If I owed something for having been brought on, the obligation was surely not a heavy one.

There were two other facts about me, two other explanations of my prompt willingness to depart. They also serve as something else, qualifications of my slightly too rosy sketch of my departmental life. It seemed to me some deference was being required of me to Richard as Grote Professor and Head of Department, despite the department's very likely being the most democratic in the college. Now with hindsight I suspect that whatever would be true of universities shortly thereafter for a while, our department was about the most democratic in the universe. This was not good enough for me. The democracy was guided. There were one or two insufficiently advanced persons in our company. Miss Ishiguro, whose political philosophy was not so advanced as other parts of her philosophy, said on one troubled occasion that Richard should have *two* votes in the election of a new lecturer. That was not my impulse.

To my resistance to deference was added a second thing, a touch of insecurity, certainly not new. It had been less hard to hold my own as a postgraduate and then in the unsettled University of Sussex than it was now among my competitive colleagues, notably those who had recently been my teachers. Was I masquerading as good enough? Did I really have some strength different from the strengths of Richard and Johnny but as serviceable? It could be that a change of scene would not only save me from the discomforts that resulted from my undeferential ways, but would also make a final improvement in my morale. You could think better if your morale stayed high.

Of course there was also something larger at work in my putting together my brief *curriculum vitae* and asking Richard somewhat unsurely for a letter of reference, and thinking it best not to trouble Professor Ayer for one. The larger thing was ambition, understood in the dictionary way as an ardent desire for distinction. There is a lot to ambition, in anyone. Mine was a little different from that of most of my colleagues, on account of my different academic history, in two University Colleges. In part my desire was for a *means* to distinction, a desire to get inside what evidently existed, and was touched on lightly some pages back.

This was the best mutual-support and approval-conferring society in academic life, and in particular the best one in philosophy. It would take a particular innocence or complicity to think that Oxford and Cambridge philosophers got no special advantage from their station and its comfortable duties. Few were near to being Strawsons, some had very low foreheads, but almost all got a hearing, first of all from most of their colleagues. It was different from the hearing they would have enjoyed if they sent out their books and papers from other addresses. And if, having spent some time in this or that Oxford college, an undergraduate or postgraduate went to another address, it was a bit as if he also kept his old one.

There was nothing unusually honourable about my ambition. But if it was no self-forgetting determination to have truth advanced, I took no doubtful or disingenuous steps to achieve it. I had the innocence to declare to the interviewing committee at St Peter's, and in particular to the Reverend Master of the college, my offensive views on the retributive justification of punishment, including divine punishment. Also, like my views, my ambition itself was properly naked. Better that it was unconcealed rather than devious or furtive. I applied for the job, rather than try to get it by not applying for it.

Can I also conjecture that my ambition may have seemed the larger because of the chance of confusing it with something else, my active nature and onward marching? They are not the same as ambition. A lot of energy in my life goes into other things than chasing distinction. The onward marching, when it enters into the ambition, is a matter of another desire coming into play, rather than an enlarging of the one already there. Well, so it is possible to think. When St Peter's wrote to say they had elected somebody else, an Oxford man, my defeat did not stay on my mind.

As we approached the end of our third year in the nether world, Pauline and I had achieved a reform of our family financial affairs, by the unnatural means of a budget. The piano lessons and ballet classes could be fitted in. Also the laundry bill, and the monthly sums to the Family Planning Association and for Peace in Vietnam, and for shirts made for my long arms by Austin Reed and shoes got for Pauline from Harvey Nicks. But if a mortgage could be paid off in an outer postal district, why not in a locale that was not suburban? Were we by nature fitted to N.12?

Pauline with Kiaran and John, in Brighton, spring
of 1964

Wedding day, August 1964: myself, Pauline, Timothy and Giglia Sprigge, Jack Lively

Freddie Ayer later than the 1959 when he amazed me
© Steve Pyke

Richard Wollheim later than his early encouragement of me
© Steve Pyke

Vermont: Ted, Pauline, Kiaran and John, one of them thinking of England

Unscathed after the Joint Session of 1970

Stuart Hampshire, sitting apart on another hill retir'd
© Steve Pyke

Bernard Williams also later on, but still on the wing
© Steve Pyke

8

NADIR, DETERMINISM AGAIN, AMERICA

To 59 Constantine Road we went, just down the hill from Hampstead village towards college. In fact, except in the stern cartographic judgement of residents of the village, Constantine Road N.W.3 was within Hampstead. Not so good as up the hill with Michael Foot, but all the amenities. A primary school of repute at one end of the street and the Bombay Tandoori Restaurant at the other – where the 24 bus started and ended its route through what *Time* magazine had proclaimed as Swinging London. The house was three storeys, in a tolerable terrace. Again with room for a lodger, and again we carried out what was regarded as an advance. This was the knocking of two downstairs rooms into one, throwing in the entrance hall for good measure. Liberated and faintly *outré* touches were added. In place of floor-bound seating in the principal bedroom, there were two hanging chairs of wicker, suspended from the ceiling by me.

Thus, as 1967–68 began, we were members of the best postal district in London, considered from the proper point of view. This point of view, despite tolerance of *Sergeant Pepper's Lonely Hearts Club Band*, was the literary and intellectual one. The past of Hampstead, which went beyond being literary and intellectual, was reassuring. Addison, Steele, Gay, Johnson, Keats, Lady Byron, Constable, Gainsborough, Lawrence, Strachey, Wells, Stanley Spencer, Aldous Huxley, Gaitskell. Still to come from Hollywood, I think, were Elizabeth Taylor and Richard Burton. The present of Hampstead might well have in it some successor to the worthies of the past. Jerry Cohen and Margaret moved into a nearby street, Agincourt Road. Not so salubrious as Constantine Road, partly because of the traffic, as he conceded in our veiled but regular comparisons of our lives.

The Heath, the open space of greatest natural beauty in London, indeed greatest beauty, was around the corner. In the evenings I sometimes played on it with Kiaran, who was coming up to 8, and Rooney, who was 5. They were happy creatures, she settled and content in her cradle vegetarianism, he excused its rigours by his mother. We went to the Bank Holiday Fairs, and the children's Christmas Parties at University College, and it was only for a time that I succeeded in prohibiting the watching of commercial as against BBC television. None of that enables me to avoid a question now. Should it be put in the way that this later age seems to require? That way will do. So – how bad a father was I being?

If I was not in a private world, or as otherwise odd and unsatisfactory as my own father, I was taken up with myself, and mainly with my work. My awakened onward marching did not have an explicit family aspiration in it. My life was not centred on my children. In this time before feminism, I did not join in putting them to bed. There are also heavier things to record. My judgemental nature was not yet in full operation with my children, but it seems too likely that it was then perceived by them, that they were touched by it. A place, it seems, was being prepared for what they would have to overcome – self-doubt and what goes with it. If I did no punishing to speak of, my son has since said to me I was bullying, maybe when he was a bit older. I jib at the word, but plead guilty to much else, and am now more deeply troubled by this than by those three earlier disgraces in another country – First Love, photographs for *The Star*, and embarrassing offences at university.

Nor is it possible to put out of mind another thought about our children. Our marriage, by a kind of agreement, continued to be of the open variety, and it was I who took most advantage of this, coming home late an evening or two a week. The agreement, as in the case of agreements at the foundation of societies, was more the work of the party who benefited most. Whatever else was true of it or can be said for it, the agreement and our acting on it could not fail to affect the connection between Pauline and myself. Plainly there were less good marriages, awful marriages, that were entirely conventional. In one way we were not trapped in ours. But for a young marriage to be looser is for it to have some question over it, even if small. Any such marriage, too, has in it at least some apprehension of disloyalty, of the revealing of confidences and private facts. I do not mean to appear before you, reader, as one who has now seen the light, been converted to what have the name of bourgeois values. But, to persist with the subject in hand, I am uncertain that our marriage, in the respect in question, was good for our children.

Towards the end of this fourth year as a lecturer at University College, I was as unable as before to figure out a principle of equality, And, as before, I had no general feeling about the right means to the end in politics, let alone a doctrine. This did not impede me from a moment's political or anyway social activity – it is easier to be confident about particular cases, some of them, and indeed these must be the source of principles and theories. The case in hand was the Lodgings Bureau of the University of London. It had the job of helping undergraduates in that first challenge, finding a room to live in. But partly it did so by sending out a particular questionnaire to householders. This asked them a series or progression of questions about the extent of their tolerance. Were they willing to rent rooms only to European students – i.e. whites? Would they have students from the Middle East? From the Orient? Even India and Pakistan? Conceivably Africa? This, said my letter published in *The Times*, was a specific invitation to racial discrimination, being issued by a university.

Persons of a greater inclination to political activism, in the end about 10 million, distracted me from my solitary campaign. This being May of 1968, they were the French. Fed up with the state of the Sorbonne under General De Gaulle, students took to the streets, adopted the means of political action known as barricades, fought the police, burned cars, and were joined by the workers. Yet more distracting for me than these *événements* was their ripple in the Philosophy Department of University College London. Our tribunes, not much in need of the covert incitement given to them from a little above. They were Follett and Dimbleby, Ken and Jonathan, not yet come to soberer ways. Was the system of final examinations of the University of London not an outrage?

Plenary sessions were called in the Grote's room, and more orators emerged. Richard was more enlightened than the General, and also, although his secretary remained loyal, he did not have the option of retreating by helicopter to secure the support of the army. He was no enemy to our *événements*. Jerry and I by contrast were wholly on the side of our unfortunates. To Jerry, if the minutes of a plenary session tell truth, was owed a line not suffused with liberalism. 'I say bugger the Board of Studies, the University, and the College.' To me, still to my satisfaction, was owed what eventually carried the day in the Board of Studies, this being the philosophy committee of the University of London. What did the trick was my uttered thought that the philosophers of University College might go their own way, secede, leaving behind the rump of the other colleges of the university.

Meta-ethics, the Correspondence Theory of Truth, equality, and the Theory of Descriptions not having wholly distracted me from the subject of punishment, my book on it was finished in the library of Trinity College Dublin during our summer in Ireland. As it still seems to me, no mistake was made in its supposing that a single and large question arises about the moral justification of punishment, and that no new light is shed by fragmenting the question into three in the way of Professor Hart.* Further, fragmenting it could lead you into muddle rather than out of it. You could fail to see that if parts or features of the institution of punishment needed justification by the reason of desert or whatever, then evidently the whole institution needed justification partly by that reason. It could not be that a whole had no need at all of what was needed by a part. Wholes *are* the sums of their parts.

The right answer to the large question of the moral justification of punishment could not be that desert played much of a role in justifying punishment, let alone justified it by itself. What did it actually mean to claim that someone deserved this particular penalty for this particular offence? Evidently not what may come to mind first, that the penalty was right for the offence, since then the claim would be no reason at all for the conclusion that the penalty was right. It would *be* that conclusion. Not that the penalty was in a certain clear and factual sense equal or equivalent to the offence, since the two things were not commensurable in the sense of being measurable in the same units.

That was the beginning of an analysis of the Retribution Theory which ended in an offensive conclusion. It was that to recommend a particular penalty by saying it is deserved for an offence, whatever talk of desert comes to elsewhere, is to argue that the penalty will satisfy desires on the

* See p. 124

153

part of a victim or others for the suffering or deprivation of the offender. The Retribution Theory was far from occupying a moral high ground above pragmatic theories of punishment having to do with just the prevention of more offences. In effect it recommended punishment on the ground that it satisfied what high-minded persons, when they got them in view, actually regarded as vicious desires. The exactly equivalent penalty on this theory, when you cleared away the verbiage and cant, was the one that did no more and no less than satisfy the desires. Seen clearly for what it was, this could be no justification on its own of punishment, and not much of a part of one either. You could not put a man in jail for ten years, or one, just to give this satisfaction to people.

Does this rough handling of a long tradition still seem right to me? Indeed it does, more and more. Nothing has changed my mind about the Retribution Theory, least of all unspeakable politicians concentrating on more jails for vengeance and profit. I retain about as much confidence in something else. It is that the whole question of the morality of punishment cannot be carried forward in abstraction from the morality of societies themselves. My fellow philosophers of punishment have shown a remarkable ability to pass by an easy proposition. It is that the justification of punishments will always depend on the worth of the ends they serve, and that societies can have good, bad or appalling ends. It is near enough true that to justify a punishment is to have to justify a society. A thought of Hitler's laws gets you well on the way to that conclusion.

From these various reflections, something seemed to me to follow as day follows night. It was that punishments would be justified in an ideal society, which would be a society of equality, when they served to prevent more offences and also in so doing re-established the fundamental equality of the society. It also followed that in our actual societies, the best that could be said is that *some* punishments are right because they prevent offences and help avoid greater inequality. So I wrote, failing to linger over the fact that my sentences on equality, as you might say, needed more attention. I should have listened more to my uncertain lectures on the subject.

No one had left the department since my coming, and so my room remained the attic eyrie. I might have kept it even if offered the chance of moving down, since it was prized by me for its seclusion. It was a place of contentment. At its window table more notes on determinism were made. From the sofa I listened closely to the weekly round of under-graduate essays, on all of philosophy save its ancient history, having any suspect sentences read out twice. On Saturday mornings the window table had on it manuscripts for *The International Library of Philosophy and Scientific Method*, the unsolicited flow of them from California, Stockholm, Sussex, and sometimes Oxford. A quicker progress was made through them. I lingered over Daniel Dennett's *Content and Consciousness*, but not nearly long enough to save him from announcing in my series that my being conscious was just the neural clicking of my brain's speech-centre.

In October 1968 I was 35, starting my seventh year as a lecturer, my fifth at University College. In most respects I was doing fine. Unlike my eight or nine colleagues, save perhaps Richard, I had a book in press. It was not a hope eternal, but would actually exist on shelves here and in America within a year. An article, the truth about Truth, was in the *American Philosophical Quarterly*, a journal of note not aspired to by many of my colleagues, if any. The truth about John Stuart Mill was in print in another respectable journal, and the truth about the Theory of Descriptions would be. I was reading papers to the philosophical societies of provincial universities rather more often than most philo-sophers, with severe aplomb, and, as reported already, had been neither silent nor discomfited at the Joint Session of the Mind Association and the Aristotelian Society. An approach had been made to me about coming to a Readership at Birkbeck College, the rank of Reader being one of dignity between Lecturer and Professor. A note had come too about a Professorship at the University of Sussex. Might I come back and continue my mission?

But something was contributing a lot to my *not* progressing so nicely within the department, and particularly in the seminar of colleagues on Wednesday afternoons. Here a paper would be read and then some part or parts of it seized on and discussed exhaustively. I regularly did not shine. I was silent quite a lot, and did not ask my questions with enough insistence to get them lasting attention. Johnny was often to the fore in these discussions. I was more often in his wake than he was in mine. There was a nervousness about him, one that suggested incomplete confidence in his resistance to a certain fact – a distinction akin to one between officer-class and other ranks. But, partly because of his seniority, he had less need than I of what would have been useful to both of us, some public school and Oxbridge panache.

These were not meetings of passionless minds, selfless reasoners, seekers after truth alone. We did not leave behind at the door our desires, hopes, ambitions, intellectual investments, and acquired standings. Johnny's perspicuity and persistence, and the feeling in them of personal uncertainty not entirely mastered, did not always make for the easiest of atmospheres in the room. Other participants also made their contributions to atmosphere, sometimes larger. Certainly these less agreeable occasions could owe something to my own special judgemental gloom.

I do indeed see now, from the later vantage point of this sunny Sunday morning, that I was not an easy comrade in inquiry. There was grimness in my concentration, suspicion in my bafflement. It was as if blessed Ruthie had never taught me that a Mennonite severity was not the only mode of relation to the Elspeths and Deirdres. My state of mind in the seminar, too often, was that some pretentiousness or modishness or contrived distinction was going unexposed and unarraigned, in particular by me. Richard, being the most intricate, mannered and interesting reasoner among us, was often the object of this attitude. It was about this time that he paid a visit to my room seemingly to ask me one serious question, without any prelude and followed by silence. Did I, he asked, consider him to be a ridiculous figure?

The intent of the question was not wholly clear. Was it possible that it implied a partly detached curiosity about the depths of my mind, or an invitation to me to look into them, prompted by the plumbing of his own depths in the psychoanalysis he was undergoing? That was one possibility, but there were others. Was he seeking reassurance from me against some other colleague's attitude to him? Was it this kind of self-doubt? He was larger than us, and inevitably attracted a kind of wit, sharpish but usually not devoid of esteem and good feeling. Some said if he discovered the fundamental truth of the universe and it was not complicated, he would not publish. Our own relations were not terrible, despite my resistance to deference and guided democracy in the department, and despite my having lately noted to myself, without having in mind my own editorial habits, that his reading of my manuscript on punishment had been cursory. Pauline and I were still making an expedition out beyond Shepherd's Bush to make a purchase at Day Wollheim's annual sale of her pots.

Despite my degree of uncertainty about Richard's question, a third interpretation was most likely. He was trying to clear the air between us, have out in the open whatever feeling there was. I said with some degree of truth that I did not consider him to be a ridiculous figure. We did not get much further. I should have given him my view of myself in that person-stage.That would have been useful. I could have made what would have cheered him up – a small confession of my own ridiculousness.

My eyrie was at the back of the house. At the front of the floor it was on, the sixth counting up from the cleaners in the basement, was a tiny room whose casement window opened onto a narrow walkway. It ran along the whole terrace of Gordon Square houses, each of them a department of the college. A low railing or parapet made it safe as a fire escape, but it was not intended for ordinary use. It is remembered by me because a few times in this year and the one after, I took my way along it, into the casement window of the Psychology Department, down their staircase, and out of their front door. The purpose was to avoid another seminar with my colleagues in the Grote's room and, additionally, not to be seen on our own staircase doing a bunk from the atmosphere and the challenge. If these two years and the different one that followed were not wholly unlike all my others in terms of morale, they were a nadir. Pretty bearable except on one occasion of which you will hear, but a nadir, and, from the perspective now of this later sunny Monday morning, a little batty.

My nadir in morale does have various bits of explanation that now are not too disconcerting to me. One is that in my travels around the provincial universities and in my external relations generally I was fortified by being from University College London. In my own department in Gordon Square, I was not merely no prophet but also an ex-student. Another and larger consideration is also not too disconcerting. It has to do with the fact that of the philosophers who listen to a good paper directed to them as peers, only a fraction follow it closely all the way through. Confessions after the meeting establish the fact. So do fallings-out in the meeting about what has just been said. Most of the fraction of followers of the paper, further, will already have thought about the general subject long enough to have written about it themselves.

I did not have a good hold on such general facts about good papers. And, in so far as I did, I wanted on *every* occasion not to tire, but to be a member of the fraction that finished up with an explicit understanding of the whole performance. The defeat of this boyish aspiration for our Wednesday afternoons could not but make me unhappy. Despite this, I was not distracted by the prospect of the seminars, made no preparation for them. That is not to say just that no reading was done in advance. It is a good idea, if you want to be in the fraction of understanders, to save some powers of concentration for a seminar, not spend the dawn of the day and intervening hours grinding away at your writing table.

There is yet another recollection of this period that is not unsettling. As lately intimated, and for reasons touched on before in this narrative, I felt a kind of division in the department. In my view of things, there existed a successor to the rift between old guard and young Turks which, it had been hoped, my recruitment from Sussex would heal, and maybe did. The new division did not have much to do with age. As may not surprise you, it was essentially between Oxonians and others. Johnny and I, in my feelings, were the others, perhaps joined by Peter Downing. His Cambridge credentials were obscured by the diligence with which he looked into backwardly saying that if Jim had been rude to Jack this morning, then Jack would have hurt Jim's feelings yesterday.

Another reflection on the first part of my nadir in morale is not yet perfectly manageable, and of course has to do with my actual philosophical abilities. Was my want of regular good spirits in part all too rational, owed to a truth about my personal share of cognitive capacities? Was it a smaller share?

Well, it is clear that I did not have and do not have all of the things that are called philosophical strengths. Fortunately, it is also clear that that is the condition of my entire profession. It has in it excellent judges of things, understanders, natural logicians, realists, reasoners, clever cats, talkers, seers, mere elaborators and complicators, mere Oxonians, county pushers, bumblers, and dimwits. It has in it, so far as can be ascertained, no one with all philosophical strengths and hardly anyone with most.

We unhappily make do with our share. On most mornings mine seems not bad. But it is clear too that any question about pure intellect, as distinct from what may release or encumber it, itself needs thinking about. Is the question of pure intellect the right one? If the result in actual philosophy is what we are thinking about, how important is intellect? Taken as distinct from confidence, fortitude and other traits of intellectual character, how important is it for finding things out? Was Hume *clever*? But enough of this maundering.

Low spirits in and after some of our seminars, as already indicated, did not get in the way of the ongoing attempt to get good philosophical propositions down on paper, preferably in superior sentences. Nor in the way of something else. An undergraduate, having agreed with the tendency of my lectures in political philosophy, proposed to do more about the Lodgings Bureau of the University of London than write a letter to *The Times*. I did not join the undergraduate campaign of protest and militancy, which soon had the name of the February 17th Movement, since academic dignity might be prudent, but did ring up a functionary at Senate House one morning to check a fact about the university's policy. It might find its way into the undergraduate leaflets. He answered my question, but must also have thought it wise to bring it to the attention of Sir Douglas Logan, the Principal of the university.

Later that day, by messenger from Senate House, there arrived a letter from Sir Douglas. He was, he said, very surprised. Was I not aware that his Lodgings Officer kept in the closest touch with the Race Relations Board, and that her questionnaire to householders was perfectly lawful, and that constitutional means of change were preferable to commotion and occupations? That did it. Here was monstrous intimidation attempted, capped by impertinence. Could a philosopher contemplate bending a knee to a mere prince of administrators? One whose entry in *Who's Who* listed no publications, but did list membership of the Northumberland Committee on Recruitment to the Veterinary Profession?

I became, so to speak, a committee myself, the University of London Teachers Committee on Discrimination. Perhaps there was a cup of tea over which another lecturer or two agreed to be sleeping members, but any such agreement escapes my recollection. Letters from the committee went from my attic eyrie to colleagues in all colleges who might be of a progressive turn of mind. Signatures for a petition to the university

Senate, 175 of them, flowed back. Michael Dummett at All Souls, of whom it was known that his principles were as good as his philosophy, wrote with tactical advice. *The New Statesman* strongly commended the University of London Teachers Committee on Discrimination.

Sir Douglas closed his Lodgings Bureau for a day to prevent its being occupied by the February 17th Movement. I had conversations with Lord Annan, our Provost at University College, lately come from being Provost of King's College Cambridge. He was as sagacious as what he always seemed to be, a Roman fresh from the baths, pate shiny, now concentrating on matters of empire. Yes, said he, he would convey my points forcibly to the university, particularly the point about the inevitability of more student unrest. He did, and I thought he might have done so even if deprived of his good sense of the way the wind was blowing. Plummy he was, a proper custodian of the remains of the Bloomsbury Circle and of culture generally, but apparently also human. Sir Douglas made his first concession. His questionnaire to householders would no longer list the lesser races in descending order by skin colour. It all ended, some time later, in success.

Will some acquaintance of mine with a long memory think a postscript to this account of my campaign is needed? I put it in in case. At this time the connection for which my open marriage allowed was with Parveen Adams. She had lately become a lecturer in psychology at another university in London, and was striking, dramatic, tall, and, despite her sweetness, forceful in the cause of Women's Liberation and if necessary raucous. Her marriage to the artist and sculptor Kenneth Adams was behind her. For purposes of the footnote, however, her relevant attribute is that she fell into the third category of human beings about which the University of London raised a question in a landlady's mind, those from India and Pakistan.

Did Jerry pensively remark, in the mimicry of Richard at which he was so adept, that in my campaign and in this personal connection were achieved what Marx or some other comrade prescribed? Unity of theory and practice? Well, I did not mind giving a proof of my credentials in my love affair, but my becoming a committee-of-one came out of my life as already settled, my own ethos. My parents did something for me there. There was no black in Baden, no Jew either. My parents would have invited any in for a Pepsi Cola. Parveen and I dreamed sometimes of rearranging life, but my children were around 9 and 6 at this time. Breaking up the family was unthinkable to me. In the summer of 1969 we maintained family unity, in our way, by making a progress through Galway in a horse-drawn caravan.

In the course of the holiday I mostly forgot a new hurt, a further indication of the imperfectly balanced personality. My book on punishment did not fall dead-born from the press. It was welcomed into the world by *The Scotsman*'s announcing its lucidity and ruthless logic, and had a window in Foyles bookshop in the Charing Cross Road given over to it, which I went to see several times. The publishers Hutchinson & Co. wrote to say Blackwells bookshop in Oxford had immediately ordered more copies, and the American publisher reported rave reviews on the way. Count on me to concentrate on something else. Mr Giles Playfair in *New Society* thought differently from others. 'Honderich is, to say the least, an ungifted writer of English prose.'

I was not buoyed up by the truth that it was the response of a non-philosopher to a philosopher's book. Nor by the knowledge that Mr Playfair gave greater plausibility than I to the idea that punishment should be replaced by therapy. I am glad not to have been rendered speechless, but instead to have composed a letter to the editor. 'Sir: Giles Playfair's review of my book is dismal, and these are but some of the reasons. (1). . . .'

None of the later reviews, of which there were very many, managed wholly to take away the early sting. It was gratifying to have the imprimatur of Anthony Kenny in *The Listener*, and the warm if anonymous approval of Mary Warnock in *The Times Literary Supplement*. Above all it was elevating to be bracketed with Isaiah Berlin in *The New Republic* in America. But none of these gratifications dislodged what remained my sharpest memory of the publication of my first book. A sad fact, made by me more than Mr Playfair.

The mishap had not, by the way, stood in the way of my becoming Dr Honderich. The book when it was in proof was submitted to the University of London for the Ph.D. degree, in place of my thesis on determinism and freedom, which never got written. My examiners were Professor Peter Winch and a criminologist. Professor Winch was a philosopher of a more detailed sensitivity than myself, somehow connected to the Welsh lodge of Wittgensteinians. He had views, limned in *The Idea of a Social Science*, about the impenetrability of primitive and other societies by outsiders. Conceivably he had views about the uselessness of universal principles about punishment, as well as the right height for door handles.

When we three met for my *viva voce* examination, he said with resignation there was no proposition of mine with which he agreed. Also, we three had no common ground from which a philosophical discussion might take its departure. Another case of social impenetrability, it seemed. And so, since the university regulation requiring a meeting had been satisfied, and I was to have the degree, we might as well have lunch. We did, not boisterously.

In this, it is better to report, there was little sting. Perhaps about as much as in my occasional thought that my book, and my position on the university salary scale, had in this year made me in some sense eligible for promotion. There were also those notes from Birkbeck College and from Sussex. Could I not be a Reader in University College rather than a Lecturer? Such an elevation would need to be proposed by Richard as Head of Department to the college committee on promotions. They would then think about it. He had not spoken to me about the matter, and I had not broached it.

This period also had Russia in it. Stalinism was about 15 years into the past and its critic Khrushchev about five years. The Brezhnev Doctrine, very like the declarations of American presidents about what neighbours could not be allowed to get up to, had lately been offered in justification of the Russian tanks that ended the Prague Spring of 1968. In London, up the street from Gordon Square in Friends House, the Quakers hoped for an improvement in understanding between East and West. Why not begin with professional understanders, Soviet and British philosophers? I was selected as one of four delegates to go to the Soviet Union for a fortnight, as a result of my book.

In Tbilisi and Leningrad I laid out my thoughts about desert and a kind of determinism, distinguishing the latter from Marx's grander variety. Oleg and Lev, if they were not dissidents, may have approved of me for my real uncertainty expressed in our private conversations about the Russian intervention in Czechoslovakia. Also my ready agreement that human rights came in more than one kind, and definitely were not exhausted by the American list, let alone freedom of speech. In Leningrad, there was a most terrible of places, the boundless memorial cemetery of war dead in mass graves. 'With their whole lives / They defended thee, Leningrad.' They were honoured not only by the inscription but, to my ear decorously, by the Shostakovich played from loudspeakers. I could not bring home to England the enthusiasm of the fellow-traveller who pretends no doubt, but I could feel overcome by feeling for Russia, its struggle, its suffering, and its achievement. The war was the defence not only of homeland but also of the Revolution. At about this time, my disinclination to visit Germany on account of the Holocaust became a resolution.

There was no question of my becoming a Communist, no toying with the idea. Necessarily this had much to do with its suppression of important freedoms, the purges and trials and labour camps, the visiting of the sins of fathers on children, all the awful means to the end. But my feeling was not a common one, that the means were simply monstrous, that there was no need to look further, that no end could conceivably justify them. I was not certain about that. My feeling was rather that it was impossible to escape doubt about any supposed justification of the suppressions and the purges in terms of the real fact of full and proud lives for so many, a kind of ending of social injustice rather than just its slow reduction. In particular, to suppose the awful means to the end could be efficiently explained by a philosophy of history calling itself scientific, the iron law stuff, was very far from sensible.

That is half the story. What is as true, as already indicated, is that my scepticism about justifications of the system had a perfect counterpart with respect to denunciations of it. My disdain for Cold Warriors in *The Times* was large. It seemed to me clear that more and different social control was needed in a society such as the Russian, where it was in a way a stronger and more resourceful class that was being controlled – those who were once the masters and were desirous of being so again. Pauline, a couple of years later, gave me David Caute's *The Fellow-Travellers* for my birthday, on the principle, which she inscribed on the fly-leaf, that it's never too late to learn. Well, it was. My sympathies with the Soviet Union remained intact. What stayed in my mind from that good book were several of Sartre's utterances. They were made some time after his denunciation of an earlier Soviet intervention, in Hungary, and his partial defection from support of the Party. 'Collaboration with the CP is both necessary and impossible.' 'An anti-Communist is a dog, I do not depart from that, I shall never depart from it.'

The series of philosophical books edited by me until now were the stiff monographs of *The International Library of Philosophy and Scientific Method* for Routledge & Kegan Paul, and the more accessible items for Penguin. My having been of two minds about these editorial roles did not prevent me from now adding a third. There would be another Routledge series, a new one, *The Arguments of the Philosophers*. It would be analytic and critical philosophy, rescuing the great philosophers from the past. Plato could be understood, on the way to judging him, without the aid of noticing that he was an ancient Greek. The book on Kant might abandon the conceptions of Kant, and carry on his inquiry with up-to-date ones. Maybe that is what Hilary Putnam of Harvard would do with Marx, Engels and Lenin, who could be got into a single volume. Might Barry Stroud of Berkeley perform that service even with Hume? Robert Fogelin of Yale with Wittgenstein? Would philosophy not be better if it was like science, which left at least most of its past behind in museums?

It is not clear to me what explains my lumbering myself with more manuscripts and hanging another Editor label around my neck. Perhaps my active nature and determination to be marching onward? It did not have to be in the right direction. It got me onto the Professorial Board of the college too, an elected non-professorial member looking out for the interests of the lower orders.

Just before Christmas 1969, I found myself on television for the first time, pleased to be there. Malcolm Muggeridge, his time of editing *Punch* and annoying the monarchy well behind him, was no longer concealing his spirituality. My role in the programme was to cast a rationalist chill on Christmas. This I tried to do by means of predictable propositions delivered forcefully. No bad idea to have a winter festival, I said, and to retreat into the family and give presents, but why not admit that the English Christmas had divested itself of spirituality and was now pagan? A good thing, too. The morality that went with Christianity did not have an effective content, and so, as history showed, could serve the purpose of any man or monster.

It was pleasing to be a public philosopher for a moment, not that much philosophizing could be done on such occasions. It was as pleasing a bit later to appear in the current art scene. Pamela Zoline was an engaging and ongoing American at the Slade with an interest in philosophy. Her idea was to intrude some real reality into the history of the portrait. Thus her show had in it three kiosks, larger than telephone boxes but on the same lines. To go inside and shut the door was to get in touch with the subject of the box, myself in one case, the apocalyptic science-fiction writer J. G. Ballard in another. You could paw through a lot of personal belongings of the subject, mine including my brother Robert's log-book, photos of Kiarney and Rooney in the horse-drawn caravan, a velvet necktie, my mechanical screwdriver, a menu from Bertorelli's, and a bottle of Barbera, this being the rough Italian wine favoured by me. The subject of the third portrait box, more emancipated than I or Mr Ballard, included her current contraceptive device, or maybe the one before.

My couple of pages of autobiography, in accord with the spirit of the enterprise, were not in rounded sentences but in incomplete and inexplicit messages, as if from my stream of consciousness. They included the messages 'Monday and Thursday' and 'the principle of effrontery'. The second item there refers to a principle I was thinking of embracing. What you had to do, if your seminar morale was low, was to join the ranks of the confident. You could really try to do this by engaging in what would seem to yourself to be effrontery. My resolution was not a panacea, but it was of some value. As for the mentioned days of the week, our open marriage was now more advanced, if that is the word. It had its weekly schedule, my being out until about midnight on Mondays and Thursdays.

On them, in this period, I had kept happy company for a while with Ruth Brandon. She was not yet the composed and astute writer she would become, but very able to give as good as she got on the Muggeridge show, and very jollily. It was there that we got acquainted, comrades in arms. That we did not persist had to do with marriages: mine to be maintained and hers entered into. Another principal connection was with Rachel Bush, also engaged in a liberated academic marriage, evidently of some value. She too was a turner of sentences and a reasoner. There was great affection in this connection, even though it crossed my mind that she was, so to speak, being unfaithful to her marriage in order to keep her end up in it. We frolicked in the country and she taught me some Philosophy of Geology in town.

The ending of this academic year 1969–70 was the Joint Session of the Mind and Aristotelian Societies, in Aberdeen. To it, I gave my paper 'A Conspectus of Determinism', retorts to a mixed bag of critics of determinism. They were then in the ascendancy in English philosophy, superior in supposing that determinism was somehow conceptually flawed. That is, there was no clear and otherwise conceptually respectable doctrine to examine for truth or falsehood – no solution to the determinism problem. Hence, also, there was nothing to examine for its consequences with respect to freedom and responsibility.

I ploughed through the brambles of various objections, most of them of Wittgensteinian inspiration. (1) No, that some causes got described in terms of their effects did not make our causal statements and hence determinism truistic or worse. For example, it might be that I could describe what caused me to have a glass of Barbera only as my inclination to have a glass of Barbera. But that did not reduce me to the uselessness of saying something of the useless form 'The cause of X caused X'. (2) No, it didn't matter that our actions could not properly be conceived as only bodily movements. Why shouldn't actions, when rightly taken as being those particular bodily movements deriving from our intentions, be shown to be effects? It was mysterious what the obstacle was supposed to be. (3) No, determinism was not wrecked by the thought that if we take it to be true, we also have to think we are caused to believe it, and so we can't take our belief in it as true. For a start, we might not be caused to believe unless it was true. I do not claim credit for seeing off these quibbles. They were not much heard of after this time, but it is most likely that they died of inanition.

My paper did not get forward in construction as distinct from what I took to be destruction. It certainly was true that a doctrine of determinism had not recently been articulated and completed. There was no up-to-date formulation. Difficulties in the Philosophy of Mind, notably the relation between mind and brain, stood in the way of that. My paper was no help. Nor was any light shed on that issue as large as those of the conceptual adequacy and of the truth of determinism – the issue of what follows from it, its import for us.

My coming away at least unscathed from the Joint Session led me to speak a couple of times to Richard about the matter of becoming a Reader. In this I was not deterred by having without success put in for a second Oxford job, at Balliol. Richard had written very strongly indeed on my behalf, but the job went to the sitting tenant, a sound Oxford man who had been doing the teaching without being a Fellow. I was now at the top of the salary scale for Lecturers, several levels past the one at which, according to some college presumption, a Lecturer could be contemplated for promotion. It is unlikely that in speaking to Richard I was able to put myself forward gracefully. He wrote to me later that he would be making no recommendation to the Appointments and Promotions Committee for their consideration in the coming year. But he would in due course make some recommendations for the committee's reflections during the year after, that I and Hidé Ishiguro be raised to Readerships and Johnny Watling to a Professorship.

It is widely held to be a good thing for an academic to spend an occasional year away, in another university, to broaden the mind. It is not unknown, either, for one to feel the need of a breather, or for colleagues around him to look forward to the same benefit from the one air fare. From whatever causes, all the arrangements having been made, I arrived in August 1970 at John F. Kennedy airport, its name having been changed since my last visit to America. It was a happy arrival. America had become a different and larger thing in my mind since my travels with Elvis, no doubt because it had become a different and larger thing. President Kennedy had come and gone, with his brother. The ongoing war in Vietnam, for some, had finally confirmed that the United States stood to Britain as Rome to Greece. For me, if that analogy came to mind, it had another side, not having to do with imperial power. English philosophers stood to American as Greek to Roman, the relation being superiority. I, having gone native, was an English philosopher.

Yale was not exactly Harvard, but in ways it was its rival, an old university of calm distinction. Some said its philosophy department had been constructed on the zoo principle, which required the inclusion of a member of every prominent species with no thought as to their congeniality. Hence, in their cages within the department, you could see Metaphysician, Phenomenologist, Analytical Philosopher, and so on. It was later, I think, that Metaphysician metamorphosed into Philosopher of Sport. They were all let out to come to departmental meetings, of course, and some said this was not the wisest of institutional arrangements. They disagreed, mainly about who was to get the next empty cage.

My self-image burnished, my arrival at Yale was as happy as my arrival at JFK. I was not only Guest Fellow of Pierson College but also a professor of the university, since in this enlightened country, so very different from my adopted one, all who gave lectures had that designation. Happy letters of married love came to Teddledy from Pauline, and vigorous postcards from Kiarney and Rooney, and a sad love letter or two. A house was found in Connecticut with a large lawn overlooking Long Island Sound, and Pauline and the children arrived to settle in for our American year. They approved of the used car that had been purchased, a Pontiac station wagon. In its great length and girth I felt myself, Englishly, to be more helmsman than driver. As the semester began, invitations arrived, prompted by the reception of the American edition of my punishment book and also by my editing. Would I perhaps have time to come to Toronto to read a paper? Princeton? Columbia, Philadelphia and Amherst as well? Yes, I could fit them in. One other invitation was to have larger consequences.

At Oberlin College in Ohio there regularly was a colloquium, in fact a philosophical conference. The organizer of this year's was Norman Care, who had improved my life by bringing me together with Isaiah Berlin in his review in *The New Republic*. Could I not easily apply my reflections on punishment, he asked, to the subject of this year's colloquium? It was to be violations of established principles in legal and political structures, but not violations for profit or personal gain. Could I not write a paper on political violence? After the Watts and other race riots, the Black Panthers, student battles with the police in Vietnam demonstrations, the shooting of students at Kent State, the Red Brigade in Italy, and the troubles in Northern Ireland – after all this, should a philosopher not have something to say on the means-to-an-end that was political violence? Professor Care seemed to me to have the right man. I could write a paper quickly, without being distracted long from determinism and what it seemed to be pulling me into, the matter of the nature of the mind.

I hadn't counted on my personality. Within a month of my happy arrival in America, my spirits were falling. Was part of the story that there was no chance of maintaining my chosen identity? My hosts were not led astray by the fact that my philosophical achievements, such as they were, had been in England, or by my three-piece suit of green corduroy from Austin Reed, or by the examples in my philosophical expositions. When a sample mental event was needed, it was likely to be my remembering a walk on Hampstead Heath rather than up the Baden Hills. Americans, as I say, were not led astray. They seemed to me to adjust their attitude somewhat when the visiting speaker, billed in advance as from University College London, revealed to them by his accent that he was not so exotic.

America was not exotic either. I was no English traveller entertained by an alien culture. New Haven was to me limited in its charm to the frame-houses with verandahs, and they were not peculiar to it. Nor was America in a certain general way uplifting. Its ideologists had a purpose, being carried forward in Vietnam by burning people to death. Many estimable students had a purpose, which was to stop the wretched war. The Blacks had a purpose. But, for me, there could be no illusion that the society as a whole or a large part of it shared a moral purpose. Not like the ones I ascribed, different though they were, to England and Russia. Here in God's Own Country there was little real resolution to deal with deprivation. Rather, there was apprehension about it, notably apprehension about such ghettos as the one near Yale, where it was not a good idea to go. There was also the fantastic dream, although less deep than it had been, that America was as the world ought to be, or anyway would have to be. If I was not then impassioned against this, it was no source of sustenance. Ordinary Americans were innocent, generous, good buddies, and they had other virtues. But for me there was none of the thrill of esteem for a people, even uncertain and troubled esteem.

Something needs to be added. Despite the good efforts of the genial Fogelins, we were a family thrown back on our own resources. We were alone, as academic families generally are when they set out to broaden their minds. This was a creditable cause of my giving up, during our American year, my habit of making good use of the policy of the open marriage. So I myself was lonely in a second way. I had an adventure or two, remembered now with fondness and guilt, but Monday and Thursday evenings were spent at home, looking out through the picture window at Long Island Sound or surviving the television commercials. If it is improper to call this loneliness, it was a life from which something of value to me had been subtracted.

These various items contributed not only to falling spirits but to an anxiousness. It could find new subjects easily. It was President Nixon, although still a few years away from final disgrace, about whom it was being asked whether it would be a good idea to buy a used car from this man. I should have asked if it would be a good idea to buy a used car from the man from whom I bought a used car. As the Pontiac's transmission followed its tailgate into collapse, so too declined my confidence about being able to deal with America.

Dealing with England was also at the edge of my mind for a while. Johnny had written especially to tell me that the department had discussed promotion in general terms. Of course I had been talked of, but that Richard had surprisingly said that Hidé Ishiguro's claim was almost as good. I read surprise and warning in the line as well as support. It was this communication from Johnny, among others, that goes into my story that academic ambition was at first pressed on me, that the asp was put into my breast by others.

Our pilgrim, I am pleased to remember, could get himself out of his slough of despond often enough. There was consolation in improving my new paper on determinism. When it was first read out, in Yale, the audience had in it a physicist-philosopher. He not only declaimed the existence of undetermined or random events down at the bottom levels of reality. He contentedly proposed that such events, since they turned up in persons as well as elsewhere, were what made for our moral responsibility. One implication of the second bit was that determinism if true would have the consequence of our not being morally responsible.

This had been heard before in philosophy, and a good reply had been made. In my version, it was that if our being responsible agents was threatened by our decisions and actions being inevitable effects, it was even clearer that our being responsible agents went out the window if our decisions and actions were owed to undetermined events, events of pure random or chance. Who could be responsible for shooting a used car salesman if that was owed to something of which *nothing at all* was an explanation? Having said that much, I got another idea.

No doubt my physicist-philosopher would think of retorting that while the action was, so to speak, physically undetermined, it was still somehow in the control of the disappointed owner of the Pontiac. It was, so to speak, in his mental control. But here there was a contradiction. Was physics, the ultimate science, not supposed to be about all of reality? Did it not aim to give a complete account in its terms of all that happened in reality? Was this not its fundamental claim on our attention, and the reason for my questioner's confidence? If so, and if he swore by it, and if it said certain events had no explanations, then for him they had no explanations. To come to the crunch, it was inconsistent for him to add in something about mental explanations, whatever they were supposed to be. This, so to speak, was physicist going against physics. Self-contradiction.

My paper and I survived its hearings in the other philosophy departments that had issued invitations, partly because it rested on a main proposition offered in formulation and in defence of determinism. It was a general proposition about the problem of the mind–brain relation, a proposition that no one had the face to take as unclear, about the general connection between mind and brain. Suppose, I said, I was thinking a moment ago about being home in England, and that my brain was in a certain physical state. Could my conscious or mental state or event have been different but the physical state or event exactly the same? Could I have been thinking of French beans?

Surely not – my conscious and physical states were somehow bound up together. If the unlikely thing happened that my brain got into exactly the same state again, I would again be thinking in just the same way about being home in England. What clear-headed American would want to go against this mind-and-brain Correlation Hypothesis? Not much less confidence was displayed in my other two propositions, both predictable. One was that brain states were effects of long causal sequences made up of other physical states. The other was that our actions were effects of our brain states.

Ergo determinism, or one particular theory of determinism. Its main proposition assumed optimistically that you could carry conviction just by making the stated general connection between mind and brain, without becoming more particular. You did not have to clarify and defend a sharper picture of their correlation. Was physicalism true – were mental states in fact somehow identical with brain states? Were they different although correlated, maybe causes or effects of brain states? You didn't have to say. You could leave that for further reflection another day.

To pass beyond formulation and truth to the third question about determinism, the large one about its upshot or consequences, was it not clear that our ordinary conception of responsibility was such that we could not be responsible if the theory was true? According to that ordinary conception, each of our actions had a kind of *personal* explanation. This was no general thing of the sort implied by the rule of same cause, same effect. By taking this elevated view, although with qualification, I abandoned Hume and joined the tradition of thought with Kant in it, to the effect that determinism is incompatible with responsibility.

My keenness was considerable to have the good sense of this one theory of determinism not confused with the determinist speculations of Marx and Freud. This issued in my paper's title, which was indeed 'One Determinism'. An editor of independent judgement might have said the title would not be translucent to all comers. Well, there was an editor, but not of independent judgement. The paper would be appearing in a book edited by me. Getting papers for this collection out of Professor Donald Davidson and others had been another of my projects. If I did not think a lot about the translucency of my title, I was taking care to be in good company.

As Yale's first semester ended I had farewell lunches with its philosophers and heard of their renewed hopes for better relations in the zoo, which were not to be fulfilled. The department thereafter suffered such departures as the admirable Fogelin's to Dartmouth College. It then suffered the final indignity of being put into receivership – since its members could not agree about things, the running of the department was put into the hands of an outside committee of non-philosophers. But that was in the future. As the first semester ended, I too had renewed hopes. I would be happier. The second semester would be spent at Brooklyn College of the City University of New York, and also at the university's Graduate Center, in 42nd Street along from Times Square and Broadway. I had some further credentials, having now been offered jobs at Rutgers and Vassar. Yale had raised the matter too. It had not been quite so forward, partly because of knowing about my defeat by the used car and thus my doubtful suitability to the American way of life, not to mention my profound attachment to Hampstead Heath.

Our Brooklyn, Brooklyn in the winter, satisfied no hopes. To me it was grim, a uniform grid of hutch-houses unrelieved by the trees. I would have been willing enough to enter into the pervasive and not very cosmopolitan Jewishness, but was incapable of doing so, and in fact was got down by it. I acquired no affection at all for the bagel, and never discovered the nature of lox. If Pauline was again delighted by graduate courses, now at the Graduate Center and Columbia, Rooney was miserable in his alarming school. It stuck in my mind that black girls on her school bus had tried to make Kiarney pick up the sweets they spat on the floor. As for Brooklyn College, it was not elegant. If its students were rewarding learners, they showed a good grasp of the principle of effrontery in trying to get me to change their Bs into As. My first room in the Graduate Center was windowless. I saw wonderfully little of my colleagues, and only a little more of the sweet Professor Arthur Danto at Columbia. There was also the matter of political violence.

Towards the end of March 1971, just after I became 38, the Oberlin Colloquium was a few weeks away. Despite my labours, it had not proved possible to bring my past reflections on punishment to bear on political violence. In fact no attempt was made, since the aim had to be to go forward, say something new. Could I conceive of understanding people who set bombs in order to improve lives? Could I summon philosophical calm and overcome a predictable apprehension about expressing my ambivalence? I did something of the sort, but after getting through a certain state of feeling.

This, if you will tolerate the solecism, was the nadir of my nadir in morale, not so bearable as the rest. As recorded a month later in my diary, I could not escape a kind of frenetic thinking on my troubles, fell to weeping for a while one day, and was afraid to be alone. Pauline did well by me. Later she said she might have been alarmed if I had not had the obligation of our children. Do I think I might have done myself in? Driven the Pontiac off the beltway, thereby sinking two problems? It did not occur to me, and no other means of departure did either. Things weren't *that* bad. They never have been. I'm ordinary enough to be saved that.

My paper for the colloquium, as I saw on the plane, was not short of manufactured spirit but consisted in something very like two book reviews, in fact reviews of two journal articles. The American radical Robert Paul Wolff was clearly beside the point in his veiled contention that we could have no political obligation of a certain funny kind. That is, we could have no obligation to obey the law in a way that offended against one of Kant's principles – obey without seeing good reason for doing so. Of course, said I, we were not obliged to engage in this automatic and unreflective obedience, like the soldier who kills the peasants only because his officer says so. But that left room for the possibility of something different, a real argument for political obligation.

The American liberal John Rawls was also mistaken. He should not suppose that his chosen method in political philosophy, based in the idea of an imaginable social contract, could issue in an argument for civil disobedience, this being non-violent, but could not issue in any argument for violence. Furthermore, his chosen method in political philosophy should not detain us. And he like Wolff was mistaken in supposing that violence of the Left could be treated from a certain height of political philosophy, well above the grim facts of both bombs and ghettos.

Having not attended any other papers given to the conference, and arrived on the night before my own, I got very drunk. My delivery of my two book reviews in the morning, very hung-over, consisted in my reading the stuff out word by word. I might not have found my way to the end of an impromptu sentence. My defence of the paper included a retort to a questioner. It was that he must be wrong in imputing two propositions to me, since I was of the rational nature that I was, and the two propositions were indeed a case of self-contradiction. They could not be mine – and other questioners were waiting for my attention. A good thing that I stood up for myself, if that is what it was. Things could have gone worse.

For the month or two that remained of our American year, we found a large cottage in Vermont, very remote. The children were happy on our green hill and down at the beaver dam, as was Pauline. I cheered up a lot, but the offer of a job in New York got no attention. We paid a visit to Florida, down the long highway through the American South past the awful shacks untouched by the Civil Rights movement. My brother

Loine was in Miami, setting up a retirement village. My sister Mary, her marriage over, was in California, and wanted to see me. I wanted to travel there, but could not get geared up for it, which pains me still. We did go over the border to Canada, and to a new motel at the foot of the Baden Hills. I mainly remember another piece of good luck. Pauline would have drowned in the motel's swimming pool save for my being 6'4" and thus able to walk in deep water.

9

ACADEMIC BATTLES, POLITICAL VIOLENCE, AN ENDING

Teachers in most British universities divide with some composure into Lecturers, Senior Lecturers, Readers, and Professors. This, as you have heard, is the hierarchy of our working lives. We also fall into other categories of a sort, these being a matter of judgements on us by our fellow workers in the world of our particular subject, say philosophy. Except in short and less composed periods of personal preoccupation with the hierarchy, most of us care more about these judgements of our fellow workers, expressed by commission or omission in articles in journals, books, book reviews, letters of reference, ordinary correspondence, and by word of mouth as gossip. It is not just promotion we worry about. This is so despite the fact that the judgements on us in our worlds can hardly be said to make for a second hierarchy.

There is too much disagreement for that, partly because little human failings, certainly reciprocity and solidarity, conceivably even envy, get into the making of the judgements, and there is no very good method of collecting them into a summary. There is disagreement not only about whether an aspirant makes it into a category, say Reputable Phenomenologist, but also about whether a category is worth making it into. There are leading lights in a subject, of course. They are much written about, and furnish the minds of graduate students. But they are not at all beyond question. It was Schopenhauer who gave to his dog Hegel's name. Conceivably it was Professor Quine of Harvard who, on hearing it remarked that a renowned philosopher of science from across the Atlantic lectured with a broad brush, said that he thought with one too.

The judgements of our subject-worlds are supposed to give rise to or at least to be reflected in our hierarchy of Lecturer, Senior Lecturer, Reader and Professor. Because of the problems with the judgements, and because other things get into the story of appointments and promotions, it cannot be said that the judgements actually rule or determine the hierarchy. Very definitely it is an uncertain reflection of current judgements. If our hierarchy is not fashion's child exactly, some of those in it can soon give the appearance of being somewhat down at wing's heel. Certainly there *is* fashion in philosophy, and it is no easy matter to see when it might also be progress.

Quite a few of us used to remain in the rank of Lecturer forever, usually on account of an internal or external impediment to the publishing of our thoughts. The rank was once what civil servants called the career grade. They meant, I think, the rank in which one could remain until the end, without either discredit or notable exertion. Few of us are destined for the rank of Professor. When we make it, we should sit in our chairs a little uneasily, keeping in mind that Edinburgh and Glasgow did not think Mr Hume fit to be of our number, but elected Mr Cleghorn and Mr Clow, of whom not much was heard thereafter. But the two middle ranks are my concern now. Senior Lecturers and Readers are on the same salary scale, but are different. Those who read the university appointments notices in *The Times* are likely to know it well. You can become a Senior Lecturer principally by being a stalwart in departmental administration and teaching. Worthiness may do the trick. To become a Reader, it is said, academic distinction is required. A book may do.

When I made it back to England and to Gordon Square for the adventure of 1971–72, it transpired that Richard had an idea. It was to propose to the college promotions committee that Hidé should become a Reader and I become *either* a Reader *or* a Senior Lecturer. She had interesting claims, being philosophically vivacious and sometimes breath-taking, wide in range, as ready to expound Frege as Sartre as Wittgenstein, imaginative as well as technical. Her book on Leibniz was on the way to publication, it too having been awarded a Ph.D. from the University of London. She had been asked about coming back to teach in Oxford, and also about jobs elsewhere. All of which would have been consistent with our thinking each other not perfectly suited to philosophy.

Richard's stated reasons for his either-or idea on my behalf were several. Out of whatever consideration, perhaps just the odiousness of comparison, or a proper sense of complexity, or an awareness of the views of others in the department, he would not be ranking one of us above the other in his two proposals to the Appointments and Promotions Committee. But, he said, would it not be prudent of me to keep open the chance of getting at least the lesser promotion, to Senior Lecturer? I had a good chance on account of my unique service as Departmental Tutor, a chance which Hidé did not enjoy. Also, might I not have difficulty in finding strong personal referees to write letters on my behalf for a Readership, perhaps because of the mischance of no Oxbridge connections?

It has to be recorded, with some rue, if not a lot, that the either-or idea did not please me at all. It set me off on some onward marching, first into suspicion. Was there not some strategy in it? Would the committee not read some hesitancy about a Readership into such a proposal by a Head? Conceivably a signal, an implicit ranking? It was a committee to which all departments and faculties of the college laid seige for the limited number of annual promotions. Would it not be less likely to make me a Reader than if that promotion alone were proposed? There was also the fact of Peter Downing. His concern with Jim and Jack had precluded administrative service, but presumably this had not left him with no chance of becoming a Senior Lecturer, since Senior Lecturer he was.

I was not detained by the unspoken truth that the either-or proposal might have in it a perfectly proper exercise of judgement by my Head of Department. Proper it might be, in terms of college conventions and ordinary proceedings, but was the judgement right? Was there bias in it? Would more bias turn up elsewhere in the promotions procedure? If Richard had not been bowled over by my thinking about punishment, I was not bowled over either by his thinking about the nature of democracy, which had got some attention from me. There was supposed to be a deep paradox in the theory of democracy, something that might conceivably join the line of named paradoxes in the history of philosophy, along with Zeno's, Bertrand's, Russell's, Arrow's and so on. It would be Wollheim's Paradox, as follows.

A man votes in an election for the party whose policy is, say, a National Health Service. In so doing he needs to be taken to make the judgement that the policy ought to be enacted. As the election turns out, his party loses to the other one, with the policy of no National Health Service. Our voter, being a democrat, must now be committed to the judgement that *this* policy ought to be enacted. So he is both for and against a National Health Service. Since he is an instantiation of democratic theory, so to speak, that theory is self-contradictory. I had found something brisk to say about this paradox in democracy, and was saying it in my lectures.

What the voter expresses in his vote is evidently something qualified – partly since he is a democrat. He does not judge that we should do *anything*, maybe have a violent revolution, in order to get a National Health Service. He does not express the judgement that we ought to get it though the heavens fall. What he expresses in his vote is really the judgement that it would be better to have a National Health Service with majority support than it would be to have no National Health Service with majority support, but that if either policy gets majority support, it ought to be enacted. That, on reflection, puts him in no logical trouble at all when things go against him and he judges, as he has to, that there ought to be no National Health Service. In the course of my lectures it came to me that I might put these useful and deflationary thoughts into a brief piece for a journal, under a measured title like 'A Difficulty With Democracy'.

A second academic struggle was also underway in November 1971, in tandem with the first. Spirits enlivened in one were doing service in the other. The department had been informed that an anonymous donor was offering the college a great deal of money to establish a new chair, The Freud Memorial Professorship. It would be the first university chair in psychoanalysis in Britain. The anonymous donor did not wish the chair to be in the Medical Sciences faculty of the college, still less the Psychology Department. The Freud Professor would be a member of the Philosophy Department. He would have a couple of rooms in it, possibly one with a couch. My immediate feeling about the idea had a lot to do with what came to my ear, that the anonymous donor had earlier made his offer to the universities of Oxford, Cambridge and Edinburgh, and to the Psychology Department of University College London, and they were not at all enthusiastic.

Initially all of my departmental colleagues were reluctant or cautious. Who was the anonymous donor? Since the department already had one less room than it had teaching members, was it not odd to be planning to take in such a professor – and would building two new rooms at the back of our house for him not be an intrusion? Would a holder of such a chair be able to be critical of psychoanalysis, even dismissive? Or was there a parallel with chairs in theology restricted to true believers? Maybe a requirement of fealty to Freud would be conceivable in some other setting, but in *a philosophy department*? Should we as a department not have a say in the appointment of a professor to our department? Could this be left safely to college barons and, as was on the cards, shadowy institutions in Hampstead?

My own reaction was of a less inquiring kind. An earlier degree of official tolerance of psychoanalysis, despite my personal disinclination, had got some expression in my punishment book and elsewhere. Now it gave way to something else. I would, if I could, be the tribune of the department. A Freud Professor should definitely not be a member of it, or have rooms in it, or rooms built at the back of it. The college should turn away the money unless the chair was in one of the most relevant disciplines, Medical Sciences or Psychology, and the filling of the chair was up to the people there.

The chair should not be in our department because psychoanalysis was not philosophy. Freud's theory of the mind, from the sexuality of infants to the Unconscious to the Death Instinct, had received no significant philosophical attention, let alone recognition. A handful of philosophers, most notably Richard, were engaged in it and committed to it, but it hardly ever got into the philosophy journals. A common attitude to it among philosophers was jocularity from a distance. Also, to me, there was a reason why psychoanalysis did not get into philosophy. It was a matter of a peculiar kind of investment and commitment, not of detached inquiry. Clearly it attracted and sometimes captured individuals of intellect, but it lacked the very nerve of decent philosophy – scepticism and self-scepticism. It was more answers than questions. As I did not add publicly, the answers were made suspect by what appeared to be a need to have them true, a resistance to any other possibility. The answers had less of their source in evidence than in their appeal to a kind of personality, indeed their succulence.

Richard greeted my declarations with incomprehension, not unexpectedly, given the fact of his *Freud* just published in the series on modern masters. In that book it was said, of him who would be the subject of our prospective chair, that by the power of his writings and the audacity of his speculations he had revolutionized the thought, lives and imagination of an age, so much so that it would be hard to find a parallel in the entire history of ideas, even of religion. Richard was true to his book and to himself. Lord Annan, Provost of the college, if his feelings about the movement were not visceral in the way of Richard's, was almost as resolute. Was Professor Popper's celebrated attack on psycho-analysis as no science not known to be wonderfully misconceived by everyone? Had it not come to him in the baths that it was *tosh*?

On the promotions front, Richard and I had sharpish meetings, on my part not stylish, sometimes with Johnny in attendance at my insistence. They issued in agreement on a number of points. The college committee would be asked, for me as for Hidé, only about a Readership. As was not then customary, I would submit my own *curriculum vitae*, drafted by me to display all my achievements, leaving none out. Also, there was the crucial matter of joint referees, these being philosophers whose opinions on both candidates would be sought by the college committee, and who might well rank us one above the other. As always these joint referees would in effect be chosen by the department, in effect the Head, and, I insisted, they had to be chosen partly for their impartiality. Here, as he did not need to, Richard agreed to something – at least that Johnny would be consulted by him about the choice of these persons. Further, he went along with the idea that his own two proposals to the committee, the ones in which he would not be doing any ranking, should have an eye cast over them by Johnny.

Was there more? Well, I wanted and asked for more. Since we were democratic as a department in the election of new lecturers, should not all of us have some say in the matter of promotions? Should all colleagues not be formally consulted and their judgements reported to the committee? In short, I came to have a keen eye for my academic interests, and a mighty resolution to pursue them. Here ended my nadir in morale.

Having secured the services as personal referees of Professors Berlin and Hare of Oxford, and Professor Danto of Columbia, I could wait until after Christmas for the committee's decision. I did not reflect much on this first academic struggle, except to rehearse to myself the points of my righteousness. I had been straightforward, and done nothing but secure a hearing by honourable means. No member of Appointments and Promotions Committee had been identified by me, let alone had a word put in his ear. As for the idea of there being a question about my having personal referees who had not taught me and whose knowledge of me was based on my writings, there was a reply. Their not being more in touch with me gave them *more* authority rather than less. And so on.

Little time was given by me to the fact that my Head of Department had forgone what some other Heads in the college took to be their inalienable right. They did not do much consulting. I would not have fared so well with those proconsuls. No time was given by me to an idea pertaining to myself, that straightforwardness can be badly overdone, and that it does not need to be replete with moral confidence. No time was given to the fact, as you might say, that I was not deepening a friendship for the future. It did not much occur to me, either, that I might be helping to make the department a less agreeable place.

I was in the grip of a determination. It had had something to do with a general resolution to get fully and forever out of my slough of despond. But the main thing was the iron need to get forward with life. As you know, it has sometimes been remarked by me, half-seriously, that the asp of academic ambition was first put in my breast by others. At this stage I was at least prompted by the good opinions of others, a considerable or large majority of my departmental colleagues, as I thought. But my determination was my own, something that felt like self-preservation. It is possible to have the thought, without grandeur, that I was further forming my nature.

What I was not forming was a book on determinism and freedom. It would have to have in it, at least, an actual resolution of the problem of the consequences of determinism – of whether it was logically compatible or logically incompatible with freedom, whether both determinism and freedom can be the case together. My assembled contributors to *Essays on Freedom of Action*, now on its way to the publisher, had given a majority vote for the answer of Compatibilism, with Davidson, Dennett and Kenny to the fore, Watling removing Hampshire's obstacles put in their way, and Mary Warnock clarifying what was suspected by others, that Sartre was confused. But the majority party had not silenced the opposition. David Wiggins, with the aid of a symbol or two of formal logic and 29 substantial footnotes, followed by further material attached to an asterisk, had proved to his satisfaction that much was to be said for the gloom and bravery on the other side.

Much to be said for the gloomy idea that determinism if true logically destroys our freedom. Much to be said for the brave idea it doesn't matter at all since you can dish determinism. You can refute it by discovering, with the help of Professor Elizabeth Anscombe in Cambridge, a student of Wittgenstein, that all humankind and their philosophers have ever been wrong in reporting what they think when they think things are cause and effect.

My situation was still one of being inclined to join David Wiggins in the gloom of Incompatibilism, if not at all in the bravery about determinism. But I was short of a strong idea – and then diverted from trying to find one. What put me on another path of reflection, was an invitation owed to my contribution to the Oberlin Colloquium, perhaps by someone interested in seeing the performance again. There would be another conference in America, an international gathering at Temple University in Philadelphia. It would be on political violence and related matters. Would it not benefit by hearing my thoughts about the relation between political violence and democracy? We had come into a new time, with political violence still more in the air and hence with a new obligation on political philosophy.

In December 1971 the front and the next five pages of a *Times Literary Supplement* were given over to Professor Berlin's lecture on Georges Sorel. This turn-of-the-century Frenchman resisted summary, having been able to admire both Lenin and Mussolini, but he had the name of being the apostle of violence. Professor Berlin did not come near to endorsing Sorel, but he did discuss wonderfully his utterances, his place in the history of ideas, and his influence. The new political time was also such that in January 1972 most of a page of *The Guardian* was given over to a statement expressing sympathy with a member of the Angry Brigade, or, to be precise, remonstration against his sentence of 15 years for conspiracy to cause explosions – his proven conspiracy had consisted in the addressing of three envelopes for communiqués. The statement was signed by 150 people, these including a publisher or two, Pierre Boulez and David Hockney, Kenneth Tynan and other theatre people, John and Yoko Lennon, and a good many philosophers, including Cohen, Honderich, Watling and Wollheim.

I do not mean to conscript any of the named persons, including Sorel, to any cause of mine. Is it nonetheless my intention to prepare the ground for some exculpation of myself? Prepare the ground for dealing with the truth that in the eyes of some I was to become an apostle of violence in a small way myself? Well, wait and see. Certainly I do mean to convey that it was less difficult then than now to do what I set about doing. This, I said, was to inquire with an open mind into the morality of political violence of the Left, and more particularly its connection with democracy. What was in an open mind, since presumably it was not an empty mind or a mind without a past, was left unclear.

It would be a good idea to begin by defining democracy realistically. We could have in mind the practice whose main features were these: (1) uncoerced choosing and then influencing of a government by the people, with the mentioned choosing having itself been subject to some influencing, (2) approximate equality in the choosing and all the influencing, (3) uncoerced and effective decision-making by the government rather than by anything else in a society. The equality in the second feature could be no more than approximate since there was no counterpart of 'one man, one vote' in the influencing of an ongoing government and in the prior influencing of the people's choice of one. It was useful to remember a remark of the foremost student of American democracy, Professor Robert Dahl. It was that the publisher Mr Henry Luce, in comparison to Professor Dahl of Yale, had maybe a thousand or ten thousand times greater control over the alternatives debated in an election.

My definition of political violence was free from a modish inclination of Marxists and others. They defined it so widely as to make possible a kind of *tu quoque* to their opponents. Political violence, to my mind, when properly conceived so as to forward inquiry, did not include the lawful activities of landlords, policemen and indeed the whole social structure and the state itself, however unjust or even vicious. Political violence, rather, was a considerable or destroying use of force against persons or things, a use of force prohibited by law and directed to a change in the policies, personnel or system of government, and hence to changes in society.

The even-handedness, if that is what it was, ran through the rest of my reflections. There were two strong arguments for democracy, having to do with freedoms and equalities of several kinds. But even if political violence broke the rules of democracy, which evidently it did, might it not sometimes serve those same ends of freedom and equality? Might this violence not be one kind of what could be called the coercion of per-suasion rather than the coercion of force? The American government was not being *forced* by anti-war riots and bombs to withdraw from Vietnam, just persuaded. And was another sort of coercion of persuasion, as defined by me, not a fundamental part of the ordinary and peaceful democratic process? What was excluded from the process was only the coercion of force. Further, did this violence of the Left not give those involved in it a kind of equality with another minority of people in their societies, those of wealth and position? Finally, could this violence not be directed to and secure the fuller realization of democracy rather than its destruction?

These answers brought some violence closer to democracy, showed that there did exist the possibility of *democratic violence*. That it deserved the name was reason to make us think about it. It was like something of which we all approved. It could only be said with dismay and apprehension, but some bombs were like votes. Did that fact make this violence right? No. No more than a policy was made right simply by its being the policy of a democratic government. If some bombs were like votes, they also maimed and killed. These thoughts, the likeness and difference between some violence and democracy, could not settle the question of justification, but they could move it forward.

In the lesser matter of the Freud Chair, there was some progress. Having gone away to America for a time, Richard missed our depart-ment's mass meeting with the Provost in his office. Noel responded well, if not without effort, to the reduction in decorum resulting from the presence of Myles Burnyeat's infant under the table. He responded in the same style to our various contributions to the debate. We colleagues were in wide agreement on some things. If and when the Freud Chair came into existence, it should not be listed permanently as within the Philosophy Department, not put permanently into its hierarchy and timetables. It should be peripatetic. In different years it should be attached to and involved in different departments in the college, who should have a say about who filled it. This official or institutional arrangement, however, would be compatible with the chair's having its physical home, and couch, permanently at the back of the Philosophy Department. This was progress by my lights, but not victory. I alone among my colleagues had persisted in my first reaction.

The other battle ended more quickly. I was informed that the Appointments and Promotions Committee had ranked all the college's candidates for Readerships in a long list. Very likely the committee counted books and papers, maybe pages, as well as weighing the judgements made on them. I was ranked fourth, Hidé being further down, and the college could elevate only three. That should have been that, perhaps, but I was persuaded that clear injustice had been done on the way to this upshot. It was my view, and Johnny's, that there had been bias on Richard's part, and in particular that the crucial agreement with him about the choice of joint referees had not been kept, but flouted. Certainly he had changed the referees after Johnny took them to be settled.

To my mind these and other things needed to be said. They were, righteously, in my letter of indictment to the Provost. I did not contemplate what some might conjecture, that the crucial agreement was not so clear as it might have been. The Provost replied that there was nothing to be done, but he would pass my thoughts on to the Dean of Arts, the chairman of the promotions committee. He had another note from me a few days later, as informative. That was after I noticed, with mortification, on looking over my *curriculum vitae* so carefully drafted by my very own hand, that I had left something out of it. This was my longest and most recent paper, 'A Conspectus of Determinism'. The consequences of a mighty resolution to defend one's interests could include at least clerical errors.

The Provost and I ran into one another in the college cloisters a while after. He could now let me have some incidental news. The Medical Faculty had insisted that the committee on promotions should reopen matters, and give it some Readers. It had got them, Noel said, and the candidate ranked fourth in the original long list had been carried along with them. Nothing at all to do with your letter about injustice, my boy. A month or two later, yet more personnel played their part, these being philosophers appointed by the university to ratify the college's decisions as to promotion. One was Professor Ayer. His note to me about their ratification showed that time had passed and he now bore me no grudge. Open and shut case, old boy, open and shut case. Professor Berlin sent a note as pleasing. He said it would have been shameful if the promotion had not happened – not that shamefulness was a sufficient cause of events, or, alas, a necessary one – but when justice was done, this gave a sense of comfort for a time, which staved off the general unsatisfactoriness of things.

The fuss about Freud carried on. The anonymous donor turned out to be Mr David Astor of *The Observer*. For good reason the news made friends for the donation. Still, Professor Drew of the Psychology Department was only mollified to the extent of making a suitably wrecking proposal. He thought the college should take the money for a peripatetic chair only if the word 'psychoanalysis' did not appear in the agreement. The ruling council of the college took the money with the word appearing, but perhaps without ordaining where the new professor would sit – or rather the new professors. At some stage, maybe early on, it had seemed best that we have a visiting professorship, which is to say a succession of different Freud Professors. It may have been thought that two or three years at the back of the Philosophy Department would satisfy any occupant's inclination to exchange ideas.

What had been proposed at our meeting with Noel became settled. The chair would officially be a wandering one, now attached to one department and now another, but physically in a two-storey addition to the Philosophy Department. This, said I to all colleagues, in reasoned fierceness, was formality being counted for more than reality. *Where* the chair and couch were – this mattered. There would be an effect, maybe seepage. And our having the chair and couch was surely against majority opinion in the department, which might be proved by our actually voting on a clear resolution. There were more departmental meetings and more declarations by me that psychoanalysis was not in philosophy. Jerry Cohen for his part sent round a note about philosophical autonomy and about amenity, the latter being a loss of light to the Grote's room.

Richard in his letter to me, copied to all colleagues, was true to the principle of necessary distinctions. It had to be kept in mind, he said, that the new accommodation would be built *onto* the department, not be *in* it, which was consistent with there being doorways between them. Hidé wrote to us all that being clear about the boundaries of philosophy was perhaps permissible only to people of very, very great talent.

My visit to America and the city of brotherly love for the international conference on political violence was brief enough not to lower my morale. I was invited to look in for a chat with an Italian professor who liked my high-handed style with the French delegation, and who was used to international gatherings of thinkers, or English novels about them. I coped, more or less, when she welcomed me at the appointed hour for the chat, splendidly proportioned, without any clothes on. Happy letters came from Kiarney, Rooney and Pauline. Kiarney, now 12, was at Camden School for Girls, not overworked, and Rooney, nearly 10, was preparing for his ascent to William Ellis Grammar School. Both of these establishments had the recommendation, among others, of being State rather than fee-paying schools, and thus of being in accord with socialist principle. Pauline was as resolute in her vegetarianism, newly interested in kinds of therapy as means of dealing with life, carrying forward her thesis in the British Museum Reading Room, and, at this particular time, getting on with me.

We had been together ten years. 59 Constantine Road was in these months the agreeable home of a vigorous and reasonably contented family, not well-off but in my view not deprived. There was the bit of extra money from publishing, including a monthly stipend for the editing of the series of philosophy books. We went to the theatre, got wine from Soho, took ourselves off to Welsh cottages for Easter, selected Rooney's small billiards table at Harrods. I took Mr Edward Heath's Conservative government to be a tolerable interlude in the progress being worked by the Labour Party, too slow but still progress.

A satisfactory marriage in these couple of months, I say, but of the variety approved of by Harry Bewick when she visited from Ireland to hear the thoughts of Krishnamurti. The marriage was of the free or open variety, to which there had been a reversion after our American year. My connection was with Sally Barrett-Williams, an undergraduate in the department who was more officially connected with a lecturer elsewhere, presumably also liberated from bourgeois convention. She was her own woman, intelligently industrious in her progress towards a future. Also mature, blonde, and a bobby-dazzler. I was greatly taken by her, and was the prompter of our connection, but remained tied by my own affection and will to Constantine Road. We settled into an arrangement by which we met an evening or two a week, sweetly. Sometimes she came on my jaunts to read papers to the philosophy societies at provincial universities, when we might stay with the local professor.

You may wonder, reader, if this carry-on was not only open to objection on academic principle but also imprudent. Was it wise, when I had been pressing myself forward for promotion and making trouble about Freud, also to be courting some degree of notoriety? It did not go well with taking the moral high ground. The thought crossed my mind, and issued in some degree of discretion, but did not detain me. I was unclear about the academic principle having to do with affairs with undergraduates, and not alone in my carry-on. There was safety in numbers. A randy lecturer known to me got an undergraduate pregnant and faced no such prospect as having a place found for him in the colonies.

Feminism had begun, with books and marches, but it did not include the charge of harassment by teachers. Harassment there certainly was, once by me in at least one mind. A young woman of good family told me of her sad marriage to an Indian gentleman, I sympathized too much, and did get an idea in my head. Something was said to Richard of this, and he found her another tutor. It was a good lesson of a kind. It preserved me from an undergraduate or two with the invigorating idea of an extra-curricular connection with their tutor.

You may have wondered too how often my marriage was as satisfactory as in the couple of months lately mentioned. The answer is that since our return from the year in America it had been in bad shape about as often. If our variety of marriage went undiscussed, we could differ on many other things. Whether and how to get homework done, freedom of the child, the spontaneous and the methodical, the usefulness of the category of the natural, a father's proper role at the dinner table, and a mother's need for the car. The rows in which these differences issued, in my records of them, ran to a pattern: a failing in me denounced, rage on my part at the excess of the denunciation, an aftermath of grim wordlessness, words about our separating, my attempt to have us reason our way to a compromise, and an indefinite ending.

It was my principal complaint that I was not joined in seeking an agreed resolution to rows, in accordance with philosophical clarity, rather than letting them fade away. Into Pauline's view of these bad times went charges against me of unfeelingness, male chauvinism, trying to be a Victorian *paterfamilias*, demanding too much of the children, incapacity to enjoy holidays and family occasions, and the rage, coldness and deliberateness. Not violence. That was political theory, not domestic practice.

At the start of the new academic year Hidé and I raked over the ashes of the promotions matter. We exchanged sad recriminations about improprieties, and in particular about who had said what to whom about what referees might have said about us. We were astonished at one another's incomprehensions. We vindicated our reputations to the Dean of Arts, Professor Ian Christie, an historian of the eighteenth century, surviving his first engagement with armed philosophers. He and I exchanged missives, and then apologies. I welcomed, to whatever effect, his kindly advice to disprove slights in future only by subsequent performance. In the next year Hidé too became a Reader, no doubt rightly.

As for Freud, Noel tired of being taken as infringing philosophical autonomy, and instructed the college bursar to consider a change of plan. Could he look into whether an addition for psychoanalysis might be made instead to another house in Gordon Square, that of the Department of Psychology? It turned out that in that place the structure would have had weak foundations. Some months later it was decreed that the peripatetic chair would have its physical home in the house of the Student Health Service. Officially, for a start, the Freud Professor would be in the Department of Psychology. In the end, a decade or two later, the mariner came to rest in that place permanently, not only in spirit but also in body.

In conversations made more ruminative by a glass of wine, it has been said by me that my spirited endeavours in this period, to get promoted and frustrate Freud, affected the rest of my academic life, at least coloured it. Although my victories caused hurts and raised feelings about me, was this to say too much? Well, it was to look away from such other explanations of my later history as my own strengths and weaknesses as a philosopher. It has also sometimes occurred to me, without aid of a glass of wine, that my two spirited endeavours reinforced a further fact of my nature, a determination to stand up for myself. It became a determination made stronger by having in it a knowledge of the possibility of success.

Sometimes too, in or out of wine, I have entertained a certain question. If I had not gotten into this resolute way of going on, would I have lost little and gained much? The quiet academic life, letting one's books and papers do the talking, and staying out of trouble, has charm, at least from a distance. It may also be a good policy for getting on in the world. Certainly you acquire fewer adversaries. Is it much less honourable?

Constantine Road had once been quiet and, as it seemed, trodden in the mornings mainly by children going willingly to Gospel Oak Primary School and by composed persons on the way to their psychoanalysts. Now it had become a rat-run. That is to say it had become a short-cut away from the main road for commuters in their cars. Residents of the street tried to have it closed to these roaring sods in their Citroens and Fiats, but Jerry Cohen of Agincourt Road, close to single-handedly, had stood up for justice at the neighbourhood meeting. It was my introduction to performance politics at parish level. Why indeed, he asked, should Constantine Road be preserved at the cost of Agincourt Road? Were they of Agincourt Road not like us? Did they not have ears? Were they not subject to the same annoyance, and should we not continue to share it out? The result was that Constantine Road was not closed, and Pauline and I got the idea of decamping. But something other than the traffic was as important to the idea. Our marriage could benefit by a new setting, perhaps a setting of greater decorum. Would that not be a fillip?

Constantine Road is just down the road from the Georgian village of Hampstead. Flask Walk is in that village, a passageway of shops and then a row of cottages. It is sufficiently tarted up to attract American tourists, but not so much so as to keep away persons of architectural taste. There was a house for sale in this known street, or at least with its back door in it, a terrace house of the later nineteenth century. Good for a family although in need of some modernization, maybe the addition of a roof-garden. We had bought our present house for £8,000 with a mortgage of £7,300. Could we not sell it now for £33,500, and, by proving our credentials again to the building society, pay £38,000 for Flask Walk, add in the roof-garden, and make all our futures brighter?

In January 1973 in time for my 40th birthday, Pauline and I again fell out, over what I took to be hurtfully uncivil behaviour and my ensuing fit of temper. My letter then written to her from college, where I would be sleeping in my room on a camp-bed until another room could be found, proposed to get back the deposit just paid on the new house. It was unbearable, said I, to be taken as the only one in the wrong. Her attitude to me was raising up a related one in Rooney. Her reply was that we had no chance of a meaningful relationship, that she had now given up the usual feminine illusions, and that we should part, in as civilized a way as possible.

Instead we slid back into a peace, and got to Flask Walk in June. That we did so had to do with affection, even battered love, and with the children. They came first for Pauline. My feelings for them, from which I could be distracted, were great. Despite charges against me, I have sometimes remembered, with pride, that I have had to sit down twice in my life for fear of fainting, and that the cause on one occasion was not a gash in my own arm. We went to the new house with some pride. We were making a gallant effort. It could turn out well. Bee, having at the past Christmas begun to give me a useful Christmas present, to be repeated thereafter, happily loaned us £5,000 for the renovation and roof-garden. Another English house would lose its interior walls in the interests of *space*. The builder would see to that, but I, not being above manual work in the aid of family progress, would do great labours myself, willingly.

They were done, willingly in the beginning, but there was also something else on my agenda. Ongoing practical and also more emotional life, in the way that the record you are reading continues to convey, alternated with philosophy, the two not being connected in any evident way. Philosophy took over the stage for a part of the day or a week or whatever, in a play part of whose continuity partly consisted in this fairly comfortable alternation. Was the more practical and emotional life subjected to more reflection as a result of the periods of philosophy? Was it subjected to that good thinking supposed to be the very nature of philosophy? Yes, much of it certainly was, but to great effect? The rest of life doesn't allow you to concentrate more on good thinking about the facts rather than getting them, about methods of inquiry rather than using them, and about convictions as to the good rather than embracing them. There's more grubbing needed. The rest of life can be harder than philosophy.

The philosophy in mine at this time was the result of the intractability of determinism and freedom and the accident of another philosophical invitation. There had been a conference in Cambridge, at which the aforementioned Professor Anscombe had gravely announced again that our common idea of an effect was not of an event made to happen or that had to happen, given the cause that went before. Our idea of an effect was just of something that might or might not happen, since we took what went before as no more than *enough* for what came after. This implied that when you hit the ordinary hen's egg on the marble floor with the ten-pound hammer it might or might not break.

This interesting view about the nature of causation drew a firm objection from me, and it caught the ear of she who caught my eye, a transfixing *Parisienne*. Marie-Pierre was, she said, seeking an Anglo-Saxon to contribute a paper to her book on the nature of time, this being another of UNESCO's investments. I had just become a British citizen without difficulty, in order to formalize a reality, and maybe out of a touch of neurotic insecurity about my unpopular political philosophy. Clearly I was the Anglo-Saxon for the job. We did not get together in Paris to discuss progress, as contemplated, but I did honour my philosophical obligation.

It was my hope to be profound. Was time not such a subject? Was it not Proust's subject, and made eternal before Proust by a dozen of Shakespeare's lines? I struggled briefly, and concluded that the subject of time, when evocatively conceived, was in fact the subject of our lives and their endings. It was the subject of our pasts and regret, the present moment of experience or consciousness itself, the future and how much of it there would be. My regular reflection on the latter question, not too melancholy, was that with luck more than a third of my life remained in front of me. And I would emulate Hume. When the end was in sight he rose to the occasion, was jocular with Adam Smith, and took his way round Edinburgh in a sedan chair to bid a decent farewell to friends.

The philosophy of life, however, was no part of analytic philosophy. Death in particular had got some attention from the early Greeks, but not much since. Nor did I have the confidence or inclination to seek to enlarge the interests of my fellow workers. There was nothing for it but to abandon time as evocatively conceived and to consider it as literally conceived. John Ellis McTaggart of Cambridge had done so, and argued to his satisfaction and famously in 1908 that time was unreal. Our conception of it was so unsatisfactory, partly because of our thinking of the same event contradictorily as future, present and past, that nothing could fall under our conception. But McTaggart could not be my subject either.

Here, as often enough in philosophy, was an argument which might entail or prove a conclusion, but a conclusion evidently false. It was evidently false that time was unreal. Events *were* in certain relations – earlier than or simultaneous with or later than others. They *did* have certain properties – those of being past, present or future. A serious fellow would therefore regard McTaggart's argument differently, as a *reductio ad absurdum*. What was proved by the argument if it was valid, therefore, since the conclusion was false, was that a premise of it was also false. Philosophers intrigued by argumentation itself could spend time on finding the false premise. That was of scant interest to me, a serious fellow who took philosophy's aim to be sizeable truths.

My paper, in the end, took up a standard question about the temporal relations of events and their temporal properties. Were the relations and the properties independent of one another, or was it the case that one of these ways of thinking about time was fundamental and explained the other? Might the soberer of my colleagues be right in taking past, present and future to be reducible to things being before, simultaneous with, or after one another? You could try on that conclusion by arguing that what it was for an event to be occurring, to be in the present, was just its being simultaneous with your saying so.

That couldn't be right. It couldn't be right because the presentness of the event passed and the simultaneity was forever. It would be as true later that the two were simultaneous, but not that either was present. Professor Ricoeur of *l'université de Paris-X* said in his introduction to the UNESCO book that time was profound because both Anglo-Saxon conceptual restraint and French spirituality were true of it. Thereafter I never knew of a human being who read my thoughts about time, save only some captive tutees. Maybe they – the thoughts – will be resurrected. Philosophers have that hope, not always sustaining but better than nothing.

My other non-manual work was less accidental. The IRA bombing campaign in England was well underway, Hampstead not being forgotten, and a bomb disposal expert had died. My two existing papers on political violence could be improved, and a third written, and three papers would make a small book. Hence my lecture to the Royal Institute of Philosophy in December 1973 would be 'On Inequality and Violence, and the Differences We Make Between Them'. It was arrogant in its attitude to much political philosophy, which it described as factless. This philosophy was presumptuous in prescribing actual lines of conduct in societies, say respect for the rule of law, without attending to relevant facts of life in the societies. If philosophy by its nature could not be as empirical as other things, it needed to be more empirical when explicitly or implicitly urging action on us, or more likely inaction. The political philosophy in question was not like traditional moral philosophy, which stayed at a high level of generality. It was like applied ethics, which did not leave out factual considerations in arriving at recommendations as to the morality of abortion and the like.

My start at putting things right in connection with actual and possible political violence had to do with inequalities – but not in the things that mainly concerned the IRA, a homeland and national self-determination. The inequalities attended to by me were differences between individuals of different socio-economic classes in length of life. An actuary in the civil service had done me the favour of extracting from the mathematics of the standard mortality indices a plain and understandable fact. English and Welsh males of the lowest social class, as officially defined, when compared with those of the highest social class, had at least 3.5 years less of life on average. American non-whites, as it was easier to discover, had on average seven years less of life than whites.

With the aid of the UN's demographic yearbooks, you could also compare the economically worst-off tenth of population in the less-developed societies with the best-off tenth in the developed societies. The lives of the former individuals, about 170 million, were shorter on average by about 40 years. They had, so to speak, one life rather than two. They were, I later added, like a different species. No doubt things would be a little better in 20 years, but how much? To the statistics and forecasts were added some human content, a woman's recollection of the dying of her daughter.

Reflection on actual and possible political violence could usefully begin with these facts. It could usefully turn next to certain other more particular matters before attending to high generalities about the rule of law, a social contract, or the ideally just society. One particular matter was our quiet moral feelings about the lifetime inequalities and our moral shock with respect to political violence – also the explanation and effect of this notable difference. Another matter was the idea of a moral prohibition on acts as a result of individuals being under an imperative to preserve their personal integrity. Being true to oneself was something of which Bernard had written exceedingly well. But conclusively? Could an individual not act wrongly in preserving his integrity? Were there not selves to which actions ought *not* to be true? Maybe the self of a torturer? It was and remains a good question to my mentor. But in my lecture it was not so gratefully put as it might have been. It would have been better without an allusion to those of especially refined moral vision. My record of gratitude and civility has not been consistent. Except for my allusion, I remain proud of my lecture, and remember its reception with satisfaction.

Like its two predecessors, this paper did not end in any general justification of violence of the Left. Nor in any general condemnation. It was indeed my contention, certainly believed by me, that political philosophy was below the standard of the rest of the subject in the ease with which it came to its proposals. I was ordinarily repelled or horrified by violence, and different in feeling from Franz Fanon of *The Wretched of the Earth* and indeed Sartre. They could speak of the spiritual liberation of violence, of the killing with one stone of an oppressor and also the personality that had been oppressed. But being repelled and horrified could not long inhibit another feeling, about the awful deprivation at which violence could be aimed.

A further passion came into my morals and politics at this time, owed first to the UN demographic yearbooks. I could not set bombs myself, for whatever reason, or come to a confident or untroubled conclusion about them. However, I could do something, in my line of life. I could try to have a rationale of the bombs heard, have them issue not only in recoil but also in thinking and other feeling.

My political feelings were also making a contribution, although not an essential one, to life at home, Pauline being no sympathizer with my internal conflict and no understander at all of the IRA. In April 1974 our house in Flask Walk had a roof-garden, whose safety rail, added subsequently by another, still offends against the symmetry of a line of roofs. But not everything was in order down below. Relations between us were grim, essentially for the old reasons. My short summary of them to myself, and sometimes to her, was my women and her hardness.

But our troubles now included, still more than before, differences about the children, concern for whom was prolonging the marriage. It was

196

Pauline's conviction that my attitude to them in connection with work was one of needless severity. I began to feel separated from them. Each of us added in less persuasive propositions about our situation. It was my responsibility, she said, that we were living in squalor and had lived in poverty. It was entirely her fault, I said, that our rows were not reasoned to a compromise. My proposition had in it my failure to note that the reasoning process as conceived by me had some manipulation in it and much self-justification. As for her proposition, she stung me more by saying that I had deprived her of a woman's confidence.

The fact of the children put me in a kind of moral fear about leaving the marriage, a fear of disgrace. But I was also persuaded that I was avoiding rows at too great a cost. Could it be tolerable that when Rooney at the dinner table asked about the problem of the justification of punishment, the ensuing lecture was given by Pauline? She was as ready with proofs of her forbearance, and the cost to her.

On 1 July 1974 we had a difference in our Fiat on the way in to college and the Reading Room of the British Museum. I said at least that the future was black. Her letter dropped off later in the day agreed that we had to part. Here ended, save for the aftermath, my second marriage and hers. That there was a necessity about the ending did not save me from weeping in the following month, or from keeping the thing secret from my friends. What did more to sustain me was an alteration for the better in my relations with the children. Rooney, coming up to 12, wrote untroubled despatches from his holiday camp, announcing in passing that henceforth he was to be known as Ruan. Kiarney, on the way to 15, sent reports from France which were as reassuring. On their return we met happily for dinners, sometimes in Jimmy's in Soho. The new easiness came from our all having escaped what needed to be escaped.

Pauline and I exchanged civil letters, and readily arrived at a general agreement. She would have half of what we had or something more than that. Since, as she said, she did not wish to be a predator-wife, I would support her for two years during which she would finish her thesis and find a job, perhaps school-teaching. She did not wish to stay in Flask Walk. We would set about selling the house, in a falling market.

After the civil letters came acrimonious ones, officially having to do with our respective monthly budgets, and who had to pay for the piano lessons, and what was financially possible after the rent was paid on my furnished room in West Hampstead. Bitter letters followed, and we began on a policy of thinking the worst of one other. We would need solicitors to defend ourselves. Letters began to flow between mine, Michael Seifert of Seifert, Sedley & Co., and hers, suitably feminist. It would be to my moral credit that Seifert, Sedley & Co., suggested to me by Jerry Cohen, regarded Women's Rights as a progressive cause.

My several histories of 13 years of connection and marriage, put in these days into the steamer trunk of my papers, shed only the light on it of which you know. There were also musings and hopes about the future. I would marry again, but it did not seem to me that there was much hope for that long-running item of commitment, the free marriage. It didn't go, I said, with the kind of thing I wanted.

10

EFFECTS, A PROUD SCOT, JUSTICE, 4 KEATS GROVE

Six years after signing a contract to write a book on determinism and freedom, and three years after it was due in, I had none of it done, having been otherwise engaged. My last paper, in the collection *Essays on Freedom of Action*, had purported to supply the philosophical and wider world with the prerequisite to further reflections on determinism, an explicit theory or formulation of the thing. But now it looked thin, just a sketch really. Could movement towards shedding real light be made by going back to the beginning and figuring out exactly what causation itself comes to? This is not something of which you have heard and to which we shall return, the matter of how we select a cause from other required conditions for something, the problem of the praising of causes. It is rather the problem of the relation between an effect and whatever precedes it. It is the traditional problem of the very nature of causation, or better, the problem of the necessitation of effects.

As always since Hume, there was no shortage of philosophical ideas. One was had by Mr John Mackie, an exceptional philosopher of the other University College, the one in Oxford, where he had preferred to be a Fellow rather than continue as a professor in a provincial university. Consider, he said, an ordinary coin-in-the-slot machine, say the kind that does or does not produce a chocolate bar when you put in a coin. When you put one in and a bar does come out, you take this to be cause and effect. When a coin goes in and a bar doesn't come out, you also take not getting a bar to be an effect, but of something's having gone wrong in the machine.

Now contemplate what some say could be constructed with the help of Quantum Theory, a peculiar indeterministic machine. If you don't put a coin in, no bar comes out. A coin is required. That is definite. But if you do put one in, whether or not you get a bar is a matter of real chance. There is no guarantee at all of either thing. There is a mechanism inside that makes this so.

Suppose you do put a coin into this peculiar machine and are lucky. A bar comes out. Would you not say that this was cause and effect? Wouldn't you say that putting in the coin caused the bar to come out? This thought-experiment, said Mr Mackie, shows that what we take to be an effect is no more than something for which a previous event was required – if the previous event hadn't happened, the effect wouldn't have.* The thought-experiment shows that our concept of an effect is not a concept of something that has to happen or is necessitated. Thus, if you remember the discovery of Professor Anscombe touched on earlier, Oxford joined forces with Cambridge.

If they were right, the most traditional argument for determinism, our own experience of the physical world, would go under. That experience is of a world of cause and effect. But, if the idea we have of an effect is not of something that had to happen, the only thing that could happen, then our experience does not support determinism. Or, if you like, it supports only a washed-out determinism that leaves room for the kind of freedom and anything else that is desired by the opponents of real determinism. After much reflecting at my table in my eyrie, I gained some confidence about Mr Mackie of Oxford and, as it was hard to resist saying, his embracing of a lost cause.

What you needed to keep in mind, said I, about his imagined machine, was that there was supposed to be a real chance event taking place in it, between the coin's going in and the chocolate's coming out. Say the chance event of a small switch's flipping or not flipping. Of course this would not be a chance event in the ordinary sense of something unplanned or in practice unpredictable, but still determined – like where the ball stops on the roulette wheel, or maybe an invitation to write something about punishment or political violence. The event in the

* See p. 87

machine would be a chance event in this different sense: whatever was happening in the time between the putting-in of the coin and the moment of the chance event, all of it could have been happening just as it was but the chance event might not have occurred at all. This was an event of which God in his omniscience, if he existed, would not know any explanation having to do with the mentioned time. He could not know one, since very literally there was none. Such a thing would be in the mentioned time, and, as we know, everything there could have been just the same without the chance event's happening. So, necessarily, nothing there explained that it did happen. If the small switch did flip, nothing explained it.

Given this part of the story, how could the emerging of the chocolate bar be the effect of inserting the coin? They were separated by an absolute mystery, something that had *no* explanation. As for the vulgar temptation you might still feel, to say that the emerging of the bar was the effect of the coin, that could be explained away. You could see why you were tempted, and escape the temptation. The inserting of the coin *was* an ordinary cause, and of something not a thousand miles away from the bar's coming out. The inserting turned on the chance-making mechanism, started its operation. Also, the emerging of the chocolate *was* an effect – of the operation of the mechanism, in particular the small switch. But that didn't make the inserting of the coin the cause of the emerging of the chocolate. It didn't make the latter the effect of the former. It didn't show that an effect is just something for which a previous event was needed.

To the devising of this reply was added my ongoing editing of the three groups of philosophy books. Despite the elements of bad conscience and imperfect rationality in this activity, the series were successful. Having acquired the indomitable Jackie Baldick as literary agent and sweet friend, I found that my honorarium from Routledge & Kegan Paul increased. There would also be a book of engaged political philosophy coming out under my name as its own editor. Contributors to it were being collected by me from both sides of the Iron Curtain. The philosophy societies of provincial universities were hearing from me. My lectures in philosophical logic and political philosophy, and my tutorials on nearly everything in philosophy, were given as diligently as before, sometimes without smoke effects since my struggle to give up cigarettes had begun. The lectures usually did not lack conclusions, firmly declared, for which the undergraduate Hanif Kureishi, in anticipation of later literary endeavours, named me Upshot. Often, on arriving at the red front door of the department in Gordon Square, I knew contentment. I arrived there *a Reader*. To have this rank was all that was needed. You could rest easy as a Reader, whatever else happened.

I saw the children a number of times a week, and was capable of thinking that they were happier not witnessing their parents at war. My feelings for them were lively on ordinary and extraordinary occasions. On 5 November 1974, I and Ruan, now 12 years old, were at a Guy Fawkes party at a house to which he was going a good deal. It was the house of a family friend and professor of standing, a father who had belatedly discovered his sexual nature as a Gay and was giving full expression to it. A man of something like my politics, he was also an intimidating figure, not feminine. Early in the evening at the long kitchen table around which parents were sitting drinking, it was merrily reported that a younger man of the same nature as our host, and as proselytizing, had been engaging in some kind of play on the floor of another room with the boys, including Ruan. The younger man now came in and joked about his coming seduction of my son. My reply was a kind of warning and threat.

My host the professor stood up, grasped the neck of a wine bottle, and smashed the bottom of it on the table edge, producing a very offensive weapon indeed, a fistful of glass daggers. In the shock, it was not clear that the action was only theatrical or a kind of speech-act, rather than a start on a blood-letting. My response was to stand up across the table and do exactly the same. There were some awful moments of our facing one another with our broken bottles at the ready when it did seem something more might happen. We were then recalled to sanity by a man to whom I remain grateful. I tell you of this episode, unique in my physically peaceful life, to indicate something of my connection with my son and that I have when necessary been braver than my nature.

Helen Marshall was not taught by me, but was an undergraduate in the department. She was in the category of mature student, being about 32, ten years younger than me, and divorced. She was a proud Scot, intrigued by philosophy and given First Class marks by my colleagues for essays in the parts of the subject that took her attention. The calm of her life, not constant, required some effort of will. She was quicksilver in conversation, well able to elude my philosophical and other logic. Her sentences were impeccable and striking, like some of the styles in capes she took over from exhibits in the Victoria and Albert Museum. She did not live only a student's life, but, despite being a miner's daughter, cut a figure in Chelsea's King's Road and sometimes in the sitting rooms of one of Scotland's great families, being a friend of a younger son. She was as atuned to the songs of Bob Dylan and Fleetwood Mac as to those of Schubert and Mahler. When she took the trouble to have regular meals and attend to herself, her looks brought Marlene Dietrich to mind. She charmed most men, all children, and some women.

She and I set up together in a furnished room in what was called Lancaster Gate, in fact around a corner from Paddington Station. We carried on well there, Kiaran and Ruan visiting often for suppers and parlour games. If there was some uncertainty in our connection, owed in part to her spiritedness and my stolid attention to intellectual duty, and if my eye had also been caught by another striking woman, I was resolved to make a fine life with her, the third woman to live with me. She enlivened the circle of my friends of the past, notably the Watlings and the Sprigges, and flourished in a circle of newer friends, one being my graduate student Sabina Lovibond, as resolutely individual as her name. Another was Professor Sir William Coldstream, head of the Slade School of Fine Art in University College and, as it seemed, Prime Minister of British painting. Having conscripted me to sit in on Slade admissions interviews, to shed what light was possible on the Conceptual Art in applicants' portfolios, he also made me a member of a proud luncheon club. It met at Bertorelli's on Wednesdays, and Helen graced the annual Ladies' Night of the club. Might he paint her? I hoped so.

The subject of causation, conceivably slightly boring, seemed less so in my new paper for the Aristotelian Society. If an effect could not be taken as just an event for which a previous one was required, what then? Well, it was an event that had to happen or was necessitated. The lighting of the match was necessitated not just by a cause in the usual sense of the word, say striking the match, but by a full cause or causal circumstance, this being the cause together with other things, say the match's being dry, the presence of oxygen, and so on. And what did the circumstance's necessitating the event amount to? How was this to be understood?

You could see one simple answer was wrong. What it was for a circumstance to necessitate an effect wasn't just that *if or since the circumstance occurred, so did the effect*. That conditional statement might be true if the circumstance was no more than a reliable signal of the event, something of the kind that always preceded such events. If this were the whole story, as mighty Hume made the mistake of thinking, then, as a fellow Scot pointed out to him, yesterday would have causally necessitated last night. Days always precede nights. But yesterday didn't causally necessitate last night. Something you could call the solar conditions did – one of them was a certain face of the earth being away from the sun.

You could get to the true solution to the problem of the nature of effects by finding the difference between yesterday and the solar conditions. What wasn't true of yesterday was that once it happened, no matter what else was happening, last night would still have happened. Last night wouldn't have happened if a new light source had come into being. So, what a circumstance's necessitating an effect came to was that *if or since the circumstance came together, then, whatever else had been happening, the effect would still have occurred*. That really was true of the solar conditions.

Essentially this had been said before me, in the nineteenth century by John Stuart Mill and more recently by my colleague Downing. But its persuasiveness was not owed to these authorities. It seemed to me an inescapable truth. Getting to it, by reflecting on night and day and the like, was something like seeing a proof in geometry. This certainty of mine about a few philosophical propositions is mysterious. Why is it in no danger of being reduced by the incredulity of other philosophers? Why is it not touched by difficulties that crop up in elaborating the propositions? Must we wonder if there is something to be said for a certain definition of metaphysics, as the finding of bad reasons for what we believe on instinct. It is owed to the generally resistible F. H. Bradley, he who not only thought that only the Absolute existed but also that to wish to be better than the world is to be already on the threshold of immorality. I prefer to think that my idea of causation came not from instinct but from a goodish acquaintance with loam, streams, bicycles, Pontiacs, and ponds on Hampstead Heath.

At last a buyer was found for the house in Flask Walk. Pauline found another house in a quiet and satisfactory street on the other side of the Heath. I toured around looking at flats for sale. The one that in late April 1975 seized my attention was Flat B, the first floor of the large house at 4 Keats Grove, a street as agreeable as any in Hampstead. Unparalleled location, said the estate agent, almost truly. He rang up the elderly and indecisive builder who owned the flat, and found he had changed his mind again. He was now thinking of selling the whole house. It consisted in the three main flats, a cottage added on at the side, and an artist's studio in the front garden.

The first-floor flat, the 1812 house and the street down to the Heath were to me a necessity. Coming in through the stained-glass porch, added to the austerity of the Regency stucco by a late Victorian, would be as reassuring as passing through the red door in Gordon Square. Necessity was the mother of an idea. The second-floor flat had in it a sitting tenant paying a small rent. She had been there only several years, but was well protected by the housing legislation of the Welfare State. My idea was that I combine with the sitting tenant and others to buy the whole property. Thereby I would end up where I wanted to be, in the first floor flat, with Helen. I left a note to that effect for the sitting tenant, then entirely unknown to me. Out of kindliness or prudence or both, she will have the soubriquet 'Green Shoes' in this narrative, derived from her favourite footwear.

She responded with happy alacrity. Something like my own age of 42, she had been a teacher of the deaf. Now she had a post somehow involved in nothing other than a kind of philosophy, in a London institution not famous in the subject. Forward we would go, we agreed, by finding two other suitable parties to join us in the three flats and the adjoining cottage. Johnny had a look round, but declined. So did Bill Coldstream, not mentioning what presumably was on his mind and came to my attention later, that in several of the rooms he looked over his first wife had carried on her adventure with the tenant and lesser poet Louis MacNeice in the 1930s.

Having seen her landlord, the elderly and indecisive builder, Green Shoes reported that he would prefer to deal with one person acting on behalf of the rest. It would be best if she, the sitting tenant who knew him, were that person. She would also find a solicitor for our enterprise. I would find our two fellow-purchasers, which was the main thing, and now and in the future deal with valuers, surveyors, roofers, builders, insurers, woodworm, and the tenant of the studio in the front garden, a tough artist given to drink, not at all a suitable partner.

She saw a solicitor in early May, and reported back enthusiastically. Some months later, to glance ahead, she signed an affidavit touching on the meeting. She then said that she remembered that the solicitor was instructed on the basis that if and when an agreement was reached about the purchase of the property on the basis of a joint involvement between herself and others, he would act for all. In the meantime, he was acting for her alone.

According to me, in my later affidavit, such an agreement was reached at a meeting in her flat a few days later, still in May. We did not have the two other collaborators to hand, and I would have to advertise for them in *The Times* and in *The New Statesman*. So we two alone would buy the whole property, essentially by raising most of the purchase price by selling off two of the four bits on the same day.

Later in May she paid a further visit to the solicitor, and he made a note of his instructions. I would not have been surprised to see it then. I was pleased indeed to see it later on, at the Discovery stage of a lawsuit, when the two sides have to reveal their documents. He recorded of her that she 'will purchase the pty in her name, as V will not deal save only with her. But her colleague, Doctor Ted Honderich of University College, London, W.C.1, will be putting up finance, and [she] will execute a deed of trust for herself & Dr TH, in equal shares, of the F/H, and sales proceeds of flats.' For the aid of my philosophical readers who have not spent a period in property-dealing, and for Americans, 'V' is for vendor or seller, and 'F/H' is freehold. The deed of trust would make us joint owners of the property, with equal shares of the freehold or ground ownership in perpetuity.

In the rest of the month, it became very clear that the idea of buying 4 Keats Grove by selling off two bits of it was one of which my mercantile grandfather would have approved. My adverts brought in shoals of would-be purchasers, 22 listed in one surviving summary. The problem was not finding buyers but choosing suitable ones. Green Shoes, however, was not so happy. It transpired that now it was her view that we should not each pay the same to become equal partners, since her role as sitting tenant was reducing the price to be paid for the property. In my naiveté I had thought my original idea and my present and future labours were also worth something. In June we agreed to vary our agreement, said my later affidavit. I would pay £5,500 more of the £55,500 purchase price – or rather, of what would be left to pay after the money came in from what we had learned to call the two sales-off. We might get £40,000 from them. The other later affidavit, hers, said something different. 'It is my contention that the negotiations I had with the plaintiff never led to any concluded agreement. . . .'

Having talked on the phone and written to our joint solicitor a few times, but not been far-seeing, I happily went off to Ghana in West Africa to act as External Examiner in Philosophy to the university. The Ghanaians were a pleasure, a gentler form of life than Nigerians. The government of army generals was more comic than grim, the avenues of the campus outside Accra were stately, and the palm wine was bracing. Among the gifts I brought home was one for Green Shoes. She was not so grateful as might have been hoped, and in her demeanour more owlish than before.

Becoming a little apprehensive, I left a message with a clerk in the office of my own solicitor Michael Seifert. The result of this imperfect communication was a letter of inquiry from the clerk to our partnership solicitor. In it he recorded our revised partnership agreement, giving figures, which was useful. But, alas, he also wrote so as to safeguard what he took to be my interests. He spoke of the agreement as 'subject to contract'. An agreement not yet finalized, that is to say. It was not good to read the letter at Discovery time. A judge might linger over 'subject to contract' one day, to my detriment.

In July it was discovered that the cottage at 4 Keats Grove had a newly broken window. The *modus operandi* of squatters at this time, it was believed, was to make premises insecure in this way one night, and return a night or two later to take up residence without breaking in, thereby gaining the protection of the law. Green Shoes rang up to say I would have to move in immediately to protect our as yet unowned investment. I moved in on the double, with Helen, whom I had introduced to my fellow property-dealer earlier. For whatever reason, she had not found Helen charming. Let me add, suspicious reader, that for discernible reasons it had been easy for me not to dally with Green Shoes, and that Helen and I would soon be engaged in trying to find out why she was not having the child she wanted.

On 4 August, deals with suitable purchasers of two flats were finally settled by me for about £40,000. I wrote the confirming letters about their long leaseholds to Professor Robert Donington, a cellist and the author of *The Instruments of Music*, and to Dr Jack Fielding, F.R.C.P., F.C. Path., D.P.H., of St Mary's Hospital. On the next day, with a weak explanation, Green Shoes returned a cheque of mine for half of the deposit on the purchase of 4 Keats Grove. On the day after, as later transpired, she arranged to borrow the whole of the purchase price herself from a bank manager who knew a safe proposition when he saw one. Over the following days she first let me know that no partnership existed between us. Our 52 or more meetings had not got so far as that.

By the time the new academic year of 1975–76 began, I had acquired a barrister, Mr Michael Tugendhat. He ploughed his way through three or four hundred pieces of paper recording the adventure until then. They included our record of equally shared expenses, with entries in our two hands on it, and our solicitor's draft contracts for the sales-off, naming me as one of the two vendors. What the pieces of paper did *not* include was an explicit written agreement between me and Green Shoes. However, at our first conference, Mr Tugendhat expounded property law and pronounced I had cause for complaint, legally and morally, and there was sufficient evidence of a partnership.

So there we were, three fish in a fine kettle. Helen and I now on the first floor, our adversary now under us on the ground floor. She was a bonny fighter, tougher than me. She would see that we went away, tails between our legs. Her central heating was being installed at 2 a.m. until I called the police, and she paid us visits with her ominous builders. We ended up not so much living in the flat as guarding it. In December, at my behest, I and Helen and Green Shoes were in court. The judge thought well enough of the plaintiff's story to order that he be allowed to remain in peace and rent-free in Flat B until the day, whenever that would be, when another judge had the time to decide finally whether there had been a partnership or just a long negotiation.

What do these eight months at Keats Grove from April 1975 say of me? The view of Green Shoes, easily reported, is that I proved myself to be squatter, liar, knave, thief, delinquent, and possibly deaf. You may take that as an option if you like. One of my own reflections is the possibility that I was naive about human nature or some human natures with respect to money and property. In saying this, I do not mean to accuse Green Shoes of being liar etc., but only to suggest that I had an insufficient grasp of the ordinary self-interest of others with respect to material things. Maybe also my own self-interest. I had a moralized conception of their likely conduct and of my own. An unreasonably high conception, you may think, having to do with a childhood without much money in it. And too much time in that other life since coming to England, the one with the good thinking in it?

But it would be much too simple to present myself as only naive and unworldly. At a certain point in the proceedings, as reported, I came to have apprehensions. They were about whether Green Shoes would stick to what we certainly had – a clear-enough agreement in an ordinary sense, involving offers made and accepted, whether or not an agreement that was legally binding. When these apprehensions arose in me, I fell into a strategy. It was to avoid a rupture and go forward, thereby making a satisfactory upshot more likely. It would be harder for my collaborator to go against our agreement later, when I had done still more work on our project.

There is something else. After my apprehension arose, I was not tough. Whatever my strengths and occasional braveries in the past, and perhaps because of being worn down by the ongoing battle with Pauline about the piano lessons, I was then no fighter. If decency put a restraint on me, there was also a want of courage, or at the very least an aversion to personal hostility and conflict. To fall into the latter was to fail to achieve what intelligence and dignity and conceivably the civilizing tendency of philosophy should always make possible. One more thing can be added about my want of fortitude, more happily. 4 Keats Grove was never the first item on my agenda.

Puzzling about causation had to give way to puzzling about a new book, the subject of a special department seminar. It was *A Theory of Justice* by John Rawls at Harvard, of whom you heard something in connection with my performance at Oberlin College. The book was the dawn of a new age in political thinking, said Stuart Hampshire in a review. He rightly overlooked what would be looked back on later as another dawn, Margaret Thatcher's election to the leadership of the Conservative Party. On television she was to me a pompous frump aspiring to the accent of the social class of public speakers, which she had not learned very well. She was mainly known for wanting to teach personal responsibility to parents by depriving their kiddies of free school milk. Professor Rawls was more serious. *A Theory of Justice* was the respectable political philosophy in terms of which all other political philosophy in our time would be defined and defended. My egalitarianism would be, if I ever got it straight.

The argument of the book has to do with what it invites us to imagine, some people setting up a society by arriving at a social contract. Certainly they have to be imagined, since they have a wonderful feature had by no actual persons past or present. This is an absolute ignorance of their personal attributes and positions in their society to come. In agreeing on fundamental principles to govern their society, the contractors do have general beliefs as to how societies can be, and about kinds of lives in them – which fact is also important. Further, each contractor is self-interested, rational, and equally able to put forward proposals. But, to repeat, each is ignorant of that contractor's own life to come, whether male or female, black or white, healthy or not, intelligent or not, rich or poor, freeholder or squatter.

Professor Rawls's basic idea was simple enough, and is now known to all undergraduates in philosophy and a few politicians. It is that we can see in advance that whatever the contractors do choose by way of fundamental principles, these principles will be the just or fair or right ones – not merely for the contractors in their coming society which we can imagine, which doesn't much matter, but for us in our actual societies. One nerve of the idea is that since no contractor can choose in such a way as to pursue real self-interest and favour his or her personal situation, the contract made will be a sure guide for us in our actual societies. The circumstance in which the choice is made confers a recommendation on what is chosen, a justification. This was given by Professor Rawls as the first premise of his Contract Argument.

The second premise, as he regarded it, was that the contractors would avoid certain principles, for good reason, and would agree on some others that add up to one of the things called liberalism. They would not choose a racist principle, evidently, since each would run the risk of turning out to be black in a white society. They would not choose the Principle of Utility, since the possible society with the greatest total of happiness might be one where some individuals were very unhappy indeed, even slaves. They would, said Professor Rawls, agree on three principles, in descending order of importance.

The first calls for as much liberty for each member of the society as is consistent with everyone else having as much. An equality in such traditional liberties or rights as the right to personal property – not to be confused, of course, with actually possessing any personal property. To have a liberty or right in this sense, in essence, is only for the law of the land not to prohibit you from having something, and maybe to help you a little bit to get it. To have such a right to something is not itself to have the power to get the thing or actually to have it. The second principle is about equal opportunity to get into upper rather than lower classes if the society has socio-economic inequality in it.

The third principle, paid most attention, is that the society can have and must have whatever amount of socio-economic inequality makes the worst-off class better off than it would be without that amount of inequality. The amount might theoretically be none – if everybody was better off in that situation than some would be if there was some inequality. But what lay behind this third principle, evidently, was the old idea, not too much proclaimed in 1975–76, that the poor might be still worse off without the rich. It was the idea later associated with that same Mrs Thatcher, that wealth trickles down from above to below.

My Jacobin piece on all this in the journal *Mind* said it was bumble at best, however impressive and well-intentioned, as you could start to see by imagining a clear-headed and sincere supporter of apartheid considering the Contract Argument. What would this racist say? He could point out that he was being invited to consider, in part, what social principles would be chosen by imagined persons who were benighted. Those principles would be owed in part to their general beliefs about society. These would not include the truly fundamental one, in his view of things, about God, higher and lower races, natural masters and natural servants. Why should he be impressed by principles chosen by persons who had not seen the light?

Suppose we invited a tough Marxist to consider the Contract Argument, one who was convinced that the traditional liberties, notably the liberal right to personal property, have always been precisely the means of depriving unfortunates in our societies of decent lives, including personal property. Would he not let us know that he had no interest in the reflections of imagined persons who were political dimwits? Why attend to hoodwinked persons whose general beliefs evidently did not include the truth about the reality of the traditional liberties? They were ignorant about a larger fact than their personal futures.

The moral of this was clear. Anyone who *is* inclined to go along with the Contract Argument must *already* have certain convictions. These do not include the racist or the Marxist one, and do include a particular kind of egalitarianism. So the Contract Argument has a hidden premise. It is a mixed bag of convictions that then issues in what is officially the first premise of the argument but really is the second, that whatever the contractors choose is right. The Contract Argument is a curious piece of machinery for summing up or generalizing or adjusting the mixed bag of convictions, a liberalism, into a few broad principles.

Couldn't you sum them up directly? Reflect on the mixed bag in an ordinary way and see what it comes to? To come to one large objection, what was the real use of all the stuff in the middle of the Contract Argument, its two official premises? They didn't add anything at all to the argument. They were otiose. It wasn't as if some obligation attached to the principles because they were really agreed to by us or any real persons, as in more traditional thinking about a social contract. And if there could be a point in talk of some imagined agreements, there couldn't be any here. Each imagined contractor, as was necessary if the argument was to be simple enough to deliver the goods, was *identical* with each other one. Indeed, exactly that is what *A Theory of Justice* invited us to imagine. So there wouldn't be much exchange of views going on among the contractors. There would be exactly that binding sort of agreement that occurs when you agree with yourself.

But persist some more, flagging reader. There was more in my piece. The Contract Argument might be no better than a humdrum piece of generalizing, but its conclusion might be right anyway. There are weak and absurd arguments to the true conclusion that the earth is round. What about the three principles of this liberalism taken by themselves?

Think about the third one – that we ought to have in our actual societies whatever distribution of socio-economic goods makes a worst-off class better-off than it would be without that distribution. This leaves us with several possibilities. Suppose the choice we face is between

(A) absolutely equal amounts of goods for all, and
(B) one class having somewhat less than that and all the others
     a lot more.

Then we are to go for (A) the absolute equality. But suppose the choice
we face is between

(A) absolutely equal amounts of goods for all again, and
(C) unequal amounts but with every class getting more.

Then we are to go for (C) the inequality. In fact *any* extent of inequality
that helps the bottom class a little, including extents not so far imagined.
So, remarkably enough, despite some qualification that might be added,
the principle on one assumption as to our choice-situation gives us
absolute equality, and on another assumption gives us extreme inequality.

   To that there is certainly a large objection. A proper principle or
doctrine of distribution must be more instructive. For a start, it will let
us know more about whether in social and economic actuality we face
the A/B or the A/C choice. This will involve some traditional social,
economic and political argument, not so olympian as *A Theory of Justice*.
Furthermore, should a proper principle of distribution not include a bit
of instruction about changing the world, and more particularly the
reward-demands of some people in it, so as actually to give us another
choice-situation? Conceivably one between the same first option

(A) absolutely equal amounts of goods for all, and
(D) everybody unequally but not very unequally better-off?

That would be the situation, if you persist in the agreeable idea that the
font is at the top of the pile, where in place of trickle-down there is flow-
down, maybe even flood-down, by way of such a pump as taxation.

   My piece on Professor Rawls was paid attention in surveys of what
were called his radical critics. It did nothing at all to impede the stately
progress of *A Theory of Justice*. It is hard to think of a more successful
book of political philosophy in the twentieth century. Another book of
political philosophy was published about this time. It was the collection
of engaged pieces under the title *Social Ends and Political Means*,

brought together by me in spare time over the past couple of years from both sides of the Iron Curtain. In it, as the jacket says, are essays which have to do in different ways with better societies than the ones we have, and with ways of getting them. *Social Ends and Political Means* did not have a stately progress, and does not count as a successful book of political philosophy.

Should I think then again about my Jacobin strictures on Professor Rawls? Wonder if my labours to improve the English of Professors Colletti and Schaff were not worthwhile? Maybe some reflection on this would not be a waste of time, but it is alien to the philosophical temper. There is no simple way in which cogency or truth is related to numbers of copies sold or the tenor of the times.

Whatever is to be said of me and the philosophical temper, which you may take to be an encompassingly critical disposition to cogency and truth, neither Pauline nor I was philosophical in a certain common sense in this year. That is, we were not inclined to being calm and resigned in adverse and irremediable circumstances – those we had created for ourselves. We did not accept one another's calculations as to how much more than half the resources of the marriage were going in the direction of her house at 11 Glenhurst Avenue, N.W.5.

Matters were further complicated by Ruan's attachment to the dashing Helen, lately graduated with a good degree, her marks in Finals having included a scattering of Firsts. She, in the feelings of Pauline, was giving vent to her maternal instinct with someone else's child. Our divorce was decreed absolute in July 1976, but Pauline and I were back in court a couple of weeks later at her behest. Essentially this was in order to have a judge decide whether she was right that I was a reckless father in wanting to provide my accident-prone son of 14 with a bicycle. He would remain, said the judge, in our joint custody, like Kiarney.

There seemed more to be said for a mother's caution some months later. Spirited as ever, my son succeeded in breaking both arms, without aid of a bicycle, which he never got. The philosophical temper prompts me to add that Pauline honourably made nothing during our war of a further grievance. I was also the biological father of another lad, about 10. His mother was the English girl of the intricate smile. I saw her and him and her husband sometimes, but kept a distance, still feeling ill-used. We had the understanding that I would be in touch at Christmases.

It was in the next academic year, in fact Christmas of 1976, that Pauline and I tired of the stream of missives passing between us, and achieved a ceasefire, prelude to a blessed peace. Green Shoes was continuing to concentrate my mind on other things, Pauline had begun her teaching job at a good girls' school near her home. My solicitor and her solicitor, having recovered their own manners after being drawn into our hostilities, had no dispute left but the bill of the second one. Michael Seifert said on my behalf, since I would be paying it too, that it had been arrived at by a too strenuous application of women's solicitor's rights.

In January *Three Essays on Political Violence* came out from Blackwells in Oxford, as did the same book under the title *Political Violence: A Philosophical Analysis of Terrorism* from Cornell University Press in the United States. It was manufactured from four papers of which you have heard, the last being the one about *A Theory of Justice*. Thereafter 30 or 40 reviews came to my attention, a couple of carping ones, most very approving, and some breathless in their tributes. Only the last were satisfactory to me, perhaps because I had become an ordinary author. Our hopes are high.

My ungrateful response also had to do with my being less aware then than now of the general fact of friendly relations between reviewers and authors. The particular fact of reciprocal reviewing, *A*'s esteem for *B*'s book and *B*'s yet greater esteem for *A*'s, may be rarer in philosophical circles than others. Hence it is wonderful to see, notably on the covers of the books of a pair of one's teachers. Of the reviewers of my violence book, two knew my virtues since those virtues had already led me to publish their own excellent work. All the rest were unconnected with me, and I should have been more grateful.

Save for the couple of carpers, one Marxist and one harbinger of a political age to come, all approved of dispassionate and inquiring philosophy about setting bombs. Most reported the truth that this philosophy did not come to a verdict on the IRA's bombs in London, or indeed any actual bombs. Should it have? It is true to say that philosophy by its nature is general, despite its recourse to particularity. It is also possible to think that what stood in my way with respect to particular judgements was not only their great difficulty, but some caution. There is a difference between an instigator or advocate of something and an apologist or understander, and it was not lost on me. If my piece in *The Times* on publication day was not dishonest, its uninflammatory heading was not mistaken: 'Political Violence: Is It Possible to Have an Open Mind?'.

The truth about my book, by my lights, is plain enough. It is that my feeling about deprivation, including deprivation in lifetimes, did raise in me an impulse to contemplate violence, which impulse was somewhat restrained by self-preservation as well as the lack of conclusive argument in support of violence. The impulse was discerned, no doubt, by the giver of a talk on the World Service of the BBC, who set about bringing it into sharper focus by free quotation. 'A bomb,' Dr Honderich says, 'is a vote.' That, as you have heard, was shorter than what I had written: 'It cannot be said without dismay and apprehension, but it is to be said that some bombs are like votes' and 'If some bombs are like votes, they also maim and kill'. My firm letters to Mr Alexander Lieven, one of those in charge of the World Service, were marked 'Without Prejudice', this being a lawyer's indication of the possibility of litigation. He, being a White Russian who had survived the revolution and also a Prince, was not terrified. He was sympathetic.

The results of his sympathy were corrections broadcast in French, German, Spanish, Hindi, Kuoyu and so on, and eventually my presence on a half-hour programme with Mr Paul Johnson. He had lately been editor of *The New Statesman* but was now en route towards an ideological love affair with Mrs Thatcher as well as a related connection with God and the Church. He addressed his remarks to The Good Doctor, and I addressed mine to The Bad Journalist, again complaining of misrepresentation. In later years we did not seek out one another at parties.

At Keats Grove and in the neighbourhood of the Inns of Court, *Honderich v. Green Shoes* had been moving forward as bracingly. Green Shoes was fighting fit. One evening I found Helen giving tea to two waiting police detectives. They had a search warrant in connection with information that I was armed. They had already carried out inquiries at University College London. Now thinking along different lines as a result of Helen's account of local affairs, they were promptly satisfied by my producing Ruan's airgun, a lad's item not near to lethal, akin to what my trans-Atlantic readers will know as a BB-gun. After that, when she went into the rear garden, my adversary might see me standing still in a window above, looking steadily at her. It improved my morale, as did the news that Dr Fielding was taking her to court for not having kept her agreement to renovate the property. It was still better to hear she would be decamping to teach in Africa for three years.

In March, in Mr Tugendhat's rooms, after documents in the case had been exchanged, he pronounced my case to have a 65–70 per cent chance of success, adding that the most he would give to any case whatever was 75–80 per cent. Such were the hazards of litigation. If my legal and moral case was strong, my financial situation was not. The legal costs to the loser if the case went to court could be £16,000, not too far from the price of one of the flats. There was also a large difference between my situation and that of my adversary.

If she won, she would get all of what was coming to us at 4 Keats Grove, but if she lost she would still get half. If I won, I would get half, and if I lost I would get nothing. Thus, if she had a greater chance of losing than me, her situation if she lost would be a lot more tolerable than mine if I lost. It had been an innocent and bad idea not going along with her on her trips to see our solicitor and the vendor. That is what had allowed the possibility of the present all too actual situation, as was clear from my summary of the supposed partnership for Mr Tugendhat in 131 pages.

It did not entirely distract me from the other life, with my determinism book in it, of which there were now about as many pages, more tentative. But the publication of my three essays on violence gave rise to other distractions, one being a lecture tour of the Canadian West. The news I brought to my five audiences from London, a London still beset by IRA bombs, had the title 'Clean Hands'. Initially my new paper was about a *tu quoque* that might be offered by defenders of violence of the Left. This *tu quoque* was that we who do not set bombs do nevertheless contribute essentially to terrible circumstances of distress and degradation, famine for a start, not by our acts but by our omissions. More particularly, the paper had to do with our natural reply that there is a large moral difference between acts and omissions. Mrs Philippa Foot in Oxford, after allowing there surely is something wrong with our letting people die of starvation, had expostulated that nevertheless there *is* a distinction between sending out poisoned food parcels and omitting to contribute to Oxfam.

The paper proceeded from the premise about the nature of morality, of which you have heard, that the general question of the rightness of actions, be these acts or omissions, is different from the question of the goodness of agents and their intentions. You could do the right thing out of a bad intention and the wrong one out of a good intention. As an M.P., you could vote for the National Health Service, despite your own principles, a hypocrite with an eye to re-election. You could vote against it, conceivably, out of a dim but honest conviction that something else would work better. What made actions right were their probable consequences of harms and benefits, first of all distress and deprivation. This, also touched on before in this narrative, had the name of Consequentialism.

From this general premise, and a survey of supposed and actual differences between acts and omissions, there emerged the conclusion that in our ordinary omissions we are acting terribly wrongly. Could this conclusion be defeated by a *reductio ad absurdum* argument, to the effect that it entails that we are all moral monsters, which is absurd? No, the conclusion was safe from that objection, on account of the lesser kind of intentionality involved in most omissions. As for the *tu quoque* on the part of the violent, that we who do not set bombs also do wrong, this proposition was accepted by me, but of what relevance was it to their own activities? It could not make those activities right, but it should indeed lead us into a wider view of things.

Do I believe it all still? More or less, although it raises more questions in my mind now. One thing to be said is that it was not so clear to me in 1977 what the nature of the persistent dispute is between Consequentialists and their opponents – those who find the rightness of actions in intentions, the integrity of the agent and so on. It is a ground-level *moral* dispute. It is not, as the opponents and I managed to suppose, a philosophical difference, a difference in meta-ethics about the nature of morality, decideable without recourse to ordinary moral convictions.

Back in England, back home, an opportunity arose for something closer to political action. *The Daily Telegraph* carried a piece by one Robert Moss on what was said to have been in the past a unique British institution, not just another publishing house. This was Penguin Books.

Now, said Mr Moss, Penguin had been subverted by Marxists, Trotskyites and radical Left-Wingers. In *The Self-Help House Repairs Manual*, there were not only instructions on doing your own plumbing but also on being a squatter. And, Penguin did not publish what had arrived on the scene, the antidote to Rawls's *A Theory of Justice*. This was Robert Nozick's *Anarchy, State and Utopia*, a right-thinking work whose distinctions included the proposition that taxation is forced labour. Also, as might be added, the proposition that in the perfectly just society, there is no moral obligation on anything or anyone to help unlucky members who are dying of starvation.

What, asked Mr Moss, should be done about Penguin? The implication of his answer was that the capitalist owners of this tedious bird should sack Mr Neil Middleton, who was Red in tooth and claw, a lapsed Catholic, and at the heart of the rot in what had been the British institution. It gave rise to a thought on my part. I and my colleague Myles Burnyeat, who in my estimation gave Ancient Philosophy what good name it deserved, had been engaged in bringing together an anthology, *Philosophy As It Is*. In it, along with contributions from a cast of stars and some others, including Ayer, Hampshire, Wollheim, Williams and Honderich, would be nothing other than the heart of *Anarchy, State and Utopia* by Robert Nozick. This was a stick with which to beat the tedious Mr Moss in my letter to the editor of *The Daily Telegraph*.

Private letters went out from my eyrie to invite others to come to the defence of the Penguin Plotters. The wind was changing. Some didn't and some did. To Mr Bryan Magee, Labour M.P. and the boy-philosopher of whom you have heard, I sent the same letter of invitation as to others. It seemed to me stylish in its brevity and assumptions, but things didn't need to be spelled out to a Labour M.P. He said to me in his note back that he had been hesitant about meeting my request, since he believed strongly in editorial freedom. But he had decided to do so – the political degeneration of Penguins was a shame and a scandal. He had written formally to its chairman to object to the subversion of the British institution by the Plotters. We exchanged sharpish sentences on this sad misunderstanding. At a lunch at Penguin Books in Harmondsworth, Dr Anthony Kenny, soon to be Master of Balliol, appeared with me on behalf of the accused. Perhaps it did some good, for Mr Middleton survived.

He was luckier than the miserably paid Asian women who thought they could form a union at the Grunwick film processing laboratory in west London. Having been sacked, they picketed to try to change the minds of the persons who took their jobs. They were joined by Mr Arthur Scargill's miners. The mass picket eventually came to have thousands of persons in it, including Shirley Williams, M.P. In the early mornings for a fortnight, the Association of University Teachers, not renowned for militancy, was represented by me, self-nominated. 'Scabs' did not come easily to my lips as the name for Grunwick's new employees in their bus. But to the massed bobbies safeguarding them through the picket line, I shouted 'Company Police!', which was not liked. Collared and sent on my way, but not arrested, I could return to my duty. We did not win. Victory went to Mr Moss and friends, he having popped up behind Grunwick & Co. as the thinking member of the National Association for Freedom.

At Keats Grove, as this academic year approached its end, so did Helen and I. It is difficult to say what this had to do with the legal and other struggle we had survived, if anything. We were not defeated, but Green Shoes had turned away an offer from me to settle the case, and waiting for a distant resolution of the thing did not improve my morale or Helen's. Certainly our fate was more in our personalities and characters, mainly mine. I loved her, but there was resolution in it. If she loved me, which I think she did, she had to tolerate my less free spirit. But the confession and truth that must be salient in this recollection is that my resolution not to fail in a relationship again, and to escape from free marriage or free partnership, had been less strong than something else. That was my attraction to the other striking woman who had caught my eye.

I have reported the emotion of earlier endings, above all with First Love and two wives. This ending was more terrible. Helen had offered me a slight opportunity, by herself speaking of separation, but she was no less stricken than I. She fled to Edinburgh and came back. For some weeks, while she found a place to go to, we existed in the flat together, never angry, usually distraught, always desolate. We had not had the time to wear down love. I could not look at her. My endless weeping was for guilt, first of all, and then for loss. She was the stronger. Yes, she promised she would eat enough, and she would write a clear statement about Green Shoes, but it would not be a good idea for us to meet for lunch until December.

11

THE HIGHER SOCIAL LIFE, CHANCERY COURT, MUCH ELSE

Myles Burnyeat and I were finishing our work on *Philosophy As It Is* as 1977–78 began. More particularly, we were finishing our brief prefaces to the included lectures, articles from journals, and chapters from other books. The official idea of the anthology was that the nature and worth of philosophy is not preserved in popular accounts of it, introductions of a general kind, interviews with practitioners, philosophy-made-simple. The general reader needs for his own good to be in touch with the real stuff itself, as it is. Do you remark, cruel reader, that in the book in your hand there is some potted philosophy? Very true, Your Honour, very true.

Still, my potting of philosophy preserves some logic and argument, which is not entirely common, and anyway my potting is not offered as a substitute for the real thing. It has those other higher or lower aims itemized – to open up a kind of life, the academic or university philosopher's, by way of a good example or instance, and to see about explaining it. Do you now seize the opportunity to grump or complain, in connection with the first aim, looking into a kind of life, that while there can be different good examples of a kind of life, the one you are getting is not humdrum and respectable enough? Untypical beginning? Too many women? The court case? No doubt more adventures to come? That to be a useful example of the academic philosopher I should have to be still less of a real individual? The same thought has been troubling me.

But then you weren't promised a standard example. Would you really prefer one? In fact, could you really be supplied with one, something that would deserve the name? If you lift the covers of academic philosophers, you find many lives that are not humdrum, but crowded and colourful. Perhaps less uniformity is required of academic philosophers than of any other personnel in colleges and universities. As indeed I know, much lies behind the membership cards of we in the philosophical section of the Association of University Teachers.

To confine myself to standard eccentrics, there is my friend Timothy, who does good work on behalf of the rights of animals, and is also both a panpsychist and a vegetarian, presumably hardened to the little expiring sighs of the meatless steaks and the lettuce leafs. My colleague Arnold Zuboff has proved that we are all one person, and defied many Korean fortune tellers to win through to his happy marriage to himself and others in Belsize Park Gardens. The envy of my small colleague Colin McGinn, also vegetarian, extended even to wanting to be Martin Amis. Several of my colleagues have private pasts much more vivid than their grey presents. To return to myself, isn't there a chance of finding out more from an extreme case? Do we not look for over-developed cases of things in order really to see the properties of the things? Is this not so with infections, abnormalities and other human conditions of interest?

Despite this pleading, it probably has to be granted by me in the end that there does exist something like a standard example of the kind of life in question, academic philosophy. You can try to get its protagonist in view. Mates early and once, stays out of trouble, thinks there's something in Wittgenstein, Senior Lecturer. It has to be granted, too, despite the thought about extreme cases, that you would in a sense learn a bit more about the philosophical life from this sort of thing. By definition, there are *more* philosophers in something like a standard category as against another, if maybe only a few. So let me retreat a bit. A kind of life, as we have been speaking of one, evidently itself consists in more particular kinds. It is a genus of which there are species, one of them being the more or less standard example – mates early and once, etc.

From me and my story, as I retreat to saying, you learn of the genus academic philosopher by first learning of one species of it – certainly with many other members than me in it. The species shares an awful lot with the other species of the genus, but not everything. What species is it? What general label goes on it? Maybe *Philosopher, academic, not much more than middle-sized, seeking culmination in mate, can think, likes things clear, mostly stands up for himself, feelingful, moralistic, not a prisoner of convention, not Conservative, imperfectly rational, hopeful.*

My writing of my prefaces to *Philosophy As It Is* was a pleasure, for a particular reason. The philosophical temper, that critical disposition with respect to cogency and truth that does not leave assumptions unexamined, comes in different forms. My own has on the whole been assertive or combative, not always genial, not always genteel. It has been a disposition to put a case directly and forcefully against views which to me have shortcomings all too evident. It has been close to an adversarial method. It has not been given over to understanding why strange things are said, or making a sympathetic entry into another's reasoning, but dedicated instead to displaying the strangeness, strangeness being next to falseness. The time has not yet come, if come it does, to repent this usual way of going on. If it can lead to error, it can also lead to truth. Do you learn less? Maybe.

Certainly there is an alternative. The method of empathy, to group several alternative things under that heading, is an agreeable one. There is a pleasure in a kind of amicable suspension of judgement, indeed suspension of disbelief. In fact this was my pleasure in writing my introductions. It was no less real for being owed to the good sense and good manners that require an editor not to cry down the wares he is offering to the reading public.

It was a pleasure of another kind to write my five introductory pages to Freddie Ayer's contribution to the book. This was his current view, laid out in *The Central Questions of Philosophy*, on the problem of the nature of sense perception or of our perceptual knowledge of the physical world. You could also call it, with reason, the question of our fundamental relation with reality. He had given up the unequal struggle to stand firm as a residuary legatee of the sense-datum theory of Locke, Berkeley and Hume, the doctrine that what is given to us directly in seeing and the like is only sense-data or phenomena, these being subjective or private images as distinct from objective things or physical objects themselves. Still, he understandably could not bring himself to embrace the idea on which he had hung the name of Naive Realism, that we are somehow or other directly aware of ordinary things. After all, he said and argued, those objective things by definition can be perceived by more than one person, and perceived by more of our senses than sight, and exist when not perceived at all – and in perception itself we are not aware of these three facts, least of all the last.

There was, he said, another way of conceiving our perceptual knowledge of the world. It involved the idea of direct awareness of stuff that was *neither* subjective nor objective, and also involved something called our *positing* of physical objects. Freddie's life was not one in which pride was constant, although some suspected so, with reason. But pride was never far off, and when he felt it, you couldn't miss the show. You couldn't miss it in connection with this final solution of his to the problem of the British Empiricists. If it seemed to me contrived, and not far enough from sense-data, I did not seek to unsettle or dent it in my introduction.

The words were written with a kind of affection, since he had indeed ceased to be Professor Ayer and become Freddie. I was 44 and he 66. At the last Joint Session of the Mind Association and the Aristotelian Society, he had read a paper, and I had asked some questions. We had then fallen in together nicely, ending a decade of at least coolness that began with the fracas about editing in the Senior Common Room. We now saw a certain amount of one another in London, whose social life he rightly rated above Oxford's. Some of his earlier friendships had worn down, his second marriage was ending, the one to the journalist and novelist Dee Wells, and he was in sight of retiring from his Oxford chair.

I did not find much difficulty in overlooking Freddie's usually being full of himself, his wonderful vanity and cocksure performances, sometimes his sour despair. There was a distinction you could try to keep in mind, that he was sometimes not full of himself exactly, but of the logic of what he was about to say. There *was* a difference there. I was pleased to be on familiar terms with England's Logical Positivist, and did not lose sight of the excusing boyishness of the vanity. Nor of his being a fighter, his humanity in politics, and, above all, the reasoned sense of his transparent philosophy. It did not matter a lot if, on speaking into the entryphone at the door of a gentleman's club, he could draw himself up and announce himself as '*Sir Alfred Ayer*', conceivably even '*Professor Sir Alfred Ayer*', thereby giving a passable imitation of being his own butler.

Someone else, the striking woman already mentioned, was at this time leaving her marriage to move into Keats Grove with me. Janet Richards had come to my eye in the course of my looking out for someone to write a philosophical book on feminism, in fact a philosophy of feminism. On further inspection and inquiry, when she had come to lunch at college, she was the very person. Dark-haired and tall, she wore a longish skirt of sort later learned to be her invariable uniform, made by herself.

Here was she who could regiment the outrage of the sisterhood into good sense. She came of an unworldly Unitarian family, her father being a minister of that faith – or at any rate denomination, since, as is well known, it believes in one God at most. She was independent-minded, another vegetarian. Her research as a graduate student in Oxford had been in the Philosophy of Science, which might give some stiffening to Women's Lib. These attributes, with the addition of a meandering girlishness, melancholy, some righteousness, and beauty, at least impressed me. Our state of feeling in Keats Grove issued promptly in a private language deriving from affectionate names for one another. We were Blossom and Bruin.

In this academic year, my sense of this and others of my merits led me to distinguish myself from my colleagues, by making my third, fourth and fifth applications for an Oxford fellowship in philosophy, with the sixth following a year or so later. Having written two well-received books, and edited two others, might I not ascend to the dreaming spires? Might I not be an exception to the rule that fellowships in Oxford went to Oxford and Cambridge men, usually men younger than me? I already went to the spires to read papers and came away in good heart. Had I not heard of Oxford men, unable to face the unrarefied air of the outside world, who stayed on for years living off bits of teaching, put in for every fellowship going, and succeeded on their ninth application?

In addition to some chance of success, other things moved me in my campaign. There was the higher rational consideration that Oxford had a good deal of strong philosophy in it, by which I might profit. There was the lower rational consideration, of which you have heard before, that Oxford and Cambridge philosophers despite their very mixed merits got more of a hearing than strivers in other places. A further consideration was my uneasiness in our department in Gordon Square. If congeniality was the rule, and social relations were maintained, it seemed to me that the Readership and Freud episodes were with us still, alongside my residual insecurity and my adversarial method in philosophy.

My sharpest recollection of what moved me in my applications, however, is of something different. There was inside me, still, 18 years after sighting England's green and pleasant land, a captured person – a Canadian lad captured by Englishness. Oxford was a quintessence of it. How agreeable it would be to join the form of life that was The High and The Broad, college eccentricities, named staircases, High Table, and of an unexampled academic history. There was truth in this, but also dream. It was, perhaps, the last but one of my more or less impersonal dreams, the other having to do with inevitable progress in the decency of a people's politics. But I got none of the jobs. All, I think, went to Oxford persons, already known in the college in question.

In one case, my kindly local supporter put my fate down to my politics and in particular my recent impolitic letter to *The Times*. It doubted that the moral and political rot at Penguins had spread so quickly to the publishers Routledge, Macmillan and Heinemann, as reported. It also denounced a spot of McCarthyism in English academic life – a list of names and guilt by association. This, said my supporter, had earned me the malign resistance of Professor Hugh Trevor-Roper. He who could assert his influence across a lane from a greater college to a lesser, and later gave pause to his own career by authenticating Hitler's diaries, briefly, for *The Sunday Times*. Whatever the truth of the comforting speculation about his not authenticating me, the other reasons for my not being preferred were several. I had not set the philosophical world on fire. My demeanour could leave the impression of a good deal of principle, and not much promise of collegiality at High Table, or effervescence. I did not have on my side the maxim that has got as many persons elected to academic jobs as any other: better the devil you know, even the plodder.

These were aspirations unfulfilled. They stayed in my mind for a while, but not as weights. It was not necessary to be an Oxford don, only desirable. Nor, after the first discomfiture, did the judgements made in favour of my competitors fasten themselves on me as proofs of very much. There was too much going on in academic appointments, over and above purely philosophical appraisal, as intimately demonstrated to me by the mass interviews in Gordon Square and indeed promotions to Readerships. I did not feel unjustly treated by Oxford. This was the way things could go in a life otherwise fortunate.

The particular thoughts that at this time abstracted me from it, not that this was necessary, were on mind and brain in connection with deter-minism. Something was wrong with the rising orthodoxy of physicalism in the Philosophy of Mind with respect to the problem of the nature of consciousness and the problem of the mind–brain relation. It was not just that mind and brain are bound up together, but that the mind simply *is* the brain, that events of consciousness are brain events. First of all, the idea was unclear. In his celebrated piece 'Mental Events' reprinted in *Philosophy As It Is*, what did Donald Davidson mean by saying mind and brain were *identical*? What did he mean if he also said that he was *not* reducing mind to brain, not embracing Eliminative Materialism, not joining those Australians for whom conceiving the *Art of the Fugue* was nothing but a complex physical event – no sweetener for the pill? I had managed to write my brief preface without finding out.

When news came to me of the death of my eldest brother Loine, on about his 62nd birthday, I wrote to my sister-in-law Charlotte that he had succeeded in what was fundamental, the carrying forward a decent project with spirit. Loine Christian had exhausted himself early by good works passionately done. He was no mere presider at evensong, no possessor of a good benefice, but outside in the world, trying hard. What was needed outside in the world, at any rate in the Florida Keys, was parks for trailer-homes of hard-up families. He practised what he preached. Bee wrote to me of the funeral, and his sadness about not having had sufficient forbearance for our brother's ways, Loine having always had faith that the Lord would provide, often by way of the resources of his other servant Bee. I felt Bee had less to reproach himself for than I. Religion had divided me from Loine in feeling, and I had been slow to answer letters that presaged another visit to England, perhaps with the Full Gospel Businessmen of Florida.

Bee's generosity to me continued. The helpful loan for the roof garden of the house that did not save a marriage, Flask Walk, was being paid off by annual Christmas gifts from he who made it. A self-liquidating loan, said the accountant, a good kind to have. Some of my salary could go to first furnishings for Keats Grove, including a good table for the dining room. In January 1978 its full length could seat 20 for Kiarney's 18th birthday dinner, certainly vegetarian. Ruan, once Rooney, now took advantage of my foresight about names 15 years before and became John. Like his sister, he was no model pupil. They were notably, even wonderfully, unindustrious, to their parents' dismay. But then I had not been industrious myself, so there was hope.

Janet and I continued to fit our personalities together with some success, if not like clockwork, and the absence of Green Shoes made us mostly forgetful of the cloud over Keats Grove. We had an aspiration to social life of the highest kind, this having little or nothing to do with social class but being intellectual and literary, academic only in part. Freddie had taken up with Vanessa Lawson, on the way to her divorce from Nigel, a Conservative M.P. on his way to being Chancellor of the Exchequer. Happy in their new connection, Freddie and Vanessa came to large dinner parties at Keats Grove – Vanessa of the hieroglyphic profile, an Egyptian priestess of spirit and dash, she to whom men's eyes were captive. Peter Vansittart, novelist and presider over the Wednesday lunch club at Bertorelli's, came too. He corrected my English history and sought amiably to correct my politics. Eric Hobsbawn corrected *his* history once or twice, and my utopian socialism. He too was amiable, and did not exercise whatever authority attached to being an actual Communist. The sisters Antonia Byatt and Margaret Drabble, necessarily on separate occasions since their relations were imperfect, reflected on sensibility as against theory in literary criticism and on the depiction of men in the woman's novel.

At table, after a shortish period of chat to left and right, there had to be general talk, robust but not too serious discussion, preferably a happy hubbub. Nothing else would suit me. A lot of drink helped, and laying down an inflammatory proposition from the head of the table. I wasn't bad at that – not Samuel Johnson, whom I had in mind, but helped by having a better stock than he of outrageous propositions. He was limited to the idea that Shakespeare was overrated.

We passed September 1978 away, in a genial institution ready to make a special contribution towards my legal bill. This was the University of Lethbridge, in the province of Alberta in Western Canada. It also had the attraction of being rather to the side of the march of history – being a visiting professor in it could be rest and recuperation. My seminars on determinism were respectfully received, and the weekly public lectures in the public library, drawn partly from *Three Essays on Political Violence*, were reported at length in *The Lethbridge Herald*. Janet and I got on well, despite an incident or two. My inclination to wine, a lot of it, had increased. We had a dispute in the car and I cuffed her, an action rightly described by exactly that verb, but a disgrace remembered by me thereafter even if it did not reduce her dignity. She allowed that she had been infuriating, and our satisfaction with our month of retreat was not greatly reduced by this Bruinousness.

On returning to London, I arranged through an intermediary, and without alerting Michael Seifert and Michael Tugendhat, to meet Green Shoes. I would try yet again to come to some agreement. It is possible to think, remarkably, that what moved me was not only self-preservation, but an aversion to hostility, a consternation about it as distinct from its consequences. My adversary was not so averse. On a morning in October, our two sides assembled in Chancery Court, bearing our bundles of documents, including Helen's firm and graceful statement on my behalf and Johnny's equally true one. It transpired outside the door of the courtroom that my two Michaels, and the legal personnel on the other side, were further convinced that a deal had to be done.

The negotiations between my side and the other side consisted in the main in calculations of a kind. They concerned the worths of parts of 4 Keats Grove and my free accommodation there for three years. Also the sizeable damages that had been secured by Jack Fielding against Green Shoes and conceivably against the putative partnership, and many other variables. The figures were not easy to master even for the legals. So I was thrown into unhappy consternation when Michael Seifert absented himself early, and left my side playing one man short, indeed playing one man against three. Having prided myself on having a solicitor of progressive political views, I might in consistency have accepted that there could be higher calls on his services. On that occasion, if memory serves, it was the embassy of North Vietnam.

If the partnership agreement back in May 1975 had gone ahead without trouble, I would have got my flat, sharing of the rear and front gardens, and half the freehold of the whole property, for something like £13,000. The negotiations in Chancery Court resulted in my getting 150-year leaseholds on my flat, the front garden, the studio in it, this being a domicile on its own but with a legally immoveable tenant in it, the perambulator store off the front porch of the main house and three years of free accommodation, for £24,000. In sum, I would be paying out a good deal more for what seemed not quite so much more.

You could look at the thing differently, not in terms of the original partnership agreement, but in terms of what my situation had been on my arrival that morning at Chancery Court. There was a 20 per cent chance of disaster. It would be financial, certainly, something like £25,000 to pay as the loser in legal costs for both sides, and also back rent and damages. Departure from Arcadia too, and no other place to live, and no money to hand to buy one. The disaster would also have been yet more personal. It would have been no good at all for a moralistic philosopher to turn out a cad in the eye of Mr Justice Slade. I could also reassure myself by another way of looking at the adventure. Jack Fielding was now selling his flat for £54,000, doubling his money. You could add up the 1978 market values of the four items I was getting, forget about having lived for nothing in a sought-after place for three years, and come to a figure something like £62,000. Getting that for £24,000 was all right.

Finally, what about moral vindication, on which I was exceedingly keen? What did the settlement worked out by the legals say about that? It is certainly true that I cared more about this question than any other. You could look in the three ways at what I had got and be morally self-satisfied, vindicated. They showed how I had been judged by well-informed and experienced persons. These persons were my solicitor and barrister and also those of Green Shoes. It is not only judges on benches who judge us, but those lower legals who may or may not appear before the judges. Lawyers are a little too inclined, for my liking, to say they are not in the morality business. In fact, what solicitors and barristers demand on behalf of their own clients and, perhaps more important, concede on behalf of the clients on the other side, is plainly influenced by their own moral senses and their anticipation of a judge's.

Not being so persuaded of the law's morality in all respects, I would not have been moved by their judgements about something else that remained unresolved. In this year, I did try to come to an actual verdict of a general kind on what now seemed the terrible fact of the time. This was political violence of the Left, not yet given the name of terrorism. An invitation had come to read a paper to a UNESCO conference in Paris. Mine was 'Four Conclusions About Violence of the Left'.

It began by giving attention to two ways of approaching this violence. One, issuing in a prohibition of it, was by way of the old claim that there exists an actual social contract, nothing imaginary about it – an obligation on each of us in virtue of our having by our conduct somehow agreed to our societies. The most that could be said of this, it seemed to me, was that we make no contract or agreement with anyone or anything, but do raise an expectation that we will be law-abiding. And whether we need to satisfy the expectation must surely depend on the alternative, conceivably law-breaking that reduces great misery and great injustice. I dwelt on the misery and injustice, rightly, and added to my statistics some human testimony from a black mother, without clean water or enough food for her children, but thankful to God for Cokes to perk them up.

Might a general prohibition on violence be based instead on what Stuart Hampshire called *moral necessities*, these including things that in humanity simply must not be done or tolerated? His estimable moral passion, regrettably, could not avoid the fact that moral necessities could conflict with one another. Those having to do with violence could conflict with others having to do with the misery and injustice. My paper's first conclusion was that the only possible way of drawing a conclusion about political violence of the Left was the method of attempting to judge between alternatives, taking into account the well-being or lack of it of all persons without exception in whatever societies. Nothing else had even a chance of being decisive. The second conclusion, for which explicit argument was given, was that in the end this method, a kind of Consequentialism, would not work either. Mainly because of difficulties having to do with probability judgements, a moral agnosticism was forced upon us.

The third conclusion was that violence aimed at ending misery and injustice, as against violence of the Right, should have somewhat different treatment. For example, the IRA should have what was denied to it, the possibility of stating its claims in public forums in Britain. The fourth conclusion, again about the misery and injustice, was that there was no avoiding a judgement on the individuals who are the reality of governments and sovereign states. For one thing, *they* have a unique possibility of improving lives without recourse to violence, and they fail.

Consider the agnosticism that could neither justify nor condemn violence of the Left generally, my second and main conclusion. Did it have in it what has been mentioned before, a self-regarding caution, an idea of self-preservation? It did, and also some moral resolution. In addition to those, it also had belief in the argument in it. Despite the discovery a while later of a confusion in the piece that galled me, I did not lose my belief. Nor did I give in to what had to come to mind, another *reductio ad absurdum* argument. That was the idea that if judgement between alternatives does not issue in an answer to a large moral question, that method must thereby be thrown into doubt. Not so. It was a dark possibility that the only real method does not always work. There cannot be a moral obligation to find what does not exist.

Writing my paper for Paris was fitted into a life that was growing still fuller. Christmas of 1978 had in it both the vegetarian feast at Pauline's and also festivities with Janet's sister and her rescued greyhounds in a Derbyshire village. Nor was life without incident. Michael Dummett, a distant ally in connection with the University of London's lodgings bureau, and who had been elected to Freddie's old chair in Oxford, gave the Shearman Lectures at University College in January. These were London's most prestigious visiting lectures in philosophy, and after the first one there was a large dinner for him at Richard Wollheim's house. I got drunk, and fell into what was supposed to be amiable and maybe Johnsonian badinage with the guest of honour. It had to do with our respective anti-racisms – and, conceivably, the superiority of one that was based in a good politics rather than Catholicism.

His final eruption was Vesuvian, I would not apologize, women cried, and the dinner party ended in disarray. In the morning, I regained my senses and a fragmentary but all too sufficient recollection of what had happened, which was that I had been stupid and awful. I delivered an abject note of apology. He came to my room in college and generously did all that was possible to put things right. He reported Richard's view, which took me aback and aggrieved me, that I would mainly be concerned about possible effects on my career. He said there would of course be absolutely none of those. Janet was slower to forgive. As you will gather, wine was in my life. Would it, despite my resolution, help me into more incidents?

There was good cheer to be had, soon after, from Kiarney's results in the Oxford entrance examinations. Wisely choosing papers not requiring knowledge of any syllabus, but only innate reason, she won an open scholarship to the other University College. It was not good cheer that was to be had from Mrs Thatcher's victory over Mr Callaghan of the Labour Party in May, but not great dismay either. Her performance as St

Francis of Assisi in her victory speech, bringing harmony where there is discord and hope where there is despair, was comic but not reassuring. But she would not be on the stage long, or do any great damage to the theatre. There had been Conservative governments before in my experience of England. If they had slowed more the slow rise of decency, or even stopped it for a while, they had not done more than that. The 1979 election was disappointing, not serious.

The first-floor flat at Keats Grove was, as we said, done up. In the extensive renovation no walls were knocked down, rightly, and all walls got back their dado and picture rails. Each room took on two shades of the same colour, a slightly lighter one above. My life of academic industry, affected slightly more by failure in the wine resolution, took me to or back to more English and Scottish universities to read papers. Sometimes they were on political violence but now more often on mind and brain – on which light was also shed for Trinity College Dublin and at Queen's in Belfast. I was invited on tour more often, it seemed to me, than any of my colleagues. The editing of series of books went on apace, still less delayed by the idea that it was necessary to read every word of the manuscript of a good author. More invitations arrived to take up professorships in America. California in particular had no charm for me.

But now, seven years after having become a Reader, and being at the top of the salary scale for Readers, and being 46, might I not think of becoming a professor without leaving Gordon Square? Having mentioned the thought once before to Richard, might it not be time to do so again? Some other departments had more than one professor. Along with named chairs such as the Grote, and other established chairs attached to the headships of departments, there were personal chairs. These were brought into existence for persons thought to deserve them and went out of existence with their departures from the college.

The idea of being a professor, along with its charms, had a drawback. It was that Johnny Watling was my senior, had been my teacher, was my friend, and was not a professor. I told him of my idea, which did not noticeably dismay him. He too would be a candidate, he said. He would be writing papers, and would be taking forward his book on the Philosophy of Science.

Richard, when we had a chat, said he would turn my idea over in his mind. It struck me in the course of his sentences that he might do that for quite a while. Indeed, given our history, that seemed probable – might he do it for some years? Something as huffy also occurred to me. University College, enlightened institution that it was, had a good promotions policy. It took into account that a member of a department could get it into his head that his claim to promotion was not seen so clearly by his Head of Department as natural justice required. In that case, if the member did not mind paying whatever penalty attached to forwardness, he could simply propose himself to the college for promotion. His claim would be considered by the Provost and the promotions committee without reference to his Head of Department. I said to Richard several times in the course of our chat that if he was reluctant about singing my praises, I could sometime save him the trouble by doing it myself.

As the academic year ended, so began a coda to *Honderich v. Green Shoes*. My consternation about the extent of my solicitor's absence from the negotiations in Chancery Court had been considerable, and my grievance against Michael had persisted. The settlement, embodied in an order of the court, had needed to be translated into an ordinary leasehold agreement between freeholder and leaseholder. This happened only in September 1979, eleven months after the settlement, with a certain effect. To the £24,000 to be raised mainly by a mortgage, but also by a further useful loan from Bee on the same brotherly terms as before, £3,000 had to be added for interest payments. I took Michael to have been less than efficient in making the leasehold agreement. Also, I would have preferred the slight psychological–legal advantage in neighbourly relations of owning half the freehold as well. Slowly I got into a temper. On account of his negligence he would have to reduce his final bill to me for his services. Looking back, it comes to mind that he may have had a good sense of something. It was that my dismay about my own decision not to fight on to a famous victory in Chancery Court, which existed alongside my satisfaction in the settlement, had as much to do with my temper as any dilatoriness by him.

I did not have so good a sense of myself. I would need a new solicitor to deal with my old one about his bill. Best to have a solicitor who would be zealous in the matter, not too inhibited in setting about a brother lawyer. Who could be more zealous, in dealing with the solicitor to the Communist Party, than the solicitor to the Queen? A capital idea. The services of Farrer & Co. were acquired without difficulty. Maybe they thought a Reader in Philosophy at the godless college of Gower Street would be yeast to leaven the heavy dough of the rest of their clientele. Michael's bill, by means of their negotiations, was in the end reduced by £825. Their bill to me for this, not without some forewarning, was £833. So ended, not to my credit, my first brush with the law.

As a result of philosophical and other distractions of which you know, the products of my attention to determinism and freedom by the year 1979–80 were three published papers and less than half a manuscript for a book. The latter pile of pages, because it had to do with the nature of the mind, was inconclusive. One thing now added to my output was a proof of the continuing need for my book, a proof that I had not been overtaken by time. Following immemorial academic custom, this took the form of a review of someone else's book on the same subject, inconsiderately finished on schedule. My proof of the necessity of myself, more particularly, was a very long review in the journal *Mind* of two books by Anthony Kenny, a friend to the Penguin Plotter and now Master of Balliol.

His basic idea was that a person's mind consists in capacities or powers involving the creation and use of symbols. In the main, the mind consists in the two capacities of the intellect and the Will. This basic idea was not left as the ordinary unreflective notion that the mind is something that issues in thought and in action. Rather, capacities or powers in general were given philosophical attention. A thing's power to do something was said in a philosophically traditional way not to be the thing itself or an ordinary property of it, say a knife's sharpness. Nor, of course, was its power what it did, cut the bread. Hence the mind was not the brain or its properties, or the resulting pieces of thinking, feeling and acting, but something more elusive, something in line with our inclination to think that powers lie or lurk in a thing.

The plot was thickened by taking the Will not to be a natural power, like the power of a knife to cut bread, but rather a special kind of power, rational power. In the case of a natural power to do a thing, the thing happens when all the conditions of its happening are in place. Bread gets cut. But with a rational power everything can be in place, everything necessary and sufficient to do the job, and then the thing may or may not happen – it's uncertain. The decision to go down to Sidcup may be made, but it may not. The Will, in short, is really free.

The two books, said I, were admirable and wonderfully elaborate attempts to make us think again about a doctrine attractive to a strain of strong philosophers, reaching back through the mediaeval churchmen to Aristotle. The books gave the doctrine new definition. They were audacious, ingenious and reasoned. Also, in all respects save the slight one of not identifying the mind with the brain, they were dead wrong.

For a start, whatever you went on to say of a power to cut bread generally, the knife's power just *was* its sharpness, that plain property of it. The power of the knife was just a property of it such that when other conditions were satisfied, such as the bread's being in the right place, the effect was sliced bread. This power was not even residually mysterious, despite our inclination to think so. It was just part of a possible causal circumstance. What of the idea of a rational power? In this case, given the uncertainty of the upshot, there evidently was no such causal connection. What could this idea be? When you subtracted a decent understanding of causal connection from an idea of power, what was left? My answer was not self-doubting. 'The idea of a rational power is no more than the denial of connection together with the gesture of putting something in its place, which gesture comes to nothing.'

There was a lot more like that in my 13 pages of admirable, audacious, ingenious and reasoned stuff about the books *Will, Freedom and Power* and *Free Will and Responsibility*. Being wholly committed to the ideal of philosophical truth, I was not restrained by the worldly consideration that the second book, to speak a little grandly, had been published by me. By my invitation to the author, it had come out from Routledge & Kegan Paul. If my 13 pages showed me to be above petty propriety, they also demonstrated something mentioned before in these pages – no great inclination to enter hopefully into a way of thinking not one's own. It was not as if the doctrines in question, by the way, in the judgement of my private soul, were not more or less admirable, audacious, etc. The trouble was that they were also a disaster. This being philosophy, they could seem to be both.

Life also included lectures given by me at the University of Leiden in the Netherlands. There I was pleased to appear a week in the wake of the French Marxist Louis Althusser, the previous visiting lecturer, who had the special disability of being mad. If memory serves, I was a week or two in advance of the English Marxist Jerry Cohen, my learned colleague at University College. With him I was on intimate terms that included rivalry, the latter accompanied by our disavowals of ambition, mine less fervent. He was, as it seemed, yet more industrious than I, being in the department not only on Saturday mornings but also on Saturday afternoons. Certainly we were confidantes, somewhat deceptive ones. The deceptiveness was not only the effect of our rivalry.

It seemed to me we sometimes played to one another's curiosity, chose to satisfy expectations, or said what the other wanted to hear, and sometimes in the course of this might preen. He let me know about the wonders of Jewishness, and how certain he was to vote for the Jewish candidate for any lectureship, and the attraction of *shiksas*. Ancient Philosophy, in my usage drawn from our boyhood past at the movies, was Loony Tunes. I also had something to say, I now dangerously report, on the general subject of women, and my having been with a lot of them. If he got no details, I could favour him again by performing the locker-room jocularity that women were, among other things, *tarmac*. Something rolled over or landed on in the course of life's journey. My confession costs me less than some will say it should, certainly some in the sisterhood. About my relationship to women, have I not got enough things to say for myself on the other side?

In my eyrie on the Saturday mornings, the editing of series of books did indeed go on apace. For Penguin, in accordance with John Stuart Mill's ideal of tolerance of all opinions, a work was commissioned by me to leave some written trace of the passing moment of Conservatism in British politics. It would be by Dr Roger Scruton at Birkbeck College, the worthy night school of the University of London. It now proved to be more possible, too, without abandoning high editorial standards, to see the worth of manuscripts of colleagues and friends. Malcolm Budd was a Cambridge man who had been taken into the department some years before. Like Wittgenstein, he was fastidious in the casualness of his costume, and not given to careless engagement in philosophical discussion. His *Music and the Emotions: The Philosophical Theories*, despite his inability to choose between them, could honourably be accepted for the Routledge list. So could another of Timothy Sprigge's works for Penguin, this being *Theories of Existence*. Alastair Hannay, now in Oslo, could be invited by me to throw whatever light was possible on Kierkegaard, a lot as it turned out, in the series *The Arguments of the Philosophers*.

Robert Fogelin's *Wittgenstein* would come out in paperback. Its pages, sadly, would still have the appearance of being typewritten rather than printed, as the result of a momentary economy in production at Routledge. When *Wittgenstein* had first appeared in hardback, as fortuitously comes to mind, Anthony Kenny had not been keen on Robert's somewhat deflationary account, and mused in his review that it was a good thing that the manuscript had not actually been published.

Having settled into monogamy with Helen until towards the end, and resolved successfully to resist the temptations of undergraduates, I now found myself in something like conjugality with Janet. She was more of a homebody than Helen, and had impressive collections of pliers and other household items. I seemed to be engaged in what it had taken the genius of Wittgenstein to draw to our attention, this being *a form of life*, previously known only as a way of life. It was complete, it seemed, without legal marriage, which institution was not necessary and for that reason not mentioned. Vegetarian dinners with the Watlings ran true to the form established over 20 years, somewhat adjusted to suit the style of my new hostess. Helen and I met for innocent lunches, my affection for her undiminished and my guilt touched by her reports of her new connection.

In December 1979 a Christmas party was given at Keats Grove, of an academic sort. There was an immense tree, the rooms were festooned with greenery from the garden and poinsettias fashioned from red tissue paper. Richard's urbanity with respect to the brass frowa caskets was consummate, his fastidiousness virginal. Along with Hidé Ishiguro, there was my colleague Bill Hart, a Harvard man who had come to us by way of his first teaching job at Ann Arbor, Michigan. His *curriculum vitae* revealed he was Wilbur Dyre Hart III. He was still more severe than required by this history, and by his duties as formal logician in our department, but capable of some geniality on special occasions. Also capable, as you will eventually come to hear, of what might be called acerbity. It was a good party. Might there be another next year? Might it become a fixture in a better part of the social calendar?

In the second term of the academic year, from Christmas to Easter, I turned up to read a paper to the philosophy societies at four British universities, thereby coming close to the goal of having read papers in all of them, without recourse to the known method of inviting the invitations. The paper this term was about the problem of justice and more particularly equality, on which subject my mind was at last made up.

Could equality, equal shares of something, be a good thing in itself? Could it be that there was an intrinsic moral recommendation in the bare fact of relationship between people taken by itself, the fact that their situations were in some way the same? The answer was no. One thing that helped you to see so was thinking, not about levels of income or power or whatever, but about levels of *well-being* – this being the product of satisfaction and frustration of desires and aspirations of all sorts, including the frustration of seeing someone else being better off than you, also known as the experience of relative deprivation or the pain of envy.

Compare, said I, two possible situations, the one where all are at the same decent level of well-being, and the one where they are at different but higher levels. Was it not clear that it would actually be irrational or self-hurting for *anyone* to prefer the first situation, and thus that sameness or equal shares could not be a good in itself? Equality in something or other often *was* a good, and very important too, as in the case of 'one man, one vote'. But it was a good in virtue of leading to something else, in the end to well-being. With well-being, plainly, an inequality could be better.

The real Principle of Equality and the foundation of egalitarianism, of which you heard some details in the self-revelations at the beginning of this book, was not aimed at producing a sameness. The tradition of egalitarianism, despite its name, had not been aimed at producing a sameness. The Principle of Equality was not directed against people being unequal in well-being, but against some people being at such a level of it that they were miserable, in distress or suffering. The reason it depended on for giving food to the starving was not that they had less of it than the well-fed, but that they were starving. What was good in itself was not making them *like* the well-fed, but replacing the pain of hunger by the good life of having food. It was just a calumny to suppose that the tradition of egalitarianism had an aim which might have been perfectly realized by the equality of universal disdain, or burning down all the schools.

The Principle of Equality was indubitably the supreme moral principle. We could have no higher purpose than making well-off those who were badly-off by way of certain policies specified in the principle. The policies were (1) increasing the total means to well-being, (2) transferring means from the better-off without affecting their well-being, which certainly was possible, (3) transferring means which did affect their well-being, but not thereby increasing the number of the badly-off, and (4) reducing the demands for rewards on the part of those who really do make larger contributions to the means to well-being – all of these policies involving certain rules of equality, notably 'one man, one vote'.

I remain proud of this plain thing. It skates over a lot, certainly, including matters that have exercised political philosophers since. Yes, there is a small problem about the imaginable case where a few members of a society, very odd ones, can only be kept from being miserable by every day getting a new surfboard made of gold, and hence need a relatively immense share of the society's resources to be saved from their misery. Yes, there are wasters of resources, and yes there are the lazy. As with any principle, there are in fact a hundred difficulties to be resolved. Attend to them we must, which we can do while making sure we are still marching in the right direction, behind the right flag. As my piece in *Mind* on my principle said, a good flag is not of an uncertain colour. Also, you should arrange to keep it flying while tying your shoelaces.

It is a pity that my own personal marching at this time, however much or little directed by the Principle of Equality, was in one way too expeditious. *Three Essays on Political Violence* had had in it essays of which you have heard, pertaining to our obligation to be law-abiding, and democracy and violence, and such things as inequalities in lengths of lifetime. Since then there had been my ruminations in Canada on acts and omissions, and my conclusions in Paris on violence of the Left. The five pieces now went quickly into the new book *Violence for Equality: Inquiries in Political Philosophy*.

If I had not been so keen to make a further attempt at securing immortality by authorship, and had waited a month or two before despatching the manuscript to Penguin, it would also have had a foundation. That would have been my piece on The Principle of Equality.

My reviewers did not discern that my book was, if not floating on air, in need of more support. As before, the reviewers were many. Save for some neutrals, they were at least congratulatory. *The Times* said that I swam strongly against the current, and *The Observer* that I had caught up to Hannah Arendt. As for the philosophy journals, the man in the *Canadian Journal of Philosophy* extended his Critical Notice to 26 pages. He was enthusiastic, evidently not gestating his own book on the subject.

There were also interviews with the author. The one in *Corriere della Sera*, the Italian newspaper, recorded my resolve to believe something. It was that despite Mrs Thatcher's selling off the nationalized industries and increasing the National Health Service's charges for medicines, the long-run tendency of history was to the Left. *The Guardian* alerted its readers to what could be read inside it by putting my photo at the top of its front page. In the measured despatch from Gordon Square, there was a certain amount about Dr Honderich's height, history, marriages, attic room, pacing, and especially his bottle-green suit. Several of my colleagues were not mollified by the despatch's discovery of an inconsistency between my egalitarianism and my standard of living. As reported on the grapevine, they found me unseemly in having got my picture on the front page.

Nor were other appearances in the press taken as only redounding to my credit. In Ghana as external examiner for a fifth year, I came to admire Flight Lieutenant Jerry Rawlings, for good reason. He, by a revolution, had rescued his country from the army generals who had become rapacious, and then had promptly arranged a democratic election. He was, they and I said, the saviour of his people. My own feeling for him had not been reduced, when I met him for the first of several discussions, by his possession of a copy of *Violence for Equality: Inquiries in Political Philosophy*.

It was to the lunch club at Bertorelli's in Charlotte Street that some other publicity was owed. This gathering every other Wednesday had as another member Mr Peregrine Worsthorne. He was still the voice of true Conservatism in *The Telegraph*. We had talked one week about a common idea of the day, that the Thatcher government lacked compassion. Perry took this not to be the very first of governmental virtues. But, on reading Roger Scruton's *The Meaning of Conservatism*, he was taken aback by the direction in which this other standard-bearer of his party was heading. In *The Spectator*, he wrote that the book was a plot, my plot in my role as the distinguished Marxist philosopher. I had contrived to get published this version of Conservatism, which he guardedly associated with Fascism, in order to discredit the Conservative Party. I wrote a letter to *The Spectator*, happily admitting to have never yet buckled down to reading a page of Marx, and Perry gave a graceful apology in reply. When we next met, we did so as friends.

When I kept my nose to the philosophical grindstone, the result was again unseemly. You have heard something of the interesting view of Professor Elizabeth Anscombe on the nature of effects. These were taken by her to be mysterious items that may or may not happen when their causes are complete, very like Anthony Kenny's rational powers. It was she who was chairman of the Cambridge Moral Sciences Club when I came to read a new and lengthy paper that touched on causation. My temper was uncertain, which fact had to do with an unconnected subject – Janet's new idea that feminist independence required that we should carry forward our lives not in one domicile but in two, the second being more hers. Professor Anscombe announced at the start of the large meeting that recent papers to the Moral Sciences Club had been too long. Maybe she remembered that Wittgenstein once shared his thoughts with it for four minutes. So I should stop not in an hour or so, the usual time allowed, but in 20 minutes.

I did not agree, she stopped me on the dot of 20 minutes, and we fought, ostensibly about causation. It went on for 40 minutes, after which, by audience request, I read the rest of my paper. She was a bear maddened by having been made a moment's fun of by me in print recently for its view of effects. On this occasion true to one of my designations in the private language at Keats Grove, I was of the particular species *Ursus Arctos Horribilis Ord*. As a good Grizzly, I gave better than I got. However, this history was put right in the official minutes of the meeting, read out to the next one by a loyal undergraduate. Myles Burnyeat, now himself a professor in Cambridge, protested about the falsification, as did others, and invited me to make a formal protest. It didn't seem necessary. I remain vanquished in the minutes of the Moral Sciences Club.

Would I succeed with the last of my unphilosophical endeavours in this academic year? Freddie had been knighted ten years before and, like me, took himself to be due for promotion. Would he not perform well in the House of Lords? Neither he nor Vanessa suggested this to me, but it was in the air. He also had a rueful memory of having been superior with Mrs Thatcher at a party but said he had not insulted her. Vanessa said he had. Surely this did not guarantee failure? Having learned something of the arcane machinery of peer-making from Isaiah Berlin, I invited the support of philosophers and grandees. The Ceremonial Officer wrote to me that Sir Alfred's distinction would be brought to the attention of the Prime Minister at the appropriate time. No doubt it was, and, whatever else is to be said, no doubt the Prime Minister's memory of Freddie did not fail her. Knight he remained.

12

MIND AND BRAIN ETC., ANATHEMA

It was a distinct relief to begin the new term with no obligations to write more political philosophy, and in particular more on political violence. Also, did I not have an actual disproof, every philosopher's satisfaction, of rising doctrines about the nature of consciousness and its relation to the brain? These mushrooms were to the effect that the mind does not just go with the brain but is identical with it, that conscious or mental events *are* physical events. A first and essential bit of the disproof was just the fact that there was something different to being conscious. As my undergraduate lecture audiences were reasonable enough to accept, the room had come to contain a different kind of fact, missing overnight if there were no mice, when the first person came through the door that morning.

We knew this, although there was no satisfactory *analysis* of consciousness as yet, because we all had a grip on it, a grip of the special nature of our own experiences. An experience in itself was partly a matter of something that led such philosophers as Descartes to talk too grandly of an inner subject, an ego or a self. It was better to be more restrained and think instead of a subjective aspect of an experience – and also of the experience's particular content, say of Richard's blue jeans brought back from America, the two aspects being somehow interdependent. This subjectivity of consciousness, whatever more needed to be said of it, was evidently not in itself a physical property like weight, being an electrical impulse, or transmitting a chemical substance.

The main idea in Identity Theories of mind and brain, as remarked, was that a conscious or mental event, an event with the property of subjectivity, was identical with a brain event. But what did that come to? Certainly it was the opposite of something called dualism, regularly condescended to in the Philosophy of Mind and a source of satisfaction to those to whom a superior understanding had been given. But what was this dim dualism? To me there was a standing disgrace in the Philosophy of Mind in that the advocates of Identity Theories did not slow down to tell us what was actually meant by saying the conscious event was identical with the brain event – and hence what they understood by the opposite doctrine, dualism. In talking of identity, did they mean that the two things always occupied the very same space? No, partly because there could be two things there. Instead of making their meaning clear, they *gestured*, sometimes using highly theoretical notions acquired from their brethren in the Philosophy of Science.

On reflection, all that Identity Theorists could usefully mean by their equation was what the philosopher Leibniz, an honorary Englishman, said was meant by saying that anything was numerically identical with something else. This was that the first thing had all and only the properties of the second. In which case, there was a first question to be answered by Identity Theorists. *What* properties were had by the conscious event said to be identical with the brain event? Or, if you like, what properties were had by the brain event? There were different answers, issuing in two kinds of theories.

(1) The first answer was that the conscious event had only the property or properties of subjectivity. But this gave us absurdity, since it issued in the conclusion that the brain event involved only subjectivity – nothing of electrical impulses and transmitted chemical substances. This was the madness of mentalizing the brain. Things were just as bad if you started at the other side of the equation, more naturally for an Identity Theorist, and said the brain had only neural properties. That was the absurdity of Eliminative Materialism. You might emphasize, of course, that those neural properties functioned as causes and effects, thereby embracing Functionalism. It was still the brash nonsense of neuralizing the mind, making our consciousness into just cells, taking it to consist only in neural facts and nothing of subjectivity.

(2) There was another answer to the question of what properties were had by the conscious event. It was better, in fact innocuous. You could say the conscious event had *both* the property of subjectivity and also

neural properties. Indeed, that seemed to be what was in the minds of such sensible persons as Professor Davidson. You escaped the madnesses this way. But what did saying that the conscious event *was* the brain event come to now? This was obscure, but presumably the answer was that the property of subjectivity was had by some *one* event or thing that also had the neural properties.

If so, there seemed room for some uncomfortable self-reflection on the part of the sensible persons. Clearly a dualism of two kinds of properties remained when the dualism of two events had been discarded. This deserved the name of being a Dualistic Identity Theory. If dualism was awful, if there were problems about the relation of conscious events to brain events, as indeed there were, these very problems were inherited by this second kind of Identity Theories, the sane ones. These were now problems, so to speak, about how the consciousness of one thing was related to the rest of its nature, problems not at all solved by saying the two attributes were of one thing.

This was the prideful start of the paper 'Psychophysical Lawlike Connections and Their Problem'. My friend Alastair Hannay honourably published it in his journal *Inquiry*. Yet more honourably, he gave over the rest of the issue to papers about it from four other philosophers. As you may gather from my title, my general idea about the mind–brain problem was that the important thing about properties of consciousness and brain properties was not that they were properties of one thing, which obviously in some sense they were, but that they went together simultaneously as a matter of law. As you have heard before, they were *correlates* – lawlike or nomological or nomic correlates. Two such properties, although not a causal circumstance and an effect, were to be explained along the same lines. In the simplest case of any two such items, what was true was that if one happened, then whatever else happened the other went with it. If a brain state happened twice, the same thought or feeling or whatever would go with it. If the thought or feeling didn't happen, the brain state wouldn't happen.

There was the problem of showing this was true, but this was not the problem mentioned in the title of my paper. That arose from also thinking that when what you could speak of as one conscious event caused another, and caused an action, this was just a matter of its neural properties. This derived partly from the good thought that anything

246

physical, say an arm movement, had to have a wholly physical cause. So it was just the neural nature of a first mental event, say wanting an olive, that caused the neural nature of a later one, deciding to reach for the bowl, and it was the neural nature of the later mental event that caused the reaching. Didn't the whole doctrine then fall into something more awful than dualism? Wasn't it a new instance of the momentary nineteenth-century delusion of Epiphenomenalism – that earlier mental as against neural facts are no part of the explanation of later mental facts, and both are no part of the explanation of our actions? That our conscious lives, as Thomas Huxley thought, are just steam given off while the real work is going on down below? Aided by baffling diagrams, and by my lawlike correlates being somehow necessary to one another, I struggled to escape the disgrace.

Five or six other papers, more work in the direction of my determinism book, would be coming out in the following year or so. Hard at it I was, harder than all my colleagues but Jerry Cohen, who was a bit behind because of being younger. Should my labours and merits not be as recognized in Gordon Square as presumably they were in 15 or 20 other institutions? In the last few years, these had written to me about their professorships and about whether I might fancy a change of scene.

A year or so ago Richard and I had had a chat and he had again begun to turn over in his mind the idea of my being a professor. This had had no noticeable effect, and six months later I had raised the matter with him again. He said he had spoken to the Provost of the college and the new Dean of Arts about it. Was I to understand from his chosen phrases that the Dean did not like my idea of my not waiting for my Head of Department to apply for me, and my singing my praises myself? This could be clarified – a note had gone off from me to the Dean of Arts asking to have a word. Somewhat surprisingly, no answer had come back. Having spent some time on college committees, I was no neophyte in academic conspiracy theory, in particular nobbling theory, and so had not speculated on whether the internal postal system was breaking down as a result of the financial stringency in the college. As it had seemed to me, battle between Richard and me had again been joined, if more decorously than in the past matter of my Readership and the Freud Chair.

Now he left me a note that he would not be making a recommendation to the college on my behalf in this academic year of 1980–81. He did intend in the next academic year to propose that all of Johnny, Hidé and I be made professors, which one or more of us might be in the academic year after that. Not being persuaded that the heavens would open and rain down chairs, and not being inclined to have a competition delayed until my competitors were better placed, I decided on the other option. This was proposing myself for promotion immediately without the aid of my Head of Department.

This alternative route for such malcontents as me, by college rule, was of course something that by definition did not involve one's Head at all. He by his inaction had already lodged his negative opinion in the matter, and was excluded from further activity in it. There was no need to bring one's forwardness to his attention, and it would save embarrassment. Also, there was something to be said for making it less likely that a member or two of the promotions committee or the Provost received a further negative opinion from him informally. I mentioned my forwardness to Johnny, who of course could take such a step himself, and was reassured that he would keep mine to himself, and that it could not unsettle our long friendship.

Sir James Lighthill, an eminence among the world's applied mathematicians and especially those who knew about fluid dynamics, and now our Provost, welcomed my *curriculum vitae* gratifyingly. He touched on the idea that I might follow in his august wake. When I met the Dean of Arts in the flesh some months later, he turned out to be easy to communicate with and funny. He was Professor Douglas Johnson, the historian of France, Gaullist but not Machiavellian, as good as his blue beret. He let me know that my referees had performed very well indeed on my behalf, as had two other philosophers unknown to me who were consulted. But the committee had taken my application to be possibly premature. Some members had noted that my main project, the determinism book, was unfinished.

As Christmas approached there was published *The Sceptical Feminist: A Philosophical Inquiry*, not by Janet Richards, as recently known, but by Janet Radcliffe Richards. New principles had required that women should not be bound by the surname of only their male parent. They also required something else. Janet had been saving up her Open University salary and had bought a house in Oxford, at 2 Glebe Street. Our official plan was to live together in both places, dividing each week between them. Aided by the growth of our private language, Bear, in which language our Citroen car was Special Paws, we seemed for the most part to be in a state of settled affection.

Jack and Penelope Lively were instructed by my consort on feminist justice, and Amartya and Eva Sen by me on economics being disguised politics, but contretemps in our socializing were few. We sought to accommodate our imperfections. One of mine in her view was my moods. These, of which more might have been said in this book, could be black and without hope. But to my mind they did not often issue in the punishment of others, being states entirely devoid of energy. Another of my shortcomings in her view was drink. Here, plead guilty I do, although grumpily and with inner reservations, and with the codicil that my usual daily consumption was about two-thirds of a bottle of white wine in the evening. Could I nonetheless succeed in this fourth attempt to live together in full and final connection with a woman?

What perplexed me more was still causation, and in particular the problem of effects. My struggle to perfect my definition of an effect was a struggle that itself had both an effect and several side-effects. The effect was a paper which again demonstrated my unerring eye for the catchy title. It was 'Causes and *If p, even if x, still q*'. The general idea behind it was the doctrine of which you have heard. An effect is something necessitated by a causal circumstance. The fact of necessitation is that if or since the circumstance occurred, even if other things had been happening, the effect would still have followed. The paper was about the detailed understanding of that conditional statement. I read it out to my colleagues in the Grote's room, and may unwisely have conveyed by my demeanour that I thought it impressive.

My colleague Peter Downing had thought about these subjects. He had now retired as a result of a terrible car accident, and was not the man he had been, not himself. He had not been present for my paper. In the course of a conversation about it later with Jerry Cohen, he got it into his head that I was giving him insufficient credit for his contribution to my thinking. He came to my room to accuse me, and to threaten legal action. There was an awful scene. The threat was made more significant by his having been a solicitor in the past. What was much worse was the imputation of philosophical theft. It was paralysing, and kept me awake at night. I chose a prudence not entirely honourable in footnotes

1 and 27 of my piece that would come out in the journal *Philosophy* for 1982.

The second side-effect of my struggle to perfect my definition of an effect was yet to come. What I got into my head was that my comrade Jerry had not been comradely in this instance. He had made at least a contribution to my discomfiture. That resentful thought became a grievance that was hard to shake off. In the end, it issued in another paper. This one was on Jerry, more particularly on his book *Karl Marx's Theory of History: A Defence*.

Marx's doctrine of historical materialism, as all used to know, was that history at bottom is matter or material facts and things rather than ideas or Hegelian spirit. Productive forces, such as the steam-engine, somehow give rise to economic class systems, such as capitalism. The class system of a society somehow gives rise to a superstructure, including political ideas, law, morality, religion, and so on. This doctrine seemed to face a great objection. Was it not true on the contrary that ideas, most piquantly the idea of Communism, sometimes gave rise to a class system? And that a class system affected productive forces, as in the Soviet Union?

Jerry's book was a defence of Marx, based on Aristotle's infuriating idea of teleological explanation. This, recently rechristened 'functional explanation', was different from standard causal explanation, where a cause explains its effect. The idea came from a thing's sometimes being explained by its goal or end. The sculptor's activity is partly explained by what he is aiming at. In fact it was the idea, if usually somehow obscured, that an effect can explain its cause. Do read that again, reader. The effect itself is supposed to do the explaining of the cause, as distinct from a thought of the effect or a desire for the effect or anything else whatever. This got into curious accounts of the mind, and curious defences of Free Will against determinism.

In Jerry's use of it, if I had him right, Marx's steam-engines gave rise to and explained capitalism in such a way as to allow for capitalism's also being explained by its effect on the steam engines. So with capitalism and the superstructure. Could that really be Jerry's idea? Well, what *was* clear was that the great objection to historical materialism was somehow being incorporated into that very doctrine by the means of the general idea of teleological explanation.

I did say in my article that G. A. Cohen in his admirable book had attempted to save Marx, and commanded great respect for his effort, and that he had given some definition to historical materialism that perhaps was missing before. But what followed was by my lights a refutation of ancient nonsense. The real truth about any so-called teleological explanation was of course not that a mentioned cause was explained by its mentioned effect, or in some other way was explained by that causal relation, or by being the cause of the effect. Rather, any such explanation was just a claim that there existed some *standard* causal explanation of something, which explanation involved the mentioned sort of cause and effect. Consider the so-called teleological explanation that a bird has hollow bones because that results in its flying better. Saying so is just saying that there exists a standard causal explanation, in this case an evolutionary one, that involves the mentioned sort of cause and effect.

Trying to write my sensible kind of thing into Marx would not save his doctrine of materialism but wreck it. I spare you the details. What needs to be confessed is that my well-known commitment to philosophical truth notwithstanding, I would not have published 'Against Teleological Historical Materialism' except for my feeling about Jerry's role in *l'affaire Downing*. I remain tolerably satisfied with the paper, but not proud of its origin in my passions.

The year did have calmer feelings in it. A sweet letter from my sister Mary in California did more to release my love for her, kept down too long by my aversion to her religion. Bee on a visit to London, although he pained me on the subject of what he called my sensitivity, again made me feel that I had a fatherly brother. Ruthie wrote me spirited letters, as endearing as her sister's, about Canada left behind by me. My son John, having finished school, had an article accepted by *The Guardian*. Kiarney, having been sent down from Oxford for want of attention to essays, wrote from Paris of her new resolutions. Pauline and I conferred peacefully and hopefully about these children. It was with some calm that I received the news that Richard would not be staying on in the department and in the Grote Chair until the obligatory retiring age of 65. He would be resigning early to go to America, but not just yet.

Michael Foot's having become leader of the Labour Party after James Callaghan was quite enough to persuade me to join it. I was not discouraged by the defection of the Social Democrats, or alarmed by Mrs Thatcher's new verb 'to privatize'. My review of books on equality in *The New Statesman* corrected Paul Johnson on the sexual depravity of the Marxist-Fascists. In Venice in September, the *vaporetti* routes were mastered by Janet, perhaps mistressed. Late at night in the *Pensione Accademia* I was delighted by her Boadicean routing, in her nightgown, with eyes flashing, of the Duke of Kent. No doubt he had not before kept a feminist awake by carousing, and perhaps has not done it since. The Dean of Arts Douglas Johnson liked the story when he had us round for drinks at his house up the hill in Hampstead.

Marx's doctrine of historical materialism was a determinism of sorts, one carrying particular implications for the future. Some of these were the digging of the bourgeoisie's grave by the bourgeoisie, the replacing of religion as the opium of the people by a better habit, and, to look a little further ahead, the withering away of the state. My brief contemplation of all this drama put me in mind of political consequences, possibly more modest, of my own growing doctrine of determinism. If such a thing came to be accepted as true, what would the consequences be for the main political traditions? An invitation had come from the editors of a rising American series, *Mid-West Studies in Philosophy*. An article on determinism and politics could go into the next volume. This would help our college promotions committee to a fuller appreciation of my international standing.

The article first asked if the truth of determinism was compatible with our being responsible for our decisions and actions in a particular way – in such a way as to give rise to our deserving various things for them, rewards in particular. Whatever might be the relevance of determinism to responsibility conceived in other ways, what about this responsibility involving desert? Having reported the results of looking into myself, at my feelings about deserving things, but not delayed long enough to provide a proof, I began with the proposition that determinism was incompatible with our deserving things. Determinism was inconsistent with the Principle of Desert. This was the principle that people are to have what they deserve, something different from and larger than a reason for punishment. In essence, this was persistence on my part in something of which you have heard,* the Incompatibilism of Kant and his regiment of successors, as against the Compatibilism of Hume and his regiment.

There followed an inquiry into the nature of the political tradition of Conservatism, taken as including political parties past and present in different countries, and also inquiries into the natures of Liberalism and of The Left. If you considered my eight distinguishing features of Conservatism, including anti-egalitarianism and enthusiasm for private property, was it not clear that this politics was founded on the Principle of Desert? Was this not discernible even in Conservatism's ideal of an organic, hierarchical, ordered or balanced society? That was the society of which it had been said by one Novalis, a German, that a citizen would pay his taxes to it in the spirit in which a lover gives presents to his mistress. As for Liberalism, did it not rest in good part on the Principle of Desert? And was it not clear, despite annoying complications, that The Left was different, and based mainly on nothing other than my own Principle of Equality?

There was opportunity, too, near the beginning of this year 1981–82, to continue my tutoring of Richard in the matter of John Stuart Mill. Richard had freely speculated that the principle of individual liberty in *On Liberty* was that an individual is to be left alone by the state and society so long as any harm he does to others is of a certain kind. Such harm depends not only on his action but also on *their* moral belief that his action is wrong. Morality-dependent harms, or anyway harms dependent in this way on wrong morality, are irrelevant and not to count at all. This would allow Mill, without going through any Utilitarian calculation of consequences, not to call the police on behalf of Sabbatarians upset by Sunday football. Nor would he have to call them on behalf of clean-living proletarians upset by the homosexual commune on their housing estate.

My piece in reply was as enlightened in opposition to the Sabbatarians and the proletarians. Its main line, though, was that for Mill their unhappiness was not irrelevant, but entirely outweighed by other considerations. My reflections started with a philosophical low blow,

* See pp. 9, 105, 182

that Mill in his ten statements of his principle in *On Liberty* never uttered a word of morality-dependent harms. Was this not odd? Might it not constrain us for a moment in our theorizing about his doctrine? In philosophy and in the interpretation of philosophers, though these were higher callings than science, was there really not a small place for Bacon's dictum, of which you have heard before, that the imagination needs to be hung with weights?

I was also not neglecting another of my postgraduate mentors, Bernard Williams. In my role as reviewer of philosophy books for *The New Statesman*, attention was paid to a collection of his papers, *Moral Luck*. This was the occasion when Bernard was preserved from his detractors by my taking him to be too clever by only an eighth. *Moral Luck* had in it the idea that one's being blameable in some course of action, say abandoning one's family to go off to Tahiti to paint, could depend on luck – on whether or not one then turned out to be Gauguin, a great artist. My feeling about this ethics was of course a simple one.

Being blameable was a matter of the state of mind of the agent when he acted, perhaps whether he was thoughtless or rash. How things turned out later, certainly, could affect our view of that earlier state of mind. Some years later, when a painter turned out to be wonderful, we could alter our view of what he could have taken to be possible when he left home. Luck, on reflection, was no part of this story at all. It didn't and couldn't get into the matter of culpability or the lack of it. This could be shown by special examples where the upshot didn't at all lead us to revise our thinking about agents' states of mind. Take the case where two awful thugs, neither leading the other, use their revolvers to play Russian Roulette with someone else's head. It would take a lot to persuade me that the lucky thug, whose gun did not go off, should have less on his conscience. To my mind, morality could well withstand the diminishing of it by the idea of moral luck. This was a good thing, since I was a moralized person alarmed by the idea that chance could make me bad, and apprehensive about use of the idea by others.

It was about this time that Richard let me know he would after all not be proposing to the college that each of Johnny, Hidé and I be given a personal chair. My response to his reasoned dilatoriness on my behalf, as in the case of the year before, was to intend to sing my own praises to the college myself – or rather, to inquire politically of the Dean of Arts and the Provost about whether they would listen. They were duly impressed by my having eight new papers accepted by journals or in press. Sir James Lighthill, he of the fluid dynamics, having read some of the papers himself, to check the philosophical dynamics, said my case was very strong. But my applying to be considered for a personal chair this year would be complicated by the matter of the election of a new Grote Professor, in anticipation of Richard's vacating the chair at the end of the year. Would it not be better to wait another year? The reasoning was not clear to me, but it was wise to agree.

On a Saturday night in November 1981, I was having my supper on my knee in the sewing room on the attic floor at 2 Glebe Street. My dissatisfaction with the Oxford life of Blossom and Bruin came into sharp focus. Our differences in the matter of domestic organization and other things had not been reduced by each of us having a primary space but increased. Also, if my affection for Janet was great, life was quite often a dark burden for her, and her burden was mine. After I took myself back to Keats Grove, we had melancholy telephone conversations, of which the result was her proposal of a trial separation, for a month.

My sadness, resignation and relief persisted until the day of the Christmas party, when I rang up Oxford, weeping, to beg her to come to the party and to give us another chance. This she did. The party went well, 41 merry-makers being present. Ronnie Dworkin, he of the jurisprudence, was august in the American way, being outranked only by Perry Worsthorne being yet more august in the English way. Colin McGinn essayed a vegetarian alliance with Kiarney, who had got the news that she would be let back into Oxford. It was all very sustaining. After the party, when all had gone except Janet, I was not at all in the way of weeping and begging.

Janet put it down to drink, but my mood persisted after she went back to Glebe Street that night. She rang up on New Year's Day to give me the news she had heard on the radio of The Second Coming, as Ghanaians spoke of Jerry Rawlings' second revolution. We did not speak of meeting. It *was* sad. We might have turned out to be the perfect couple. But this ending was unlike the terrible one with Helen. The main difference for me was that I was not guilty and not the first cause of our ending. Also, I had done well by this woman, as the acknowledgement page of her book really recorded after my small suggestion as to its revision.

The Grote Professorship of the Philosophy of Mind and Logic is named for George Grote, the author of a 12-volume history of Greece and a three-volume work on Plato, neither forgotten. He was a Philosophical Radical or all-purpose reformer along with Bentham and Mill and Mill's father James. He was also a founder in 1826 of University College, in which role he was aided by being a banker. The greatness of Grote was not transmitted to the early incumbents of the chair. Its rank and desirability now in 1982 owed much to Freddie's having sat in it. From Freddie it had passed to Stuart, and from Stuart to Richard, in each case, or so it was said, to the great surprise of the predecessor. Who would succeed Richard?

As always in the past, the chair would not be advertised, for whatever reason – one was the idea that distinguished people did not answer advertisements. Rather, a special college committee under the chairmanship of the Provost would survey what was known as the field, and in the end choose a winner. The committee would be helped in several ways, one being intimations from persons wishing to be considered as runners. In 19 Gordon Square, there were thoughts of several Oxford dons reputed to have tired of the spires, or to be attracted to the station of professor and cosmopolitan life. There were also speculations about a handful of rising American philosophers. Our concentration in the department, however, was as much on candidates within it. Richard had been an internal candidate. Stuart had been a lecturer in the department not long before his election.

Johnny was necessarily a candidate on account of his philosophical character, great acuteness and seniority, as well as affection for him. He was comradely, and not pushy. However, he had not written a great deal, his one book being a thin one on Russell, in an unlikely literary series. I was a candidate because I took myself to be one. So too was Jerry, on the same ground. If I had published most, and could bring myself to say to Jerry that he was premature in his ambition, others could usefully say to me that I was under something of a cloud in the department. I was divisive, no bringer of harmony, as shown by my earlier campaigns. There was a truth there, and also strategy.

Bill Hart, as you have heard, was our department's severe formal logician and propounder of well-formed formulae. He was also the department's representative on the Grote committee, having been thoughtfully nominated on our behalf to the Dean of Arts by Jerry, as he reported to us after the event. The other members were the Provost and professors of other departments. It was primarily Dr Hart's role to convey to the committee the general state of judgement and feeling in the department. In my awareness, there was at least tolerance of each of the three internal candidates, but also the opinion that it would be best to get someone new from outside, a rising star or anyway a breath of fresh air. In this opinion the internal candidates concurred, although not so hopefully as their colleagues.

Dr Hart's report to the committee included something different. What is said in private in university committees on these special occasions is rarely private for long. For dissemination of a thought, express it on a chair committee under conditions of strict confidentiality. What quickly reached my ear in March 1982 was that Dr Hart, in conveying the general state of opinion in the department, had included the well-formed proposition that my being the Grote was *anathema* to the department.

It caused me rage and grief. This was not abated by propositions some-times rehearsed in my mind over the following weeks – speculations, appearing in the guise of necessary truths, as to the explanation of his fatal sentence. Bill had become committed to psychoanalysis, gave occasional lectures on its philosophy. It was said he wished to become a practitioner of it himself. One of his utterances, heard occasionally in sonorous and slow American accent, but probably not by the committee, was 'Richard is my hero'. As the committee would not have known, his utterances in general were verdictive, to say the least, notably on the subject of some of our undergraduates not keen on formal logic. Moral leprosy might be diagnosed as their condition at our department meet-ings, not plainly light-heartedly. Our laughter was a bit uncomfortable. He was certainly odd. At dinner in his flat before Christmas, when he was in drink, had he not touched a burning match to the side of my forehead to extinguish it? It did me no great harm, but had led me to write in my diary 'He will do a lot worse'.

My reflections on the extinguishing of my hopes for the Grote Chair did not include much on my odd colleague's purely philosophical judgement on me, to which he had every right, or much on the philosophical judgements of my other colleagues. In fact, I could hope that most of the latter judgements were as temperate as their makers.

I gave up thinking about it all with the help of philosophy and Miranda Seymour.

She was compared by more admirers than me to Flora, the goddess of spring, who appears with Venus as well as the three Graces in Botticelli's *Primavera*, the allegorical painting around which all but the most superior tourists congregate in the Uffizi in Florence. I am not so comparable to Mercury in the painting, but note the similarity between us that he does point up to a small cloud drifting into the orange grove. Miranda and I, 33 and 49, had fallen in together just before Christmas, during another of her husband's long absences abroad. By as soon as January, a cloud over us was larger and darker. Her marriage, in her view, had become sad and precarious before we met. But if we continued and it ended, that very likely would not be independent of me. She had a child. I said and wrote more than once that she must not go forward on the assumption that we had a future.

Some reality was given to my sentences by my being open about the general fact of a number of other new attachments or inclinations of mine. Over these months these three Graces, or rather four, were a publisher and a law lecturer, each characterful and winsome, and a *Guardian* journalist Left-Wing and blue-stockinged, and a winning personality sometimes seen on television. There was no concealment by me of the Graces, or of Janet's overnight visits to Keats Grove, affectionate but not sexual, or of our Easter holiday in Wales. The new mess of my life was not kept from Em, as she had become, but I did not disappear from hers, demonstrated no iron will. For reasons having to do with her need for a year's independence, agreed to by her husband, and also for reasons having to do with me, she took a flat on her own in Primrose Hill. It was, in his official understanding, not the ending of the marriage but a hiatus. In my understanding, it had her determination in it, both endearing and alarming. We had sweet times with good talk when the cloud was in recession.

There was a darker fact. It had transpired, since the letter from my sister Mary that had further affected my feeling for her, that she had cancer. She would soon die of it. In July I went to stay with her for a fortnight in California. In the mornings, she said, I must write my important book. For the rest of the day, she said, we would talk of Baden, John William Honderich and Rae Laura Armstrong, all of the past, our brother and sister, marriage, religion, and life and death. This we did, with few tears. We toured Hollywood in her prized Jaguar, and I heard of the actor with whom she went out and who had also gone out with Katherine Hepburn. Mary was calm, and had my full love and admiration. Would that I had seen the quality of my sister earlier.

The darkness of Pasadena was followed by the darkness of Toronto. Unexpectedly, I went there rather than back to London, for the funeral of the husband of my sister Ruthie. Elmar Victor Spielbergs had decided, for reasons of illness, that his life was insupportable. Ruthie, strong in her suffering, had no less of my love and admiration. At least the women in my family could deal with adversity.

Towards the end of the university year, there was news about my son John. His independence had led him away from home and into the ranks of the squatters. But he had written an admissions essay that wholly persuaded Tony Byatt to admit him to read for the degree in English at University College London. There was satisfaction too that my programme on punishment for Radio 3 had annoyed judges. Richard liked it, though, and said I should take over his general lectures to our first-year undergraduates. There was also the mortification of sexual failure, with one of the four Graces. Part of the explanation was that I had not at the right moment wholly persuaded myself that we had a future. Might Em and I have one? Having had accusing letters from her husband, I had had a meeting with him in which I conveyed that our affair was not different in seriousness from some others. Now I began to feel more uncertain. But a bracing weekend at the country seat of her parents was followed a month later by another letter saying we must end. This in turn was followed by a happy time at her house in Corfu.

In September I rounded up six referees to support my application for a personal chair, and deferred to the wisdom of Douglas Johnson's successor, a new Dean of Arts. Professor Martin Swales, Head of the Department of German and well used to the *Sturm und Drang* of college life, said it would be better not to include at the end of my *curriculum vitae* the list of professorships offered to me elsewhere. My application would be considered in the coming year. Freddie said he would be fulsome in his letter of reference. He, like Professors Alastair Hannay and Timothy Sprigge, was not debarred from doing me a service by being a friend. Timothy was not debarred, either, by my having helped him towards his professorship in Edinburgh. If such high principles of propriety were embraced, university promotions might grind to a halt. Also, as was sometimes suspected, friendship and gratitude could turn out to be consistent with independence of mind. My three other referees were distant acquaintances of good standing. Peter Strawson in Oxford, don of dons, cheered me by saying that for some time it had seemed to him an anomaly that he was not writing 'Professor' before my name on his envelopes to me.

4 Keats Grove, main house and entrance, with The Studio on the left

At home

Helen Marshall, proud Scot

Janet Radcliffe Richards, sceptical feminist

1986 television: Ronald Dworkin, Paul Sieghart, Neil MacCormick, and me
By kind permission of Anglia Television Ltd

Farewell to my college eyrie

Jane O'Grady, looking for quotations

13

PROFESSOR,
PSYCHONEURAL INTIMACY,
DISARRAYS

Another anomaly on my mind was Anomalous Monism, the best-known and most intriguing version of the idea that mind and brain do not merely go together but are one thing. It was owned by the aforementioned Don Davidson, the Pied Piper of Berkeley, California, in whose train so many English postgraduates followed, often not to their doom. Anomalous Monism is one of the two kinds of Identity Theories identified some pages back, the sensible and innocuous kind. It does not actually get rid of the mind by neuralizing consciousness – Eliminative Materialism – or of course get rid of the brain by mentalizing it. Rather, it takes a conscious and a neural property to be properties of a single event. Some single thing has properties such that it is both your thinking of Charlotte Street, as that is ordinarily understood, and also an electrochemical episode in your brain.

This Dualistic Identity Theory has more to it, which flows from a novel argument for it. The first proposition is the humdrum one that there are causal relations between mental and physical things, such as your thinking of Charlotte Street and, some time later, your car's being parked there. The second is that wherever there are causal relations between things, the things are connected as a matter of natural or scientific law, nomically connected. So far so good, you may say – especially if you join me in supposing that causal connections in the world just *are* the main lawlike or nomic connections. The third proposition is that there are no lawlike connections between mental and physical things. Mental things are not a matter of law but are *anomalous*. Your thinking of Charlotte Street escapes being nomically tied to anything physical before it, at the same time, or after it. The only lawlike connections are between physical things. Do not ask me, querulous reader, why you should believe it. Rather, having by now heard enough philosophy to have learned suspension of disbelief, ask only what follows *if* it is true.

The three propositions seem to be inconsistent, an inconsistent triad, which they cannot be if they are true. The only tolerable escape from the seeming inconsistency, we are told, is by drawing a certain conclusion: that mental things *are* also physical things. Ergo an Identity Theory of the sensible kind, but necessarily one with more to it – a certain addition about your thinking of Charlotte Street. Since there are no lawlike connections involving mental items, the addition is that there is no lawlike connection between a thing's having been your thinking of Charlotte Street and also having been a certain electrochemical episode in your brain. That they were one thing was not a matter of law, but in this sense an accident. *Anomalous* Monism.

A very cheerless doctrine it was to a would-be pied piper with only a couple of postgraduates in his train, and carrying forward 500 pages of determinism, definitely including the idea of mental and physical properties being in lawlike connection. The journal *Analysis* was devoted above all to snappy refutations. Why not one of Anomalous Monism? Even better, why not one that did not get bogged down in the large matter of disproving the third proposition – no lawlike or nomic connection between mental and physical things? You could just peer at the internal consistency of the finished doctrine, see if the Emperor had clothes.

We could all agree, to put it plainly, that the thing that was in part your thinking of Charlotte Street and in part an electrochemical episode in your brain was a cause of your car's later being parked in Charlotte Street. A question arose, and kept on arising despite attempts to smother it. Was it the mental part of the thing that did the causing of the effect? Or the neural part? Or both? Whatever actually did the causing, plainly, that would be in lawlike connection with the effect.

Well, if the mental part did the causing, then, according to the first two propositions in the argument for Anomalous Monism, there would have to *be* lawlike connection between the mental cause and the parked car – which was flatly denied by the third proposition. There would be the same trouble if both parts did the causing. Try the neural part, then. Here was another sadness. If the neural part did the causing, what was the use of the mental part? It played no role in the explanation of where the car was. The mental part might have played a role, of course, if it was in lawlike connection with the neural part, and therefore somehow necessary to it, but it wasn't. So what we were being told here, unbelievably, was that our conscious lives were beside the point, not explanatory of our actions and their effects. Anomalous Monism was an Epiphenomenalism. Very bad news for Anomalous Monism.

Professor Davidson being otherwise engaged, perhaps resting in his tent, Mr Peter Smith of Sheffield University said in the next issue of *Analysis* that I was confused. In the next one, I said he was very confused. In the next, he said I was extremely confused. The next carried my contribution 'Smith and the Champion of Mauve'. In the household of the Champion of Mauve there are many things painted mauve. Here his bedroom slippers, there a bottle of gin, here a light-switch. They do their respective jobs, he says, because of the fleece lining, the alcohol content, and an effective circuit-breaker. Moreover, their being mauve is not nomically necessary to these facts about them. But, adds the Champion of Mauve, do not underrate mauve. Do not underrate it in connection with my warm feet. The slippers with the fleece lining *are* the mauve slippers. Nor let us have any diminishing of mauve with the other two items. Could Mr Smith and Professor Davidson distinguish themselves from the Champion of Mauve? Was the mental efficacy they assigned to events as uncompelling as mauvish efficacy? Answer came there none, for a while.

It was during this year 1982–83 that I began to have Charlotte Street on my mind at least once a fortnight. The lunch club at Bertorelli's had originally been got together in 1953 by Ben Nicolson, art historian and editor of the *Burlington Magazine*, and Philip Toynbee, principal book reviewer for *The Observer* and a writer of novels informed by literary theory. There remained a few of the original members, notably Freddie, Stephen Spender, Bill Coldstream and Peter Vansittart. It had in it mainly public school men, but its exclusiveness was a little more complicated, and certainly had to do with its members having made a mark, preferably by way of the printed word. It now had about 45 members, of whom an unpredictable dozen or so would turn up for the ordinary lunches, 35 for the special Christmas beano, and a couple of dozen for the annual Ladies Night. Peter had been presiding over the lunches, and, having had a conversation or two with other members, made me his successor. Conceivably the selection process would have been longer if the absent member Richard still turned up.

Certainly I was an unlikely chairman of this English thing, although the unlikelihood was somewhat reduced by the chairman's also being factotum of the club, sending out the cards giving the dates of meetings and collecting the money to pay the lunch bill. You will anticipate that my role pleased me well. It also suited my inclination to table talk. At the first lunch under my auspices, we considered the proposition that minorities are almost always in the right, hazarded by a nineteenth-century essayist and to my mind still in need of attention. Victor Pritchett, he of the short stories, thought so too.

As for Keats Grove, there was news in November 1982 that Green Shoes had sold out. She would be decamping forever. My Christmas party was again true to Mill's injunction to allow all voices to be heard. It had at it not only at my neighbour Lennie Hoffmann, happily down from his judicial bench, but also Roger Scruton, not yet so public a figure as to be beyond the pale for Prosecco socialists. At the end of December, Richard's feelingful and moving note of departure from 19 Gordon Square thanked us all for everything over the years – help, encourage-ment, existence. Hidé Ishiguro had resigned as well and gone to America some months earlier.

The Grote Chair being unfilled, another Head of Department had to be found for the coming term. Johnny was the department's first choice, the ideal man. He took the view, however, that he should have the compensation of being made a professor. This the college declined to do, on the grounds at least that it could not overleap its own annual promotions machinery. Jerry and I thus became candidates, and did some canvassing in our small constituency. Representations to the Provost by some of my colleagues, unprompted by me, confirmed agreeably that anathema I was not. The upshot was undecided, but by my calculation looking promising, when Johnny relented and took the job without the compensation.

There was no real discomfiture for me in this, since a headship without a chair could indeed be looked at as doing a job without having the honour of it. In any case, any small disappointment did not occupy me long. It gave way to much more feeling in January when Bee rang up to tell me of our sister Mary's death. Her daughter Bergeth's letter was harrowing, but rightly proud, since Mary had died well. This remained a shadow in the following days, but did not fill my mind. Life edged out death. Just in time for my 50th birthday, 30 January 1983, a note was left for me by the non-professorial member on the college's promotions committee, not to be confused with the Grote committee. The note said only 'Congratulations!', thereby preserving committee confidentiality. Professor I was, or soon would be.

This elevation to a personal chair was savoured. It was not only splendid in itself but an avoidance of what had come to seem the disaster of remaining a Reader forever. There was *worthiness* about being a Reader. The splendidness of my elevation was not much reduced by being a few years late, Richard and Stuart having got chairs at 40 or 45 rather than 50. There was also a touch of rue in the fact that this honour of mine had been struggled for, first asked for three or four years ago. But there was no need to record more than once in my diary that my predecessors had had good starts in life, by way of Repton and Westminster and Balliol. The Dean of Arts confirmed that my referees had been, while of independent minds, nothing less than an unrestrained chorus. My promotion had sailed through ahead of all others. I was a member of something, the English professoriate.

In fact, as it quickly turned out, I was not. The decision by my college would have to be ratified by the University of London. This would involve a university body and the taking of opinions from more members of my profession. Bernard would likely be consulted, and the names of more possible referees were needed from me. Three more were arranged from Oxford, the unreassuring ratio of acquaintances to friends being 2 to 1. It came to my ear that Richard had written from America protesting that my application for promotion had been kept secret from him, or at any rate not brought to his attention by the college. Very certainly, I myself had not supplied him with the information. The point was that my claims were to be considered independently of him. He had voted already.

Might the university body and the referees have the benefit of having another vote from him now? I could worry about that. If there was small chance of the university going against the college's recommendation, might there still be a fuss, say someone's resigning in protest from the deliberations? Such a thing had happened with a successor to Professor

Popper at the L.S.E. I went over the matter in my diary, and wondered if my apprehension was partly another symptom of withdrawal from cigarettes. Would nicotine chewing gum help? It did. So did philosophy, that most trusty bracer and succour. The strengthening of my determinism manuscript went forward pretty steadily. Will you expect, reader, knowing me as you do, that I nonetheless did not have the fortitude to concentrate absolutely on this as against other work?

There was the collection *Philosophy Through Its Past*, contemporary writings on the great philosophers. It, like its predecessor *Philosophy As It Is*, was informed by the high principle that philosophy is the best introduction to itself. It was a grind getting the 19 brief prefaces right, even to those pieces by friends, and to 'The Individual as an Object of Love'. The latter was the ideal piece on Plato by Gregory Vlastos, he who had been charmed by the grace of Helen at a Hampstead lunch. It was easier to run off the thumbnail biographies of the great philosophers, and easy to succumb further to small temptations, as in the last line of the one on Nietzsche. 'Friend of Wagner, praised by Freud for self-insight, died deranged.'

In another task there was more than loyalty to a firm, Routledge & Kegan Paul, and connection with another line of editors, the current one being the pleasingly unworldly Stratford Caldecott. There was feeling for John Mackie of University College Oxford, suddenly dead. Acute Mackie of the lost causes. Although not a close friend, it fell to me to edit *Morality and Objectivity*, a volume of papers in his memory, on account of reservations by his widow about another possible editor. This book too had strong things in it, many of them on or against Mackie's admirable Penguin, *Ethics: Inventing Right and Wrong*.

These two editorial tasks, it discomfits me to recall, were insufficient distractions. Until then there had been three series of books under my general editorship: *The International Library of Philosophy and Scientific Method*, *The Arguments of the Philosophers*, and the philosophy books brought out by Penguin. To these series was now added *The Problems of Philosophy: Their Past and Present*. Each book in this vicarious onward marching would deal with a great, significant or persistent problem of philosophy, first by presenting its history, then by giving its solution, according to the lights of the authors. I was keener on the second part. In due course rationality, conditional statements, personal identity, the foundations of ethics, scepticism, democracy, private property and various other problems were laid to rest.

At about the time the college committee had promoted me into a state of apprehension, Miranda strengthened her resolve to get a divorce and persuaded her husband. She allowed this had something to do with our intermittent connection, but affirmed she would have gone ahead anyway. There was overdetermination – more than what was needed for the effect. I wrote yet more letters saying that we were not suited to one another, which fact very likely was to her credit rather than mine. She replied so sweetly and often as to increase my own weakness of will. My threat to end our connection with barbarous efficiency was never carried out. There were only interludes when I carried forward elsewhere my eternal project of seeking a relationship without foreseeable end.

With respect to one of the four Graces, my hopes sprang up quickly, more than once, and expired somewhat less quickly. As with Em, this Grace did not sufficiently prize herself, and so was insufficiently prized by me. It would all seem very promising to me, and then in a fortnight imperative not to go further, not to store up more disappointment, not to try. *Trying* no longer seemed so good an idea. There were also several new candidates. Also, at the end of a family gathering, having had a lot to drink, I did what my son John later charged me with. This was at least the eyeing-up of a girlfriend of his. No defence is offered by me. Through it all, Janet and I remained in touch. She stayed overnight at Keats Grove before and after her weekly appearance on television, in a programme called *Credo*. It was uplifting and offered food for thought.

In June I was offered food for thought about England. Mrs Thatcher, who already could better be called 'Thatcher', won her second election, over Mr Michael Foot. It had something to do with the political good luck of the Falklands War. That war had been made necessary in my own mind by England's self-respect and made horrible by her sinking of the *Belgrano*. But the election also had quite a lot to do with the electorate. It could not only stomach but give a large majority to this unspeakable woman, whose pomposity was no bad guide to her morals and politics. Certainly I was not among those who had been reassured by her declaring 'The National Health Service is safe with us'. It was no longer as clear to me that England's normal condition was one of slow progress in decency.

In 19 Gordon Square, Johnny as our new Head of Department was not keen on what had long been our departmental habit of meeting our tutorial students briefly in the first week of each term to assign essays to them. This delayed the start of our actual teaching to the second week. He firmly said we should mend our ways. It was a teacherly idea, and well supported by the loyal departmental secretaries, but not one that endeared him to our colleagues. They were equally keen on what was now called our research obligation – more keen than me on hanging onto every free hour traditionally possessed for the writing of their works and thus the improving of their prospects. Our Head had also been forceful, perhaps impolitic, in conducting our external relations with other philosophy departments in the university. Birkbeck College was unhappy, and perhaps Kings too. He was no practised academic politician.

Now in June there was consternation of another and sharper kind. Our Provost, Sir James, had got the idea that Ronnie Dworkin of Oxford, whose jurisprudence gave him philosophical credentials, would be right for the Grote Chair, better than any internal candidate. Delicate negotiations were being carried forward between Provost and candidate, with pleasure at least on the part of the Provost. The negotiations were importantly about the hours of teaching that would be required from the candidate if he came. Johnny was caught up in the matter. After some uncertainty he acted. He stated a large number of hours to Ronnie, allowing not a minute off for jurisprudential distinction, and thereby brought the delicate and pleasurable negotiations to a crashing end. This was to the dismay of colleagues, myself included, and certainly the Provost. He expressed his unhappiness pithily. Departmental affairs, unexpectedly, were not in ideal order.

My own life's domestic disarray reached a climacteric one morning in July as I went out the front gate at Keats Grove. My car, an orange Citroen the night before, was now largely pink. The change had been brought about by the emptying of a can of paint over it. I hoped that the culprit was the artist in The Studio, Mr Peter Hobbs. This could be his way of discouraging his landlord from sending him more notes saying it would be nice to have some rent, or might he let in the plumber this time to replace the WC cistern and pan? But it seemed all too likely that the culprit was not Mr Hobbs, but a husband. My reaction was complicated by the large question of my own contribution to my discomfiture, but I also allowed myself some moral outrage. The policeman who came round was not greatly sympathetic, and asked if it was about a woman. I did not need him to reinforce my good understanding that this was the sort of thing I might expect.

Soon enough there was no need to turn to philosophy, the other life, for solace. News came from the University of London that from 1 October 1983 I really would be a professor. Good wishes came from various quarters. They were wonderfully cheering, notably the ones from Oxford. The Provost wrote that my appointment was widely acclaimed and warmly welcomed. The card from Professor Coldstream was as agreeable. 'Dear Ted: Proportionate congratulations. Love, Bill.' I thanked him when ferrying him away from his marriage in my Citroen. In September Janet and I went to Tuscany. Our time there, some of it in front of the *Primavera*, was recuperative, but did not lead me to propose resurrecting the past. We would, however, be in touch by telephone forever.

It was persistently agreeable, a sweetness, on climbing up to my eyrie, to register that the door now had on it 'Professor Ted Honderich'. My new tutorial students at the start of the university year, I hoped, took in my grandeur. They might note that it was unique in the department, Richard having taken his official departure, although he would be a ghostly presence in this term and some others in the future, doing useful teaching for us. I did not begrudge myself my small pleasure in my door-plate, but did reflect on titles, and did look up George Bernard Shaw's relevant line in *Man and Superman*. 'Titles distinguish the mediocre, embarrass the superior, and are disgraced by the inferior.'

That was more food for thought. One thought was that the title of Professor did not much embarrass the superior members of my profession, at any rate in anticipation. None turned it down. Also, all those with any chance of getting it certainly acted on the chance, sometimes by the well-tried method of disclaiming interest. It came to mind too that intellectual ratings are touched not only by the ambitions of the raters themselves but are also in other ways accidental, as remarked before in this narrative. There was also the good idea that one proper and rational response in the troubled mist, sometimes the fog and filthy air, is to stand up for oneself.

The first draft of my improved determinism book was now on the way to being finished. About 650 pages existed, leaving me with no shortage of material for my inaugural lecture as a professor. As for what to call the lecture, I was in no mood of academic diffidence. Something traditional like 'A Few More Remarks on Free Will' would not do. Much better would be 'A Theory of Determinism: The Mind, Neuroscience, and Life-Hopes'. Also, that might attract an audience from more than the Arts Faculty in the college, and from both of the two categories of philosophers distinguished by William James, the tough-minded and the tender-minded. The former could come along for the neuroscience and the latter for the life-hopes.

My view of the problem of the nature of consciousness and the problem of its relation to the brain, of which you have heard something, was that the conscious mind was no more than the flow of conscious or mental events, these having a certain subjectivity, that they were as efficacious as the brain in giving rise to our actions, were not identical with the brain in the sense of being no more than the brain, but were in lawlike connection with it and hence not what you could call auto- nomous. You could hang onto this view without being very clear about the distinctive subjective nature of the flowing conscious events.

The first aim of the lecture was to prove the last proposition, about lawlike connection between conscious events and the brain, the Correlation Hypothesis. So far it had been more or less assumed. You could prove it by a chain of argument, its first link being something called *psychophysical intimacy*. This, perhaps against expectation of something racier, was the intimate connection between mental events and simul- taneous events in the brain, neural events. The basic idea was that a type of mental event always goes together with a type of neural event in a certain locale of the brain, or rather one of a set of types, and that the explanation of this co-occurrence is not coincidence but some kind or other of intrinsic necessity. This idea, as it seemed to me, had not been so forceful as it should have been in the thinking of philosophers of mind. They needed really to be persuaded of it, by the rubbing of their noses in the current achievements of neuroscience.

That mental events were bound up with simultaneous neural events in the given way was indicated, first, by my impressive Figure 1, projected on the large screen in the lecture theatre. It showed the known mapping of sensations and of actions, in terms of parts of the body, onto parts of the two hemispheres of the brain, the dominant and the other one. There was the connection of what is called the unity of consciousness with the corpus callosum, this being the bundle of neurons connecting the right and left hemispheres. There was the cerebellum and motor control. Also the Wernicke and Broca speech areas, grandmother-recognition cells, the transfer of memories between goldfish by transferring neuro-chemicals between them, and a good deal else.

The upshot was indeed that you could not doubt psychophysical intimacy. The upshot of *that* in the chain of argument was that only certain philosophical theories of mind and brain were left as possibilities. The best of these, other than one, were certain Identity Theories. But they were open to the fatal objections having to do with neuralizing the mind and with Epiphenomenalism. The only possibility left was lawlike connection between mental and neural events.

It was impossible to resist spending some minutes, too, on something less serious, a mile away from Identity Theories. This was the large book by Professor Popper, lately of the L.S.E., and Professor John Eccles, a neurophysiologist with the temerity to let a philosopher know that neurophysiology did not support the basic idea of psychophysical intimacy. The book *The Self and Its Brain* had announced that the Self or Self-Conscious Mind was not tied to the brain, but was its proprietor, somehow free-floating and magnificent. Such a view may have suited Professor Popper because it consorted nicely with his doctrine of the creativity of science, which had won him many friends in the labora-tories. The mind's freedom from the brain may have suited Professor Eccles because his distinctions included not only a Nobel Prize but unshakeable Catholicism.

It proved possible for me to leave out these low diagnoses of their doctrine of the Self and its brain, fortunately, and to concentrate instead on the basic reason given for the doctrine. This was a piece of Californian nonsense owed mostly to one Benjamin Libet of that state's university. Wrapped in much experimental evidence in nine scientific papers, it was about a conscious sensation occurring on its own before the brain caught up with it. My refutation, wrapped up in much conceptual clarification, had been accepted as an article by *The Journal of Theoretical Biology*, thereby establishing to its readers that philosophy was not merely the handmaiden of science.

Certainly my inaugural lecture audience was large, far larger than any such audience of which I had ever been a member. The Chemistry Auditorium, as later established, was the largest theatre in the college, 334 seats, and there were people sitting in the aisles and standing at the back. It unnerved me. I read my way stolidly through the lecture, never departing from the security of the text. A standard arm movement was made at regular intervals throughout at least much of the hour. Purportedly this was to get my hair out of my eyes, but seemed a little suggestive of a loss of motor control, something amiss in the cerebellum.

Why were they all there? Evidently both the tough-minded and the tender-minded had gathered, and presumably some readers of my works on punishment and violence. Maybe some curious college persons who had heard of *événements* in the Philosophy Department, maybe people who kept up with academic appointments in *The Times*, and certainly friends and family. Persons down from Oxford looked attentive, the college neurophysiologist J. Z. Young looked approving, authors of books in my series looked loyal, Richard and Jerry looked challenged, Bill Hart no more verdictive than usual, Peter Vansittart respectful in his puzzlement, the Virago publisher Ursula Owen independent-minded, Janet serene, Miranda happy, Pauline composed, and my son John conceivably proud. Kiarney, having compensated for a lesser Oxford degree by a stunning performance in the American exam for entrance to graduate schools, was carrying forward her career in economics at Columbia in New York, and so missed the show.

In the department at this time, there were small upsets fairly easily managed. It was made clear to Johnny that it could not be I who was responsible for a dark fact. This was my name's no longer being on what was called the establishment-list of the department, sent annually to the Head by the college administration, and thus my salary's not being revealed to him. Evidently this great irritation to him was a matter of college policy, having to do with the fact that professors' salaries were not on scales but individually settled by the Provost.

As for the new personal letterhead ordered by me, carrying my name as a professor, I allowed that this was all too human, but noted it was in line with the practice of others in the college, and that certainly I had expected to pay for it myself. But was his secretary not being odd? Why was she not allowing me to give her a cheque, pay for it in the ordinary way through the departmental accounts? Did the accounts need to be *so* purified of human failing? Surely he could not have given her that instruction? Over this matter, I spoke my first angry words to him in 24 years, but we put it behind us.

We did not confer about the Grote Chair, this subject being a sensitive one on account of the possibility of my again being a candidate or making myself into one. It was not that I ranked myself as a competitor against all comers. There would have been no discomfort in having Ronnie Dworkin, and I wrote to Bernard wondering enthusiastically if he had had enough of being provost of King's College Cambridge. Would he care to relax in the chair of his friend Richard? But was it clear that I should not be out of the running if one or two Americans, not widely known, were now being talked up?

Fortunately there was little to be done. I had made an application two years ago with the dire result you know, my being anathematized. It was possible, as my diary recorded, to bask in my personal chair and to feel that all that really mattered was my determinism book. I did have a higher self, and, if it was not so autonomous as Professors Popper and Eccles supposed, it could take an ascendancy over the lower for a while.

Social life was also enlivening. Miranda, in the periods when we were together, thrived on it and improved it. I, in the periods when we were not together, still pursued it vigorously. The Berts club chuntered on agreeably, its urbanity increased by new members elected by the chairman and factotum, three being Jonathan Glover, Eric Hobsbawn and Douglas Johnson. There were parties given by Nigella Lawson, made in the image of her mother Vanessa, and pleasingly literary dinners called together by Tony Byatt, and the stylish drinks of the satirist Eleanor Bron in Harley Street. There was good food and talk in going out to dine with Faye Maschler, on duty in connection with her restaurant column. Occasions in Keats Grove continued. Among the further entries proposed for Dan Dennett's jocular philosophical lexicon was one on 'Honderich'. This was defined as a cry against inequality heard at Hampstead dinner parties, a contraction of 'Hound the rich!'

In December 1983, I was among some of the rich, not doing much hounding, and also a lot of other people, at Peregrine Worsthorne's 60th birthday party, in a large restaurant on the Thames. Charmed by Nigella, by chance placed next to me, I was also apprehensive of hearing myself say a word or two to a government minister, indeed the Foreign Minister, best known as Bunter. So I drank a lot, and on the way home in my black tie and orange 2CV, I drove with sufficient spirit through Parliament Square to attract the attention of a policeman. The result was a £100 fine and disqualification from driving for one year.

It seemed a good idea to keep quiet about my discomfiture, which in the main I did. As for the suspension of my career as a motorist, that might not be the greatest of hardships. Cars were a curse anyway. They needed servicing, and funny things happened to them. Why not a bicycle for my early-morning runs down to Bloomsbury and the evening returns back up to Hampstead? Thus a pleasure began. It was, like some of the best of pleasures, boyish. It might not be given up after the year of disqualification from driving. I might be a boy eternal.

The Christmas party had added to it the fetching Irish novelist Julia O'Faolain for literature gloss and the Provost for scientific ballast and other purposes. Then early in the new year I found myself appearing in hubbubs of another kind, recording television programmes with Professor Eccles and Professor John Searle and others. Did Professor Eccles not sometimes fancy escaping the boredom of mystery? Mad Identity Theorists added up the conscious mind and the brain into one sort of thing, but did Professor Eccles not outdo them by adding them up into *three*, these being brain, the ordinary flow of thoughts and feelings, and also the proprietorial Self? Did he stand by Professor Popper's scientific conjecture that the young Self, after hovering for a while, like a spiritual dragonfly, chooses to alight on the side of the brain that then becomes the dominant one?

Professor Searle, by contrast, was not easy game, but formidable. He was good on his feet, and funny with it, a stand-up philosopher. I made no real headway when his own Californian naturalism came up for examination. My thoughts about it were that it was all very well for him to say that the brain had lower-level properties and also higher-level properties, the latter being thoughts and feelings. Of *what general sort* were those higher properties? All very well to say they stood to neurons as the liquidity of water stands to H_2O molecules, none of which is wet. But *what* were thoughts and feelings? It wasn't as if their nature was as clear as water.

In May Miranda and I achieved escapes from one another. There had been lovely evenings of days when the writing of two books had gone well. But certainly she saw that I was not what she wanted me to be. We had struggled towards our end throughout the past months. Scores of letters had passed between us, all tender and almost all either hopeless or too brave in their resolution. In the end, the charge against me, never laid by her, but in my own and several other minds, was that the affair had at least contributed to the ending of her marriage, and then not replaced it.

My own guilt, if that is what it was, could not be my having failed to put into words my curious conviction that we did not have a future. Nor could it be deception about the existence of others in my crowded life, temptations felt or succumbed to. Rather, what I had failed to do was to act on my words. It needs to be added, too, that she and I were the victims of my moods. Certainly they were not only bad ones. Good ones came upon me, and I had not learned to outlast them. She said in the end that the right thing had been done, that we would survive and become friends.

In the department Johnny and I were friends still, but dealing imperfectly with what academic life had allotted to us. The college's promotion machinery in this year's operation, uncharitably, had not added a professorship to his Headship. He would remain a Reader. What academic life had allotted to Jerry Cohen was enviable, the Chichele Professorship of Social and Political Theory in Oxford. This was a chair that to my mind was like the Grote in owing its desirability to having been sat in by someone, in this case Isaiah Berlin.

The seminar on Mondays at five, the great institution of postgraduate life in the years of Professor Ayer, had withered away under his successors. Now it did not exist at all. Invigorated by my professorship, and inspired by memory, I proposed to try to revive it. My colleagues agreed happily at our meeting. We would put in a good effort. We and our postgraduates would in the last term of this year look over *Reasons and Persons*, partly on the philosophical problem of personal identity. This was the large work by Derek Parfit in Oxford, new friend to Janet Radcliffe Richards. It had needed to be published and well-received to ensure its author's future at All Souls, and my review in *The New Statesman* honourably celebrated it as extraordinary, an exemplar of unflagging and meticulous logical sequence, only sometimes a higher doggedness.

It became clear Johnny was unhappy about the proposed seminar. He foresaw timetable clashes, those great icebergs of academic life. Alone among colleagues, he would not be coming. Above all, he could not see why a special notice should be sent to postgraduates about the seminar. Could they not just keep an eye on the bulletin board? My response was to say I was happy to resign in advance as convenor of the seminar and to propose that he organize it rather than I. This was no help. I was to do it, but none of the department's resources, including paper, were to be used in sending out my special notice.

14

MENTAL AND OTHER EVENTS, JOHNNY, DETERMINISM DONE

A nice new thought to go into the completed first draft of my determinism book made this year 1984–85 begin better than it would end. My theory, as it sometimes seemed a bit grand to call it, contained three connected hypotheses. The first was the Correlation Hypothesis, about the lawlike correlation of mental or conscious events with simultaneous neural events, or, as might better be said, mental properties with neural properties. The second and principal hypothesis, the heart of this determinism, took these correlates to be effects. But of exactly what? There was a long causal sequence involved, made up of causal circumstances and their effects, each effect being part of the next causal circumstance. But exactly what was in the chain and where did it start?

You have heard from me of the good attitude, hard to shake off once you escape from common sense, that the causes of anything that is physical are wholly physical themselves.* This had seemed to me true, and from it had come an idea about my psychoneural items. Take for example your consciously intending a moment ago to reach for the bowl of olives, and more particularly what guaranteed it, the neural or electrochemical correlate. This guaranteeing correlate, given the physicalist attitude, had itself to be the effect of wholly physical causes.

The problem about this explanation of your intending was that it seemed to leave out earlier mental facts. The problem was essentially the same one as could arise with the explanation of actions. Just as the

* See pp. 246–47

explanation of an action itself, say your actually reaching for the bowl, needs to include earlier mental facts, so too the explanation of your intending to reach needs to include earlier mental facts, say your seeing the olives and wanting one. The problem was again Epiphenomenalism. A paper or two of mine had struggled to avoid the disgrace. Now there seemed to be room for a simple improvement.

Mental events or properties did indeed have a unique nature, their subjectivity – each one had a subjective aspect as well as a particular content. And, as it had always seemed, this nature was not physical, not like weight or being an electrical conductor or being able to transmit the stuff called dopamine between neurons. Now it came to me on my bicycle, for good or ill, that rethinking might be in order about the general idea of anything's being physical. Some pages in Anthony Quinton's book *The Nature of Things* were a help. Generally speaking, physical things fell into two categories. They were things that took up space and had perceived properties. This was the case with sofas. Or, they were things that took up space and caused things that took up space and had perceived properties. Atoms went into the second category.

What about wanting an olive? If it *were* physical, it could, in accordance with the physicalist attitude, help cause the intending, and there need be no more struggle to avoid the disgrace of Epiphenomenalism. *Might* the wanting fall into the second category of physical things? Well, we all believed that it did some causing of perceived things. What also had to be true for it to be physical was that it took up some space. And, on reflection, why shouldn't it? Certainly we didn't ordinarily think of wantings, thoughts, feelings and other mental events or properties as taking up space, but exactly why shouldn't they take up a bit? Why shouldn't they take up a bit of space in our heads? Why should their subjectivity get in the way? No doubt we were tempted to think of them in terms of what they were *of* or what they were *about*, and thus to remove them from our heads, and then to be lost for a location to which to assign them. But the temptation had to be resisted – your wanting an olive was not the olive itself, after all.

The nice new thought that mental events could be physical, of course, was not to be confused with the mad Identity Theory that mental events have only neural properties, Eliminative Materialism. My happy discovery about the nature of consciousness was not the disaster of neuralizing the mind. To say that mental events were physical was not to say that they were the particular kind of physical events that were neural. They weren't electrical impulses and dopamine. They were some other kind of physical thing. I wouldn't talk about 'psycho*physical* intimacy' anymore, which implied that mental or psychological states weren't physical. Only 'psycho*neural* intimacy' would occur in my future.

There was much more to be done in making clear the hypothesis that each mental event, including each choosing and deciding, along with its neural correlate, was the effect of a long causal sequence – and hence was made necessary by the initial elements of that sequence, things for which the chooser or decider could not possibly be responsible. If the hypothesis was a version of the idea that we are products of heredity and environment, it had to be a lot more precise. Still more effort went into something else. This was the question of whether opposed ideas of the mind, indeterminist or Free Will ideas, however important in the living of our lives, could be made clear.

How were we supposed even to think of such an originator of choices and decisions as the proprietorial Self? Or such an originator as the Will, or a funny cause that was 'enough' for an effect but might not work? Such an originator was supposed not to be physical, but it wasn't just the flow of a person's mental events either. It was not only a third thing, in addition to the brain and the ordinary flow of thoughts and feelings, but evidently a third sort of thing, of a nature different from each of the other two. What sort, pray, was that? Professors Eccles and Popper hadn't begun to explain. Also, if an originator wasn't really caused to give off choices and decisions, *why* did they happen? Also, why did they happen *when* they happened? What *was* this relation of origination? As for the addition of Quantum Theory to loosen the grip of neural events, that deepened the dismal murk. My own second hypothesis, by contrast, was a heaven of light.

The autumn term had another charm. Catherine Lamb was a striking editor of art books who had rung the bell at Keats Grove to collect my subscription to the Labour Party. Like most members of the Hampstead Heath branch of the people's party, she seemed to bear no close relation to the working classes, save for her general support of them. I was approaching 52 and she was about 35. She was very comely indeed, Irish, characterful, had lately separated from her husband, and she lived down the street. She was often quiet, for the good reason that she was thinking. Her orderliness of thought and precision of speech were those of a good class of natural philosopher. To this rigour was added a sensitivity with respect to contemporary English poetry. If ambition got hold of her, she could certainly write some.

She was irresistible. We had lately been to Ireland, and stayed happily in the guest room at Trinity College Dublin and at the Anglo-Irish farm of Frank and Jennie Goodwin, brother and sister-in-law of Pauline. They had proved themselves, as always, admirably able to take it as part of the course of nature that each of my visits would be with a new companion. They especially approved of this one. Catherine had a daughter at school, her first concern. She would always be on hand for her. I, despite my having been charmed, was not more confident now about another experiment in living together than when Janet and I had parted. Hopes I had, fine ones, but insufficient resolution. For these several reasons, no question arose of our abandoning our separate flats. Our lives still fell together nicely, if uncertainly. If things were not settled, they were orderly. Here was a very possible answer to the woman question.

It was her composure as hostess that helped to preserve decorum on an occasion when the idea that I personally owned the subject of political violence led me to be superior and surly to her friend Michael Ignatieff, man of ideas and another escaped Canadian. She did the same at a Sunday lunch when Freddie set about what he described as teaching logic to feminism. The Virago publisher Ursula Owen was not to be tutored, any more than Liz Forgan of *The Guardian*. Ursula would not sit on the same balcony with him, but was prevailed on not to abandon the premises entirely. Freddie's lecture from Vanessa on social logic began as they took their departure down the staircase. He sounded unimpressed but was better behaved a later Sunday with Doris Lessing of *The Golden Notebooks* and *The Grass Is Singing*, another of my heroines and for a moment in our social round.

No influence of Catherine could prevent a performance of mine in Edinburgh. After my paper had been given to the Philosophy Depart-ment, a glass or two was drunk in celebration of it. We and the hospitable Sprigges then went on to a public meeting in the university. The subject under discussion was the accepting of money for a professorship of parapsychology, perhaps under the will of the dubious character Arthur Koestler. After pompously excusing my intrusion into Scots affairs, I said a word about the idea of academic institutions having chairs on ghosts. Perhaps I left the impression that University College London had an imperfect but slightly better record in the matter of accepting gifts with strings. A written apology by me followed the next day, rightly of little avail. It was of as little avail as feelings expressed by such as myself in a few magazine interviews about the advance of the New Right of the Conservative Party, the changing of England, the driving of people into an underclass by policies of social victimization.

One of my moods contributed to an ending with Catherine at Christmas, about which she was coolly efficient. At parties, in the weeks after, there seemed the possibility that my future might be a decorous one with the Hon. Susan Baring. Sweet Sue was a looker who unaccountably had not been elected an M.P. for the Social Democrats. She might tolerate my feeling against her political party, whose founders had culpably weakened the Labour Party, our only possible engine for decent social change. She might also put up with my nicotine chewing gum, if not so readily. We contemplated one another for a while, and the differences between our two lives, and the luggage in them, and concluded amicably that a future was not to be.

Catherine and I, reunited in our way, had more hope. She approved, perhaps, of another of my small pieces of resistance to the changing of England. This was 'Equality and History's Dust-Bin', a talk on Radio 3. In it I put to rout the Duke of Edinburgh and others, who were seeking to put my ideal of equality in the dust-bin. His Royal Highness in some writing had raised an arch question about helicopters. Since only a few people own one, or get to ride about in one, surely the machines must be socially unjust and quite wrong, and should be put down? I brought my reasoning for the Principle of Equality to his attention, firmly but amiably. No such peeps stirred England at all. Nor, really, did Oxford University's louder note in January 1985, when it voted against its binding tradition and refused to give its daughter Thatcher an honorary degree. In March there was another increase in prescription charges, and more privatization planned. To England, privatization was not profitization. To England, it was some reasonable and necessary thing, as taught to it by its daily papers, its press so free to express any opinion of its proprietors.

My social honour, despite my peep, was not great. It was agreeable to invite to the lunch club at Bertorelli's such guests as Salman Rushdie, who was starting work on a new book called *The Satanic Verses*. We got on well enough but he was curiously satisfied with himself, and so not regarded by all as membership material. Might I myself be membership material for those more stately clubs that had their own premises in the West End, the gentlemen's clubs? One was the Beefsteak, of great exclusiveness and very percipient about good breeding. Another was the Garrick, larger and more outward-looking, but no less careful in its election of new members. Both clubs had in them only representatives of the English regiment noted on my arrival 25 years before, the one that makes its private conversations in public places audible to all.

Peter Vansittart proposed me for the Beefsteak, and Perry Worsthorne and Isaiah Berlin for the Garrick. With the Garrick, the past and present members included thinkers, and some who were unconventional. Some present members did not pretend to believe that making the rich richer was guaranteed to help the poor. Others did not pretend to believe that the guilty log-book of the British submarine that sank the *Belgrano* had been misplaced entirely by accident. There were greater powers of belief at the Beefsteak.

In 19 Gordon Square, more hurts had been felt, seemingly by all colleagues. One of mine, not lasting, was that it had proved impossible for Johnny as Head of Department to secure for me as professor what could be secured for Jerry as post-graduate advisor, an unshared telephone line. There was something like affront to colleagues generally in his thinking better about our agreed decision at a departmental meeting to advertise in order to find a temporary lecturer to replace Jerry. There had seemed to our Head good reason just to go ahead and appoint one of our own good postgraduates instead, which he had efficiently done. To hurts were added an apprehension. Was our department on good terms with the college, and in particular the Provost? In these straitened days many posts were frozen, which is to say left unfilled. Would the college find its way to replacing Jerry Cohen and our other departing colleague Colin McGinn? What of the Grote Chair, now in its third year of being unoccupied? Philosophy departments could dwindle. Several in the provinces had actually been closed. Ours surely could not, but would it prosper?

Helen Marshall and I, partly because she had been happily taken up with a new connection, had fallen out of touch. In January 1985 I learned that she was dead of cancer. She was 42. During the funeral in Golders Green Crematorium, I did not think of Burns Nights with her, or first-footing in Edinburgh, or her staunchness in *Honderich v. Green Shoes*, or the holiday with my son John at John O'Groats, but only that she was dead, that she was gone forever. There was no help in the Strauss song or Dylan's 'Mr Tambourine Man'. There was no room for pride for her in hearing that she had chosen the time of her death, and in the funeral's having no smell of religion in it. She was gone forever. I had not done enough while she was alive. Weeping had only those two last things in it.

The day of the funeral had become known to me only on the day itself, and a note had been left by me on my door apologising for my absence to a tutee who could not be reached by telephone. She was an older woman whose jolliness may have concealed considerable self-esteem. A fortnight later, there was a note for me from Johnny. He was sorry to write about a certain matter, but thought he ought to. The note had to do in part with the missed tutorial, and was a reprimand. This sort of thing was not at all characteristic of me, he said. And he was sure that I did not believe students should have to prise tutorials out of their tutors. But he had the impression that I was not keeping a necessary balance in my priorities, not respecting my obligation to teach as much as my obligation to write.

My letter in reply to all points seemed to me conclusive, but it reduced neither my hurt nor what was greater, my rage. I was proud of my record as a diligent, popular and successful tutor. Official notes of reprimand, as if for a personal file or even a dossier, were no part of good relations between colleagues and friends. You should have had a word with me, I said, rather than go by an undergraduate's tittle-tattle to a secretary. His brief note back neither soothed nor pacified me. Nor did it deal with what was different from hurt and rage. This was a sharper sense of my future in the department. As it seemed to me, my prospects with respect to all things, perhaps with the Grote Chair if other candidates fell away, would be a matter of more passions than my own.

At a departmental meeting in the Grote Professor's room, I made a brief and interrupted speech. Its gravamen was that all members of the department had the highest opinion of Johnny's philosophical ability, but they were also unanimous in thinking that he had suffered mishaps, and that his gifts were not the lesser ones of administration, and that he should step down as Head. The persistent silence of my colleagues verified this. It was a speech of a kind heard before in other departments of the college, and in other colleges, and on those other occasions a cause of mortification but not disaster. Being a functionary could not be the first thing in the life of a scholar or scientist or historian or philosopher. It was not what one prided oneself on.

My first sentence had been about our departmental problems being the result of all our difficult personalities, mine included. It was interrupted by Johnny's charge that my personality was the main cause of our problems. I was a swine. My sentences about someone other than me being Head in place of him were stopped by more imprecations. My saying that no doubt he would want to hear the opinions of my colleagues, perhaps privately, was met by a declaration. It was that if he was not to be Head, he would resign from the department and from the college. Indeed he would do that right now, if a piece of paper could be found. It could not, and he ran from the room.

My six colleagues, having uttered hardly a word, were stunned and unstrung, but stood by the proposition that we all valued him, all wished him to stay with us, and all thought another Head would be best. The Provost, informed of the department's view by me, spoke with him about it. At my suggestion Malcolm Budd, as fastidious as ever, took over his role, as Acting Head. Students demanded and got a general meeting on what might have been the injustice done to Johnny by the Provost, and concluded that there was insufficient evidence to enable them to decide. He was rarely seen in the department thereafter. At the end of the academic year he left it and the college forever. He would not have a retirement gift or dinner. He was about 61, about four years away from the time when it would still have been too early to leave us.

In so far as there was concern about my future in my action, it could turn out that I had done myself more harm than good. It could be forgotten that a jury had all been of one mind, and a prosecutor could be remembered instead. If bad luck ought not to touch one's reputation, it could. As for the hurt and rage, seemingly so sharp and so strong, they had in fact been bearable and governable. Hurt and rage almost always are. Should they not always be with a friendship of 26 years? It was Johnny's own view, passed on to me by intermediaries thereafter, that trouble between the two of us was inevitable, and that he was most affected by the silence of the others. No doubt he would say more to you, reader, if life and books could run on the greatest principle of the law. *Audi partem alteram* – Hear the other side. You have only me to hear. For myself on the day, if apprehensive and saddened, I lacked conviction that I had done wrong. But I would not be among those who gained no title and who lost no friend.

Before this dark chapter, and alongside and after it, ran another chapter in the history of the Grote Chair. Visible in it were David Wiggins, his wife, the department, the Provost, the Dean of Arts, and University College Oxford. Were they not in perfect communication, settled in a common intent? At an early stage we understood that David would come from the Oxford college to our chair with haste if it were offered to him. It would be, to my mind, a pretty good appointment. Subsequently, there was as much to be said for something else. This was the idea of his being accompanied from Oxford by his wife Jennifer Hornsby, successor to Hidé Ishiguro, who might become a Reader among us.

Then, at about the time of the dark chapter, there was the idea broached to the department that David might just have a leave of absence for two years from University College Oxford to do good to us at University College London. He did prematurely play the strongest hand in the appointment of the two young men who succeeded Jerry and Colin. It all ended unhappily, in recrimination. The Provost said, reasonably, that he had never thought that the Grote Chair could be held as a temporary or missionary appointment. It deserved better. A sharp note saying so went off to University College Oxford. Had David ever wanted Freddie's old chair? Or had he really wanted to have it on his c.v. without, so to speak, actual labour and loss of job opportunities elsewhere? It could put you in mind of those gents from the Indian subcontinent, sometimes publishers, whose business cards carried the words 'B.A. Failed, Bombay'.

As this year neared its end, it seemed that I was no longer anathema but again a candidate for the chair, maybe even to the fore. Some said this was the Provost's view. If my life did not depend on another title, and might not survive it, my hopes rose. They fell again when I heard from Malcolm of a visit paid to the Provost by Bernard Williams, down on a day-return ticket from Cambridge. He was, in my view, an upholder of standards in philosophy, a well-wisher of the college, and also an emissary and perhaps piqued. As I understood it, perhaps correctly, he persuaded Sir James of at least the proposition that he should take more thought about the Grote Chair, wait for a while.

Catherine and I passed a fortnight of August in Venice, peaceful comrades in step. The islands of the lagoon were further explored, the lecturing pulpit of Galileo at the university in Padua revered. Another death by cancer awaited me back in England, Vanessa Ayer's. She was 48. When I took him to dinner, Freddie was in an awful state, and said he had thought of committing suicide. She had died well. As an obituary said, the summoned undertaker responded to her spirited instructions about a funeral with a question, 'May I know the name of the deceased?', and got the firm reply 'The deceased will be myself.' That she had died well was not much solace to Freddie, and my powers of consolation were wholly insufficient.

It was being borne in on me more strongly that I was not only a definer and defender of egalitarianism, and a member of the Labour Party, and a sympathizer with the impulse to revolution, but also a landlord. It could be kept in mind that my being landlord of The Studio at 4 Keats Grove was a kind of accident, that it had grown out of a local historical process that began with the idea of a cooperative purchase, maybe a commune. It could be kept in mind too that the rest of the process, *Honderich v. Green Shoes*, had taken on a will of its own. That was all very well, but landlord I was, if fortunately not one in profit.

Mr Hobbs had added to his natural superiority as an artist and a drinker some barracks experience in the R.A.F. He was well able to deal with the soft landlord class. Whether or not he still painted canvasses, he would paint no walls, unblock no sink, whatever the lease required, these being activities unsuited to the artistic temperament. More money was being spent by me on keeping The Studio standing up than was coming in from it, and so the Fair Rent Officer, one of the few remaining functionaries of the Welfare State, did raise the rent slightly. This was no problem for my Mr Hobbs, who was consistent in these matters, and paid neither unfair nor fair rents.

As for the inconsistency involved in being a socialist landlord, my attempts to clarify it were of an ordinary kind. If I supported fundamental change in society, a whole new system, did that entail self-denial by me in the existing system? What I supported, maybe, was no landlords at all. Did that entail excluding myself by my own fiat from their present number? Certainly the existing economic and social system was appallingly unfair in all respects, private property first of all. But my personal resignation from the system would not weaken it much. Also, resignation would involve an unfairness conceivably not trivial. If I *had* to compare the prospects of my children with the prospects of children in the new underclass, I *could* compare the prospects of my children with the prospects of the children of my colleagues. If I *had* to compare myself with the English beggar now brought out of history and into existence again, I *could* compare myself with my colleagues.

Should I remember Bernard's moral philosophy and be fastidious? Would I be better if I kept my own hands clean? Would my giving up most of my salary to the Labour Party, and also giving up The Studio, have the recommendation that by so doing I would preserve my integrity, be true to myself? Well, as you gather, I wouldn't be being true to *all* of myself. In any case, what was the worth of truth to self, considered in isolation from the effects of the actions, including real effects on oneself? Zero worth, was the answer. There was some balm in this reflection, as in the others. There was not enough for me to be free with the information that I was not only among the philosophers of the Left but also, in my way, *rentier*.

There were other small flies in the ointment of what was otherwise a time of contentment. My editing of the several series of philosophical books went on, and since it did, must have been more satisfaction than dissatisfaction to me. I had been or would be accessory to the shedding of light on the Pre-Socratics by Barnes, on Augustine by Kirwan, Locke by Ayers, Nietzsche by Schacht, Santayana by Sprigge, Frege by Kenny, Frege by Sluga, Russell by Sainsbury, Russell's political philosophy by Ryan, Wittgenstein's philosophy of psychology by Budd, Ayer by Foster, Popper by O'Hear, and all of philosophy by Hamlyn. Also light on rationality by Brown, private property by Grunebaum, scepticism by Hookway, actions by Hornsby, and *if p, then q* by Sanford.

Still editing could be a fly in the ointment. It was a source of bad conscience, as you have heard. This was increased early in December 1985 by a review of a book that promised us a new basis for moral philosophy. I cannot guess, said *The Times Literary Supplement*, how such a farrago has appeared in a well-known series. More mindful than I of the use of diplomacy in academic life, the reviewer conveyed more of his amazement by noting that the series was edited by a philosopher of remarkable clear-headedness, etc. I now read the book through, and resolved that I would take more time over the manuscripts of authors unknown to me, and did for a while.

My Christmas party, sixth in the series, was also in a way imperfect. To it came Lewis Wolpert and Jill Neville, scientist and novelist, both of generous dispositions. Jill's led her to bring along a fellow Australian, a waif in England at Christmas. Proud of my party's membership, I was not keen on an uninvited guest, but was welcoming enough. The waif liked the Beaujolais. Having been left behind by her two benefactors when they went on to another party, she engaged in the Australian national sport, this being a variant of *épater le bourgeois*. Mildly described, it consists in reducing the complacency of the intelligentsia, demonstrating that Yvonne's as good as her master. Poseurs and pseuds were discerned on all sides, and this fact was brought home to them.

Professor Karl-Miller, whose shortcomings included the editorship of *The London Review of Books*, may have received the news with Scots stoicism. No doubt Nicola Lacey, good friend and Fellow in Law at New College Oxford had reserves of legal applomb. But Sir James Lighthill, my Provost, was not pleased with his new standing of pseudo-scientist, and showed it unmistakeably. I remain grateful to the waif that despite his sharp retorts she excused him the *coup de grace*, this being a glass of Beaujolais to the shirt-front. Another guest got it, and in the end a professor of psychology whose name momentarily escapes me, possibly a behaviourist, got into the spirit of the occasion, and replied in kind. The waif, now pink, was unabashed. But I save you, reader, a continuation of this low-life scene. On the next day, I turned over in my mind, slowly, the reassuring proposition that Sir James in committee was surely not a man to bear a grudge to a hapless host.

Very likely I thought of the feelings and choosings of the Australian waif, and of Jill Neville's in her graceful apology, and of the waif's in sending me a large bouquet of flowers, in the way it now occurred to me to think of all mental episodes. This was in terms of my philosophical preoccupation, my determinism. Its second and principal hypothesis seemed more or less clear, and my main concern now in revising my manuscript was again with whether this hypothesis was true. Was each mental episode, including each piece of choosing and deciding, really an effect of a long causal sequence whose initial items were inherited and environmental ones?

The best source of evidence for the hypothesis about a long causal sequence was neuroscience. To look into it was to find a large and ramified set of causal connections between neural events. Only the most fundamental of these had to do with the functioning of each of the elements basic to everything in the head, each neuron. Certainly the electrochemical activity of each of these cells was taken as a matter of cause and effect, as was the connection between two of them. If a brain looked at in terms of these elements was causal, how could there be *any* true way of looking at it, in terms of relations between systems or levels or whatever, that was not causal? You didn't have to spend time on the idea of mysteriously 'emerging' properties or the like, if those were supposed to be something other than effects.

The fact of individual neurons could be buttressed by an awful lot more. That was all satisfactory, but what it added up to was a general truth only about neurons. All *neural* events are effects of long causal sequences that include other neural and bodily events and also, of course, environmental events that impinge on the person in question. For outrageous Identity Theorists, those who believed that mental events, including choosings and decidings, were only neural events, the general truth in neuroscience would itself amount to most of a determinism. It would itself nearly amount to a causal picture of ourselves that at least raised a question about our freedom, responsibility and so on. But, having been saved by good sense, I was not among these theorists, many of them Australian.

So the general truth from neuroscience did not itself produce a determinism for me. It became clear, as it should have before, that the scientific truth about neurons played a good role in my whole philosophical picture of determinism, but no more than that. For me, each mental event was something subjective in lawlike connection with a simultaneous neural event – each momentary thought or feeling or intention, and each choice or decision, was a correlate of a neural event. As for my story of how such correlates were caused, they were the effect of a long causal sequence, one that included other such correlates.

Considering two correlates as an effect, there admittedly was a problem of how one bit of it could be necessary to the other if that other bit was necessitated by the prior causal sequence. The right move was to take the neural part and the mental part together as a *single* effect. The truth, if a little breath-taking, had to be that strictly speaking neither part was to be taken as an effect on its own. Thus they made up what you could call a psychoneural pair – two lawlike correlates that are a single effect. The complication about being one effect was tolerable, wasn't it? Reality didn't *have* to be simple, especially human reality. This Union Theory of simultaneous mental and neural events, as you could also call it, might be exactly right. It was in fact one of the sane or sensible Identity Theories, surely the best of them.*

The general truth from neuroscience, that all *neural* events are effects of long causal sequences, was not identical with my bundle of philosophy. Still, there was a connection. Neuroscience sharply limited the possible answers to the question of how thoughts, feelings, intentions, choices and decisions came about. My story was certainly a possible one, and a lot better than Australian Identity Theories. In fact you could suppose, although neuroscientists officially restricted their findings to neurons, that they were inclined to exactly my whole philosophical bundle. You could get one in a corner, maybe, and get him to agree that it was what he really believed. Neuroscientists were not Epipheno-menalists, despite some loose talk. And *of course* they did not take us to possess a faculty of The Will or to be proprietorial Selves or miraculous originators of choices and decisions.

The third hypothesis of my theory was that all actions or doings are effects of causal sequences beginning in certain psychoneural pairs. It needed more clarification and support, but not much. So, if troubled in my confidence, a completed determinist I was on the way to being. I was on the way to being a member of a brave tradition that included Spinoza, Hume, Newton, Einstein and a host of lesser luminaries. Should we be

---

* See pp. 246, 261

troubled by Quantum Theory? Not much. As you may remember from some paragraphs at the beginning of this book, we did not need to be so deferential to wonderful interpretations of the mathematics of Quantum Theory. So I lacked Free Will, as that term is usually understood, and so did we all. Did it follow from this that we were not in any sense free, that we were not in any way responsible? Was that the consequence of determinism?

Catherine and I came to an end in March, mutually enough, with weeping on my side and stoic gracefulness on hers. We thereafter went our separate ways quickly and without further fuss, and said that after a respite of some months we would go forward as friends. We would not be writing another properly condescending letter to *The Guardian* together if Freddie needed defending again from Ernest Gellner, the merely sociological adversary of analytic philosophy. But we would be in touch. She had made my life better and prouder, and, as it became possible to see, I had done no great harm to hers. She had preserved what she rarely spoke of but valued resolutely, the autonomy of women.

As it seems possible to see now, of this and other connections of mine, their endings were in a way accidents. At the beginning of this book, something was also said of what has not been talked of explicitly since, but has received illustration. The subject is *the persons we are* or person-stages. This is not the philosopher's question of personal identity or the persistent person, and in particular not the subject of one mysterious thing that persists through each of our lives. The person you are, in the different sense in question, is not settled by the consideration that you share a body with a certain child, or are connected by memories with that child, or are the same inner self.

The person you are is unlikely to be, very likely cannot be, the person you were. The person you are is a matter of dispositions and attitudes that now exist, and did not exist earlier in your life and are unlikely to exist later. Questions arise about these transient persons and the persistent person. To one question, the answer is simple. Yes, relationships end because of the persons that two people are, persons they then cease to be. If one party or the other had got to a later stage earlier, there might have been no ending. There would not have been the accident of mistiming. Is it an accident that can have negligence in it? Insufficient foresight? Negligence that can lie on the file, stay on a persistent charge-sheet?

Not long after the ending with Catherine, I was in Venice again, this time with Dr Kerry Greer, neurophysiologist and psychologist. You are right, reader, that in this part of my life like others, the woman part, I did not let the grass grow under my feet. My diary for the week in Venice records a good performance of *The Rake's Progress* in the Fenice. We also drank a lot on some evenings, and survived the deflation of my 52-year-old aestheticism by her 34-year-old empiricism.

When at home, Kerry enlivened the Psychology Department at University College. She contributed to what it was keen on, its sense of rightful membership in the Faculty of Science rather than the Faculty of Arts. She was the author of a clear-headed piece, 'Physiology of Motor Control', and it was in the bibliography at the end of my determinism manuscript. I would continue my life as a visited and visiting bachelor, but something else could very well grow out of our connection. If passing some evenings of the week by myself in Keats Grove was sustainable, sometimes pleasant, and if we had sharp and dramatic differences, there could be a fuller life to come.

In what remained of this 23rd of my teaching years, and our fourth year in the department without a Grote Professor, I carried on with not much less spirit. There was more television, with better motor control. On one occasion I and the Master of Birkbeck College, the Baroness Blackstone, combined what intellectual forces were needed in order to deal with the simplicities of Thatcherism. At Keats Grove, Kerry sought to accelerate the stately pace of Conrad Russell's table-talk. In the month of June, I was At Home, as the invitation cards said, at the Beefsteak Club, giving drinks to 40 assorted friends and acquaintances. The Provost could not fit it in, which saddened me, but my son John came as a representative of the college, having lately got his good English degree from it. My colleague the gentle reasoner Marcus Giaquinto liked the fine room, and to my satisfaction Freddie reported on our conversing the week before with Harold Macmillan at the club's common table.

Then there was Ghana and another room, high in The Castle, with guns in the corners and under the table. My conversings with Jerry Rawlings, also on social reality, went on for many hours, to my edification. The *People's Daily Graphic* reported on its front page my view that the Provisional National Defence Council appeared to be making progress towards the ideal of egalitarianism. Back in London the World Service of the BBC transmitted an interview with me that carried much the same good news, and my piece in *The Times* partly survived an attack on it by a sub-editor who knew his proprietor's politics.

As the new year started in October 1986, all of my manuscript on determinism was being subjected to a final inspection for philosophical virtue, and doing well. Some time was being given to further clarification and fortification of the third hypothesis of the theory, about our actions. Yes, I was right in my conception of an action or doing, say tossing wine or making an apology or sending a bouquet. Actions in general were of course not merely bodily movements. If it should happen that exactly the arm movements that went into a wine-tossing occurred again, but in a very unusual way, without any intention on the part of the person, this would not be an action by the person. The movements would not be my action if they were entirely the result of someone else's grip on my elbow. Nor would they be anyone's action if they came about as a result of some neural commotion in my motor cortex unconnected with anyone's mental life.

But nor were actions to be taken as compounds or mixtures made up of movements and of mental facts before them, perhaps intentions or volitions, as Colin McGinn and predecessors had supposed. Maybe he'd got the idea in an afternoon of practising his rock-band drums next door to my eyrie, but he should have had second thoughts afterwards. On this view, no one could ever see all of an action, which was odd. Still worse, a throwing could begin before an arm moved, a nod begin before a head moved. Surely no conception of an action could be satisfactory if it mislocated it in time? The right idea was that actions *were* movements, or stillnesses, and no more than that, but only the movements and stillnesses somehow owed to an active intention or intending on the part of the agent. An active intention could be explained, too, rescued from mystery. As for the result of these reflections, that actions were effects of standard causal sequences beginning in psychoneural pairs of which one element was an intending, this third hypothesis of determinism also got good support from neuroscience. That it was not much needed did not lead me to omit the details of it.

Thus there was finished the pile of manuscript whose title had already been tested with my inaugural lecture. *A Theory of Determinism: The Mind, Neuroscience, and Life-Hopes* was very long, long enough to make a book of about 750 pages. Here was a substantial thing, the product to be expected of labours, although interrupted, that had extended over 25 years. It was something that might earn me a future. In cooler moments it seemed very unlikely to be a great book, something to earn me a place in the pantheon of philosophy. But it might still be on the shelves of some succeeding generations of philosophers, or anyway borrowed by them from college libraries in desultory summers. Limited immortality.

To make the chance larger, and to save me from what colleagues and other interested parties might allude to as my having published my book myself, it should not be brought out by Routledge & Kegan Paul or Penguin. Certainly it was not the easy introduction to the subject for which Penguin and I had made a contract many years ago, now well forgotten. Four years ago the philosophy editor at Oxford University Press had got the idea, on the basis of some draft chapters, that maybe the book would be no major landmark. Since then, fortuitously, he had given over his editorial role to the sagacious Angela Blackburn, wife of the philosopher Simon Blackburn. She had sent me a manuscript or two for reading, and had liked my advice and its promptness. Might she not have a better eye for major landmarks? Might she settle for a minor landmark?

At about this time, on a television programme about thoughts of death, a subject more familiar to me than others that got my public attention, I made use of the bracing line from an ancient Stoic. Life is a banquet room from which it is our obligation to leave gracefully at the appointed hour. Hume too was remembered for his farewell by sedan chair, and Blake for singing songs near the end, and making a last drawing of his wife Kate. But, as my notes for my performance record, I also intended to make use of the idea that you can tell you are with the right partner if you would like to have her on hand to see you off.

In my case it had seemed at times that Kerry, who came along to the television studio, should have that privilege, but now in my judgemental way I found my way to the datum that we were unsuited. The prospect of having a child concentrated both our minds, and brought apprehension about a settled future. This apprehension, on my part, had little to do with the differences of 19 years in our ages, but a good deal to do with the unlikelihood of compromise by two wilful spirits. If I saw some edge or corner of my own unreasonableness, I could not contain it. Nor did I wait on time. It seemed to me necessary to be resolute. In addition to resolution, efficiency was needed. In February 1987, as I should not have, I alone went where the two of us had planned to go together. This was to Leningrad with Janet and her new friend Derek Parfit.

Derek, as meticulous in his photography as his philosophy, waited through days in Palace Square for the necessary moment of weather and light that might never come, sustained by resolution and also his battery-heated gloves. Janet and I, meanwhile, exchanged views on large numbers of pictures in the Hermitage, giving only a judicious amount of attention to the Impressionists. In the plane home, Janet looked over her shoulder to see me weeping. My familiar feeling was disgrace. It was not a feeling diminished by the sharp recollection that Miranda, with whatever reason, had failed to greet me in a restaurant.

On getting back to Keats Grove the news was that Bill Coldstream had died. We had not been very close friends, but how many of those had he had, anyway in the later part of his life? How many had I had in my life? I remembered pictures of his, and going to see him at work in Church Row in Hampstead, and the joke about falling asleep on the bus home and missing his stop, and ending up in Stoke Newington, and thinking it was Belgium. He had not been able, because of health, to come towards the end of his life in decent spirits. He could not be content near the close of his hours in the banquet room. Maybe I would be luckier.

By degrees over several weeks, more quickly than retrospect would prefer, more news revived my spirits. The best was that Oxford University Press might be my new publisher. The Press's decisive advisor on my pile, not by my doing, but no misfortune either, was Derek. He discerned that my aim had been encyclopaedic. Indeed it had been, and indeed the aim had been owed to an insecurity, as well seen by me then as now, but inescapable. It was clear to him, from an Oxford perspective, that the Professors Popper and Eccles did not require so much refutation. A cut of 12 per cent in the pile, which the Press might be got to tolerate after having earlier required more, would be in order. Since the pile was a *magnum opus*, said Derek, the author of course would like to see it come out as one volume, but afterwards it should be two paperbacks, one containing the philosophy of mind and the like for the tough-minded, and one on the human consequences of determinism for the tender-minded.

The Grote Chair was now in its fifth year without an occupant. One reason given was the college's unsettling or even dire financial situation. As with other places of higher education, this was the result of the government's priorities, unprofitable truth not being high among them. Another reason why the chair was unfilled was that no candidate for it scintillated. Richard was sending thoughts and general advice from America, but so far without success. This had partly to do with the familiar fact that philosophers no more agree about themselves than about their doctrines. It was at this time, I think, that Professor Searle was mentioned by me for the chair. He was in no need of its distinction, being in the international firmament, but was judged by my colleagues to be only a dull star, if star at all. Some thought, too, that the chair's being empty owed something to the Provost's having been tired by his attempts to fill it.

Might it happen, as external candidates rose and fell, that a candidate from within the department would emerge? With an internal candidate, at least you knew what you were getting. Might a candidate who had once been anathema emerge? Even if someone with a very good memory for a dinner party might propose, as it transpired they did, that an opinion on the candidate's harmoniousness be taken from Professor Michael Dummett?

The chair committee, by college tradition, had seven members. Five were the Provost and professors of allied subjects. Two were representatives of the department, these being Malcolm Budd our Acting Head, and Bill Hart. The two philosophers, if they could be outvoted, would certainly be listened to. It was my firm impression that Malcolm, although given to sitting on philosophical and other fences, was well-disposed to me. He would support me in the absence of a bright star. Bill Hart, despite my civility, would not. I was certainly not his hero. So the philosophers on the committee would be divided, leaving the upshot more uncertain.

It was at this stage that an excellent idea was had by somebody disinclined to my further progress. It was an admirable stratagem. At my instigation, the ordinary promotion machinery of the college was in this year raising Malcolm from Lecturer to Reader, which he would be next year. He was now proposed by Bill as a candidate for the Grote Chair, albeit a self-deprecating and officially unwilling one. It gave me more than pause. If I had found myself in his position, I wondered, would my self-deprecation persist? Would I not be struck by the fact that Malcolm reported to me, that he had been told that powerful referees could be arranged for him by his promoters? Would no ambition be aroused in me? Would I not be captured by hope? Could I face the disappointment of hope? I saw the Provost and left him my new *curriculum vitae*, with some optimism but not a lot, and reassured myself that all that really mattered was limited immortality.

To my college's honour, it did not seriously cross my mind in these Thatcherite months that my having been taken as an apostle of violence in a small way might give pause to a committee member. Prudence did not require that I withdraw from a debate in the Oxford Union on the motion 'This house believes that IRA violence is not justified in pursuit of a political solution for Ireland'. Other invited speakers did publicly withdraw when the Union revealed to the press that a further speaker would be Mr Gerry Adams, M.P. for West Belfast and head of Provisional Sinn Fein, the political wing of the IRA.

There was a little self-preservation in my not simply defending the IRA, but speaking instead as the only cross-bencher in the debate – neither opposing nor supporting the motion. There was also truth to my convictions. It was not so hard, said I, and might be morally imperative, to support the campaigns of violence of the African National Congress in South Africa and the Palestine Liberation Front in Palestine. IRA violence was different, on account of the difficulty of probability-judgements about its success. It was harder to support. The main thing to be said, however, was that the British government was wrong in prolonging a situation of injustice in which Irish patriots would certainly fight. Only light and transient moral philosophy could absolve the British government from a responsibility for the predictable actions of others. To support only the condemnation of the IRA would be morally blind partiality. All present should abstain in the vote. In the event, 348 did support the condemnation, 47 opposed it, and 305 abstained. The condemners were thus outnumbered. It was a good night for the IRA, as the press said in the morning. I remain satisfied to have been a cause of it.

The labour of shortening my manuscript took three months, and was done just in time for a celebratory dinner at Keats Grove in May. Michael Foot and his wife Jill Craigie were on hand, my forwardness having lately added them to my list of friends and acquaintances. Freddie came with his acquaintance Verity Ravensdale, evidently life-enhancing and at that point not tightly married to the novelist Nicholas Mosley. Janet too was present, along with my son John, who did me proud in what my diary happily recorded as the blazing talk. Some of it was about the election that Michael's successor Mr Kinnock was about to win. My piece in support of the Labour Party had been declined by *The Independent*, I had thought, because of the banality of the truths it contained against the government, truths that would necessarily be acted upon by a people. Instead, on 12 June 1987, the people elected for a third time a government whose righteousness was transparently self-serving, and whose policies were vicious.

This at least touched my confidence about the place in which I had now spent most of my life. Here was no slow progress in decency. A democracy, manipulated by a press prating of freedom to serve its owners and their party, had voted to do nothing much about three million people without work. A democracy had voted to continue what was already apparent, making the rich richer and the poor poorer, feeding self-indulgence and adding to misery. It did not matter that Oxford again refused her daughter Prime Minister Thatcher an honorary degree.

Half of July was a holiday with Freddie and Dee Wells, his second wife and the predecessor of Vanessa. In their house on a hill above Le Beausset, along the coast from Toulon in the Var, we talked, worked, drank the *vin de pays* despite its being *rosé*, and played bowls. Freddie's son Nicholas and his friends made friends with French girls and crashed cars, without serious consequence. Coming up to 77, Freddie continued to be taken up with himself, but he had my great affection, as real as my feeling for any man outside my family. It was increased by my overhearing, in the mornings as he made his tea, his pensive reciting, as if to the cat, of some lines from Tennyson about the time that was left to him. What is also true is that we were not on perfect terms, for the reason that he suspected me of a kind of *lèse-majesté*, this being affection for lovely Verity, by whom he too had been smitten, without result.

We were, so to speak, working on the same book. It would be published some years later as *The Philosophy of A. J. Ayer*, a volume in the series *The Library of Living Philosophers*. It would contain papers on him and his replies to them. Mine was on his view of causation, his elaboration of Hume's idea that a causal circumstance and its effect are just two items such that all others like the first are followed by others like the second. It was not believable, said I, essentially for the old reason having to do with yesterday and last night not being causal circumstance and effect. There was no deference at all in my laying-out of my different view about a whatever-else connection, but pleasure in paying him a forceful compliment in my first paragraph. There was pleasure too, if also a touch of uncertainty, in taking my examples in my paper from our holiday and from the doings of Nick. For him, as Freddie had written, he had a love which was a dominating factor in his life. Might my examples have been better avoided? They will not be edited out to avoid the charge of flattery in any future reprinting, which, perhaps fortunately, is unlikely.

In London we more or less made up the difference between us, and went on as before. There were more lunch parties, several graced by Catherine Lamb. I and the book-packager Elsie Donald, a belle of the American South transformed into an English hostess, contemplated one another hopefully. We had the idea that we would get on amiably on a Spanish holiday, and, despite the residual effect on me of various vegetarians, that we could agree to differ about the bull-fight. Freddie, despite his affection for her, might give us a blessing. There was reason to try to bring our lives together. But my courage for yet another connection was not great, not so great as my fatigue. Her realism was firm, as indeed was the realism of one or two others who fell under my contemplation.

The Keats Grove house ran true to form. The new freeholder in improving his basement sought to have me and my fellow leaseholders in the house pay for the repair of a damp-proof course that did not exist. My solicitors Farrer & Co. dealt nicely with this ambition, sticking to the logic that you cannot repair what is not there. Mr Hobbs, presumably pleased with the fine new roof on The Studio, must also have been pleased to discover that the Welfare State was in some respects not dragged down. It would pay off his arrears of rent of £2,000, and also pay his rent in the future. This further fortified his capability of dealing with the landlord.

Money was also a subject elsewhere in my life. In my role as chairman of the London philosophers, it had fallen to me to negotiate further with Mr Jens Jacobsen, a singular Dane of 76. He had already made a decent benefaction to the university. His whole fortune from import-export, he now made clear, might come to the university. Could we have the money without undertaking to propagate his personal philosophy? It had to do with Life-Forces, and the primal disaster for human affairs of the first-person pronoun 'I', and was elusive.

At a culminating meeting, also attended by the chief clerk of the university, I completed the work of other university personnel, some of whom had given up too soon. Jens's agreement was got to what seemed an honourable proposal. The University of London would at least get the worth of a vanload of bonds on which the Chinese and others had defaulted after their Communist revolutions. There had been a speculative trade in these bonds, and monies had now been lodged by the Chinese and others with a British government body called the Foreign Compensation Commission. Claims could be made to the commission. The bonds might turn out to be worth something.

15

LIFE-HOPES, THE GROTE,
AN IDEA'D GIRL

My determinism book was now being brought into being by Oxford University Press, its advent not underestimated by me in filling in my Author's Publicity Form. You have indeed heard some grounds of my hope for its future, and my own, but not much of the main ground. I was confident that the book contained a resolution of the problem about determinism most argued about by philosophers in October 1987, as it had been since Hobbes, Hume and Kant in the seventeenth and eighteenth centuries. This is not the problem of formulating a conceptually adequate theory of determinism, which came into view when the philosophy of mind became an industry in the twentieth century. Nor is it the problem of the truth of such a determinism.

It is rather the problem of the human consequences of determinism. What follows *if* a proper determinism is true? Nothing, said Compatibilists airily. Disaster, said Incompatibilists gravely. My own inclination had been to join the latter crew, Kant and successors as against Hobbes, Hume and successors. Almost all Incompatibilists however, made themselves more comfortable than I ever could. Almost all of them escaped their gloom by making an addition to the proposition that *if* determinism is true there is no freedom or moral responsibility. The addition, of course, was that determinism is *not* true – thanks be to God, moral necessity, or Quantum Theory.

In trying to deal with the problem, it had seemed a good idea to give up a philosophical habit, at least for a while. That was the habit of peering at the words 'determined' and 'free' and 'responsible' to see if the first word could be shown by some contrivance of argument to be logically compatible or incompatible with the second and third. It seemed a good idea to look more directly at life itself with determinism in mind. If you did that, what turned up first was not about freedom-in-general or morality. It was that determinism raised a question about your hopes, and above all about something you could call your life-hope, your main hope. Such a hope may shape at least a stage of a person's life.

You may hope to succeed in a struggle against adversaries, or to enter into and be enriched by an unending relationship with another person, or you may hope to do both these things. Indeed you may. Or, if you find yourself in different circumstances, you may mainly hope to be an actress, or own a car, or live where you are not condescended to, or have enough to eat, or to live for a while longer. And what is such a hope? Well, it is a particular *attitude*. Like attitudes in general, as against true or false beliefs, it takes things to be good or bad, and, what is part of that, has desires in it. More particularly, a life-hope is an attitude to the future, almost always a desiring thought about possible actions of yours, about what they will be and what will flow from them.

Let me not be fastidious or prolong this approach to a certain proposition. It is that each of us has two sorts of hope, including two sorts of life-hope. In one sense they share the same content. Both are about adversaries or relationships or acting or owning cars or whatever, but they are still different. Certainly you can recover this fact of your experience by reflection on your life, the inside of your life.

One sort of life-hope carries the thought or is based on the idea that maybe nothing will get in the way of your desires and your nature. Neither someone else's desires or nature nor any other adverse circumstance will frustrate your attempt to get what you really want and value. It will turn out that by your actions you will succeed. You will not just be putting up with things. The other sort of hope carries an additional thought, that your future is not already settled, that you have a kind of chance. Your future is open in the sense that questions about it are not yet answered. The situation isn't that the answers already exist, that they are stored-up and waiting, but that they do not yet exist. Your future will consist of moments when what you do and what happens is not fixed by the past, and in particular not fixed by what you have been. Your future doesn't already have failure in it. You can get away from things, from yourself in particular.

It did not seem difficult to make clear that indeed we all have, or at the very least can find in ourselves, the two kinds of life-hopes, different in their bases and also their feelings. This could be shown to be true at least of all of us in Western culture. Contained in the proposition, evidently, was something else. We have rooted in our lives *two* images or notions of actions and their initiation: as voluntary or flowing from our own desires, and as both voluntary and also unfixed by the past. We all have and are affected by the image of actions worked up into a definition of freedom by Hobbes, Hume and toiling successors, but additionally we all have an image of actions, quite as tenacious, as also being escapes from the past. That the image is murky and has not been turned into much clear philosophy by Kant and his tradition is nothing to the point, and does not reduce its role in our lives. It may even have enlarged it.

The general argument of Hobbes, Hume and successors has been, first, that our single and settled idea of a free action is of a voluntary one. Therefore, secondly, a free action can be fully determined. All that is needed is that an action proceeds from one kind of cause, say the agent's embraced desires, and not from the constraint of prison bars or heroin or the like. And so, thirdly, determinism if true changes nothing.

The general argument of Kant and successors has been, first, that our single and settled idea of a free action is of one both voluntary and also originated. Such an action might not have been chosen given the past and the present exactly as they were and are. So, secondly, a free action cannot be determined, and, thirdly, if determinism were true, there would be the disaster that we are never free.

The proposition about our having two kinds of life-hopes, containing the two notions of freedom, surely rocked these venerable traditions, both still having more knobs fitted to them. Consideration of other consequences of determinism, also overlooked by Compatibilists and Incompatibilists, finished the job. We also have two attitudes of confidence in the truth of our beliefs. One involves our free inquiry as having been voluntary or unconstrained, and one involves free inquiry as also being in a way unlimited. So too with personal attitudes to other persons that are not moral attitudes, say gratitude and resentment, to which Peter Strawson had paid attention. So too with the long preoccupation of Compatibilists and Incompatibilists, moral responsibility. The attitudes of holding people responsible for actions and crediting them with responsibility for actions come in the two forms. Holding people responsible in the second way has a retributive desire in it.

What you needed to say in sum about freedom generally, having looked at the various particulars on the ground, was that there are two ideas of freedom that have a hold on us. So, both Compatibilism and Incompatibilism were plainly wrong, failures in the very first step of their general arguments. What I particularly liked about the conclusion was that it seemed to be provable. You could prove it by forgetting about linguistic analysis and modal logic, and considering our attitudes. The proof was well on the way to being that fine and public thing, a behavioural one. In part, it *was* a behavioural one. If a man behaves in a certain way in certain circumstances, it is in human terms certain that he has the idea of a glass of wine. If we act in *two* different ways in punishing people, as we do, it is in human terms certain that we have two governing notions of their responsibility, not one. The rejection of both Compatibilism and Incompatibilism could not be the final resolution of the problem of determinism, since it raised a new problem, but it was well on the way.

In 19 Gordon Square we philosophers began to have less confidence about the Grote Chair, now in its sixth year without anyone in it. Might it conceivably be consigned to the attic of University College London? Thatcher's political philosophy, rightly laid out in the magazine *Woman's Own*, was that there was no such thing as society. Whatever else this came to, it promised no money for the declining universities. In the first term of this year, while replacing Malcolm Budd as Acting Head during his time off, I continued his supplication to the college and particularly the Provost to fill the chair.

I also did a bit of supplicating on behalf of myself. Was the present college committee for the filling of the chair ideally fair? One philosopher on the committee was greatly influenced by he who was still about the college during some terms, the previous holder of the chair. By a very good tradition, he was supposed not to be concerned in the matter. Judging a candidate for a chair should not be a matter of carrying on any old battle, but looking to the future. The second philosopher on the committee, being human, must be influenced by having been made into a candidate himself. He would have got over his diffidence, wouldn't he? How could he judge the matter impartially?

As for the idea that had come up of the chair's being advertised, there was no possibility of my opposing such an enlightened break with tradition. It did cross my mind that the rise of the idea might have as much to do with tactics in the present situation as a belated conversion to the idea of the career open to the talents. But also, as Martin Swales said, calling on his sagacity as Dean of Arts, an invitation to all comers might well issue in judgement in favour of me.

Such was the Grote situation, in my view of it, as Christmas approached. My party went off nicely, 49 being present, the guest list having been pruned of those who appeared actually to believe in Thatcherism, and had added to it such newer acquaintances as the amiably confident Margaret Jay, member of two Labour Party families. The last meeting under my chairmanship of the Bertorelli's Lunch Club, after five years in the role, was as orderly, despite some consideration by Noel and others of my idea of admitting women to the membership. Both of these gatherings were less consequential than a third.

This was the annual party of the publishers Duckworth, in their offices in what was called the Old Piano Factory, in Camden Town. It was, more particularly, the party of the firm's presiding spirit, Colin Haycraft, a convivial man who saw both the profit and the higher worth of philo-sophy books. As always, the party was congenial. The first Oxford personage with whom I fell into conversation, when we turned our minds without great delay to academic politics, declared what an awful disaster it would be if my friend David Wiggins were elected to the Oxford chair being vacated by Peter Strawson. Many in Oxford felt that, he said. The second Oxford personage with whom I fell into conversation said what an awful disaster it would be if my acquaintance Simon Blackburn were elected to the professorship. Many felt that, he said.

It was reassuring to have this further evidence that philosophical passions, even *odium philosophicum*, were not peculiar to University College London, and could be directed to two fellows of Oxford colleges. It was thought-provoking too. It raised questions in the mind. If the two local candidates for the Oxford chair had local parties ranged against them, might an external candidate not slip between them? Might the board of electors for the Waynflete Professorship of Metaphysical Philosophy not turn its eye to someone not of the spires? A candidate who had lately defeated all of Hobbes, Hume, and Kant? The St Thomas's Day feast at New College to which Jonathan Glover had taken me the other week had been grand. It had been agreeable to be placed at the high table, opposite the Warden, for the dessert course. There was also another and different thought to be had about it all. Might my Oxford ambition and my chance of realizing it not concentrate the mind of University College London?

It was fortuitous that I had new credentials to hand, certainly weighty, these being the page proofs of *A Theory of Determinism: The Mind, Neuroscience, and Life-Hopes*. The 640 pages were being read not only by me, but also by the sagacious Mary Warnock, with whom I would be discussing them on Radio 3. They were also being read by various philosophers who would be contributing to a special issue of the journal *Inquiry*, this having been proposed as fit and proper by Alastair Hannay. From these personages, new referees in support of my claim to the Oxford chair might be drawn. They would include a clutch from across the Atlantic, since it was becoming desirable for English philosophers to have American accreditation. Peter Strawson himself, furthermore, having been supplied with another set of proofs, although he was likely to be called upon by other aspirants as well, would write a letter for me. So too would David Hamlyn, the professor at Birkbeck College, well-informed not only on the history of philosophy generally, but also on the recent history of philosophers in the colleges of the University of London.

More sets of proofs could be Xeroxed. Five sets went with me for distribution to members of the board of electors for the Waynflete Professorship of Metaphysical Philosophy when I took my application to Oxford in January. It was not the only visit that had been under contemplation. One was soon paid, out of academic courtesy as you might say, to my own Provost. Sir James listened with attention to my tale of the Duckworth party, and of my day-trip to Oxford.

Very interesting, he said, but it would be a pity to lose you. Might some of these persons informed of your new work, say about five, send me an opinion for the use of the Grote Committee? Indeed they might. To eight persons, including my referees for the Oxford chair, went more notes and telegrams from the eyrie. Most of these communications reported on my reading of Hume, who had said 'tis natural for a Man, that has not been much accustom'd to solicit for Favours, to be a little shy in that particular. Not half so natural, said I, as the shyness produced by asking for a second favour hard on the heels of a first. But, having overcome it, it was possible for me to solicit support for the Grote as well as the Waynflete. Freddie, Derek, and Peter would say a word for me. Also, among others, Professor Jaegwon Kim, the rising American philosopher of the nature of events.

It came to my ear that the Grote Committee had been summoned to meet on 9 March 1988. In the meantime, my diary could have in it some reflection on academic careers in general and on mine in particular. If mine prospered further, would this be owed to improprieties? Yes, I had conveyed to interested parties in the college that opposition to me had to do not only with my present accomplishments but also with a local history that included an accomplishment in connection with Freud. Yes, when serving as a member of another of the Provost's chair committees, I had been moved by something in addition to principle in making a certain remark that he might take in. It was that none other than Professor Sir Alfred Ayer had been elected to a professorship by a committee whose philosopher-members had opposed him. I concluded my diary reflections, confidently, that I had been more sinned against than sinning.

It seemed yet more true, perhaps an instance of moral luck, when the news came through at noon on 9 March that the Grote Chair was on offer to me. No time would be taken for advertising. It also came to my ear, perhaps mistakenly, that all but one of the seven members of the committee had been in favour of me. Malcolm, being unwell, had not been at the meeting, and had been rung up at home by the Provost for his opinion, which he gave. He was reported to the meeting as being for me. A year or two later, however, it transpired that there were two views of what he had meant in expressing what was taken by the Provost as support for me.

In Oxford, the committee on the other chair was still taking thought, and might go on doing so for some time. It seemed, correctly as it turned out, that the two local candidates would not succeed. What were my chances? No doubt against another Oxford man serving elsewhere at the moment? A conclusion was reached after a drink that evening with my friend the historian Juliet Gardiner, during which we contemplated the course of history and its *de facto* unpredictability. There was no way available to me of judging my Oxford chances confidently. But, even when thought about in the best of moods, they could not be higher than

75 per cent. In considering even a 75 per cent chance of the Waynflete as against a 100 per cent chance of the Grote, my prudence and my precipitateness easily won out, and produced exhilaration. My application for the Oxford chair was promptly withdrawn. In the next term Grote I would be, with delight.

Life was complete, or at any rate half of life was complete. A long struggle for academic certification had succeeded. A book different from its predecessors on punishment and violence was being announced in a special leaflet from OUP, to my mind excusable in its breathlessness. The recording of the radio programme with Mary Warnock in Keats Grove had been carried off by me with a mixture of *gravitas* and boyish audacity. Michael Stevenson, who had already endeared himself to me by his management of my radio propaganda for Ghana, abandoned the requisite severity of a BBC producer and said yes, Plato had been onto something in taking dialogue to be the proper vehicle for philosophy. Still, there was also the other half of life. A solution to the woman problem was not yet apparent. Perhaps renewed diligence could find it. Perhaps it could turn out that the past Christmas party in the Old Piano Factory would have more consequences. At it, I had also had a third conversation, bracing in a different way.

Jane O'Grady had been an undergraduate in the department during my Janet period, about eight years ago. I had not tutored her, and we had barely met. Not much had been seen of her in the department because of her social life elsewhere, some left over from her having done some acting in Cambridge while taking a diploma course to become a teacher. Fine eyes, fine lips, fine everything. Entirely English to the uninformed eye, she was also of an Irish Catholic father and in terms of her grandparents one-quarter Jewish. Intent on showing her superiority to fashion, femininity and womanliness, she bought her clothes from the Oxfam charity shops, without close attention to their gender. She was definitely an idea'd girl. Her sentences had caught the eye of Auberon Waugh, son of Evelyn, and she was now writing a column for *The Literary Review*, rightly entitled 'O'Grady Says'.

We met again at one of Jean Gimpel's literary salons in Chelsea. Yes, she agreed, after my exposition, Compatibilism and Incompatibilism were *over*. But, to turn to Wittgenstein, my scepticism about his greatness was perverse. His saying that if a lion could talk we could not understand him was pellucid. We went on to Covent Garden for another drink, and began what might be our own fruitful pilgrimage, some of it by bicycle, since she too was a pedaller. Thereafter I worked out a good route from Hampstead to her cottage in North Kensington. It was as characterful as she. It was pretty under its vine, and, having been an electricity sub-station, stood its ground a little formidably.

We were in some agreement about the Thatcherite thinking, transparent in its cupidity, that remained in a kind of general ascendancy. If its pretensions did extend to the point of considering itself a philosophy, it could do with attention, not for its intrinsic worth but for its contribution to the new England. Neil Kinnock had asked for some reflections on it for his speeches, which I was trying to provide. There was also another idea, of which he much approved. Penguins on my advice had brought the thinking of Roger Scruton to the attention of readers of books, his audience until then having been restricted to readers of *The Times*. Should Penguin not publish another kind of work on Conservatism? Jonathan Riley, a rational young editor, agreed. I looked around for a suitable author, and, remembering that I had already had some thoughts on the subject, found myself.

Thus began again some desultory research in the short shelf of the classics of the Conservative tradition, English and American. Save for the sentences of Edmund Burke in his *Reflections on the Revolution in France*, the shelf was not engrossing. My attention remained more on the philosophy of mind and the coming reception of my determinism book. Still, something on Conservatism would get written. It would see what Conservatism was, improve on my previous view, and also see what could be said for and against it. First analysis and then judgement. The analysis, above all, would find the real rationale or unifying principle or best summation of Conservatism. Had I been right before in thinking it was the large Principle of Desert? The book might salve my landlord conscience and make a small contribution to the next election.

There remained one thing to be settled in our philosophy department. Malcolm had been its Acting Head for three years, since Johnny's disappearance. Still superior to the necktie, he had nonetheless discharged this perilous duty safely and well. Maybe it helped that he lived in Cambridge and so was not on hand regularly to get reforming ideas. It was possible to think, despite disclaimers, that he would not mind continuing his success. It had generally been assumed, however, that a new Grote would also be Head. My feelings were divided between a real disinclination to the burden and a thought or two or three. Might any new endeavours of mine, perhaps more *esprit de corps* in the department and the reinvigoration of the postgraduate seminar on Mondays, go better if the department's resources were in my keeping? Including paper for special notices? Might my several Grote perquisites be safer too? Also, by being Head might I at least loosen the label so long attached to me, of being at least a stormy petrel?

Malcolm and I met with the Provost in April. Each, traditionally, said he would prefer the other to be Head. Malcolm went on saying it only a moment longer than I. Head I would be. In preparation for the new dawn, as the Provost had already said, it would be far better if the two departmental secretaries, wedded in soul to Malcolm's predecessors, were not encouraged to give up stated intentions of theirs – to seek employment elsewhere in the eventuality that had now come about. These intentions, however they had come about, had been brought to the attention of the Grote Committee, but had not had anything like the desired effect on its deliberations. Also in preparation for the new dawn, Sir James thought he could see his way to dislodging the college cleaners from the basement of 19 Gordon Square. In future our department would have more room for manoeuvres.

Although capable of ructions, Jane and I were getting on well. If she was self-willed and exasperating, was this not a small price to pay? We spent a weekend in the Devon barn of the artist John Latham, our literary enthusiasms untouched by his works of art. These were books sawn through diagonally or otherwise partly destroyed before being tastefully mounted. I was, I recorded, in love, and there was no need for conceptual analysis of the idea. That I was 55 and Jane 36 was no impediment to the marriage of, at least, true minds. In Sienna and Florence in June, we subjected the proposition to further testing, and it survived. Was credibility attached to it by our holiday companions, including her astute and calm sister Selina, my acute and comradely postgraduate Paul Noordhof, and the unsevere Stevensons, Michael and Deborah, of the BBC and the law? Well, we would not abandon our separate London residences, but would work out even better cycle routes between them.

George Grote was honoured in the college by busts outside the library and in the Senior Common Room, and, less predictably, by a marble profile high in a passage on the way to a gentlemen's convenience. In the term when his name got attached to mine officially, the passage got a lower ceiling, presumably leaving Grote in enduring darkness above it. I did not seek into the meaning of this entombment, but did not report it to my colleagues either. Several might exercise on it that rollicking form of humour, academic wit. Nor, when the Bursar reported that the profile had been taken into safekeeping, did it seem prudent to accept his offer to install it in the Grote's room, to which I had descended from my eyrie. This might be perceived as hubris, conceivably not an exercise of power in a mature and responsible way with proper processes of consultation.

I was becoming aware of the advisability of this policy for a Head of Department, having transgressed again in the cause of departmental seminars. In addition to my mission, failed in during the Watling hegemony, of reviving the Monday postgraduate seminar, it was my aim to resurrect the Wednesday seminar. This was the one limited to teachers of the department, the exclusive drama in which Bernard had starred for a while. I had had a word in passing with colleagues about this, and encountered no dissent. It was no revolutionary proposal. Such things were common.

It is true that in having a word with colleagues, and encountering no dissent, I had not found a universal enthusiasm for philosophizing together for an hour or so on Wednesday afternoons. Some might have to travel to college especially. Universal enthusiasm, thought I, was not an absolute necessity. Was it not part of my new role as Head amicably to jolly and nudge us all into new activity? This was not merely nostalgia for a Golden Age but a higher purpose, the greater good of philosophy. To that higher purpose was added the thought that the government's policy of improving universities now included an assessing and official rating of the research done in each department in each institution. It would be as well for us to be true to our history and in the highest category, a five-star establishment.

The charge laid against me, not too decorously, was not only that I had misconstrued as assent an absence of dissent, but in this way had misled some colleagues in reporting the responses of others. Above all, I had not submitted a proposal formally to a Departmental Meeting. There had not been, in the words of a later indictment, an exercise of power in a mature and responsible way with proper processes of consultation. Malcolm withdrew his offer to read a paper to a first gathering. There would be no philosophizing together on Wednesday afternoons, it seemed.

To my woeful misjudgement in this matter was added another. Some part-time teaching by postgraduates of undergraduates had already begun, an economy in money and time. Should this foot-on-the-ladder, prized by all postgraduates, not be more widely shared out among them? Would that not be better than its being left to the pair favoured by the previous administration, understandably loyal to it? Certainly my redistribution of favours, however sanctioned by the history of politics, had no wisdom in it. Nor was there much wisdom, despite the college's having lately had to go cap in hand to the National Westminster Bank to borrow £5 million, in acceding to the Bursar's economizing in the repainting of the department. The repainting, for the moment, would not be carried higher up the house than the level of the Grote's room.

In these several ways did I follow in the fateful footsteps of that earlier Head, my teacher Johnny. In January 1989 my meeting with Bill Hart proved it is not always a good idea to try to clear the air, rise over the past together and have hopes for the future. No air was cleared. Part of the difficulty was that he had this month not been promoted to Reader. Since he took the line that my powers of machination were great, I needed to absolve myself of responsibility for the choice of referees made on his behalf by the Acting Head before me. One of these, Bill let me know, was a total twit, only accidentally a professor of philosophy of the university.

In February, another visitor was more congenial, if also unsettling. A tearful student was concerned for the common good, and mine, and let me know that one postgraduate, a severe young man, was in the habit of bringing down to the student common room animadversions on my philosophy, career and character just learned from his supervisor. Not Dr Hart, by the way. The postgraduate would be giving these feelings wider currency at the next meeting of the Staff–Student Consultative Committee, that lasting tribunal owed to the events of 1968. Indeed he did, by implication, in the silence of his puppeteer, who looked on impartially. Was I restrained by the severe young man's also being odd, and once seen dashing towards the department in a skirt? I said not enough in reply to him, and nothing to puppeteer.

Hoping not to follow further in the footsteps of my teacher, and having better things to do than exercise power in whatever way, and in accordance with my own past principle of departmental democracy, I resolved to continue to be Head by a certain means – not being Head. In fact if not in name, Chairman I would become. Factotum, maybe first among equals, but far from departmental proconsul. There was some incredulity on the part of my colleagues at our next Departmental Meeting, as my 26 items on the agenda were agreed. No Wednesday meeting of minds, a committee to choose postgraduate instructors, candidates for promotion to choose their own referees so far as that was within my power, no suggestion that colleagues should attend my Monday postgraduate seminar. Departmental xeroxing by students to cost 6 pence a page, thereby being no tax on knowledge. It was not exactly an abdication of responsibility, but it was a piece of politics, democratic politics, and it might work. Time would tell.

As much and as lively attention was being paid by me to reviews of *A Theory of Determinism: The Mind, Neuroscience, and Life-Hopes* – in particular to how the news was being received of my final resolution of the problem of the consequences of determinism. Having to my satisfaction dished Compatibilism and Incompatibilism as accounts of those consequences, something else had needed to be said. Our true situation was indeed that each of us had two kinds of life-hopes and other attitudes, differing in their bases and also their feelings. One kind involved an idea of voluntary or unconstrained actions, the other kind also involved an image of origination or Free Will. Neither kind was in any way mistaken in itself, and the two were perfectly consistent. But the matter could not be left there. What would the upshot be if determinism were now wheeled onto this scene? What is the upshot for you if you are inclined to believe it?

Well, thinking just of your first kind of life-hope, you can be intransigent and plough on, since determinism does not logically rule out voluntary actions – in essence your doing what you want. Roughly speaking, you can take everything to be okay, declare that nothing changes. But, thinking of your second kind of life-hope, you will be dismayed, since determinism certainly does logically rule out the idea of origination. Here, roughly speaking, things go black, hope ends. All of this is at least unsatisfactory. The intransigence is a kind of bluff, hard to keep up. It is dependent on temporarily not thinking about your other kind of life-hope. Also, the dismay is dismay, not agreeable. Moreover, there is a kind of inconsistency of moving back and forth between taking life to be okay and taking it to be black.

The *real* problem of determinism's consequences is dealing with this situation of troubled feeling. It is not the old theoretical problem of seeing what our single settled idea about the initiation of actions is, since we don't have one such thing. It is the problem of how to go on when we have two ideas, feelingfully, and then contemplate determinism or take it to be true.

The way to go on, said I, was to try to give up the kind of life-hope whose contained idea has to be false if determinism is true – give it up by trying to see that the other hope you can persist in is sustaining and there are other compensations, enough to enter into a celebratory philosophy of life. So too with our confidence in our beliefs, and such personal attitudes to others as gratitude and resentment and even love. Also with ascriptions of moral responsibility to people, including oneself. This is neither the response of intransigence to determinism, nor the response of dismay, but the response of affirmation.

One means of trying to make this response is by seeing what is certainly true, that there is a sense of failure and a kind of guilt, both sharp, that cannot be part of a determined world. We cannot say to ourselves in such a world, after a defeat or a disgrace, that we could have done otherwise to prevent it at the moment we acted, given things as they had been and were. Nor, less happily, can we say to ourselves in congratulation, after a victory or right act, that we might have failed to pull it off given things as they were and had been. But is this loss not outweighed by the gain?

This and various other attempts to look on the bright side, said I, are not certain to succeed. They cannot guarantee success in getting into the way of affirmation. Only one thing may succeed in the end, maybe for those who come after us. Few of us now, at least in these parts, do really believe determinism. It goes against the very stuff of the life we are brought into. We can be persuaded by arguments for it, and yet, paradoxically, not really believe it. But for those in the future who really come to believe it, a contentment will be possible. People may wish for what they know they cannot have. But they do not go on fully desiring it, where that is bound up with trying to take steps to get it, maybe thinking purposefully about it. Undistracted, they can value what they know they have.

This resolution of the problem, in the end a kind of pointing to the light, was approved as original by all but one or two reviewers of my book, which was gratifying. But did they also believe it? Well, several owned up to conversion, a state not natural to the philosophical mind, and no refutations were attempted. Freddie's long piece in the *London Review of Books* made more progress towards the fulsome than was usual for him on these outings. He doubted whether anything on the subject in the previous history of philosophy was the product of such intense research, which comment presumably carried some implication as to the worth of my product.

Daniel Dennett's piece at the front of *The Times Literary Supplement* was very approving. But stung I was by the implication that he had thought of my resolution of the determinism problem himself, that he too was neither Compatibilist nor Incompatibilist, and that he had written this down before me in his own book, *Elbow Room*. For his Compatibilism, said I, try his pp. 19, 51, and 131, and for his plain intransigence, pp. 4, 6, and 18. In fact we were as much at odds about something else. This was the rising idea that the philosophy of mind is properly to be done by computer, or, if I must show more restraint, such rising ideas as that there is a full characterization of the mind and consciousness in terms of the abstract states of a computer programme. I was not nearly grateful enough to a good reviewer, who unlike Freddie did not cavil that my book ran to 640 pages. My appreciation should have been closer to what was felt in connection with a piece in *The Literary Review*, a periodical not dragged down by high principles about possible reviewers. 'I must admit a slight bias in that I know the author,' said Jane, 'but it seems undeniable that this book. . . .'

Still, no Hampstead intellectual fell under my eye increasing his dignity in a coffee shop by visible ownership of my volume. A few dozen reviews came to my attention, not enough. Nor were they paeans that could satisfy me. The heavens did not open and rain down praise. I suspect that nothing else would have been sufficient. Can it be, as sometimes it seems, that this is the condition of all authors? There is reassurance in that, or at least company. I sought to solace myself by the fact that the price of *A Theory of Determinism* was unprecedented in my experience, £55. That helped, but not much.

Towards the spring of 1989, the writing of what would be called *Conservatism* took on momentum. Hours were spent on it daily, and some on a programme about Wittgenstein for Radio 3. Of this programme I was in my view a suitable presenter, not having undergone conversion to its subject-matter. It would have been hard for me to do so, given my recent history and a particular piece of brazen nonsense by him in something called *Zettel*. '. . . no supposition seems . . . more natural than that there is no process in the brain correlated with . . . thinking. . . .'

It was the law of Jane's nature that no party, and no fag-end of a party, was ever to be missed. We went to all. I kept my end up in the all-star cast at the Whitakers, defended the shortcoming of my heterosexuality elsewhere, maintained my professorial dignity among Labour Party leaders on Ken Follett's voyage down the Thames, and survived the launching of books in all manner of places, not excluding the Tavistock Clinic in its Freudian dignity. My suggestion to the Provost at this time, that despite being the Grote I might not be an ideal member of the committee to elect a new Freud Professor, was not accepted. It would not be wise, he said, to rock the unstable little boat which that body was. The Tavistock might claim further representation.

In Keats Grove took place one of the dinners celebrating Michael Foot's lovely *The Politics of Paradise: A Vindication of Byron*. Also dinners with such friends as the Cohens, and one for the new young lecturer in the department, whose American gravity earned him some public speaking by Jane. Pauline came to Keats Grove gatherings, and news was received that there might be a second Professor Honderich, although a professor in the American sense and of economics, she being Kiarney. John hopefully wrote his film script on London's history, and rightly maintained his independence of me. All three, showing no visible signs of fatigue, welcomed my new partner into our family after-life.

In April, Jane and I passed a week in Russia, still the Union of Soviet Socialist Republics, but now being reformed by Mr Gorbachev's policies of *glasnost* and *perestroika*. Through her openness to me in her opinion of the hotel's plumbing, my partner sought some reconstruction in my political tolerance. On the subject of socialist social justice, she noted that quite a few Russians were more equal than others. Our political discussions in ensuing weeks were vigorous, but did not affect the first line of a number of diary entries. 'Things perfect with Jane.'

In the department, things were not so perfect. Malcolm privately volunteered to me his opinion that a majority in it were unhappy under my chairmanship. Being unsure of what this came to, since I certainly had friends and allies, and not being inclined to the embarrassment of being replaced, I did not write out my resignation. It was not yet required by honour, or, more to the point, academic politics. Maybe there would be a Departmental Meeting to which somebody would make a speech, maybe an interrupted speech, with other people sitting silent. I could wait.

Since Freddie was 78, and had already had a near-death experience and told the world about it, the BBC thought it right to commemorate the grand old man of British philosophy. Its best-known practitioner he was, whatever his future standing. Remarried to Dee, contentedly, they were living in the house at 51 York Street once graced by Vanessa. There, in May, we recorded something other than the philosophical conversation planned. He was full of himself, and gave a lecture prompted by questions from the audience of one. The alternative would have been a wrangle, and my affection made it possible to defer to him, but did not save me from rue later.

Towards the end of the hour, I did succumb to remarking that we all struggle against vanity. Do you carry on a great struggle, Freddie? I asked. 'I'm vain but not conceited,' he replied. 'A vain man is one who's proud to display his medals. I am vain. A conceited man is one who thinks he deserves more medals than he's got. I'm not conceited.' He once said to someone that I had dropped him socially, as I had for a while, less long than others. But often he seemed to me not so much vain, or conceited, as wholly taken up in his campaign, determined to deserve another medal. In June, in University College Hospital with his lung trouble, he kept at it, and was in no danger at all of succumbing to nonsense.

A committee that had lately elected someone to a chair in Oxford must have gone stark staring mad, he said, and gave reasons. When he could not talk, he wrote sharp sentences on his clipboard. As I left him, he would return my clenched-fist salute with a big smile. He died on 27 June. There were obituaries, articles and letters to the editor, mine feelingful and those of Dummett, Quinton, Strawson and Wollheim cooler and better. There were also two other things, vile pieces of politics by Robert Jackson, Conservative M.P. and Minister for Higher Education, and Roger Scruton. The former derided Freddie's contribution to the era before the present Conservative one, the poverty and superficiality of its thinking. The latter remembered Freddie with gratitude for showing by his life how paltry philosophy becomes when the path of wisdom is abandoned. Dogs at a corpse, I thought. The funeral in Golders Green Crematorium was private and small, with records played of songs he liked, but no single word spoken, exceedingly sad.

Life went on, including departmental life. The government's committee finished its assessing of the research of university departments over a five-year period. We in Gordon Square were judged not to be a five-star but a four-star establishment. It did not much trouble me. My personal research contribution was not in doubt, I had been Head for only one of the 15 university terms in the five years. My colleagues could not be persuaded, at a departmental meeting, that each of us would be expected to publish one philosophical paper a year or more. We were all fully aware of the need to publish, some said. No mechanical rule was needed, which might get in the way of long-term thinking.

My own new book was going well, writing itself. Coming to a new analysis of the tradition of Conservatism in Britain and America, by finding more distinctions of the tradition, was easier than thinking about mind and brain. You could merrily put aside most claims as to Conservatism's distinctions by those it knew as its thinkers. The first of them, the all-too-eloquent Burke, spoke of resistance to change in societies and a wise toleration of reform, but he notably failed ever to produce his 'manifest, marked distinction' between change and reform. It was inconceivable that Conservatism could be enlighteningly described as the tradition of freedom. However awful, *every* political tradition espouses and if successful secures *some* freedom or other, the removal of some obstacle to desire.

I would not, of course, in my high-minded inquiry, take up John Stuart Mill's description of Conservatives as The Stupid Party, but seek to do better in finding its distinctions. Some had been discerned in my earlier reflections on it. It was in favour of one kind of economic freedom, having to do with a market. It was for a certain sort of political freedom, falling as far short of a democratic ideal as history allowed. It resisted certain social and civil freedoms, such as the right to a job. Eight distinctions having been found in my earlier reflections, 19 were found now, adding up to a true analysis of Conservatism.

They raised the old question. Why were they together in this bag? What brought them together into a political tradition? Why some freedoms and not others? There must surely be a rationale or unifying principle. At the very least, there had to be a best summary of these various commitments, something brief and enlightening. What was it? More effort could go into *that* question. Once, all too recently, it had seemed to me the answer was the Principle of Desert, but you could have second thoughts about that.

As the new academic year got underway, Jane and I carried forward our reflections on marriage, hers shared with her readers in *The Literary Review*. O'Grady said that she had freed a fly trapped in a window, and thought of the traps that marriages became. But, she said, she was being overtaken by life. It aimed us at the institution. She would have to give up her dear liberties, including disorder, no timetable, and listening to radio chat-shows at 2 a.m. while cleaning the floor. Having let the fly out of the window trap, she said, she killed it, thinking that flies spread disease and that she particularly hated this fly.

As you gather, we were not without some realism. To reassure ourselves, we signed marriage agreements. We would be independent in the ownership of my flat and her cottage, and in all other such matters. I would keep my worldly goods and she would keep hers. Should this third marriage of mine go the way of the others, and be without children, we would fly out of it as free as birds.

In December 1989, the happy deed was done at the registry office in Chelsea Town Hall, the bride in scarlet. The party afterwards, in the library of the Reform Club, 150 being present to hear no speeches, went swimmingly. My old and new Provosts at University College, the second being the admirable Dr Derek Roberts, said that no doubt we would be philosophical about married life. My colleagues, almost a majority of them, drank well and contemplated a regiment of North Kensington women advanced in their feminism. Also for the bride was Uncle Peter, once our man in Washington, who kept his end up along with the other Ramsbothams. Ruth and Bee and a good selection of the next generation of my family confidently added to and liked the show. I was gratified by it, and pleased at the political truces arranged by me between Foots, Worsthornes, Hobsbawns, Folletts and Waughs. Should I have had second thoughts about this, and wondered about the depth of my political passions?

Freddie's memorial meeting followed a few days later, under the auspices of University College London, of course free of religion, with 400 in attendance. In a good company of speakers, I did well, best according to a newspaper or two. Freddie was not only a kind of hussar against nonsense, who never recanted the intention of *Language, Truth and Logic*. He was a philosopher whose audacity it was to be true to truth, the truth of sense and not the truth of aspiration or predilection or theory. He did not write to intimate, or to evoke, or as the apostle of a specialism, or to strike a prolonged pose, or to do any of the things that are better done by choosing a calling other than philosophy. He eschewed what perhaps he might have engaged in, kinds of originality which gave greater fame to some others. He went on saying the truth when, as truth recurrently does, it became a little dull. He lived fully, and died well.

In 19 Gordon Square, we were in no danger of being under-promoted. Any promotions were difficult to achieve in the current state of the college's finances. But it was with zeal that I carried out my obligation as Head to advance my colleagues' claims. In February came news of a great success, three promotions in one year in a small department. Dr Jerry Valberg, my metaphysical friend and the restrainer of my passions, would be a Senior Lecturer. Malcolm Budd would be a Professor. Bill Hart would be a Reader. I had not been restrained in my letter on Dr Hart's behalf by his response in a departmental meeting to my idea of our having a chair named for Freddie. Better have one for Joe Shmuck, he said. The promotions would be an aid to my three colleagues in affirming life, and maybe improve mine. In March, however, there was a brief test of my own powers of affirmation, Dr Michael Rosen.

He was a scholar in German philosophy who had come to us from teaching politics in Oxford. We two started out well, and he did not find in me the antisemitism that, he said, had stood between him and a permanent Oxford job. But we then had a difference about Rawls at a departmental gathering in Bill Hart's house. It seemed to me later that Dr Rosen got some help in catching a local infection left over from the past. Now, in his resignation letter to me, he said that in six months he would be going back to a prestigious and extremely desirable post in Oxford, this being a college fellowship – but he would be going for the sole reason that I was Grote and Head.

I had got the Grote somehow improperly, he implied, and reaction to this in the department was testified to by the fact that our emeritus professor, Richard, was no longer seen in the college, and also by the departure of the two loyal secretaries. As Head, I had not exercised power in a mature and responsible way with proper processes of consultation. I had by partiality, non-consultation and secrecy produced mistrust, inhibition, wretchedness, demoralization, a gloomy prognosis, the departure of yet more secretaries, fewer graduate students, his own departure and that of another young lecturer, and our being rated as only a four-star establishment. Copies of the indictment went from him to all members of the department, and, yet more unprecedentedly, to the Dean of Arts, the Vice-Provost of the college, and the new Provost, Dr Roberts.

Sue him, was the first reaction of Jerry Valberg. I propose to, said I to the Provost. Don't over-react! said the Dean of Arts. I wrote a reasoned defence against the indictment, with supporting documents and also statements by such secretaries as the splendid Helen Betteridge. In my opinion the mood in the department, although improved, was owed to actions by others of which Dr Rosen's was the best example. My defence went to the Provost, etc. with the request that he meet with all my colleagues individually to ascertain their views, and make a reply to Dr Rosen.

The Provost's firm idea in response was that Dr Rosen should immediately be shown the door of the college. He should not be around the place until his official leaving day in about six months. A related thought was also expressed about Dr Hart. If Dr Rosen were to be expelled right now, said someone else, six months early, might that fact be of interest to his prospective colleagues in Lincoln College Oxford or its head? Might he find himself between two stools? Who *was* the head of Lincoln College?

Having for long been officially committed to the iniquity of retribution, I restrained Dr Roberts, as he reported in his brief reply to Dr Rosen, also copied to all parties. Dr Roberts was relieved to hear of Dr Rosen's eventual departure, but, if Dr Rosen were to make another contribution to departmental mood, his leaving day would be earlier than six months on. A note of my own went to Dr Hart. It was about his trying to find a job elsewhere, which he was doing, and which now seemed to me in the department's interest. I would be amenable to waiving the rule that resignations for the next year should be in before the end of April. He could let me know later than that. Anytime at all, really.

Quiet ensued. In the quiet I sometimes reverted to the truth that I had been ordinarily above-board in pursuing my academic ambitions. I had been pretty much a straight arrow. It was notable that Dr Rosen's letter contained no specific charge of impropriety, since there could be none.

There had been no comic episode where a candidate arranges for a telephone call to be made by someone else to a higher power, in order to get a further understanding of the attitude of the higher power, this being best got by the candidate's eavesdropping on an extension phone. Higher Power would not have been amused. Nor had my progress involved an honourable arrangement whereby a member of an appointment committee did not inform his preferred candidate of such things as the questions he would be asked in an interview, but happened regularly to chat to a mutual acquaintance with a good memory. I had been reported to no college committee as having tried improperly to influence a member. I was in no private connection with any of my referees, such as the connection of having been to bed with them. I hadn't secured that criticism of my doctrines was less heard of by buying up all the copies of a recent publication at the local bookstore. Nor had I done any like thing. Failings I had, but not in the way of low stuff. Should I, in reassuring myself, have thought more about my self-righteousness, maybe moral simplicity?

In the quiet, too, I contentedly took in the reception of my Conservatism book, and in particular its principal conclusion. The tradition of Conservatism was distinguished by the 19 marks. There was, for example, a coyness on the part of its thinkers as to its rationale, this being part of a general theme that all of society, politics and Conservatism are too deep for words. There was the defence of the particular kind of property-rights most useful to entrepreneurial and efficiently acquisitive persons, and to persons already owners of large things, and to others whom these two categories of personnel choose to benefit, above all their children.

Above all there was opposition to the Principle of Equality – that we must make well-off those who are badly-off by effective policies, including transferring goods from the well-off to the badly-off and also reducing demands for rewards or incentives by those who do contribute more to the means of well-being. This principle, whatever you thought of it, and as discovered before now, was the rationale of the Left in politics. This was the moral principle of the Left, its moral foundation. What was the rationale, presumably the moral principle, of the tradition of Conservatism?

There were three obstacles in the way of saying that it was the Principle of Desert – that each individual is to get what he or she deserves on account of personal qualities or his or her actions and activities. Supposing first, as you may be inclined to do, that the words do convey some useful and definite general principle, there is the trouble for Conservatives that it seems as useful to their opponents. The Left does indeed say that we all deserve decent lives and social freedoms, that miners deserve to keep their jobs, and that unmarried mothers deserve special help. The second obstacle, still supposing that there really is a useful general principle to talk about, was that surely it could not defend Conservatives in the possession of all the world's goods they do possess. Does the languid heiress, three generations away from the early capitalist, *deserve* the mansion? Could *his* deserts reach so far? What of the wonderfully enriching windfalls for the directors of the privatized public utilities?

Still, the third obstacle was the best. Admittedly we never stop talking about desert, very naturally, in connection with more things than people. Some books, we say, have bits in them that deserve slower reading. And admittedly the Principle of Desert trips off the tongue – each individual to get what he or she deserves on account of personal qualities or his or her actions and activities. But do the words supply a useful general principle for Conservatism? If so, they certainly can't be taken to mean the truism agreed by all sane parties, that in distributing things we need to pay attention to differences between people and their situations. *That* is agreed to by a supporter of the Principle of Equality.

By these reflections and others, progress was made to the proposition that in fact there is no useful general principle of desert. The only philosophical book on the subject said so too. You can find particular arguments about desert in connection with particular subjects, say the argument about retributive desires in connection with punishment, but that is all. From this it followed, with the help of another proposition or two, that Conservatism was based on *no* moral principle. Was the tradition unique, then, in being a tradition of self-interest, even selfishness? No, things were a bit more complicated, since evidently there was self-interest in the politics of the Left.

The principal conclusion of my labours was that the tradition of Conservatism, unlike the Left, was *only* a matter of self-interest, that it had no other rationale. The self-interested Left, in contrast, also had the moral support of the Principle of Equality. Conservatism was the political tradition whose true nature was no more than selfishness. I laid it on. The conclusion, like all of my book, was in a way like what unfortunately will last longer, Burke's *Reflections*. My stuff too was written in an anger that things had gone wrong in a society.

As postcards said, friends and the Labour Party were delighted by it. Fifty or so reviews appeared quickly, mostly by Conservatives. Many were unstrung not only by the principal conclusion but also by a personal paragraph. It was about my having come to England in 1959 and my now being in a place whose government had had some success in degrading human nature, dragging down the character of a people. Enoch Powell, M.P., said that I was trying to be too clear. Conservatism was more like a song than a theory, and I had not heard it. Conor Cruise O'Brien, the great defender of Burke, said it was not difficult for a logician to expose fallacies in anything, and it didn't matter. Ian Gilmour, a kindly and civilized Conservative, and for this reason dismissed by Mrs Thatcher from her cabinet, declaimed at length that there was no such thing as the political tradition under study in my book. Perhaps he was moved by the thought that if the tradition existed, there would be something of which he and she were both members.

Ferdinand Mount, lately at work in the Prime Minister's office in Downing Street, and not yet editor of *The Times Literary Supplement*, kept in mind the full title of the Grote Chair and so his piece in *The Spectator* appeared under the heading 'Small Mind and Less Logic'. My conduct on television with David Willetts, reportedly a Tory of intellectual and other rectitude, was properly high-handed. The magazine *Marxism Today*, having lost its nerve and begun to see the real worth of market mechanisms, interviewed me at length about my degree of political realism.

Roger Scruton, having been identified in my book as 'the unthinking man's thinking man', for his role as a non-intellectual party's intellectual, had taken thought by the time of our debate in a bookshop in the Charing Cross Road. He identified me as 'the thinking man's unthinking man'. To his saying I was part of a Left Wing establishment of a censoring kind, it was possible to remind him of something publicly. It was that after others had declined to support his becoming a professor of philosophy in the University of London, I had at least said a word to enable him to become what he did become, a professor of aesthetics. My savage review of his own book of essays some weeks later said that the politics of the Authoritarian Right should neither be confused with Fascism nor disconnected from it.

Letters by way of the Editor were passing between me and my critics. My main refrain was that none of these Conservatives could produce an alternative to my short summary of their politics. The possibility of some real philosophy was also being contemplated by me. It would be a kind of personal philosophy of mind, based on and written out of what could be called first-person empiricism. Other endeavours were as satisfactory. Freddie had made arrangements with publishers to bring together two books, one of them a dictionary of philosophical quotations. He had not got far forward in this worthy enterprise, but, in the view of the publisher, far enough to justify the use of his name on the cover. He would need, so to speak, a co-editor. Having failed to enlist Timothy Sprigge and others, it became clear to me that another candidate was close to hand. Jane would do it, and bring to the enterprise a wider sympathy than her co-editor, certainly literary *élan*. Work began in the study in Keats Grove.

In August, for regeneration, we had a holiday, first in Wittenberg where Martin Luther began the reform that did not include toleration for Anabaptists, and then in other German and Czech towns. The wall between West and East Germany had come down. This, to my way of thinking, could be taken as ending a German era that included the Nazis and the genocide of the Jews. Thus it was possible for me to go to this place of some of my ancestors. On account of some of Jane's, we survived a visit to Auschwitz. Germany was also one of the places where another ideology, not mine but not monstrous either, had come to an end. Thus the holiday was also a farewell to Marx. We talked a lot about politics, but had a lovely time.

16

HARMLESS DRUDGE,
FUNCTIONALISM,
SOCIALIST LANDLORD

Mr Jens Jacobsen, the singular Dane of the pre-revolutionary bonds, filled up suitcases with his scribbled thoughts. The most fundamental of these, according to one of my arrangements, was that Reality, all of what exists, is a single and indivisible whole. This is Nature or Life, more particularly Life-Forces and Physical Forces. The Life-Forces, more primal, are Self-Preservation, Inquisitiveness, Sex, Balance, Logic, and Compassion. The whole thing, Nature or Life, is most certainly not to be thought of as God, a vulgar fiction. However, only Nature or Life is truly conscious. Like the amoeba, midge, newt, donkey and elephant, we are Nature's products, subject to determinism and evolution. Our derivative consciousness is trivial. What is basic about us, as in the case of amoeba, midge and the rest, is that we are not selves or egos. The pretence that we are, including the primal disaster of the first-person pronoun 'I', is the source of the awfulness of human life. Jens sometimes contemplated the setting up of a Jacobsen International Philosophy Essay Competition. Use of the first person in a submitted essay, being an insult to Nature, would disqualify the candidate absolutely.

Now 79 and a widower with no children, he seemed to have as his life's primary aim the propagation of his thinking. As chairman of the philosophy committee of the University of London, the federation of colleges whose clerks were housed in Senate House, the grey erection of Malet Street, my conflicting obligation was to meet his continuing campaign with a lesser truth. It was that the university, being committed to inquiry, could not properly undertake the endeavour of propagating Impersonal Naturalism. We could take his money for the advancement of philosophy generally, into which his metaphysical vision evidently could be said to fall, and accord him a kind of hearing. He could meet the annual Jacobsen Lecturer, say John Searle, and impress his doctrine upon him.

Might University College itself do what was possible for Jens under the same proper terms? At a dinner with the Provost and some of my colleagues, having already got £40,000, we gratefully accepted another £100,000. It was not the most comfortable occasion of my academic life. While our understanding was clear enough, it might nonetheless give rise to hopes on the part of our benefactor, for whom I had come to have an affection. It was easier sending out the hundreds of begging letters for donations to the A. J. Ayer Scholarship Fund. In sum my department's invested capital, the interest from which would go for bursaries, was getting on for £250,000, making us unique in London philosophy. I was pleased with this success, the good that would come of it for our students, and the thought that it added greater stability to my Chairmanship.

My fund-raising had to do with the Thatcher government's policy on the universities. This was to make them ever better by making them ever poorer. In November 1990, the government also had a further idea, about the tuition fees of students, paid from the public purse. It would be impolitic for a troubled government to take its marketism so far as to legislate that students themselves should pay all or part of their fees. What it did do was to nudge the universities to do its work for it. They could 'top up' the insufficient fees from the public purse by charging additional fees to their students. Any institution could take such a decision for itself. Our Provost, Dr Roberts, called a meeting of the Academic Board of the college, and, with whatever anticipation, asked me in advance to make a speech. If he asked others, only mine got heard.

You will know, reader, that it did not accept the invitation to realism. These fees would discriminate against the sons and daughters of poorer families, would deny them equality of opportunity. There was a lot more said along these lines, ending with the proposition that while a college has teaching and research as its primary obligations, it also has another. It has an obligation having to do with independence of mind, truth, and social justice. In a society whose government had lost the moral confidence of most of the people, and of virtually our entire profession, a bit of courage in discharging our social obligation was in order.

As the newspapers reported the next day, the 175 members of the Academic Board voted unanimously, with two abstentions, against the college's charging discriminatory fees. The *Times Higher Education Supplement* reprinted the speech, our house organ *UCL News* said the Grote had killed top-up fees, and Oxford's house organ said that UCL had stood up for an educational and social principle, not for the first time. My diary necessarily recorded that the thing had not been stylishly done, as maybe my four radio talks on the words 'cause', 'free', 'freedom' and 'deserved' had been. Karl Miller did not say to me I was an orator, but did say I had done well in seizing the moral high ground.

It was no bad thing to have been a local harbinger of a larger event in late November. The Conservative Party itself had had enough of its leader. It chose to replace her with Mr Major, mainly on account of his having all possible convictions on all issues. The newspapers said she had destroyed many of the sacred cows of Britain, and tended to forget that her ethos was the one in which, for the sake of better profits, Britain was catching an appalling disease from secular and mad ones. She would not have won the election to come, and, plainly, neither would he.

Early in 1991 it was my turn to give a lecture in the celebratory series on Freddie's philosophy, arranged by the Royal Institute of Philosophy in the hope that he might be in the audience. My lecture had to do with ordinary perceptual consciousness or awareness, in particular the experience of seeing things. Freddie, as mentioned in connection with his contribution to *Philosophy As It Is*, had to an extent persisted in the sense-datum theory of Locke, Berkeley and Hume.* In seeing a tree in front of you, he said, what you are aware of is *not* an objective thing. That is, you are not aware of one and the same thing that others are also aware of, and the same thing you can be aware of by more senses than sight, and the thing that goes on existing when perceived by nobody.

Rather, said he, what we are always aware of is *qualia*, in one sense of that modish term. They are related to various philosophical predecessors, including sense-data, in that they are not objective things. Out of this original and somehow neutral stuff of experience, by reasoning and imagination, we build up a conception of a kind of objective world. In

* See p. 223

the language of Professor Quine at Harvard, we *posit* this world. That is to say in the end, alas, that the tree itself is just part of *a theory* that explains the experience. The tree is a theoretical entity, thought up to explain the *qualia*.

As perhaps indicated by my lecture title, 'Seeing Qualia and Positing the World', Freddie's new argument for shutting each of us into a private world, solitary confinement, needed attention. The argument for the conclusion that you see *qualia* seemed to be that (1) you do not actually *see* that anyone else is aware of exactly what you are aware of, or (2) *see* that what you see is what you touch, or of course (3) *see* that anything goes on existing when unperceived. Those propositions of objectivity are not delivered to you in your actual perceptual experience.

Well, said I, if that is the argument for my being aware only of qualia, I am out of solitary confinement. The argument is a *non sequitur*. The three premises can be granted. It does not follow, from my not being aware of the three properties of a thing in my experience, that I am not aware of exactly that thing. It does not follow, from my not being aware of what makes the tree in my awareness a perfectly objective thing, that I am not aware of that perfectly objective thing. No more than it follows from my not seeing the other side of the tree, not seeing the bark there and so on, that I am not seeing exactly the thing that has that other side and the bark and so on. *Exeunt qualia.*

Freddie not being on hand to delay progress, my lecture could go on to what could not be taken as settled. If our perceptual consciousness does not consist in awareness of *qualia* and in positing the world, what *does* our perceptual consciousness consist in? Well, like all consciousness, it raises the temptation given in to by Descartes and many others, even English philosophers. That is the temptation to think of a person's experience and all of consciousness in terms of a self or homunculus, some inner thing that is somehow related to the content of the experience or episode of consciousness – a content being whatever it is within an episode of consciousness that distinguishes it from other episodes. But, nonetheless, there still did seem to be two different facts within any piece of seeing, thinking, desiring or intending. There was the content, and, bound up with that, some fact of subjectivity, a subjective aspect to the episode. The relation between them wasn't awareness – what you could say was that the two facts were *interdependent*, that there couldn't be one without the other. You might go as far as saying subjective aspects existed-through the contents, and the contents existed-for or existed-to the subjective aspects.

This was to be realistic about the nature of consciousness, anyway mine – not driven off a subject-matter by its obscurity, or distracted from its reality by computers. But, even with additions made to it, this mental realism and first-person empiricism consisted in a kind of gesturing. It was not a real analysis of consciousness, but vague. To this embarrassment was added another. There is a real difference between perceptual and other consciousness, say between seeing a tree and then later on thinking about it or having a belief about it. *What* is that difference?

Clarification from me came there none. But it was better to have no good clarification than to embrace a fiction, and my lecture went well, and I got compliments that pleased me. Some were from Swedes and Danes when I read it out again in their countries. There was also one from Ingrid Coggin Purkiss, previously a teacher of philosophy and now The Secretary of The Royal Institute of Philosophy. She was a Platonist, restrained by reason, and an instance herself of The Form of the Good. Also The Form of the Good-Looker, if there was one of those. If I had not been committed to success in marriage, more than my eye might have strayed.

To my ongoing struggle with the nature of consciousness had been added what first presented itself as a worthy relaxation. Oxford University Press published what were known as Companions. Each of these was a one-volume encyclopaedia, authoritative but of an amiable kind. As you listened your way upwards to Mozart and Bach, you could consult the Companion on music, and, as you got deeper entangled in *Honderich v. Green Shoes*, turn to the one on law. As you read George Eliot and the rest, you could have at your elbow *The Oxford Companion to English Literature*, provided by Margaret Drabble. Well aware of the encyclopaedic nature of my determinism book, Angela Blackburn at OUP saw in me the Margaret Drabble of philosophy. Edit *The Oxford Companion to Philosophy* I would. Hardly a word would have to be written by me, but it would mainly be my inclinations that would determine what was included and what left out. If the entry on Hume was 2,250 words long, should the one on Wittgenstein be as much as 1,350? Would 450 not do?

My list of 1,500 entries, eventually to be written by conscripted experts at £50 per thousand words, went out first to stern examiners. Several of them had reservations about putting into the book not only Thales to Sartre, but also a selection of living philosophers. This anointing of contemporaries might not only endanger the editor but be invidious. For whom was it necessary? asked one of my examiners. Your ordinary commuter? Someone potters along to the station bookstall, sees OUP's latest bestseller, and says 'I really must get this dictionary so I can find out who David Wiggins is'? I was chastened by all this, learned again that philosophers have their own fish to fry, but remained resolute. My second list of entries, if different, would not be a transformation of the first.

Spring was not dramatic, but had more moments as it advanced. The obligations of a university teacher and Chairman of Department did not leave time for unhurried lunches in two gentlemen's clubs. Also, the common table at the Beefsteak was not made congenial by my propounding my proposition lately published in *The Guardian*, that it was not Saddam Hussein who was starting the Gulf War, but President Bush. It was not ideal, either, that for the convenience of members, the individual identities of the club's servants were submerged, all of them being addressed as Charles. It would be sufficient to my social needs to be a member of the Garrick.

College was surviving more financial crisis, and so it was good that some more money came to the Philosophy Department. There would be an annual colloquium to honour the name of Stanley Victor Keeling, a teacher in the department when Freddie arrived as Grote Professor. The engaging donor of the £55,000 was the best kind of American, aware that Cincinnati needed to be supplemented by Paris. He chose to remain anonymous, and became a friend. A note came to me too from Bill Hart. It said that he would be leaving the college in nine months. Mine back to him, also a sentence long, wished him the best in his new job in Albuquerque, New Mexico.

In April, the clerks of Senate House presumably permitted themselves an extra glass of dry sherry. The Foreign Compensation Commission had taken the view that the Chinese and other bonds were indeed worth something. The final cheque to the University of London for philosophy, added to Jens's earlier contribution of £67,645, was for £522,643. A benefaction of this size for philosophy was unprecedented in living memory. If it did have precedents in the history of English universities, they were few. My own satisfaction in the matter was troubled. Jens had approached us persistently, and chosen to make the best deal on offer. He had, four years before, turned over to us things of uncertain value. He was now unhappy about what turned out to be his largesse. In return, he felt, more should be heard of Impersonal Naturalism. It had not turned up in the subsequent work of Professor Searle. The university's philosophy committee expressed its gratitude to me for my efforts, and I said I would not mind its gratitude being recorded in the minutes of the meeting. It was, but the clerks of Senate House were ahead of me. As discovered by later research in their archives, the chief clerk had already put on record that I had played but a consultative role in the matter.

Jane and I, in the fourth year of our connection, were not only surviving the institution of marriage but often enough affirming it. If, to my discomfiture, she had taken the view that our first wedding anniversary did not need celebrating, we had decided to have a child, or anyway not impede Nature in its productivity. In June we took ourselves off to the United States, and to Williams College, where the other Professor Honderich was happily promulgating her economics and feminism. It was sweet to see Ruth and Bee in Toronto, indeed to be welcomed by them as a visiting dignitary in their different ways. It was instructive to attend the reunion of diverse Honderichs on the 1825 farm to which our ancestors had come. Neither Jane nor I was charmed by Baden, Ontario, Canada. I was, truth to tell, embarrassed by the village of my birth. I did not rise up over the past. Unfortunately there was a firm connection between the person I now was, looking at the telephone house, and the boy who lived in it.

This was the 32nd year in which work in philosophy was as large a fact as any other in my life, whatever my adventures. There were my graduate students too, not all so instructive as Brown, Magill and Walsh, who would teach philosophy to other persons thereafter. There was no slackening of my efforts at age 58, but some sense of the worth of rest and recuperation. For more of it, I went to Paris for a week, by myself. That Jane was not with me, and had not been in Ravello either a year or so ago, was in accord with her principle of independence in marriage, but not the best omen. It was exasperating too. In Paris, if English I somehow was, and still loyal, it was clear to me that this capital outshone London.

I wished that the translation of *Conservatism* was in French rather than Spanish.

The Provost rang up on my return to say that he had learned by experience to settle in advance the headships of his departments. My appointment had been for four years, to the end of the academic year about to begin. Might I serve another four after that? My reflections on the question were not prolonged. There had been no *putsch* at 19 Gordon Square, and the chance of one was now reduced by my new colleagues, Tim Crane and Sarah Richmond, independent-minded and comradely. So far as could be noticed, they had caught no local infection. But the prospect of four more years of service was not engaging. My perquisites as Grote Professor would be safeguarded by the Provost. Our new Head, or Chairman, would be the other professor in the department, Malcolm Budd. He made it very clear he did not seek the chalice, but did not take an eternity to say he would drink it.

At the beginning of the new academic year, October 1991, the Senior Seminar on Mondays at five became a yet more pleasant occasion. It was now conducted not only by Mark Sainsbury of King's College and myself, but also by Professor Nancy Cartwright of the L.S.E., wife of Stuart Hampshire. However great such distractions were, and however large my need to discover the nature of consciousness, the General Election was six months off. Some time needed to be spent, proudly, on a request by the leader of the Labour Party, Mr Kinnock, for material for speeches. Perhaps my stuff about freedom and power wasn't hopeless, but, despite bullet paragraphs, it had the sound of the lecture hall in it, and an impolitic disdain. The state of Britain would win the election for us anyway. Before then, my obligation to arrange guest lectures in the department was nicely discharged, and my equanimity demonstrated, by arranging three performances by Bernard Williams. In my chairman's remarks, I did not stint my praise. We had heard, I said, from the most creative of living English philosophers. Richard too was asked back to lecture in the department, but could not fit it in.

At a conference in Barcelona, my paper on the need for the Principle of Equality in international relations was gracefully if sceptically received. At the conference banquet Jane chose to preserve decorum rather than act for feminism when a noted British sociologist, impeded neither by crutch nor age, paid special attention to the inside of her thigh underneath the tablecloth. Informed by her of this afterwards, but being aware of the greater impropriety of regarding my wife as private property, I said good-bye to the gnome civilly in the morning. On television in London I was as enlightened about the case of the allegedly freely consenting circle of homosexuals who engaged in the torture of one another. Still, all I was called on to deny on *Newsnight* was the proposition that such practices would bring down civilization, a proposition akin to that of the Roman emperor who reasoned that sodomy caused earthquakes.

These recollections bring to mind that in the present era of brazen confessional writing a reader or two of this chronicle may be feeling deprived. It is nearly 30 years past in these pages that you heard anything much of me and sex. You have not been deprived of a great deal. What I was in Sussex in 1964, close to *l'homme moyen sensuel*, decorous and orthodox and even prim, I more or less continued to be, except for a shortish period. For this period, spurred on by what seemed to be the sexualization of the world, and feeling myself a little deprived, I and an agreeing partner or two experimented mildly with a riding crop. For good or ill, it was not much of a success, but soon an embarrassment. I returned to something like my previous dogged spirituality, with only the addition of talk. Silent sex I did escape.

There were more junkets than to Barcelona. I went to Zurich without Jane, somewhat forlornly. The philosophers there, deferential to Professor Popper, did not unsettle my convictions in the discussion after my lecture on determinism. But they were not so defeated as to agree to publish my paper in their journal. It was, in truth, just a summary of my big book on determinism. Their attitude, if sensible, did not please me, and put me in mind again of Hume. His great work, the *Treatise of Human Nature*, as all know him to have reported, 'fell dead-born from the press'. He dealt with this by reworking much of the material into the slim and greatly more readable *Inquiries*, and so raised Kant from his dogmatic slumbers. At the start of 1992, a precis of *A Theory of Determinism* got written in the dining room at 4 Keats Grove, under the reproduction of the Carrogis portrait of tranquil Hume. The 46,000 words of *How Free Are You?* were finished in a month.

In it we went to one of the small dinner parties laid on to enable Salman Rushdie to put up with his tribulation. This one was given by the notable and genial pair Drabble and Holroyd, around a corner from Keats Grove.

With armed policemen upstairs on the lookout for the assassin of the *fatwah*, we carried on ordinary Hampstead social life downstairs. In the end it required a sympathetic inquiry into Salman's situation. He had, he forcefully said, even less hope of real help from an incoming Labour government, if there was one, than from the Tories. Indeed much less hope from the Labour crowd. This pleased neither me nor Michael Seifert, my solicitor in *Honderich v. Green Shoes*, now fully rehabilitated in my affections. It may be that Salman's superiority did not wholly impress others present, one being Doris Lessing. It fell to me, however, with the amiable support of Michael, to say a word for our side, and therefore against the condemned man. The question of whether he *had* insulted Muslims was in a way broached. He and the policemen took their departure suddenly, although at 2 a.m. The next morning I felt that I had been remiss, but no more than that.

The election of April 1992 finally awakened me from a dream of England. Despite my faxes to Mr Kinnock on the philosophy of the Labour Party, which did not disdain self-interest on the part of voters, and despite my knocking on doors with Glenda Jackson in Hampstead, Mr Major won. This was the fourth victory in a row for the Conservative Party, by 21 seats. Michael Foot was not alone in thinking, until the day before, that we would certainly win, that we could not lose. The victory was won, partly, by lying exaggeration of the truth that Labour would raise taxes in order to help those who were doing badly. But the people had an ear to half-believe the wretched lie. They could listen to the unspeakable crew who were trying to make it true that everyone is out only for themselves. There was no generosity, no decency at all, in this outcome of democracy.

There was little solace in thinking the outcome was owed less to English human nature than to something else. This was the English press in both its reputable and disreputable parts, in the end Rupert Murdoch's *Sun* with its front-page photo on election day. The photo was of Neil grinning in a lightbulb, with the mixed cargo of implications being that it would be a good idea to switch it off, that he was not very bright, and that if he won, the good times would be over and we could turn out the lights. The thought came to me of going to live in Paris. The politics were somewhat better there, and anyway I wouldn't care so much about France.

If philosophy was a consolation, it was also a necessity, since there would be a conference in Oslo, partly to celebrate the 60th birthday of Alastair Hannay. At it would be formidable judges of my new paper on the nature of consciousness, including Professor Quine. Struggled over for about six months, before and after the month for the little determinism book, the paper was restricted to ordinary perceptual consciousness and called 'Seeing Things'. It was a long way from computerized philosophy of mind, and had in it further stubborn thoughts on a perceptual mental event's having within it a content and also some subjective fact. The subjective fact was kept undramatic, not reared up into a self or whatever. Indeed, in place of talk of the subjective aspect and the content of a conscious event, we could just speak of the experience and its content, or maybe of mental space and what it contained.

The paper's main concern, however, was something else, or at any rate what seemed to be something else. This was the relation between the content and the outside world. In the case of my seeing the line of trees, how does the content, which is whatever it is within the experience that distinguishes it from seeing the portrait of Hume and so on, stand to the actual line of trees? What is it for the content to be *about* or *of* the trees or to represent them? This problem of which you have heard before is oddly spoken of by philosophers as the problem of *intentionality*.

A solution natural to philosophers of a naturalistic bent is that the content of my seeing the line of trees is in its details *caused* by them. But, while it had to be true that this causal relation existed, it could not by itself shed any light. One reason was that the line of trees, after all, was in causal connection with a lot of things, including its shadow on the grass. What was special about the particular effect that was the seeing as against the effect that was the shadow? That question, the question in hand, remained unanswered. In any case, the seeing was the effect of more things than the trees. It was the effect of the real image of the trees on the retinas of my eyes. Clearly the seeing's being an effect of something didn't make the seeing about that thing. The seeing was of the trees, not of the impression on the retinas.

Could it be that the fact of aboutness, the relation between content and object, was somehow to be understood by way of the other relation, between content and subjective fact? And did all of the story have to be brought into connection with something else? This was the conviction brought to bear on Freddie and his sense-datum forebears – the conviction that in seeing the trees, I am aware of precisely the trees, and only such things as the trees. I am not given both the trees and something else, this other thing being the content of my experience. Seeing isn't seeing double. There is just the givenness of the world. Was this tangled story a disaster, as I have sometimes thought since? Being in a better mood with myself today, my contribution to Alastair's birthday seems marginally better.

Life with Jane had remained full of talk, walks, socializing and her dictionary of philosophical quotations. For some months we tried to take prescribed steps in order to have a child, maybe in order to settle our marriage. To these ingredients of life, however, we had by now added battles and wrangles, sometimes grim. Unforgiveable things could be said, on various subjects. Did I still have an eye for other women? Was she reformed in this respect? Although she despised the Conservatives, was my Principle of Equality not grotesquely utopian? Was it not sad that England, on account of immigration, conceivably including Canadian immigration, was no longer England? Were her cycle routes not better than mine, and should she not lead? To such soluble problems we brought her indomitable spirit and my conviction of my transparent rationality. If she was the daughter of Major Robert O'Grady, decorated for valour, I had been toughened on that other battlefield, academic life.

The first-floor flat in Keats Grove, as I had failed to learn earlier from Janet, was not spacious enough for a couple used to space. Let alone a couple and, should there be one, a child. In May, the flat on the floor above was for sale. It could have a nursery in it. Should we not buy it? It was my idea that Jane and I should do this together, partly by way of some family money to which, it could be said, her feminism had made her claim indubitable. She declined. Our independence in marriage needed preserving. I, in my transparent rationality, did not take this well, but went on with the purchase on my own, by way of a very large mortgage. Things might still turn out nicely. They *could*. We were merry when not at war.

In September, fittingly, to the Graduate Institute of Peace Studies in Korea we went. The large international conference, starting on an anniversary of the United Nations Day of Peace, was on Democracy and the New World Order. My paper was the one that thereafter acquired the title 'Hierarchic Democracy and the Necessity of Mass Civil Disobedience'. It went down pretty well, even if my morals and politics were coming to have an antediluvian aspect, and were not at all concordant with the New World Order, this being the hegemony of the United States.

In the paper two things were recanted. One was a piety of mine in the past about Western democracies, an illusion about their egalitarianism, an absurd illusion about their involving approximate equality in the choosing and influencing of governments. My news was that our democracies are nothing like egalitarian, but are hierarchic, with awful effects. The other thing given up was in a way of a different political tendency. It was my long-standing moral agnosticism about political violence of the Left, and in particular Democratic Violence, the kind aimed at democratic ends. The news here was that violence of the Left, except in certain national liberation struggles, will almost always be defeated. The final result will be maiming and killing, with not enough to show for it. That the governments of hierarchic democracies are wrong not to give in to such violence does not put those who resort to it in the right. Things are different with mass civil disobedience, where there is a chance of success. There should be a lot of it. This is so partly because this kind of struggle does not so quickly drive out truth, and hence disarm one side of its best weapon.

There was another conference banquet. At it, ranks of Korean school-girls danced shyly in their uniforms and Korean women maintained their immemorial silence in the company of their men. It was a decorous and lavish occasion, attended by hundreds seated across a vast garden. For the speeches, there was an elevated podium. Mr Davidson Nicol, former United Nations Under-Secretary General, used it to thank our hosts, and to make a joke about the husband who went to heaven, joined the section for men not dominated by their wives, and, when asked why, answered that his wife had told him to. He did not reckon on Jane. She, having seen the Korean sisterhood to be in need of support, needed no invitation to storm the podium and correct his closet chauvinism, not omitting a useful reference to her grandfather the Viscount Soulbery. From this *coup de théâtre*, Mr Nicol retired wounded, with some of my sympathy. He may have made the mistake of thinking that in this enlightened company, he had the safety of being a black.

A few months after the list of entries for the *Oxford Companion to Philosophy* had been settled and I had begun finding contributors, the size of the job was clearer. Maybe 200 would have to be found for 1,500 entries. Dealing with them could involve not hundreds of letters, but a couple of thousand. In giving up the Headship of the department, and thus becoming the first of the Grotes who was not also Head, I had taken thought to have the Provost guarantee me some services of she who was slyly designated by me in college records as the Grote Professor's Secretary. Alas, I had not been foresighted about what could be discerned, by our new Head and maybe another colleague, and herself, as the large size of the other demands on her time. After fairly decorous negotiations, I resigned myself to grinding out my letters and addressing most of my envelopes myself. It was better to keep the departmental peace than fight to the death over envelopes. Did I not have a past to live down? It was there to be perused, incidentally, by my successors in the Headship, in my personal file in the department's locked filing cabinet. I had not followed a precedent, and emptied my file before turning over the key. In my case what was there to hide?

The list of contemporary philosophers to be included in the book was looked over by a jury of 12 leaders of our profession, British and American. The jury turned out to be far from unanimous. They agreed about a large core of the list, but about no one else. No suggested addition to the list got more than two votes, and no suggested deletion more than two blackballs. The fortunates who did get two votes were added in, but no names were dropped from my list. It would be sensible, though, to say in the preface that another editor would have chosen differently. Indeed he would. He would not have got, and succumbed to, a supplication from another professor of the University of London, who in sorrow could not conceive that his industrious scholarship in Loony Tunes did not place him among the elect.

Within a week or two after the finishing of the commissioning of entries and celebrating it, a message came from the agreeable pair of editors at Oxford University Press who had taken over my guidance.

Tim Barton and Peter Momtchiloff had discovered a past miscalculation. If the *Companion* ran to only the 350,000 words now arranged, it would lack heft in the bookshops. By an iron law of publishing, it had to be larger by a third. Telling the 225 contributors was made more bearable by my being in favour of heft myself, and the promise of more money. My mortgage would be reduced by more than the £15,000 that had originally been guaranteed to me in order to make a worthwhile endeavour still more worthwhile.

Marriage now had in it fewer battles and wrangles but more suspense. Not forgotten was the portent of our not having come together to buy the flat upstairs. Janeso and Tedso were engaged in an honourable struggle to accommodate one another's natures. The struggle was tiring and not entirely victorious. That Tedso was happy in his harmless drudgery of dictionary-making did not make him less of a drudge. Also, at 60, he remained convinced of the power of reason, the latter being identical with his allotment of it. Janeso's independence extended to her meal times, these being regular but a few hours in advance of ordinary. It was as if two time zones coincided in 4 Keats Grove. Taking myself to have nature as well as convention on my side, I did not re-set my watch.

If we did not battle much, we had a ready supply of other issues over which to disagree, from the state of the flat's study, of which Nietzsche would have approved, to the state of my politics, of which only I approved. What was done in the marriage bed while awake was the reading aloud of novels to one another. Tony Byatt's *Possession*, while wonderful, was not a source of full contentment. We had by this time agreed that our having lovers had to be regarded as permissible and that it seemed to be inevitable.

There was another smaller dismay to be borne, sharp while it lasted. The government's committee of inspectors of research in philosophy departments made its report. 19 Gordon Square again got only four stars, while other departments in London got five, along with Oxford and Cambridge. I had been in charge, so to speak, for the three years in question. It was not much good being disdainful about the whole machinery of assessment, possible though this was. Nor was it much use explaining that we were now a young department, and that my new colleagues Michael Martin, Lucy O'Brien and Sarah Richmond had not had time to make their mark. There was not much solace in remembering that the other senior members of our departmental democracy had defeated my idea of a term free of teaching for *having* published, not for the promise of publishing. If by my history in the department I had not raised up resistance to myself, might I have succeeded in making us five-star? My note of apology to the Provost had in it not only rage but also mortification.

It was a relief and a pleasure to lay hands on *Mental Causation*, a collection of new papers in the Philosophy of Mind. It was edited by Heil and Mele of North Carolina, both of them up-to-date philosophically and otherwise, their preferred mode of communication being E-mail rather than snail mail. I was among the contributors, in the good company of Donald Davidson, Jaegwon Kim and other risen or rising figures. My paper was 'The Union Theory and Anti-Individualism', the first of several in which my long-held truths about the nature of consciousness and its relation to the brain were defended against what I hoped were passing fashions. Is it conceivable that you need reminding, reader, of some of those glowing truths? It is conceivable. Take as an example one of your own passing thoughts – say your thought a moment ago that this particular page you are reading promises the higher pleasure of philosophical enlightenment as against the lower pleasure of mere personal revelation.

Your passing thought about the page was somehow a matter of a content and a subjective aspect, these things being respectably physical, and the subjective aspect certainly not so large or so much as a Self. Your passing thought was not what some other Identity Theories suppose it to be, something that had only neural or electrochemical properties, including causal ones. The conscious event did stand in lawlike connection with a complex neural event at the same time. This kind of connection is like causation but not the same. Roughly speaking, the connection is such that if the conscious event hadn't happened neither would the neural one, and, most relevant at the moment, since the neural one happened so did the conscious one – it guaranteed it. This, and their being a single effect, gives us the Union Theory. Also very relevant, the two events were an effect of a causal sequence that included various causal circumstances *within* the history of the individual in question.

It is implicit in the mentioned truths that your passing thought about the page had an *individual* explanation – that it could be explained by or was dependent on facts of the individual who is you. More precisely, there were causal circumstances and a neural correlate in you, whatever their origin, that were quite sufficient to bring about the passing thought.

Enter Professor Putnam of Harvard, armed with an idea about the meaning of the word 'page'. It was, in my understanding, that *what a word means is part of its meaning*. This seductive idea, although connected with speculations about our Earth and a possible or imaginable Twin Earth, was not new, but had recently not been taken so seriously. There was the upshot that part of the meaning of 'page' was a large number of pieces of paper. Now add in a further idea, possibly also seductive, that the meaning of 'page' was part of your own passing thought. The conclusion follows that your passing thought, all of it, could not conceivably be dependent on any causal circumstance or neural correlate in you. The real pages of Hume, bed-time novelists, Putnam etc. are not dependent on you. The general conclusion, the doctrine of Anti-Individualism or Externalism in the Philosophy of Mind, is indeed that passing thoughts and many other conscious events do not depend on their individual owners in the way supposed. Exit the Union Theory and much else. Exit, more or less, the mind–brain relationship problem.

Enter Professor Burge of California, on a similar mission, with a thought-experiment. Imagine a man saying to his doctor that he has arthritis in his thigh. The thought is false, since by definition arthritis is an inflammation only of joints. Now imagine a different possible world from ours, W2. It is the same in its past and present as ours in almost all respects, including the neural or brain state of the man talking to his doctor. He utters the same words, that he has arthritis in his thigh. But, in W2, 'arthritis' means something you *can* get in the thigh. So, the thought he reports to his doctor may well be true rather than false. In which case you are invited to a general conclusion about thoughts. It is that they somehow depend on something other than neural facts in an individual's head. That is slightly vague, but can be taken as denying that there is a causal circumstance or neural correlate in an individual for such conscious events. There is not anything in an individual that by itself guarantees such a conscious event. In the Philosophy of Mind, we need to be Anti-Individualists. Exit again, if it re-entered, the Union Theory. Also much else.

Professor Putnam had been entertaining at dinner in the Garrick when I was deputed by the Royal Institute of Philosophy to take care of him after his lecture on Freddie, but he did not have to be joined in his peculiar idea about meaning. Evidently there was *another* idea of the meaning of a word – as conventions or rules for its use. This idea had the desirable consequence that you could not take your pen and actually make a marginal note right onto a part of a meaning, otherwise known as a page. Did his idea have some superiority? On reflection, it did not. What was more, if you thought long enough about it, this large idea of meaning collapsed back into something like my plainer idea. Such a meaning was a *conception* of a set of things, albeit a scientific conception, rather than the things themselves.

Professor Burge had not long ago given some acute lectures at University College, and rightly remarked to me that it would be better if Bill Hart and I were in different possible worlds. My resistance to him was as firm. What exactly was the general conclusion of the thought-experiment? Evidently it had to do with environmental facts of a linguistic kind, and the two different linguistic environments in the two worlds. But exactly what was meant by saying that thoughts *somehow depend* on such an environment as well as on neural facts in an individual's head?

I canvassed possibilities. One was that what either man in the doctor's office could be *held to mean* was dependent on the linguistic environment. But that sort of thing did not entail that what determined the man's thought was not all in his head. According to the Union Theory and to other Individualisms, the full determining history of his thought would of course include a linguistic environment. Earlier on he learned from it the meaning of 'arthritis', not quite correctly in the case of the man in our world. But that was perfectly consistent with the end of the story being an explanation wholly within him of his thought. What was more, despite Professor Burge's ominous invocation of Hegel and Wittgenstein at the start of his reflections, Professor Burge disavowed any non-historical or magical influence of the environment. There was a lot more to be said, some of it about the argument for the general conclusion, the argument about truth and thoughts. You had to keep in mind that your thoughts on two separate occasions, say that the wine in the cellar is cool, do not necessarily differ because someone started a fire in the time between them, making one false.

Almost all of the entries for *The Oxford Companion to Philosophy* had come in by April 1993. I survived my only undecorous battle with a contributor, a resolute and perhaps Antipodean philosopher in an ancient university. Her various entries were to include a lighter one on astrology. She thought it better to get it written by another hand, that of an astrologer, possibly her own. I said I was not inclined to print it, and my contributor said she would therefore withdraw all of her entries. The last blow struck by her in our postal battle was better than any of mine. Her final communication to the Grote Professor came in a large brown envelope, addressed in large letters to *Gross Yob Honderich*.

To rest from my labours on the book, and lesser ones with such graduate students as the admirable Targett, Martin, Kretschmer and Scott, I went off with Jane on a cycling holiday in the Dordogne. We got on well enough in our chaste way, and my rage was reserved for a hotel keeper. Her bed, said I, in a passable secondary-school accent, was good only for a dog, a French dog. Thus I could still on occasion assert the superiority of my chosen nationality, even if things were yet darker in England. The government was engaged in making the fares on British Rail cheaper by giving it to selected profiteers. I felt less inclined, with persons met in London who noted slips in my English accent, to make my old joke – that I was more British than they, having of my own volition taken on that identity and not had it thrust upon me.

The manuscript of the *Companion* was delivered by me to the stately premises of Oxford University Press only about a year after the commissioning of it began. My two guides Barton and Momtchiloff, in a way more atuned to 1993 than I, noted that the entries in the book on political philosophy included few on Conservative thinking and not many on Liberalism. This was true, said I, partly for the reason that there was not much Conservative thinking. The sum of it had not been greatly increased by the recent attempt to conscript into its history such True Blues as William Shakespeare and Jane Austen. Christopher Kirwan, the redoubtable Fellow in Philosophy at Exeter College in Oxford, sometimes present for the Christmas party in Keats Grove, was by my invitation casting an eye over the entries in Ancient Philosophy and Formal Logic. He put his boots on and made his way through the entries writing 'FALSE' and 'REJECT' on a few and doubting some others. In the end, ungracefully, I accepted that the copy-editing of the manuscript, now going forward, would stop in its tracks.

For political balance if not philosophical justice, an entry would be got on Conservativism and Romanticism, and others on Natural Aristocracy, Benjamin Constant, the Invisible Hand, and Piecemeal Engineering. There would still be enough antidote to this stuff elsewhere in the book. There would be a bit in the one entry by the Editor, on Unlikely Philosophical Propositions. And all the entries would be vetted by the combined efforts of another 13 philosophers, contributors to the book themselves, and thus with a sense of the enterprise.

In my role as landlord of The Studio, the agreeable little house in the front garden at 4 Keats Grove, there were also episodes. Not having achieved entry to the property for a year or two, I tried some more, and in the end Mr Hobbs let me in. A shock it was. The place was now a dark cave whose squalor was breath-taking. What was more alarming was the awful damp, enough to make the walls black with mould. Was it fit for human habitation? There were laws about that. Might the socialist landlord find himself up before the Hampstead Magistrates? Maybe exposed in *The Hampstead and Highgate Express*? Electrical rewiring was done snappily, greatly increasing my excess of expenditure over rent, of which I was keeping a running total, with more dismay than socialist pride.

Mr Hobbs was informed in writing of the need not to block up the essential ventilators again, and to use his electric heaters instead of the paraffin and butane ones that produced the condensation. In the course of all this, he weakened and allowed me a key to the place. It transpired that the lock needed replacing. Having fitted a new one, I delivered his new key to him in the local hospital, to which he had been admitted briefly for his bronchitis. In due course, reader, you will hear something more of this small episode of the new key.

The year moved towards its end less wearingly. Jane and I passed a bracing weekend with Janet and Derek behind the fine facade of West Kennett House. It was also in this year, I think, that we did not have a dinner with Jerry Cohen after he and I fell out over my owning two properties in addition to my own flat – or more particularly, as he said, my insensitively revealing this fact at a moment when he had no roof over his head save that of All Souls College, Oxford. Was it also in this year that he mentioned that the iron laws of history and the inevitability of the proletarian revolution no longer had a hold on him, and that he might vote for the Greens? My son John, having chucked his publishing job, made a decision that was partly to my satisfaction. He would not have a monthly subvention from me, but make his own way in the world.

I had an occasional lunch with Ingrid Coggin Purkiss in the church crypt next to the Royal Institute of Philosophy in Gordon Square. She had had a good deal of experience of the really problematic marriage, but now, after her escape, was pleased with her four grown-up children, and in a friendship with a man from the Arts Council. She herself was distracting, as were her views, her stylish calm, and her high principles. We talked of religion, and she was as good as an Anglican bishop at divesting God of his traditional attributes while still leaving him with some stock-in-trade. As well as being distracting, she was consoling. But nothing would be done to endanger my own problematic marriage. She did not ring me up, I noted. Despite experience of her own, she respected marriages.

There was the satisfaction early in 1993–94 of finishing the task of trying to remove forever another impediment to the understanding of the nature of consciousness. The doctrine of Functionalism, against which you have already heard some declamation, was owed in the first instance to Professor Putnam and Professor Armstrong, the latter having set it out in books in one of my Routledge series. Thereafter Professor Dennett was one who inventively nourished the child. Functionalism or computerized philosophy of mind or Cognitive Science with Philosophical Ambition, was purportedly the complete answer to the question of the nature of consciousness, the question of what conscious events are. They are events of which the only truth is that they have functional roles. They are in accordance, as you might also say, with certain causal rules or a certain programme. What all that comes to is that they are no more than events with certain causes and with certain effects, the effects including behaviour.

The idea owed much to the fact that beliefs and desires generally are typically effects of our environments and causes of our actions – and to such particular truths as that we explain someone's wanting a glass of wine, partly, as an item owed to his seeing the bottle and result-ing in his putting a hand out. Functionalism also owed something to a thought about what may or may not come to exist in the future – a constructed thing including a computer that actually does function as humans do. It is no merely partial and remote approximation to us, like our chess-playing machines, but indistinguishable in its carry-on from all human carry-on. This thing may act as if there is a cloud over its affection for another thing and she might leave. What could rationally impede its human contemporaries from ascribing conscious beliefs and the like to it? Does this not prove Functionalism?

Professor Searle had striven splendidly in articles and on television to rid us of all this, and I could contribute. It could be shown, first, that Functionalism as applied to us humans was exactly as unswallowable as something else, something that even Functionalists could not swallow. The charm of Functionalism, for its proponents, was that it was somehow better than Eliminative Materialism, the truly mad Identity Theory of mind and brain for which conscious events are events with only neural or electrochemical properties and no more said. Just cells. For Functionalists, conscious events were now events, involving *whatever* material or stuff, with the right causal connections. In the scientized haze of this doctrine, its conscious events can seem to be a little ethereal, a little above the brain or the like, satisfactorily so.

This was an illusion, said I. Our own human conscious events, on the Functionalist story, in fact remain no more than neural events in certain causal connections. That is no better than the truly mad Identity Theory. Near enough, it *is* that theory. I am not told more about my desire or belief, anything in addition to its being a neural event that is a certain effect and a certain cause, by being informed that some other material or stuff could be in the same causal relations. I am not told more about this neural event by being told that silicon could be substituted and it would be the same mental event – that is, in the same causal relations.

This proposition about Functionalism and Eliminative Materialism could have a second one added to it. On the story of the Professors Putnam, Armstrong and Dennett, soon to be recanted by the first of them, the category of conscious events is distinguished from all else only by way of two other categories – the causes and the effects of the category of conscious events. There is no other true conception of conscious events, no other way of getting to them. So, to find the subject-matter that is conscious events, and to write their books about it, Functionalists need as a first step to pick out two large categories of causes and effects. Certainly these causes and effects are not *all* the things that affect us persons and that we affect. They are not the only input and output.

A multitude of things affects me without my awareness, and a multitude of things is then affected by me without my awareness. At breakfast this morning I gained some weight, and thereafter flattened the cushion on my chair a bit more. The weight-gain was not a conscious event.

How does our Functionalist, in order to find his subject-matter and indeed to conceive of conscious events at all, select the right categories of causes and effects, and hence the right category of inner events? He does it, I happily informed him, by having and using what he denies to exist, a conception of conscious events additional to and different from his official one. It has something to do with nothing other than fundamental subjectivity. Functionalism, in depending on what it denies, is incoherent. This second insult, in my contribution to Warner & Szubka, *The Mind-Body Problem: A Guide to the Current Debate*, has not done a great deal to persuade my fellow pilgrims in the Philosophy of Mind to pass by Functionalism. I live in hope, though, rather good hope. If the day ever comes, by the way, when the constructed thing including a computer carries on as we do, and we ascribe consciousness to it, we will have in mind not only silicon events in the right connections.

During the first term of 1993–94, I again became contentedly compulsive about the *Companion*, since the 13 reports on its 1,950 entries had come in. Getting into the spirit of the thing, I went a lot further than suggested by my vetters in asking contributors for revisions. About 220 of the 240 would hear from me. Letters and faxes flowed out daily. Having earlier resigned myself to being my own secretary 90 per cent of the time, it now became necessary to go further to keep the departmental peace. It was galling, and a reminder of the disputability of perquisites, but soon forgotten in my onward marching. Chastened by my editing I had been, but pleased I was with the outcome. Among the small pleasures were last entries secured from further contributors as antidotes, one being the useful *Masculism*.

At 4 Keats Grove the background fact of life was melancholy doubt about the future of Janeso and Tedso. We were keeping the peace, often affectionately, and giving uproarious dinner parties, but also holding our breath. It would not be me who brought my third marriage to an end. I did find myself arraigned again elsewhere for something akin to the theft of philosophy. At any rate the use of ideas of my friend and colleague Jerry Valberg without giving him sufficient credit in a hasty and careless footnote. The paper of mine in question was one of which you have heard, 'Seeing Things,' and Jerry's book is *The Puzzle of Experience*, the manuscript of which had been recommended by me to its publisher.

My defence of myself to him was mainly that my contention in the paper was that we see the world and nothing else. His different contention in his book was that in the conflict between this realism and the opposing doctrine of phenomenalism we have an antinomy or paradox, an unresolvable question. My second defence, not happy, was that for some time I had not been a close attender to other philosophers' manuscripts. Having fought about it, very nearly as boys would, we would get back on good terms, but when? Diligent reader, I leave to you a final judgement on me, which you may make by a study of 'Seeing Things' and *The Puzzle of Experience*, the latter of which will in any case reward you for your effort.

My labours with the copy-editors of *The Oxford Companion to Philosophy*, and on its index, made an Easter holiday seem a good idea. At 61, as my college doctor Ali Alibhai said, you should pace yourself, and also give up that nicotine chewing gum. Acting on the latter advice was difficult, since the habit of furtive chewing was now ten years old. But I would relax in Rome for a week, by myself. It was lonely but recuperative. The Forum, the Sistine Chapel, paintings elsewhere, the fresh flowers for Raphael in the Pantheon, family restaurants, Keats's other house, reading Paul Foot's *Red Shelley* on the Spanish Steps, the beatification mass attended at St Peter's – these led me belatedly to another thought about London. Paris was not the only capital that outshone mine. Also, it seemed unlikely that Italy was like England, where the *British Medical Journal* now reported that the poor were dying still younger. It was agreeable that an Italian translation of *How Free Are You?* was in prospect. Maybe the Italians would also translate *Conservatism*, as the Germans were doing on the heels of the Spanish.

Having tried out of some sympathy and more apprehension to get help for the declining Mr Hobbs from the social workers of our local government apparatus, Camden Council, and installed central heating in The Studio, I learned in August that he was in one way able to look after himself. He too could get in touch with the Council. A zealous officer of it, a tribune of the people of whom I had to approve, warned me that The Studio was still in danger of being declared unfit for human habitation, whoever had caused it. The renovation he proposed seemed excessive, as he thereafter agreed it was, and as proved to be the case. But, said I, every single proposed thing would be done *immediately*. No, I did not want to have the premises declared unfit for habitation in order to be entitled to a financial grant that might pay for half the work. The cave became a building site, given over to Greenleaf Property Care. Mr Hobbs did not decamp, but occupied his single bed in the rubble.

During my several inspections a day during the two months of renovation I got more of an idea of my tenant's friend and supporter, who was on hand several times. She was about 60, a pretty woman grown older. She had been noticed by me on her occasional visits to The Studio over past years, and now she was seen a little more often. She came in a car and one of my neighbours took her for a social worker or a nurse. I had the better idea that she and Mr Hobbs had been on closer terms sometime in the past, and, out of old affection, she was now propping him up. One day when I needed to be in touch with him, I did so by ringing her at her council house – one of the low-rent houses on estates owned by the same Camden Council. She was a woman of a peculiar feminine liveliness, self-aware in her movements, putting one in mind of a child who had got attention and sought more. She fluttered between her car and the front door of The Studio. Like Green Shoes before her, she can do with a soubriquet in this narrative. *Flutter* will do.

Lectures in Crakow had been the first of a number of philosophical invitations accepted partly because of my release from labours on the *Companion* and partly because of Jane. Beijing, Copenhagen and Hawaii were also in our diary, but Tokyo came before them. Jane starred at the dinner in the traditional Japanese inn, and I took care to preserve the decorum of our double act by keeping my political opinions to myself. She was not to be present for our later engagements.

In late September, near the end of the seventh year of our connection and the fifth of marriage, we went for a walk on the Heath, along the path where I had last seen Johnny a year before, when he didn't stop to talk. Jane said, again, that we had to split. My momentary calm could not overcome her resolution. Nor could her true propositions about our situation overcome *my* resolution. If hope was faint, and if I would not struggle more against our ending, I would not agree to it. It would be her doing. Back at the flat, she prepared to go. We spent a half-hour of tears and hugs. To show we were able to deal with life, we snapped separation-day photos of one another. I went out for another walk myself, so as not to see her leave.

Perhaps you have some decent sense of why it happened. Perhaps more than I in my allotted degree of self-blindness. What was last said about me by Jane, whether or not as her final opinion, was that I was by nature dominating, and that it was no great relief to her if I gave up the exercise of my power but still possessed it. As for the feeling of the ending and the days afterward, it was pain. I had failed again, and my tenderness for Jane was as ever. But the pain and tears could alternate with relief, and clear memory of exasperation. We had wanted things of one another which, surely, we could not provide. The age-difference of 19 years was part of the story. We had tried, not done much culpable hurt to one another, and I had not given up.

In the run of suppers arranged to fill my evenings, I was tolerably stoical. The first was with Ingrid. She was ideal in adversity, and her friend Peter Bird of the Arts Council had died. Other suppers were with Pauline, John, Janet, and the friends-in-need Janet Whitaker, Faye Maschler and Reg Gadney, Karl Miller, Robin Blackburn, Robert Audley, Tessa Blackstone, Gillian Hoffmann, and Ingrid again. All need to be recorded as doing well by me. Kiaran was sweet in her E-mail messages from Princeton, and the Sprigges in their letters from Edinburgh, and Janet of regular help on the phone. When walking again on the Heath with Pauline, my stoicism wore out at the wrong moment, when our path crossed with that of Claire Tomalin and her Michael, and I was caught weeping a tear. They too did well. In my diary I earned less good marks, by recording, if not in full reflectiveness, that I loathed feminism.

Ingrid Coggin Purkiss, ideal partner, en route to Cintra

W. V. Quine, me, and Alastair Hannay, in Oslo, seeing things

On Hampstead Heath
© Harry Borden

Peter Strawson, don of dons
© Steve Pyke

Jerry Cohen, pilgrim of political progress
© Steve Pyke

Hidé Ishiguro, both imaginative and technical
© Steve Pyke

Myles Burnyeat, giver of good name to ancient
philosophy
© Steve Pyke

Michael Dummett, superior philosopher and
anti-racist
© Steve Pyke

Derek Parfit, meticulous and friendly
© Steve Pyke

Anthony Kenny, philosopher of powers
© Steve Pyke

Another of photographer Pyke's subjects in 1990
© Steve Pyke

David Wiggins, Incompatibilist
© Steve Pyke

With Ingrid, on departure from Keats Grove for
Iran and its dress code for women

Last lecture, Grote's room

17

INGRID, COURT AGAIN

Three weeks after separation-day, I set out for Beijing, a solitary traveller showing signs of good resolution. At the airport began what would maintain my inner equilibrium during the flight, the writing of paragraphs of retrospective diary. The conference had to do with Logical Positivism, and was in memory of the Chinese Freddie Ayer. These official facts did not constrain all of the delegates, some of whom brought along whichever of their papers was closest to fitting in. Mine was the one already tried out in Tokyo, against the doctrine that actions are right because of special facts about the agents who perform them, rather than because of certain consequences of the actions. I did not deliver it especially well, mainly because of the difference in time zones, for which life in Keats Grove had not fully prepared me.

Still, the paper seemed to be approved of by Li Li. She was a graceful philosopher of Quantum Theory who caught my eye, now free to rove. We had talks and walks, but no assignations, partly because of her socialist rectitude, partly because of my revived sense of not being God's gift to women, and, not perfectly consistently, partly because of my thoughts of Ingrid. These had come over me since separation-day. Were we not suited? Was a match not more than a reviving prospect? Would it not be a consummation as much called for by inclination as by reason? Surely it could not be that I was much intrigued by smaller facts about her, such external properties as her family history in which occurred religion, the Communist Party and old Rolls Royces?

Later in October 1994, back in my role as landlord, I was in my front garden at Keats Grove preventing damp in The Studio, by taking the leaves out of the roof gutter near the big window. Into my garden, bare-footed and seemingly enraged, came she who has been introduced to you as Flutter. She would, for whatever reason, prevent me from going about my task. The idea, it seemed, was that the task was hers. She claimed it by getting bodily between me and The Studio. She shouted out to people in the street to call the police because this fucking man was attacking her. What it all portended was clearer a few days later, with the news of the death of Mr Hobbs. It was still clearer the next day when I made inquiries of a clerk as to his next-of-kin. None known, said the clerk, except for the lady who was in here this morning. She said she was his common-law wife.

Hobbs, you remember, had been protected in his possession of his home by a good law left over from another political age. He had a right to it, and could not be got out by a landlord with scruples. The rent paid on his behalf, despite increases by the Rent Officer, had been very low indeed. It was a fraction of the rents determined by supply and demand in the blessed market. If he had been married when he died, his widow would have inherited his right of tenancy and the same low rent. So too, and properly, would a woman who was his common-law wife and had been living with him in the premises.

The landlord in me rang up his solicitors with the facts as he saw them. The solicitors were Farrer & Co., left over from the coda to *Honderich v. Green Shoes*. The facts about Flutter were that she had been Hobbs's occasional visitor, his friend and supporter, and that she lived in a council house on another side of Hampstead hill. Indeed I had telephoned her there in August. Flutter, to my mind, was plotting to acquire a second residence, in Keats Grove, but fortunately it was not a good plot. Quite so, said Farrers. It doesn't matter that she's moved in, changed the lock, and installed a telephone.

A week or so later, her fierce solicitor down in Camden Town informed mine of the facts as she saw them. They came together into a simple proposition, which was that Flutter had been living in my front garden for 20 years, as common-law wife to Hobbs. It was breathtaking, but not too ominous. It was a scandal that Flutter's solicitor was taking the view that Flutter had an arguable case in law, and hence, since it seemed she had no money of her own, that the State should pay her legal costs. The decent institution of Legal Aid was clearly a social necessity, but here was a misuse of it. Not that it would be a disaster for me if we failed to persuade the Legal Aid Board of its error, as indeed we would try to do. If the case ever went to court, the truth would out quickly. My standing in the role of landlord would be vindicated. And as winner in the case I would in the ordinary way have my legal costs paid to me by the other side.

It was a relief in late November to be out of a role and being what I took to be really myself, a decent philosopher giving a paper to the philosophers of Copenhagen, with some gusto. My struggle had gone on to make some advance in understanding consciousness – to get to a real analysis or some compelling account of the fact, as it seemed, with which we all have our most intimate experience. There was my advantage over many of my co-workers in the Philosophy of Mind of my being unburdened by technical expertise of doubtful relevance, despite being on good terms with my own computer. But no progress had been made in clarifying the three things in terms of which I tried to think of a conscious event, these being the so-called subjective aspect, the content, and the object. No progress had been made, either, in thinking of the relations between them. The tangled story was really more gap than story. If it seemed more promising on some days than others, it was not being untangled and filled in. It was deep and murky philosophical water. Might it be possible to get out of these depths, and think about the problem of consciousness in a simpler way? A proper English way? This was the idea of my leader in the struggle against mesmerization by computer in the Philosophy of Mind, Californian though he was. Professor Searle had to his satisfaction completed what gave him the title of his new book, *The Rediscovery of the Mind*.

My Copenhagen paper looked at his way of seeking to state the truth about consciousness and to despatch Functionalism – by staying out of the deep and murky water and relying on what he called humble and obvious truths about the mind. One was that a conscious event has a special mode of existence. It exists only as *somebody's* conscious event. It depends for its existence on a 'first person', an 'I'. But what did that mean if it was not a dive into the deep and murky philosophical water? Well, what it had to mean was that a conscious event is dependent on a particular person in an ordinary sense. In that sense, a person is a persisting body and/or a flow of conscious events, some of the events being memories of others.

So a conscious event was being defined as one that would not exist without such a particular person. But when we got that clear, did we actually get an idea of a conscious event different from the one in Functionalism? The sad answer was no. We did not get a conception of conscious events that makes them different from just brain events in causal connections. These latter events, it can certainly be said, *also* depend on one person in an ordinary sense.

What about the natural idea noticed in his famous paper 'What Is It Like to Be a Bat?' by Thomas Nagel, and noticed independently elsewhere by my friend Timothy Sprigge? This is the idea that when something is conscious, there is a way it is like to be that thing. So a conscious event, you can say, is one that brings in what it is like to be something. Does this sound promising? No doubt, but what is meant by this talk of *what it is like to be something*? Before answering, remember that we take it there is such a fact with humans and bats but not with stones and chairs. Isn't it inevitable that what we understand by what it is like to be something is *what it is like to be something conscious* or indeed *what it is like to be conscious*? But this is a disaster. We were going to get an enlightening truth about conscious events, but what we have got is only that they are events that bring in what it is like to be conscious. We knew that already. That is more or less what we are trying to understand. The sad conclusion of my paper, which thereafter went into the *American Philosophical Quarterly*, was that humble and obvious truths were no great help in trying to understand consciousness. More time would have to be spent looking into the murk of the mind.

Ingrid had come along with me to Copenhagen. We were getting on very nicely in our tentative connection, starting to meet for much of the weekend in Keats Grove or in her stylish flat in Belsize Park Gardens. We talked of Plato and the Forms, and of whether he showed good sense about the rearing of children in pens. We had fine meals, together, and discovered that all of life could begin again. Might our connection become less tentative? Might our undisturbed tranquillity last? Might it last because it had some roots in family pasts in some ways similar?

Although she seemed quintessentially English, she came on her mother's side from a line of Danes. It had in it a strain of politics whose present culmination was Svanholm, the largest true commune in Denmark, probably in Europe. We visited cousin Knud there, and I took in that his professorial salary went into the pot with the lesser incomes of unskilled comrades, and that he got an equal share out of it. As for Ingrid's father, he had been of a family of English churchmen and benefactors and a press lord. Like Russell, he had ended his Cambridge career by his pacifism during the First World War, and did not conform thereafter. Instead he became a Communist, and sent his daughter to a suitable place, Dartington Hall School, very progressive.

We also had more in common. She was not 19 years younger than me. She was interested in philosophy and at work in it, being the person-ification of The Royal Institute of Philosophy. She was also the mother of four children, and they were of about the ages of Kiaran and John. We coincided, too, in various conventionalities, one of these being tastes in rooms. The dramatic difference between my past career with women and her attention to duty as mother and wife, in darkest Surrey, gave rise to caution with respect to our prospects, but no more than that. She had left her husband after 30 years and could well maintain her independence of me. Other admirers were on hand to help her do so. Here indeed might be an ideal consort, in time for my 62nd birthday. The high Anglicanism with which she had replaced the atheism got from her father, and her Platonism, unqualified by teaching it in a sixth form college, and her relation to Bach cantatas were all comprehensible to me. Her disposition was sweet, her contentedness instructive, and she had little need to utilize her accent in public speaking. I loved the look of her. Tall and blonde, with hazel eyes.

In December it was reassuring to meet Mr John Litton, the barrister procured by my solicitors in connection with The Studio. Yes, if the matter ever came to court, it would be good that my witnesses would include not only such neighbours as a judge and a judge's wife but also the postman and various labourers and tradesmen who had worked in The Studio – it wouldn't be easy for a court to see my case as a conspiracy of toffs against a woman of the working class. Yes, the drinker's squalor inside The Studio, and the kitchen sink's being blocked for years, and no refrigerator, would tell against any woman's living in the place. And yes, a court would certainly be interested that Flutter's daughter and her boyfriend had been living with her in the council house and that the daughter had lately become pregnant and they had got married. There had then been the prospect for Flutter of less room in the house of which she was the official tenant.

The next day brought a new fact, a letter from the solicitors on the other side. They had eight witnesses who would swear that their client had lived in The Studio for 20 years as the tenant's common-law wife. As for our judge and judge's wife, they were trumped – by a bishop's wife who would also be speaking for her husband the bishop. As for the council house, it was just an accident that it had remained in Flutter's name as tenant after her husband died. It had in effect been her daughter's home. There was also something still more unsettling.

A bedrock of my case, even *the* bedrock, had been that my neighbours, the postman and so on and I myself had seen hardly anything of Flutter around The Studio. To this there was now a reply. She had been living there *secretly*. The idea was that Hobbs had been worried that if it were discovered he had a woman living with him, his landlord might be able to get him out. This was why Flutter was more or less invisible. This was why the voters' list, the utilities bills and the whole pile of paper attached to the address said nothing at all of her, unlike the pile attached to the council house.

Having in five months run up a sizeable bill in order to see my story about The Studio vindicated and justice done, I learned another proposition. Julian Pike, the reassuringly combative Farrers man newly in charge of the running of my legal affair, made something clear to me. If I won in *Honderich v. Flutter*, I would also lose. It had just been a mistake on my part to think that if the case came to court, and I won, my legal costs would be paid to me in the ordinary way, by the losing side. The fact was that the Legal Aid system would pay the legal costs of Flutter, but these would *not* include a claim against her in accordance with a court's finding that I was in the right.

It was alarming enough to call for an Easter holiday, in Vienna. Ingrid could speak some German there, a language learned in her university days, and I could look out for the translation of *How Free Are You?* in the bookshops. A shelf of the little yellow Reclam paperbacks was located, in good alphabetical order. There indeed was Honderich, in between Homer and Horace. *Very* satisfactory company. Conceivably a portent? Best to think so after my three legals visited 4 Keats Grove to see for themselves what I and my neighbours could see of The Studio and comings and goings to and from it. Along with Julian Pike and John Litton, for added gravitas, was Dick Griffiths, a veteran of the coda to *Honderich v. Green Shoes*, and now the senior partner in Farrers.

More dark propositions were conveyed to me. John Litton confirmed his recent written Opinion that my chances of winning in *Honderich v. Flutter* were now only 50/50, because of the ten statements on the other side by Flutter's daughter, son-in-law, and friends and acquaintances. My legal costs were now estimated at £30,000 in all if I won, and double that if I lost. In that year my annual university salary after the 40 per cent tax was under £23,000. The other side was sounded out about a settlement, and it made a confident response. Flutter would make no deal, Flutter would fight and Flutter would win.

This was the stage of my life surveyed in the opening pages of this book you are reading. My narrative has now come up to that green summer – places, the philosophical furniture of my mind, my daily round, more philosophy, and my inner life. As you will anticipate, more has happened since then. Let us carry on together for a while.

The Oxford Companion to Philosophy was published to acclaim. In the happy mood of a sunny morning, I had posed for photos lying down on the grass on the Heath. These, very large, graced *The Independent on Sunday*, starting on the front page. The accompanying piece was funny about philosophers, and bountiful in its approval of me, except for a quoted remark on my philosophical standing and prospects, which did not surprise me after I learned the identity of its maker. He remarked, very truly, that I would never be elected a member of a kind of academic club of mixed distinction, the British Academy. It was not so good as the Garrick, but had in it all of my detractors left over from past struggles and my pieces of imprudent assertiveness.

One other bouquet with small thorns in it was more provocative. Ray Monk, the biographer of Wittgenstein, was very superior in the course of arriving at his conclusion that the *Companion* was 'the most authoritative single-volume reference work in philosophy yet published'. It was not his diplomacy in having it both ways that moved me, but his superiority about certain lighter-hearted entries in the book by Jane. She and I had remained on affectionate terms since our parting. Defend her I certainly would. To fill out my waspish letter to the editor, I dragged in the fact that Mr Monk had pretty much left out the homosexuality in his life of Wittgenstein. Not my most graceful moment.

If *Honderich v. Flutter* was writing on the wall, the beginning of the year 1995–96 had its distractions, some of them comforts. It was a comfort to reflect that the question *How Free Are You?* would be considered in their own languages not only by the Germans, but also by the Italians, Spanish and Japanese, and maybe the Polish and Romanians. Social life at Keats Grove revived, Ingrid now at the other end of the table. The usual unlikely alliances were made in the talk, one being between Michael Foot and Ruth Dudley Edwards, charming firebrand but no daughter of the revolution. Later on Ken Follett gave me a drink and we contemplated our coming double-act at the Institute of Contemporary Arts. Yes, he said, it was true that the new leader of the Labour Party, Tony Blair, was cutting ties with such class-warriors as him despite their fund-raising capabilities. It seemed unlikely that I would be faxing in suggestions for speeches in the next election.

Distractions did not always succeed with *Honderich v. Flutter*. There was not much relief, either, in a letter from the tax collector that made it conceivable that all my legal costs could be deducted as an expense from future rent got from The Studio. Thus I might in the end be reimbursed 40 per cent of those costs. This showed that the world was not badly arranged for the landlord class. But it could not reduce my main apprehension, about the disgrace to be borne if I lost my case. The same was true of a cheque from Bee, prompted by a general piece on Legal Aid in *The Sunday Times*, under the heading 'Winners Face Ruin in Legal Aid Scandal'. Bee's cheque would pay a good fraction of the £32,000 if I won and help a bit with the £64,000 if I lost, but it would not help with my self-image.

On a Thursday in March 1996, our first day in court, it was clear there had been no need to worry that a judge would see me and my witnesses as toffs united against the working class. Flutter, despite the misleading council house, and her way with the language of the people, had a touch of old Vienna about her. Despite being a street trader in the Portobello Road on Sundays, she was definitely among the members of the middle class herself. On Friday, Flutter explained something that the admirable Julian Pike had unearthed. This was her method of paying the rent of the council house that on her final story she had for the most part *not* been living in – the method of repeatedly signing forms saying she *was* living in it and thereby getting £17,000 in housing benefits from Camden Council. She explained to Judge Diamond this had been only technically fraudulent, since her daughter had a right to the house, and her not actually being listed as its tenant was an accident. Also, if it was bad of Flutter not to have owned up to inheriting £70,000 from her family while getting the £17,000 from the Council, it was only human.

What affected me much more was something else. To my mind, my adversary's case consisted in gross exaggeration of her presence in The Studio and her relationship with Hobbs. But there was a little truth in it. Now, on the wing in the witness box, she added something. She let us all know, a little confidentially, that on the day in 1993 that I delivered a new key to Hobbs in the local hospital, I also personally gave a new key to her, on the doorstep of The Studio. I thereby recognized her as living in the place. She remembered it well because it was out of character for me, and reminded her that there was hope for everybody. The brazen lie unhinged me for a while. It seemed to be, and maybe even was, the most shocking experience of my life. It increased my fear, put an end for a while to a small doubt about my own general story of The Studio, threw a lurid light over hers, and gave me an excited hope. Lies are dangerous.

On Monday my Mr Litton set out to ask questions of Flutter about three days which included the one on which she had appeared in my garden bare-footed. As had since transpired from various documents, Hobbs was then lying dead in The Studio. He was lying under the big window into which I might have glanced in the course of my labours. Flutter, in these three days before a doctor had been got on the scene to certify the death, was trying to consult her psychotherapist, and visiting a solicitor about her rights.

Having been taken aback by what seemed to be Judge Diamond's evident sympathy for Flutter as a woman who had given her life selflessly to two alcoholics, the other being her husband, I was now alarmed by his discouraging John Litton from pressing questions about the three days. Maybe the question of whether Flutter was not just saying goodbye to Peter, as she said, but cooking something up. Was the judge impressed by her first two witnesses, these being her daughter and son-in-law? The latter, a Shakespearian actor, brought presence to the witness box, despite being discomfited by a fact that had accidentally come to light. It was that

Flutter had been for a time living in *his* flat in Kensington, which fact he had left out of his affidavit about her living in The Studio.

On Tuesday morning nine more witnesses for Flutter were heard, if no bishop's wife. They stuck to their written statements, but also painted no pretty picture of Hobbs, no picture of a man given over to an affectionate relationship. In the afternoon, in the witness box myself, I displayed what was to me the confidence of truth, no doubt unwisely. To the implied charge by the other side that I was a bad landlord over 15 years, it was possible to produce the details of having received £23,230 in rent and paid out £23,750 for repairs. On Wednesday, after having stood up for myself some more, I was succeeded by eight of my witnesses, Jane being one. Two others were relatives of Hobbs. These had been sought out by Flutter to testify on her behalf, but had been kidnapped by the lovely Pike to testify on mine instead. Peter's daughter was not reluctant to do so, having learned of her father's death a day or two ago, 18 months late, as a result of Flutter's need for help in a court case. On Thursday there were another eight witnesses on my side, including a gent found in a local pub by our private detective and three from Camden Council.

On Friday there was my Mr Litton's closing submission, an admirable piece of work. Certainly A++?+. It included a detail having to do with the chronology that had been worked out from Flutter's confusing recollections in court of her periods of presence in The Studio. One of the long periods of absence included the day on which, according to her in that early moment of her testimony, I had given her the key on the doorstep. Also, as my man pointed out, her story of my giving her a key was inconsistent with her fundamental story that Hobbs believed he needed to keep me in the dark about her living in The Studio.

A few days later, Judge Diamond read out his 34-page judgement. It included a thumbnail sketch of Flutter as an attractive, unselfish and caring personality, who had given her life to two alcoholics. With respect to the first question he had to answer, whether Flutter was living in The Studio immediately before the death of Hobbs, the judge surveyed the evidence, not leaving out the squalor and the buckets of urine on the table. Taking into account everything, above all the number of Flutter's witnesses, he could answer this first question in her favour. She *was* living there. She had not been there earlier, but she *had* been living in The Studio for eight months before the death of Hobbs.

The second question was whether she had been living there as his wife. The question, said the judge, could not be decided on the basis of sympathy alone. It had caused him much difficulty. His thumbnail sketch of Hobbs was relevant. He reported Flutter's admitting that for Peter painting came first, drink second, she third, and other women fourth. Peter, said the judge, devalued the women in his life. He had in his personality a strong element of misogyny. He did not make, and was probably unable to make, the emotional commitment involved in a relation equivalent to that of husband and wife.

Flutter had lost, and my character had not officially been slighted. But my relief was brief. Judge Diamond gave leave to Flutter, very readily indeed, to appeal against his judgement. On the way out I learned from my legals that it might take the Court of Appeal a year to get around to the matter. A year. Until then, Flutter would be in my front garden, unless she liked the council house better. That house had turned out to be on a unique wooded estate. A witness from the Council had said it was worth £500,000, more than twice the value of my own flat. Flutter had an eye for good addresses. Aggrieved I was, not at all philosophical. By Judge Diamond's finding that she had been living in The Studio for eight months, I felt myself unofficially accused, anyway doubted. I was not let off by his saying that I had honestly missed her, rather than known of her presence and lied about it.

But, as I am more content to report, no question arose in my mind about the justice and decency of the Legal Aid system. Flutter had had an arguable case, and had rightly been supported by what remained of the Welfare State. Despite my moral confidence, the only practical test of whether she had a case was what had happened in court. It was no good saying she was lucky in her judge. She had, as it seemed, very nearly won. Even if she had turned out not to have had a case, the decency of Legal Aid would not have been put in much question. Any social or human system, however good, will involve bad upshots. If any social provision had to be foolproof, there could be no social provision. And, finally, it was in fact no scandal in this imperfect world that the landlord class sometimes had to find some extra cash. After the Court of Appeal, it might be £45,000, if I won.

Can it be that some philosophers of mind have been deprived of such emotions as those in *Honderich v. Flutter?* Or, if they have got into a lawsuit, they only have had calm passions in it? The philosophers in question are the mixed lot who, despite their differences, say the thing about our conscious existence of which you have heard. They take it to consist in certain limited kinds of physical facts. These are neural or electrochemical facts in our head and an array of facts of causal relationship, one being the relationship between a glass of wine in the environment, the neural facts, and the production of the sounds 'Yes, please.' Could it be that these philosophers, who leave something out, have experienced fewer human relationships? Does their Ingrid make less impression on them?

It could be true, but there must be more reason for Functionalists taking up a conception of consciousness so meagre – indeed so meagre as to be, for the rest of us, just false. One further reason, of which you have heard before, is the unsatisfactoriness of the alternative, the obscure and problematic nature of a fuller conception of the nature of consciousness, a conception owed to the grip we have on it. In spring 1996, with the prospect of another lecture to the Royal Institute of Philosophy before me, I was more sympathetic to this want of nerve. In my case, however, there was more reason for sympathy than the tangle, murk, vagueness and difficulty of talk of a conscious event's subjective aspect, content, and object.

The more particular problem had been touched on at the end of my paper for Copenhagen. It was that my tangled talk was in a way outrageous. According to it, firstly, conscious events were physical events. That is, as you have heard before, they were in one of the two kinds of physical events, those taking up space and standing in causal connection with those taking up space and having properties we perceive.* Secondly, conscious events were in our heads. Where else could they be? But, thirdly, they were not merely the standard electro-chemical events taken to be the only subject-matter of neuroscience by some of its practitioners. So conscious events were funny physical events in heads. If attempts could be made to calm recipients of this news, it was not reassuring. It sounded like something awful heard of before in the history of philosophy, in connection with souls, egos and selves – *conscious stuff*, maybe a relative of ectoplasm.

* See p. 278

There was also another trouble. What force was there in saying that conscious events, being a matter of subjective aspect, content and object, were of a different physical kind from those other physical events in heads that were electrochemical? Suppose one day the Centre for Neuroscience in University College London seems to discover conscious events so conceived. It learns more of them. Will they not be, despite what has been said of a difference in physical kind, very like electrochemical events? And, to come to the end of this gloomy anticipation, will some philosopher superior to the fashion of his decade not say something? Will he not say, all too reasonably, that this conception of conscious events *leaves something out*? That it is so meagre as to be, for ordinary persons, just false?

My personal struggle with consciousness, renewed and different, carried on in Gordon Square and Keats Grove. What *was* it to be conscious in these rooms, looking out these windows at those trees? It could be got hold of, couldn't it, if I kept at it? It wasn't as if you had to give up and say the problem of consciousness was insoluble. My old colleague McGinn had announced this in an article, but for such philosophical reasons as to put me in mind of someone's earlier observation that he distinguished himself not only as the Wilde Reader in Oxford but also the Wilde Writer. Conceivably out of justified spite about a line of mine, he had earlier said in a review of Freddie's posthumous collection of essays that my memorial-meeting speech for him, reprinted as the introduction, was ill-written, plodding and faintly nauseating in places. Was it for this reason that I was disinclined to his stuff about giving up in the philosophy of mind? Not only, cynic, not only.

Outside of Gordon Square and Keats Grove, the rich were getting spectacularly richer, although less safe even in their fortified houses. There was more research into the connection between not having money and dying earlier. Mr Lilley, the cretinous Minister of Something, said that there was no real poverty in Britain. I damned the monarchy ritually on Canadian television, and went on about The Principle of Equality for a profile of myself in a Swedish newspaper. But I cared less about England and the victims in it, having worn out my feelings. The shits had won, and England had let them.

Ingrid and I also settled into what Wittgenstein would no doubt dignify as a form of life, this being the habit of joining forces on Friday evening until Monday morning and also on Wednesdays, either in Keats Grove or Belsize Park Gardens. In July the tenants left the flat above my head, purchased by me in an earlier person-stage. It needed renovation, about which Ingrid had good ideas. Against a past resolution of mine, another wall came down, making a fine, broad room looking into the chestnut tree in front and out across a balcony to the green palisade behind. Who should the new tenant be? Why not Ingrid? She was rueful about the long line of my women before her, but also about her own past of exemplary restraint and dutifulness, kept up too long. Also, it had become clear that her strength in her own life was more than sufficient to save her from feelings that would have troubled someone less favoured. She was above being diminished by taking up a place in a line, by being, as she said, the present incumbent of the benefice.

Having consulted with her four children, she moved in in early August. We would, we said, carry on our successful form of life, our weekly round that allowed for some solitude and independence. We would not quarrel with success. Still, we would not actually be debarred from meeting on other than the four official days, and of course would have keys to one another's flats.

In the Court of Appeal, Lord Justices Russell, Saville and Aldous had read Flutter's barrister's written submissions to them. One was that Judge Diamond had partly used a subjective rather than an objective test in coming to his answer to the question of whether the pair had been living as man and wife. That is, he had asked himself if *they* thought of themselves as man and wife, as distinct from the question of whether the outside world or the ordinary man would have taken them to be such. He had said there was an inner element to the matter, and had become over-interested in the personalities of Flutter and Peter.

What do you mean by this bold assertion about subjectivity? asked Lord Justice Russell of Flutter's man. There are these various possibilities. Please make up your mind. Flutter's man was tutored for two hours, very good use being made of the written submission to the court by my Mr Litton. Lord Russell allowed himself to wonder, for good reasons, whether Flutter had been living in The Studio at all in the eight months. He was wonderfully unimpressed by 'this secrecy business' in her case. He noted how very well her story served her purposes in connection with her son-in-law and pregnant daughter, and also their purposes. He elicited the fact that Flutter remained on this very day the official tenant of the council house, and thus had another roof over her head.

My man Litton rose and proposed to elaborate his case on my behalf, but the trio chose to retire to take thought. It came back soon to announce it need not trouble him. It was already perfectly clear that Judge Diamond's judgement had been a model judgement. The Court of Appeal would not dream of overturning it. No fault whatever could be found with Judge Diamond. Judge Diamond was a peach of a fellow. My man sought again to speak, this time about my legal costs in the appeal, but was anticipated again. If ever there was a case, said Lord Justice Russell, where the legal costs in an appeal of someone in my position should be paid for by the Legal Aid Board, this was it. It seemed to me possible that if this splendid trio had had the power to save me my previous costs, they would happily have done so. They could not. Those were now £50,000.

At lunch in Chancery Lane, which Dick Griffiths said would not turn up on Farrers' bill to me, glasses were raised. It got still jollier, and we all drank well. Back at Keats Grove, Ingrid and I had some more wine. I got very tight, and rang up all my family. My notes delivered to neighbours included a line from the hymn Ingrid was singing in a full soprano. 'The strife is o'er, the battle done.'

18

CONSCIOUSNESS AS
EXISTENCE, FAREWELLS

What is the difference, the difference of what we call my consciousness, between me and a chair in this room? What is that difference between you and a chair? Well, for each of us, a world now exists. In the case of a chair, there isn't one. Isn't that roughly what is left out of the computerized philosophy of mind, the meagre and timid accounts of our existence limited to the electrochemical traffic in our brains and its relations to input and output – say the input of light on our retinas and the output of movements of chairs? Those accounts leave out that *my consciousness consists in the existence of a world*. So began my report of my brand new thinking on my old subject, the nature of consciousness, in the first of the 1996–97 lectures of the Royal Institute of Philosophy in Gordon Square.

The sentence about my consciousness being the existence of a world, said I, can be taken in several ways. It can be taken as being about all of my consciousness now, including my awareness of this room and what is in it, and also my passing thoughts and feelings about other things. The sentence can also be heard in another way, as about only my awareness or *perceptual consciousness* – my seeing, hearing and so on with respect to this room and what is in it. Let us take it in this limited way. If the nature of our experience of seeing and the like can be explained, this will surely serve as a foundation for explaining all of consciousness.

There was a plain problem about saying my perceptual consciousness consists in the existence of a world. Was it worth saying? Obviously not, if what it comes to is that a world exists 'for me' – where that in turn just means that what is around me is seen, heard and so on by me. That is no use to us, but philosophical disaster, since our aim is of course an explanation or analysis of this seeing, hearing and so on, otherwise known as perceptual consciousness. To try to exclude the useless understanding of the sentence, the circularity, we can rewrite it a little, and just say my perceptual consciousness consists in a world. Is that just baffling? Well, since all the plain accounts of consciousness are unsuccessful, maybe the right sentence *will* be strange. And isn't a lot of real philosophy strange, anyway at first? Let us not lose heart – or suppose we already have something really enlightening. We have no more than a bold assertion, worth some cooperative reflection.

The world of my perceptual consciousness, so-called, whatever else is to be said of it, does have a number of features. One is that it is bound up with and depends on myself – the particular person, subject or self of which I have long had a sense. If the world of my perceptual consciousness is dependent on this person, of which we do not need any grand or daring idea, this world is also dependent on something less elusive, as reported before now. My world is dependent on my brain, on a sequence of neural events. It would not exist in the absence of some such events. Moreover, thirdly, they guarantee its existence. A fourth feature of my world of perceptual consciousness is that it is in some way private. You do not have my kind of access to it. A fifth feature, bound up with what has been said already, is that my world does not exist unperceived. It is not there when I have my nap.

These five features, it may well seem, add up to the idea that the so-called world of my perceptual consciousness is *a mental world*. It is, to be plainer, just a totality of thoughts and feelings, my thoughts and feelings about my immediate environment. The idea, if we are stuck with it, spells uselessness again, philosophical disaster. It is no use saying my perceptual consciousness is a world, boldly, if the so-called world is then just taken as thoughts and the like about my environment.

Let us not give up just yet, but instead turn back to something solid that has got attention from us in other philosophical connections. It is simply *the physical world*. Be reassured, however, that in wheeling the physical world onstage to join my perceptual world, we are not going in for ontological extravagance, loose philosophy. There is but *one* world in a primary sense, containing all that exists. Of parts, sides or aspects of it, say the mechanical or the human or the financial, we have large and inclusive conceptions. What falls under such a conception is, in a second-ary sense, a world. The usage is common enough and may be a nudge to thinking. It can be a means of getting another hold on the primary world and in particular our existence in it.

The ordinary physical world does indeed consist in one part in things like chairs, and in another part in things like atoms. In the first part, generally speaking, are space-occupying things with ordinarily perceived properties such as shape and colour. In the second part are space-occupiers that stand in causal or related connections with things in the first part. It is the first lot of physical things, *the perceived part of the physical world*, that repays attention at the moment. An interesting question arises. How much resemblance is there between the perceived part of the physical world and the world of my perceptual consciousness? How near do they come to being the same thing?

Well, my present world of perceptual consciousness seems to have spatio-temporal things in it too, somehow real, including my chair. It's not a *mental* chair that I'm sitting on, a thought or a representation or a sense-datum. And it's not a thought of the chair that has the shape and colour of which I'm aware. Do you jib, troublesome reader? Well, try to forget any old philosophy in your head, maybe some old potted philosophy. Just ask what is in your awareness now. *A chair*, surely? I happily assume you grant it, that you do not take yourself to be in solitary confinement in a cell of your own ideas. So we have one similarity or bundle of similarities between your perceptual world or mine, on the one hand, and, on the other hand, the perceived part of the physical world. Both have actual furniture in them. We therefore have a reason for hesitating before concluding that a world of perceptual consciousness, yours or mine, is just a mental world.

I will save you the whole course of reflections, but think along a bit longer. It is no strain to see that the perceived part of the physical world depends partly on us persons – above all on our perceptual apparatus. The chair in it is not brown to a bat, as everyone since Locke in the seven-teenth century has agreed. There we have another similarity between the part of the physical world and my perceptual world. Does it turn out that the perceived part of the physical world has something like all the five features of my perceptual world? Yes. In each instance you can find not only difference but also similarity. The resulting over-all difference and resemblance between these two worlds is a premise for two or three conclusions.

Despite the initial suspicion, my saying my perceptual consciousness consists in a world is indeed not philosophical disaster. It is not a case of getting nowhere – talking without explanation of a mental world, a totality of thoughts and feelings. Rather, to say my perceptual consciousness consists in a world is to give the enlightening truth about perceptual consciousness. It is to say my perceptual consciousness is a state of affairs akin to the ordinary state of affairs that is the perceived part of the physical world. The fact of my being conscious of this room just is the fact that this room in a way exists, which is mainly to say it is in space and time and has among its dependencies or conditions one that has to do with me. Right or wrong, and baffling or not, that is an explanation or analysis, with a good deal in it. To come to another conclusion, my perceptual consciousness is a state of affairs that it would be misleading to call either mind-dependent or mind-independent. Further, and despite that, this state of affairs is what our conviction of our subjectivity in perceptual consciousness is about – an unmysterious subjective world. It is not just in my head, although what is in my head contributes to it.

To get clearer about perceptual consciousness, we need to think more about this state of affairs, work on this conception. To clarify our inescapable conviction about our subjectivity, we need to look differently at the only world there is, put the primary world under a certain conception – and not get mixed up with ghostly stuff in the head, physical or otherwise. We need to be guided by the idea of *consciousness as existence*.

I was proud of my lecture, prouder than of any other before it. It was certainly different. It brought some metaphysics, necessary and calm metaphysics, into the philosophy of mind. It was a lot different from what was believed by me and reported to you when the opening chapter of this book was being written – and what was believed and reported thereafter. It upset the apple-cart of all those previous positive reflections and conclusions on the nature of consciousness and mind and brain – naturalism as against my new near-naturalism, the Correlation Hypothesis of mind and brain, psychoneural intimacy, the Union Theory, a conscious event's in-the-head subjective aspect, its content and object, and of course conscious events as physical stuff in the head yet to be

371

discovered. All those apples went flying. Some or all could be fitted in again, probably, in a story about the brain rather than consciousness. But in any case the new idea was better, and it had a chance, unlike Functionalism and the computerized philosophy of mind.

A university reading week, according to useful theory, is a week when students read books and articles as a result of being undistracted by lectures or other teaching. In the reading week of the first term of 1996–97, Ingrid and I also had a holiday, our seventh. We went to Cuba. This was not only with a rest from my labours on consciousness, but also had to do with morals and politics. We would get in touch, if tardily, with the saga of a revolution. Despite the United States of America, there had been the construction of a kind of egalitarian society in Cuba, a dream made into reality. The eradication of poverty, disease and illiteracy, as even the cautious guide book from Oxford said. A society where the life-expectancies were decent for everybody.

Now Cuba was also a society with rationing and other ills. This was the result of two things. One was the end of Communism on the other side of the world, and the other was the American trade blockade. The latter was condemned by all of the United Nations save those two so accrediting allies of the United States, Israel and Uzbekistan. Furthermore, Cuba was now pressed into some new thinking about a place for the middleman in every transaction and also the social usefulness of private profits. Fidel and his friends were making a small concession to the new global truth, that the market that some of us want and do very well by is in fact an economic necessity. They were bowing slightly to the new iron laws of history, now unchallenged, Marx's old iron laws having been intellectually refuted by the end of the Cold War. To the victors the truth.

The old iron laws never got a hold on me, and the new ones about the blessed market were doing no better. Nor was I quick to recognize certain social effects of belief in the new laws. In the lobby of our Hotel Plaza, under the palms, were a lot of girls in elastic body-sheaths that revealed every mound. Their line of life, what they were selling, dawned on me only by way of their decorous and stylish older sisters on the other side of the lobby, who more discreetly promised more. It was pretty sad, if not so sad as what could not possibly be overlooked, the dulled eyes in the queues in the heat outside bare shops. If once this had been Eden with good state security, it wasn't any more. On the flight back to Heathrow and the deprivation of our hierarchic democracy, made more squalid by one of its liars being brazen in court about who paid his hotel bill, I felt that I had gone to Cuba to say good-bye to a hope. Not exactly my hope, but a better hope than most.

My inclination to social life, once great, and then fully satisfied by Jane's religious commitment to it, was now smaller. More private life was taking more of my time, happily. There was the real interest in the book you are reading, and how it will end. Reading aloud with Ingrid through works by the Brontes was educative, as were her relations to her four children. Assisting in her transformation of the front garden at 4 Keats Grove was worthwhile, even edifying.

Flutter had had to be evicted in the end. My moral confidence was sufficient unto the day, and I chatted companionably with bailiff, policeman and locksmith. As for my final bill from Farrer & Co., it had not left my mind that I had a complaint. I should have been brought out of my ignorance of the workings of Legal Aid earlier – the fact that I would not get my costs back if I won. Negotiate I now did, and emerge from the unequal battle in the mansion in Lincoln's Inn Fields with a reduction of £2,500 in the bill of £50,000. Tempers had risen. The day after, sad about having lost the love of Julian Pike, one of my saviours, I sent in the £2,500. The Queen's Solicitors graciously sent it back, and we all celebrated at the Garrick, with wives and consorts.

The tax collector, for his part, said that some more of my legal costs could be counted as an expense against future rents. It might well be that in the end I would get back 40 per cent of my outlay on Flutter. My son John, afloat as an editor and continuing to value his independence from me, chose not to live in my front garden. Instead, new tenants came into The Studio, paying the market rent. Would *Honderich v. Flutter* turn out in the end to have been worth it in landlord's terms? Very likely, and that was not all. The Honderich Trust, set up by Bee, had been struck by my misfortune at the hands of the Welfare State, and would see that I was all right. No need for you to buy two copies of this book after all.

As the spring of 1997 came on, the state of Britain was nonetheless awful to me and others. A Conservatism despicable in its cupidity and stupidity was now at least questionable to all persons in touch with the world. All now had reasons in their own lives for doubt about the condition we were in, reasons of self-interest. When I walked Pauline home from Keats Grove at night, we did not cross the Heath, since there was the underclass to think about. But the state of Britain now, compared with five years ago, was in fact not so much more disturbing that the Conservatives could not possibly win again. They might again call up benighted selfishness and make good use of it. Mr Blair and New Labour sought to prevent a fifth Conservative government by any effective means, and in good part by playing to that same selfishness in advance. They took the socialism out of the party's constitution. They undertook not to increase existing help to the badly-off or to increase general taxation.

I gave more money to the party each month and, if asked, would have done whatever else was possible to support the cause. I did not mind being overlooked. Partly this was defeatism. England and I had already lost what likely would not be found again in my lifetime, whatever the government. Against us, there had been a change of society, a degrading of England to the level of the United States. A New Labour government would attempt no transformation. But during election night, despite this resignation beforehand, my feeling became the feeling of many, which was joy. Lovely joy. Long before morning, the shits were gone. Their electoral defeat was complete and unprecedented. Their departure had been long delayed, but they were gone. They were as disgraced as any English government ever has been by voters.

It took me aback, as my own joy did. Could it be that my paper on democracy and the need for it to be accompanied by civil disobedience, read out in Korea, China, Red Lion Square and Hawaii, was put in doubt by this glorious election? Was my politics like my philosophy of mind, in need of being more or less abandoned and started up again? Did it need to be made more tolerant, more realistic, less utopian? At moments Ingrid was inclined to consider the question on my behalf, if gently.

My plain paper about democracy had needed to be written only because of the piety of others. Its basis was that the best analysis of our democracy, the analysis most explanatory of its actual policies, is that it is a system governed by the activities of grossly unequal groups.

Among these, certain economic groups predominate. The best-off tenth of society in terms of wealth and income, which has at least 30 times more than the worst-off tenth, has at least 15 times the political influence of the worst-off tenth. So citizens stand in different grades of influence, in a hierarchy. No amount of elevated theory about social contracts, liberalism, communities or whatever else can reduce the importance of this fact. It is uniquely explanatory of what our democracies do. They make no resolute effort on behalf of the badly-off.

Did the glorious election put this in question? In obvious ways it did not. The glorious result was dominantly owed to ranks of persons of greater influence, moved in good part by self-interest. Sixty per cent of the press had been for Labour, an historical precedent. The probability that such a system would ever go further than reduce inequalities and actually rescue the badly-off was negligible. And yet. . . . And yet the result this time had been wonderful. Should I try to feel better about the capacity of hierarchic democracy? Was I not myself, if reluctantly, a hierarchic democrat? I would think again sometime.

My laurels were freshened in my last days among the B.A. examiners, one of whom was a genial dame aware that all of philosophy is but footnotes to Plato. As it seemed to me, she discerned a lack of this awareness on the part of a certain candidate in his Ancient Philosophy paper. In it he apparently corrected Plato's thinking by some paragraphs he closely reported from a recent book on the nature of explanation in one of my series. *Plagiarism*, said the dame. It seemed the wretch must not graduate with an Upper Second degree, Lower Second, Third, or Pass, but be sent away in shame. It emerged, however, that more than half his marks from other examiners in other papers were in a certain class, thereby putting him above the threshold for a certain degree. It proved possible to prompt a defence of him. He left us, and our dame, with a smashing First. I wondered to myself inconclusively if it threw a light on our more ordinary judgings.

In the rest of the summer, life consisted in tranquillity with Ingrid and the writing of this book. We differed amicably only over such matters as whether persons are collections of properties. Her flat was the most agreeable of eyries, and my flat now had in it two of her still-lifes, not out of place in my tolerable collection of stuff, since among her ladylike accomplishments, next to gardening, was amateur painting. Along with these satisfactions, however, on some days, went feelings of being 64 – past a last milestone before retirement from teaching. My tenure of the Grote Chair would end in a year, in September 1998, and advertisements for my successor now appeared. In charge of replacing me was a good committee, including Bernard Williams and Mark Sainsbury from outside of college, and Malcolm Budd and three other members of our department.

My darker spirits, on days when these were in the ascendancy, fastened themselves on ailments, first of a shoulder and then of an eye. It took some time before my diagnosis of cancer of the bone gave way to Rotated Cuff Tendonitis, otherwise known as gardener's shoulder. A night or two had to be passed before coming blindness gave way to Posterior Vitreous Detachment, floaters in the field of vision that will eventually settle down. In this adversity, recourse could be had to the old brightener, activity. I could also lean on blessed Ingrid. In a letter to Jane, I mentioned this, and also reflected on life's passages. You and I, Janeso, had a fine time together, despite my large shortcomings and one or two of your small ones. I wouldn't subtract any of our adventure from my past, save only certain bicycle routes. Still, we're on different routes now. So should we make ourselves into legally unattached individuals again, and when the divorce comes through have a smashing party? Indeed we will, she said. It's a deal, Tedso. My better spirits took over.

The 35th and last of my teaching years would not be one in which I was much burdened by teaching. At the moment when it would end, on 30 September 1998, I would have earned and been due for a sabbatical, a term off teaching, according to our departmental rules. It had been unthinkable to the prim and punctilious Malcolm, our Head, that I have some of it in advance. It seemed pretty thinkable to me, but my policy of not rocking the boat was easier because the shore was in sight. Two of our new departmental invigorators and organizers, Crane and Martin, maybe of the mind that I should somehow have time off for good behaviour, took over the Senior Seminar on Mondays.

Halfway through the term, having tested ourselves on holiday not only in Havana but also Paris and Regensburg, Ingrid and I were in Rome. We were again making use of a reading week, recalling a bit of Catullus and a Latin verb or two. Prompted by my diary, I am obliged and contented to record, in passing, that my proclivity for pet names was not diminished. It was only touched by a certain political correctness and a recourse to superscripts. She was Dollop[1] and I was Dollop[2], these being abbreviated in notes to D[1] and D[2]. Do you cringe, superior reader? I care not. As some of my best friends say, you should be so lucky yourself –

so lucky to be in Rome in such a way of feeling. The day after I got back was the last day of 40 years of the lift of nicotine, the last 15 years by means of chewing the gum.

In November I found myself across a boardroom table from the bankers who were the good trustees of the estate of the late Jens Jacobsen, probably worth about £3.5 million. They were certainly obliged to use the money somehow for philosophy. Were they also obliged to propagate *the philosophy of Jens*? 'Ought' does indeed imply 'can', said my written opinion to them. You are obliged to do only what you actually can do. There was no philosophy of Jens to be propagated, but there was another possibility.

The interest from the £3.5 million or so could be used to forward the philosophy-in-general that Jens favoured – such parts of the subject as metaphysics, as against those about which he was superior. The project could be entrusted to an institution in which he had not lost faith, and one that eschewed the technical in favour of the humanistic. The Royal Institute of Philosophy could give out annual Jacobsen Fellowships to postgraduates in philosophy, each worth £5,000 a year. The Secretary of the R.I.P., Ingrid Coggin Purkiss by public name, had the good idea of Jacobsen Visiting Teachers of Philosophy for schools, probably doctoral students from nearby universities, doing something to help the English educational system catch up with the French.

The good committee on the Grote Chair, having found the claims of various candidates insufficiently impressive, and issued invitations to two or three figures who declined, and overlooked two or three others, came to a decision. The committee chose Malcolm Budd. He, being on the committee, had of course made no application for the post. His reply to my note of congratulation was firm. His election was not to him a matter for congratulation, not something he had wanted. It would not enhance his life and would at most make a minor difference to his role in the department. I wondered if his three departmental colleagues on the committee and he had tacitly agreed that a Grote with smaller pretensions would suit all of them.

It was at about this time that I received a visit in the Grote room, still all of the first floor of the department, still stately in its extent. Windows front and rear and good plasterwork in two light blues. The two visitors were the amiably efficient Jo Wolff, an undergraduate in the department in the early 1980s and now its new Head, and a man from the Bursar's office. The department itself had thought about the further utilization of space and partitioning. You could have two or three persons thinking where one thought before.

The 19 pages of my lecture 'Consciousness as Existence' had taken me three months to get together. Impressed by them I still was, and happy to survey them at *http://www.ucl.ac.uk/philosophy/honderich.htm/* on the Net. So it was easy to choose from three invitations from different organizers of what would be the largest congregation of philosophers in all history, The World Congress of Philosophy in Boston. My reflections on being aware of chairs and the like, perceptual consciousness, would be taken forward.

The three months now given over to 14 new pages were not happy at the start, and not perfectly contented thereafter. Having buckled down actually to reading 'Consciousness as Existence' again, rather than happily surveying it, I made a discovery. It was not the small wonder-work of my grandest fantasies, but had mistakes in it. When you stepped out on your own, were the chances of putting a foot wrong so much higher? How on earth had I managed to write that the chair in my world of perceptual consciousness was *identical with* the chair in the perceived part of the physical world? It could not possibly be so, since the first chair was not in space at times when the second was. The relation between the two chairs had to be different. Worse, how had I managed to understate or obscure what was almost the greatest recommendation of my doctrine? It gave an account of the subjectivity of consciousness that respected its unique reality. Yet it did not make it impossible to see how episodes of consciousness could be causally connected with physical things – light on our retinas beforehand and chair movements afterwards. Had my philosophical wits at the time of thinking about my piece been addled by *Honderich v. Flutter*?

Well, however my mistakes had come about, the three months could not be given over to making a further advance, maybe on the subject of the nature of non-perceptual consciousness, say thinking of Judge Diamond in his absence. What had to be provided, rather, in hope of some philosophical posterity, was a reworking, development and correction of 'Consciousness as Existence'. The result, making use of my considerable ability in the titling of things, could be called 'Consciousness as Existence

Again'. It would be no bad thing to get it on view at *http://www.ucl.ac. uk/philosophy/honderich.htm/* quickly.

My last undergraduate lecture was given in March 1998 in the Grote room. In the hour they were informed by me of the news brought earlier to Tokyo and Beijing about the right way to look at moralities generally. The news was that we should get out of philosophical line. We should give up dividing them into moralities that take consequences to make actions right, and moralities that do not. In fact there is no fundamental distinction between these. Rather, there are moralities of concern, having to do with fair or just consequences of actions, and there are other moralities, one being Utilitarianism and others having to do with consequences that raise a suspicion of selfishness. The morality of the Principle of Equality, you will anticipate, went into the first and higher category.

My retirement party in my room in May, as all said, was of greater affection and better feeling than any other departmental occasion that could be remembered. It was indeed a happy retirement party. Should that latter description be disambiguated? Well, the party itself was happy, and the guest of honour was happy, and the prospect of his getting out of school was happy, but I think not many other guests were happy about that same prospect. All but one of my colleagues were on hand, some evidently wistful, as were old students who remembered 1968. A speech by the admirable Crane, a philosopher of mind fairly resistant to computerization, was all that I could wish. My own speech remembered that Richard Wollheim did not persuade me of psychoanalysis as the solution to my problems, and that it did not help him much with the ones I was causing him. The speech had in it, too, gratitude to Jerry Valberg for being a good forgiver.

I vacated the Grote room so that it could be partitioned into two chambers, one pink and one salmon, and occupied a cubicle elsewhere in college, contented enough but sometimes lethargic on account of no chews. Could it be true, as the report on rat research was supposed to show, that nicotine was as addictive as heroin, with comparable withdrawal symptoms? There was my knee too, and, as many said, the psychological effect of the prospect of being out of school forever. Having come to hear that several persons of my acquaintance were making use of the drug of good cheer, Prozac, I thought of having a go. Why not? Why put up with moods? I had a go, and stopped as quickly, having learned that the warning in the leaflet, 'may have the side effect of poor sexual performance', was a notable understatement.

I was not at my best on the telly tutoring Professor Flew about absolute moral principles, or at the University of Sussex telling them about the mind, or on the radio with Joan Bakewell discussing one of Carlyle's many falsehoods, 'Work is a grand cure for all the maladies and miseries that ever beset mankind'. Nor at my best, alas, in saying good-bye to the splendid Provost of University College London, now Sir Derek. He kindly said that I would be becoming Emeritus Grote Professor. He drew on his experience to remark that dealing with a department of philosophers was like herding cats. In July, many who had been at a wedding nine years before came to what another invitation card called Jane's and Ted's Happy Divorce Party. I leave the disambiguating to you. My speech went along nicely, ending in a toast to two paragons, Jane and Ingrid.

The second paragon brought the Royal Institute of Philosophy to the attention of the World Congress of Philosophy and I delivered a snappy summary of the truth about perceptual consciousness and chairs. Having spent good times with my daughter Kiarney in Boston, we pressed on to Canada. First the comfortable seclusion of the island in Georgian Bay of my nephew John, and then Toronto. There, Bee and I proved that being 65 and 79 is no bar to competition between brothers. There was blood on the carpet of Ruthie's favourite restaurant. With her help we would make it up absolutely, without further discussion. He would ask for some special towels from Harrods and I would promptly send them.

On one day before coming back to London I visited the village of my boyhood, Baden. Still to be seen was some of the past, a past that would be as everlasting as me. They no longer made limburger cheese or had a village softball team. The telephone house called to me to come in, but I didn't ask permission of the housewife who answered the door. She thought that maybe Florence Ferguson had died. The path along the edge of Brubacher's Dam could still be followed. I met two of the farming Honderichs, and there was nothing to divide us. They seemed very like me.

In retirement smaller things can get larger. There was the morning rat-run down Keats Grove, pushy drivers leaving the main road to race through a maze of side-streets in order to rejoin the main road ahead of their previous place in a queue. There were also the unspeakables who in the rest of the day accelerated even more offensively down or up our straight and narrow lane in order to get to the other end before being held up by something coming the other way.

Could the local council not be persuaded to do something for Arcadia? Preserving our lane for generations to come, anyway those persons able to afford it, would be part of this good cause. In pursuing it, also, we present neighbours would also escape possessive individualism and fall into some wonderful amity and community. Perhaps we would have street parties. A maypole in Lennie Hoffman's garden? Trestle tables and English wine? Readings from our poet, maybe 'I stood tip-toe upon a little hill'?

In October 1998, the Keats Grove Residents Association was called into existence by me in the local library, and, by my prior word in an ear, I was called to be its chairman. To the sweetness of our meeting would be added light and good order. In the second row, however, sat Lady Macbeth, or maybe Lady Macbeth of Mtensk. For love of her BMW, she would do many murders and reverse over the corpses. *Rat-run?* Did the professor hallucinate? And was I not above my station? When I had such experience of the great cities of the world as was her good fortune, I would appreciate the universal fact of some few persons hurrying to work in the mornings. *Rat-run?* Could the professor *count?* I did myself no credit with Lady Macbeth by having to ask her name, which was Janet Suzman. A known actress, if now resting. I did myself some credit with the audience by my own mild decorum, which was as much the product of sadness and hurt as calculation.

Definitely there would be no maypole. I had, it seemed, been subject to some innocence, a kind of high idiocy or simplicity of soul that can persist despite experience, a spreading of good will onto the world. Were my own palpable facts about the traffic, like the palpable facts of others, contrivances made of self-interest? Whether or not, I was mortified that I had not given Mtensk as good as I got. The feeling had some resolution in it too. Others were hallucinating and counting with me, and we did in due course get a no-entry sign.

There were other facts in my new life. In it, there was now one place, not two. The Grote's room was gone. Did the one place in my life, consisting in my flat and Ingrid's, still seem closer to *being* my life than just the setting of it, closer to being the stuff of my existence than its principal location? Well, that old piece of fancy had given way to some philosophy, my new existentialism about perceptual consciousness. The existence of a certain world in space and time was no less than identical with my life of perceptual consciousness, my being aware of my rooms. Charms *can* fly at the mere touch of cold philosophy, but some are traded in for another good class of stuff.

More work needed to be done on the stuff, by the way, for another public lecture and to get in training for a book to be written. The lecture would be about a considerable industry in the philosophy of mind, having to do with the *aboutness* of conscious events and states, for mediaeval reasons called their intentionality. There were many philosophical doctrines on this, almost all of them proposing a relation between the content of your consciousness at any moment and the object that the content was about. It had to be allowed that this relation of intentionality could hold or exist when in fact there was no relevant object in existence – when, say, some predecessor of mine hoped to find the fountain of youth in Hampstead, or when I wanted the non-existent bottle of wine in the refrigerator.

But, to think again, how *could* there be a relation of such a kind that it could hold or exist between two things if one of them was missing? How could my otherwise rational friend Crane say so? Something couldn't be to the left of *nothing*, and something couldn't be in a real relation to the fountain of youth or the bottle of wine either. It didn't make sense, and complacent philosophers shouldn't pretend it did. They should give up and turn to a different account of the nature of perceptual consciousness. The one that doesn't say your being aware of this room is being in a funny relation to the room. The lecture could have another good title, 'Consciousness as Existence and the End of Intentionality'.

I had my Old Age Pensioner's bus pass now, but the small pleasure of riding free on public transport, and the honour of supporting its rationality against the motorcar, would not often take me off my bike. My old colleague Heinaman, still of the one or two who give Ancient Philosophy a good name, was abandoning London for the Lake District, but would not be followed by me. I'd cycle on through the inner postal districts.

I also had my St John's Wort in place of Prozac, since it was true too that my spirits could flag as late afternoon came on, and time slow down in its passage towards 7 o'clock. Was this new, or was it something that had always accompanied early rising, and had been unnoticed in a life with a fuller diary, a life of 5 o'clock seminars? It wasn't clear. In Oxford to read the first of two papers, I was not at my most combative or olympian in dealing with the impertinence of the county dimwit out to win his spurs by doubting my truths. Spirits could be summoned, of course, and were for the second occasion when he unwisely appeared again, but they did not leap up themselves.

Were there small excesses of passion too? What came with my new computer, the programmes Microsoft Windows and Microsoft Word, raised feelings in me by their useless and unfascinating complexity, their helpfulness with the typing of my sentences, and their changing the date on my diary entry to the day when it was printed out a week later. Don't do anything on my behalf, Mr Gates, just get out of the way. I didn't pay you to think. Don't try. Was I excessive too in the e-mail to Kiarney on the primitiveness of America at the time of the President's impeachment and the awfulness of his aggression against Iraq, abetted by our Mr Blair? Maybe. Michael Foot and Jill needed defence against the good writer Frederic Raphael, explainer-away of Arthur Koestler's tendency to rape, and against Mr Raphael's ally Mr Monk. But no doubt it was not a good idea for me to have at Mr Monk in another letter to *The Guardian* about his Wittgensteinian delicacy. It was not kind to a famous scientist, either, to make use of my website to touch on the question of how good scientists are at philosophy.

If retirement had in it a thing or two grown larger, and one place rather than two, and spirits sometimes vulnerable, and small excesses, it also had in it the two large things sufficient for a life. One was forward marching, mainly on paper. The other was love. It was a kind of easiness, a pleasure not ending. Dollop[1] and Dollop[2] were getting on a treat. On D[1]'s balcony at 7 p.m., with a new wine to try, and the green palisade, we talked of injustice between children and parents, and followed the course of the finer sunsets that came with global warming. There would be no other incumbent of the benefice. If temptations could be felt by

Dollop[2] at occasional dinner parties with nicely forward dames, he could say in the morning, and did, that he fancied and needed no other company in the world than the company he had.

A first draft of this book was finished in time to invigorate me for the Beeb's radio programme *Today*. Part of it was given over to the matter of British and French philosophy, brought to wider attention by a poll conducted in *The Philosophers Magazine*. The poll identified the most overrated philosopher in history as Professor Jacques Derrida. He was the exponent of the deconstruction of literary texts, its having been usefully said of 'deconstruction' by him that it escapes all definition.

I pleased myself and some others by first saying of Continental Philosophy that I was like many British philosophers in not allowing my ignorance of it entirely to obstruct my judgement. It was a different kind of thing from ours, and aspired more to the condition of literature or intellectual show-business. It was only disgraceful by our standards. You had to remember that Sartre did discover determinism and science a couple of decades after announcing the absolute freedom we all have in creating ourselves. There had to be something to be said for him since ten million Frogs couldn't all be wrong. And, turning back to our own shores, it was noted by some of us, although of course not by me, that our current philosophical professoriate in Oxford could on a clear day rise up to the level of the humdrum. It was enjoyable to make these truthful remarks to an audience of millions, but not necessary to get a tape of them afterwards.

The 19th Christmas party went as nicely, and soon after there was the new world made clear to me by the services to my eyes of Mr Fison of Upper Wimpole Street. From the top of Parliament Hill, the Millennium Dome was all too clear. Other things now getting attention, as I owned up to Ingrid, were the breasts and cleavages of womankind generally. It seemed I had been missing a lot. Were they really there before in this profusion? Could my new awareness be a matter of new libido rather than new lenses? It was possible, but I thought not. Several later days were darker. Having sent a jolly letter to Bernard Williams inviting him to give the Royal Institute of Philosophy Annual Lecture for 2000, I got the reply that he had bone-marrow cancer and didn't know what shape he would be in. My letter back to him said the invitation stood absolutely, and that his being afflicted was a hurt to all of us in philosophy, and seemed more than that to me. It was, as I hope he believed.

Ingrid and I were in Tehran a while later, both of us gracing the World Congress on Mulla Sadra, the great Iranian or rather Persian philosopher of the seventeenth century. No doubt the flying-in of philosophers and scholars from everywhere was to serve some purpose of the Islamic Republic in its ongoing battle with The Great Satan. I wondered again if the anti-Americanism was more fundamental than the religion. One of Iran's two leaders, the Hojatollah Khatami, himself philosophical, welcomed us at length, and said the beauty of the face of God is proof, or maybe the other way on.

There was a paper on Plato's Form of the Good by the daughter of the Ayatollah Khomeini, he of the *fatwah* on Salman. My friendly question to her got us onto nodding terms thereafter. Ingrid went on the telly, indeed on 'Good Morning Iran', and did not kick up rough about the compulsory wearing of the chador or black tent by all women. My piece in *The Times Literary Supplement* on getting back pleased our hosts and was true to me. Its last paragraph noted that what had been conceivable in advance had turned out to be possible. You could go without a drink for ten days, partly since Zam Zam was better than Coca-Cola.

There ends my narrative of a kind of life. What remains is a coda of reflections, with a bit more in it of the tale of Ted.

19

CODA

You have heard what seems to me to have happened in my life until now. What does it come to? How is it to be understood in an ordinary sense of grasped, brought together, or summed up?

What has happened so far in my life, it can be said, is that after awakening in clear and restrained philosophy in Hume's tradition I engaged in it, and also lived with six women, had large hopes about others, made enemies and friends partly by being a kind of activist with respect to more things than my self-interest, and got ahead in my world. The restrained philosophy alternated with the libertarianism or dissoluteness, the assorted relationships made, and the diligence rewarded.

To hear a second voice, my life has been one of satisfactory onward marching, in my own directions. Much of the marching has consisted in thinking about determinism, subjectivity and how life ought to be, much of it in feelings for women, bits of it in going to court and editing the books of others. Despite rising and falling moods, there has been much happy hopefulness and no giving up. I have been a difficult character to a few more people than those who gave me good reason to be. Too severe in judgement, and not more than a tolerably good father.

Or, it can be said, an effective if not overpowering intelligence and a resolute personality has in my case often been impeded by other things. Those supplied by myself have been self-doubt, apprehension, and occasionally fear. The degree of reasonableness or groundedness of the self-doubt and apprehension has been uncertain. They have certainly contributed to struggle, assertiveness, grimness, relieving comedy, and a persistent arrogance. An awful lot of philosophy still seems to me not much good. That is not to say, I hope, that I have in feeling joined the hanging judges. As executor with Dee of the literary estate of Freddie Ayer, it is good that the biography of him by Ben Rogers is so fine. Still, the mighty little McGinn in reviewing it could write that Freddie not only never had an original idea in his life, but also never had a good idea, his own or anyone else's. I thought he had one or two.

To hear a fourth voice, my life has come out of a vulnerability to plain truth and plain logic, and a determination owed in some part to hurts in boyhood and in another part to my not being ideally placed in my second society. Mine has been a moralizing and judgemental life, an immoral one to conventional persons and perhaps some others. Also a life opposed to both the unreal and the real superiorities of others. You might say too that it has had in it too much and not enough ambition, too much in connection with the academic hierarchy and not enough in connection with the philosophy in my books.

These four understandings of my carry-on until now can have others added to them.

Why not say it became an intellectual and emotional existence, industrious in both those ways, but one in which accidents have played an ordinary and therefore considerable part? They have at least occasioned the largest products of my life, books on certain subjects rather than others. The book you are reading is my first wholly non-accidental book. Does it need to be added that accidents and chances are one thing, and acting on them another? That in fact I *chose*? Well, some chances are hard to resist.

You may say, differently again, without hearing any confident denial by me, that mine has been a reflective life since I found myself within philosophy but still a life of at least as much feeling as thinking. It has been one in which an inclination to truth has had added to it strong and persistent desires, often satisfied. Also a sharp sense of the means to my desired ends, and, along with an illusion or two about England and the maypole, a sense of the means by which some others seek their ends. I have had a Thrasymachean conviction about the reality within justice and in matters of reputation, standing and rank, and about the use of social and philosophical drapery.

Or, you can suppose, this life has been one in which self-interest has been in conflict with empathy, perhaps an unusual degree of empathy, owed partly to family misfortune at the start and partly to a good eye for seeing past the social drapery. The empathy has issued mainly in a moral and political philosophy, and not in changes in the world or self-denying services to it, even small ones. If the empathy and what has come out of it have not been hypocritical, they have not been very dangerous to me either.

Some, but not I, may say that this life has been one of so many women as to put in doubt the importance of any of them to me. Also a life in which I had adversaries, fell out forever with one best friend, sought out persons of achieved standing, and have not been close enough to my son. They may remember such items as an insult to the University of Edinburgh about chairs on ghosts. They may add, if they like, with Dr Rosen of the resignation letter, my failure to exercise power in a mature and responsible way with proper processes of consultation, and also impropriety, partiality, non-consultation and secrecy.

Lastly, you may consider that my life is got hold of, sense made of it, by way of a summation with slightly more in it. I thought a little as a boy in a place where most others did not, was helped by my family through my young manhood in a diffident country, and was awakened by philosophy in an England that delighted me and which I joined. I wanted recognition at least for my industry, got some, found myself theoretically in the grips of a decent political morality, and was naive about politics but not shown to be naive about what politics ought to secure. Happy work helped to make me less than a really good father. I escaped ordinary sexual convention without difficulty and became a man of many women and a libertine, despite not being notably sexually desirous, at any rate in my own awareness. I made enemies and was in several items unlucky. Despite distractions, I came to have more worldly success than most in my line of life. I enjoyed it, but certainly wanted more. I wanted to be better than I was, and not only in being more fixed on philosophy of my own. I became saddened by England and then a bit hopeful, and, in Hampstead, after tribulations, have fallen into a kind of contentment. Ingrid and I dine out tonight with our neighbours in the flat downstairs, the antiquarian bookdealers Christopher Johnson and Christopher Forster, to celebrate our plan of my buying half the freehold from them. After our agreement in principle, shall we not bargain our way to the final details of legal equality here at 4 Keats Grove?

So – there is a bundle of understandings of my life, significantly different attempts at focus and clarity. The bits in each of them could be coloured differently, have edges put on or taken off them. They could be mixed together into new understandings. Or, leaving the nine under- standings as they are, they could have others added to them, about as persuasive. Maybe one remembering more fulfilments. Maybe even one evincing some self-love. Maybe one having more of your self-deception in it and less of mine?

All such ordinary understandings, as it seems, are in a way unsatis- factory. The ones I have chosen to provide do of course tell you more about me, and something more about my kind. In effect they continue the narrative supposed to be ended. They are not only speculative con- clusions by me, but can be premises or data for you in the enterprise of drawing your own conclusions. Putting these recommendations aside, all such understandings are to my mind unsatisfactory. No doubt they can be taken together, averaged into some *impression*, but an impression is not an understanding. If it has in it some kind of truth, it does not have the truth of focus and clarity.

It is not that the nine understandings are unsatisfactory because of their brevity and simplicity. That is a mistake. For the purpose in question, trying to get hold of a life, exactly what is needed is summary. Any life is a large thing, and, as remarked earlier about something else, there is no hope of any large thing coming into focus from close up. You need to stand back to try to see and report the main shape and colour. You have to be out of sight of the detail and the shadings. There would be no gain in trying to enlarge the nine understandings.

They are unsatisfactory, rather, because none stands out as the truth over the others. None seems indisputably closer to the truth. This is so for several plain reasons, one being the great richness and difficulty of the subject-matter. A human life, any human life that has lasted a while, has a fullness that can seem greater than that of any other single subject-matter. It is possible to think there is no thing or problem in philosophy and no subject in science that so challenges perception and judgement, so challenges summary. Nothing else is, so to speak, life- size.

Each life or entire consciousness and carry-on, in a sense that may one day be made explicit, is *a world*, a world going on through time and one that includes other people and more. Mine includes the cast of characters of which you know. They are the largest things in my world. Saying so, in my philosophical hope, is not exactly loose talk. In saying that a life or entire consciousness is a world, I have in mind something more along the line of thought about just perceptual consciousness – being aware of the chairs of the Royal Institute of Philosophy and the World Congress of Philosophy.

But there is another very plain reason for supposing that no particular understanding like the nine above commands attention over all others. These ordinary understandings are not summaries called up by the facts, but also and inevitably *attitudes* to a life, passing or settled attitudes. As indicated by what these understandings do and do not include, and the shaping and colouring of what they include, they are appraisals or valuings.

Each, if it had not been constructed by me for my purposes, but advanced by a reader of this book, would come from a different reader, a different person, and would not be so congenial to any other one. The understandings would be owed partly to taste, principles, self-images, impulses, hopes, ideals, superiorities, aversions, resentments, jealousies, and hurts. At bottom, like all attitudes, the understandings would be owed to desires. Such things are not a matter only of truth. The best one can hope for is increasing agreement about them, certain not to be rapid.

Nor is it possible to get the desires out of the understandings, leaving behind uninfected and uninflected propositions having the objectivity of ordinary judgements of fact. It is not so plain a point, but surely a true one, that the request or need for this sort of understanding of a life *is* in part a request or a need for an attitude to it. What we want, perhaps above all, is an idea of how to feel about a life, or a confirmation of what we already feel or want to feel. This fact also lies behind the need for brevity, by the way. What we want is to come to something like a verdict. Not a collection of impressions but a judgement or conclusion. At least a resting-place in thought and feeling.

That is what we want one of, and seem not to be able to have. Aided by our own histories, we can lurch into one particular way of thinking and feeling about a life, and try to maintain the position or pose. But we know other ways of thinking and feeling are as possible. One cannot dominate all others. Certainly this must give us pause in contemplating a life. It is discomfiting that we cannot get into a confident and settled view of it. It is discomfiting that there are large matters, even this largest one, where truth does not settle things.

Are you inclined to reflect sceptically on this idea of mine of intrinsic obstacles in the way of grasping or summing up a life? Will you wonder if it suits my purpose too well – which in fact is to escape the one true or most defensible judgement on myself? That my idea of intrinsic obstacles is deception? At any rate self-deception, the maintaining of ignorance by avoiding the fact that something really is possible? You have my official support in your scepticism, even your Thrasymachean moment. You do not have my agreement as to there actually being a best understanding of my life that is tolerably exact. Nor my agreement that in this and other matters a reader is more immune to self-deception than a writer.

With the smallish caveats mentioned earlier in this book, about veils drawn over several episodes, mainly to safeguard others, my account of my life has been full truth by my lights. Coming later than Rousseau, and in a confessional time, I have done somewhat better than he in this respect. So too is it a truth that there seems to me no dominating understanding of a life. There seems no possibility of acquiring the one true understanding of a life in an ordinary sense, of no longer being given the pause that is owed to the largeness and richness of the subject-matter and the disputability of values and desires. Coming to the one true understanding, completing the evaluative project, would depend on better vision than we have and also on having found the good life or the like. We have our views and passions about that, but as yet nothing more.

You may say that there is the possibility of another kind of comprehending of a life. This is a comprehending of large things in it, but not so large and full as already to guarantee uncertainty. These large things come close to making up a life, or at least are pretty fundamental, but, not actually being life-size, can be taken in. What we can hope to get here, more particularly, is a particular kind of answer to the question of *why* each of these things happened or was the case. Such an answer, you say, gives what we have had in mind a lot – a causal circumstance for it, a full cause, something that must exist if determinism is true. Such an *explanation-by-causal-circumstance*, as we can call it, is free of values, inclinations, tastes and the like. It is free, in short, of the desires of an inquirer.

It was one of the two aims at the beginning of this book somehow to explain why my life had gone as it had, to where it had, and maybe why it had arrived at its philosophical conclusions. Since then, a good many informal explanations of a sort have been offered in passing, with more or less confidence. Whatever is to be said of them, we are now contemplating something more specific. It is that a life can be comprehended by finding full causes for large things in it.

What was the causal circumstance for what you may be pleased to call my pattern of behaviour, the large number of women? What causal circumstances explained in this way my traits of character and personality, the person I was at several stages? My intermittent membership worries? My degree of success in the world? Happy times? What were the full causes of my coming to my philosophical conclusions? My lonely loyalty to the Principle of Equality? You can also turn your attention to particular actions and pieces of feeling.

What brought about *Honderich v. Green Shoes* and *Honderich v. Flutter*? Why did I not see that money would keep on rolling in from *The Oxford Companion to Philosophy*, and so perhaps there *was* something to be said for my paying my own secretary to address the envelopes? Why were my experiences of the endings of connections with women as they were? Is my lesser enthusiasm today for Keats Grove owed more to inner than outer facts, more to myself than ongoing investment in houses and gardens by owners more monied than me? On one of the lawns in front of the green palisade, as I see from my study, a sheep and lamb now graze, lifelike and woolly, but in plastic, like the large garden gnome.

You have lately heard that necessarily there appears to be a kind of unsatisfactoriness about ordinary understandings or summaries of a life. There is more frustration for us with causal explanations of the kind now being contemplated. The fact was anticipated at several stages, one in connection with my first marriage and then the end of my early manhood and my leaving Canada for England.* In no particular case, it seems, is

* See pp. 81–82, 86

it possible actually to specify a causal circumstance for a large thing in a life, to say what is in the full cause with impressive or considerable exactitude. We do not get to the point that no further question arises about the content of a causal circumstance.

Each of these circumstances, you may remember, is indeed something that by itself necessitated or guaranteed the effect. On my view, to be more explicit, it is something of which it was true that since it came to exist, whatever other things had also been happening, whatever the situation had been, its effect would still have happened as it did. Despite our hopes, it is thus no surprise that particular causal circumstances cannot be specified for large things in a life. There is also a great deal outside of any individual life for which they cannot actually be specified, despite the lesser complexity and richness of those other subject-matters.

Indeed, in a sense, there are few things for which causal circumstances *can* be specified. For few things are there explanations-by-causal-circumstance. Such explanations are rare in what falls under physical science. It cannot be supposed that this science consists in laws, these being propositions reporting lawlike or whatever-else connections in a general way, above all those that hold between causal circumstances and effects. Science assumes the existence of such connections, aims to get closer to knowing them in full, does get closer, and in almost all of its parts has a long way to go. The matter is a difficult and controverted one. But, as is often remarked, laws are few and far between in science, and are not immutable and eternal. I have not yet made a close study of *How the Laws of Physics Lie*, a work by my fellow-conductor of the Senior Seminar a while back, Professor Nancy Cartwright, but commend it to you confidently.

Do you stray from our official subject, the hope to comprehend a life by way of finding causal circumstances for large things in it? Do you take heart and reassure yourself belatedly that determinism is not true after all? Determinism is, of course, precisely the doctrine that each of our choices and actions and the like *is* an effect of a string of causal circumstances. Given my belated admission that it is not possible to be certain in specifying any causal circumstance for any large thing in a life, do you feel annoyed? Do you recall my happy report of my inaugural lecture in 1983 and feel aggrieved at having half gone along with the idea that determinism is proved by neuroscience along with some

393

philosophy? Are you aggrieved at having been more persuaded of determinism by later reflections on causal connections within and between individual neurons, and against the funny idea of real effects that might not have happened.

I stray after you, but say again that there *can* be evidence, over-whelming evidence, that every relevant human event has been the effect of a causal circumstance, even if the particular causal circumstance for none of these human events has been demonstrated. Think of the final location of any pebble in an avalanche, and more particularly the proposition that this was a matter of some string of causal circumstances. We rightly believe it. We rightly believe it without being able to give a proof with respect to the stages of the course of the pebble.

The situation with human events, in my view, and in a nutshell, is that it is arguable that *all* the evidence available about them supports determinism. Such an evidence-situation is far from unusual. All the evidence about something can go in one direction, and be quite enough, without there being a perfection of evidence about any bit of it. The evidence about the human events may be quite enough, too, to deal with scientific piety about Quantum Theory and non-events. I will at this late stage try to restrain my impulse to lecture you some more, fortitudinous reader. But let me add two items, two verses of swan song.

Do not suppose, along with a philosopher or two now long retired, that the idea of a causal circumstance or full cause is, so to speak, useless, since a causal circumstance for an event contains *all* that was necessary for its occurrence, a long history disappearing into mists of the past. That is a mistake. A causal circumstance, rather, is much more manageable. It is some set of necessary conditions that is just enough to necessitate or guarantee the event. In the case of each human event, if determinism is true, there are very many of these. There are many of them in the causal sequence for the event, and of course one just before it.

The other item is simply that if we may be hard-pressed actually to specify a causal circumstance, we commonly can get fairly near to it. We can be clear and confident about a part or parts of a circumstance, some or many of the conditions that make it up. We can also characterize a circumstance roughly, by describing what includes it, a larger state of affairs. We can do this for the effect that is a rainstorm, or snowdrops coming up, or the boiling of a kettle, or the breaking of an egg. So too can I characterize a circumstance roughly for my having got into a state of desire for something, or a state of determination about it. So too with such judgements as that for me life with St John's Wort is better than life with Prozac, and life without St John's Wort has turned out to be still better. It is importantly because of this general fact, as well as our knowing parts of a circumstance, that we can be certain there *was* a causal circumstance for an effect.

Let us try to leave the question of exactly the truth of determinism – if not in order to carry forward the earlier matter of some kind or other of causal explanations of large things in my life. We will attend to that shortly. Let me for a while persist with something else about determinism that can more or less be separated from the question of its truth. This is the matter of my own relationship to it, including my belief in it, and an up-to-date report.

On looking back over this book, I see that there is recorded no moment of conversion to determinism on my part. Nor, if you consult the entries on 'determinism' in the index, and look over the years from my unstrenuous conversations as a graduate student with Stuart Hampshire, will you find a record of entirely untroubled belief. One reason was the difficulty of getting clearer about causation itself. Another was trying to get clearer about the nature of consciousness and the mind–body relation and the other two hypotheses of a decent determinism. A different reason was my personal allotment of our culture's resistance to determinism, at bottom our family of attitudes having in them an image of actions as originated rather than causally necessitated. It is a mother's mission to have us acquire them, and, as remarked, Rae Laura carried out her mission.

But if my believing determinism has been troubled, that is not to say that I have not believed it. On the contrary, when actually thinking about it, I have always believed it. The transition in the Grote's room with Stuart was not from disbelief to belief. It was a transition to belief from neither disbelief nor belief. As soon as the question came up in a serious way, it had an answer. Since then, when my mind has been on determinism alone and the evidence for it, it has seemed as good as beyond question. The theory that each of our choices, actions and the like is an effect of a long causal sequence has seemed to me really to need only clarifying, not proving. The beginning of the evidence for me, overlooked in favour of neuroscience in what was reported to you, has been our being part of the natural world, and thus our existence being as much a matter of effects as anything else.

Bound up with this naturalism and now near-naturalism applied to choices and actions has been that conviction about causation. It is that our experience of the world has issued in ordinary causal concepts that plainly presuppose that events are made to happen by causal circumstances. What do we believe in believing that the striking of the match made it light? Partly that since a number of other things were the case, the addition of the striking inevitably produced the lighting – given things as they were, including the dryness of the match and the presence of oxygen and so on, nothing else could have happened. That *is* believing that there was a causal circumstance for the lighting. You can get to the same truth about our beliefs just by reflecting on what we must take an event to be if it is an effect. That we believe the mishap of my going over my handlebars in Haverstock Hill was the result of the opening of the car door *is* the belief that the event was a necessitated one. If we did not get these firm ideas from a world of which they are true, where did we get them? Could we really have made them up? Are these foundational ideas not very different indeed from such made-up ones as those of satyrs and fountains of youth?

This is more swan song – but let me remark on one last thing overlooked until now. It has always been hard to resist an idea never got clear, and it is still hard to resist. The idea is related to Leibniz's principle of sufficient reason, which is usually said to be the principle that there must be a sufficient reason for everything in the world, that nothing exists as it does without there being an explanation of why it is that way. In my own smaller reflections along these lines, it has seemed that the definiteness or determinateness of things, indeed their very identities, require an explicit explanation, in fact a causal circumstance. But the connection between definiteness or identity and an explicit explanation remains unclear, as does the further leap to identifying the explicit explanation with precisely a causal circumstance.

So much for the past history of my relations with determinism, in particular my belief in it. To come up to date, has the writing of this book affected these relations? One thing to be reported is a fuller and livelier awareness of a large way in which determinism is irrelevant. This is another side of the fact of our not being able actually to specify full causes for large things in our lives, and also small and middle-sized ones. It is the fact that our lives remain unpredictable. Determinism in a way leaves undiminished the *amount* of unpredictability in a life.

If we become convinced of determinism, we do lack a certain reason for being uncertain about the future, and for sustaining a hope. We no longer believe that our future is unsettled and open, something to be made partly by acts of origination. We do lose a kind of hope, but retain another kind, having to do with our future voluntariness. What is as true is that on account of our not knowing full causes, the future remains unpredictable to us in practice. We still do not know how things will turn out. I now know two new lovebirds, Bee and Rina, 81 and 85. News comes from Oxford that Jerry Cohen has passed beyond both Reds and Greens and now contemplates with Professor Nozick that each of us owns himself and so taxation by the state is robbery. I hear the Grote will be up for grabs again, since Professor Budd is giving up the struggle early. Given this fact of unpredictability in practice, to come to the main point, we can hope in the one way for just as many things as before. No particular object of hope is subtracted. That determinism is in this way beside the point, beside the fact of a life, in a way irrelevant to it, has been borne in on me by my recording of mine.

What can also be reported of my authorial experience, if it needs to be, is that it has not affected *at all* my belief in determinism. My writing of this book has instead reinforced my belief. Never has it crossed my mind, in revisiting a thing in my past, that there was not a real explanation of it – which there would not be if determinism were false. I have never thought about a thing in my past that there was no causal circumstance for it. Enough of one has been showing. Nothing in my revisiting has affected, for example, those grounds of determinism lately mentioned, having to do with our settled membership of the natural world, our concepts of causation, and the Leibnizian impulse about the definiteness of things.

But that is by no means all of my report. What needs to be added has to do with Mother's mission, my personal allotment of our family of attitudes in conflict with determinism. Now that I have passed through my past life again in the course of writing it down, it would be satisfying to bring a certain piece of news. It would serve my hope of greater consistency. It would be satisfying, that is, to let you know that my attitudes in conflict with determinism have weakened. In particular it would be a happy fact if I no longer held myself morally responsible for things in the way that is inconsistent with determinism. That is being responsible in a way that involves thinking of one's actions as not having been fixed by past and present, but originated, and hence the rightful objects of feelings against oneself that may include a retributive desire.*

It would have been satisfying, but what is true is more or less the opposite. In my feeling, much of the time, I am now far from letting myself off. I am far from the milder attitude that does no more than trace traits and actions of mine to my voluntariness and my nature rather than a free will. Crawling through my life again has not helped me to make a permanent escape from what should be regarded, I say officially, as a form of self-abuse. I have not made a permanent escape from dismay and intransigence about moral responsibility, as responses to determinism, and entered securely into the higher life of affirmation. This fact, something too close to my having no less than a life of contradiction, does give me pause.

It is not that I want a kind of higher credit for decency, the kind of credit that would come with my having originated things, my having been a kind of creator rather than a creature. Would that it was *credit* that was my concern! How fine to have a life moved by exactly getting credit rather than avoiding blame! My moral impulse is usually less brave. I want to shoulder my blame in a certain way. I want to admit what I seem to have, more responsibility for my life than I can have according to determinism. No reflection about person-stages and the disappearance of past ones affects the matter and saves me from this regrettable impulse.

Is there some good news? It is a satisfaction to me, now, that this moralism is not the only thing that has resisted the truth of determinism. I have had something underdescribed as a want. I have wanted to be my

* See pp. 303–04, 313

own man, wanted an independence for itself, not in any moral connection. I still do want it, in a way that determinism cannot allow.

My persistence in the moral and other attitudes in question, you may think, is odd. Should they not at least be *touched* by what is inconsistent with them and has been reported to you, a reinforced confidence in causal circumstances and determinism? Some will say a more interesting question arises about the contradiction, not just a question about my personal psychology. Do the attitudes, not only those involving moral responsibility but also life-hopes, confidence in knowledge, personal feelings for others and so on, and also wanting to be my own man – do these attitudes have more than desire in them? Can it be, despite that big book on determinism and the *précis*, that somehow the attitudes have a suitable *truth* in them? A truth missed by me and a couple of centuries of other philosophers?

Galen Strawson of Jesus College Oxford is a son running true to his father's good form. He has nonetheless made dealing with the question of these attitudes easy for himself. There cannot be the remotest possibility of truth in them, he says, since the very idea of our originating decisions is absurd. What the idea of origination comes to is something's causing itself, an ancient nonsense. Well, if origination *is* so conceived, absurd it is. But might there conceivably be a conception of it that is not absurd? Should some of my retirement time be given to a new and ambitious hope – of transforming our thinking about ourselves, trying to work a revolution in our understanding of determinism and freedom? Showing that rationally we *can* persist in certain attitudes? Having discovered that my perceptual consciousness is the existence of a world, might I not discover another unlikely truth? I wish myself well in this new millennium.

Our concern, before determinism distracted us, was the idea of comprehending a life by way of a kind of causal explanation of large things in it – finding causal circumstances or full causes for them, circumstances that necessitated or guaranteed them. Explanations-by-causal-circumstance. Against this, it was said that in no particular case does it seem possible actually to specify a causal circumstance, say what was in it with impressive exactitude – any more so than elsewhere, including most physical science. Against this in turn, it was said that the general idea of a causal circumstance is not useless, some kind of vague history, and there is nothing confused in trying to get closer to one. In fact, and most importantly, we are often able to get in sight of the exact specification of one. We can single out a slightly larger state of affairs that contains one.

Have you been supplied with rough and large descriptions of causal circumstances, not exact but useful, for large things in my life? Say the number of women, and the determinism, and the moral and political philosophy you say is inconsistent with my worldly possessions? It is not easy to answer.

You *were* given materials to go into such descriptions. Were the brief summaries of my boyhood and then my early manhood not of some use? As we went along I was on the look-out for evidence that the rest of my life, mainly its past, was giving rise to my philosophy. Also evidence that the philosophical life was influencing or anyway touching the other one. And the possibility that there was some common causation of both lives. No such relevant materials were left out, but none were made up to serve our purposes. It did seem clear, by the way, that there was no connection worth speaking of between events or feelings on a particular day and the philosophy that was done in it – or anyway the philosophy that survived reflection later on. Nor did I learn much about myself, as I had hoped, from the court cases.

If you say all this fell short of very satisfying explanations of life, it is hard for me to disagree. Is there a different and better hope of comprehending a life? It seems so.

We are very often concerned with an apparent part of a causal circumstance for something, without our business being the getting of a general idea of the circumstance or the making of progress towards specifying the whole of it. We are settling whether an item is required for the thing – a required condition. Such an item is such that if it hadn't happened, neither would the effect. The item is also something else, as might have been remarked in earlier tutorials on the subject.* Since that

* See pp. 87, 200

particular item happened in the company of other conditions, the effect *did* happen. In the setting, the item was not only a required but also a requiring condition.

About this sort of thing, plainly, we can have a lot of confidence, even a lot of certainty. We can have confidence and certainty about what can be called *explanations-by-condition*. If I had not come to England, many things would not have happened in my life. Also, since in a certain setting I ran into the stately Stuart, it came about that determinism and the mind got a lot of attention from me thereafter. More specifically, since other things were as they were, then since I ran into Stuart, those two philosophical subjects got a lot of attention. Any good narrative is replete with truths and good guesses about such required and requiring conditions for effects.

That is all very well, and no doubt you and I have been enlightened by contemplating such conditions for a load of things. But another thought intrudes itself, one of which you have heard something before, mainly in one of those earlier tutorials. It is the oxygen thought. If my running into the stately Stuart was a required condition for the subsequent activities, so in exactly the same way was oxygen. So were many other boring things such that if they hadn't happened, the subsequent activities wouldn't have – and such that since the boring things did happen, given what else was happening, the subsequent activities did happen.

As remarked, it is understandable that we do not and seemingly cannot resist going further than taking something to be just a required and a requiring condition. We do not content ourselves with explanations-by-condition. We pick out one particular condition in the circumstance and dignify it or give it an ascendancy. We give this condition the name of being the cause or speak of it as what caused the effect – not meaning thereby, of course, that it was itself the causal circumstance or full cause. Sometimes we speak of several such items as causes. The fundamental idea seems to be that this condition or these several conditions are *more* explanatory than any other condition in the causal circumstance.

Running into Stuart, we say, was more explanatory than the oxygen in the Grote's room. This is the essence of what can be distinguished as *explanation-by-cause*. As you will remember, it raises the matter of the praising of causes. *Why* do we dignify one condition as against others, give it the name of cause, take it to be more explanatory than others? Now the matter needs further attention, more than may be expected. Diligence here at the end, please. The matter needs further attention if we are to come confidently to a certain conclusion about our lives – the conclusion that there exists a certain large philosophical problem.

Neophytes may suppose that in the activity of explaining-by-cause we always pick out the human action in a circumstance. This idea as to our principle or practice in connection with causes immediately faces counter-examples. One, remarked on earlier, is any causal circumstance that includes no human action at all. Such difficulties have led to other suggestions, one being that we pick out as cause *either* the human action *or* the abnormal or unusual item in the conditions that make up a causal circumstance. This suggestion would suit certain cases where we do not take a human action to be the cause, but something else instead. Think of the case where, unpredictably and by nobody's doing, an explosive gas gets into a place where a smoker lights yet another match, as he has been doing safely for years.

Other examples suggest other ideas as to our activity. It is said we choose as cause the thing that is an event or change, as against any ongoing state or standing condition. Another thought, from John Stuart Mill, is that we choose the thing, event or state that is most conspicuous. He added that sometimes we may insist that something is a cause for a quite different reason – when somebody else is disputing or doubting that the thing really is even a condition, that it is required for and requires the effect. But there are still different ideas. One is that we choose as the cause the very last event in the sequence of events that issues in the effect. Or remember medical research into what we call the cause of cancer. The words show that in situations where we know some of the conditions for an effect, as almost always we do, we sometimes choose as cause the particular condition that remains unknown.

There is more to be said. There seem to be cases where what we take as the cause is not an action, abnormal, an event as against a state, the conspicuous thing, the disputed thing, the very last event in a sequence, or the unknown condition. In this study with the two blues, what holds up the patch of brick wall directly above the doorway? What is the cause of this satisfactory state of affairs? Mainly the lintel or cross-beam in the brickwork above the door. This structural cause is neither an action nor, surely, any of the other things just mentioned. Advocates of several of the competing answers may try to make their answer fit the case. You can try, for example, to come to such a sense of 'abnormal' that the lintel becomes such. This is hard to do, and if you succeed, you at least run the risk of turning *every* condition into the cause.

We might find another category or two of causes. But those already on hand are enough to indicate reasons for my brisk conclusion earlier. It was that what we name as a cause is just the particular bit of a causal circumstance *that interests us*. Explanations-by-cause, it seems, are on the way to being misnamed. Certainly they are not only explanations, if they are such at all, but also the linguistic means by which we register and convey what interests us.

This is consistent, of course, with our often taking our causes from the listed categories of actions, abnormal things, events as against states, and so on. These categories are indeed things more interesting to us in some general sense than other conditions of effects. The presence of oxygen is a condition of all our diverse human activities, but, to say the least, not as likely to have our attention as such springs and sources of actions as thoughts and desires, personal strengths and weaknesses, and hurts and prides. Can these personal springs or sources of action, by the way, be fitted into the eight categories above? Probably it would be better for the categorizing philosopher to set them aside on their own. A ninth category.

Leaving all that aside, notice that a particular condition in a circumstance may interest us and so become a cause as so far understood as a result of something other than our attention, curiosity, inquiring minds, reflectiveness, impressionability, and maybe prurience. We may be being very practical. Attending to this condition may be not just interesting, but *in our interest*. That is, an explanation-by-cause may serve some purpose of ours. It may serve a personal purpose, or a social one. The civil and criminal law is a fundamental case of the latter or social sort, worth attention and some more diligence.

In the law, we or our appointed persons look for what we certainly *call* causes of things, typically causes of harms. We certainly contemplate human actions and abnormal events as candidates. The purpose can be to try to put things right between plaintiff and defendant, as in the case of Judge Diamond. It can be to reduce criminal offences in the future by the present offender and others, or to provide the satisfaction of some-one's getting what they deserve. My friend Lennie, the Lord Hoffman, tried something like that to his eternal honour with the dictator Pinochet. In short, we serve important ends by, as we say, inquiring into and deciding what caused something. The ends are so dominant in the activity, so to speak, that a certain issue arises about it.

Some philosophers of law and jurisprudents say that the legal question expressed as the question of whether a man caused a harm is really not prior to and separate from the question of whether he is legally responsible for the harm. The seemingly causal question is not, for example, really the question of whether a man's action was the only human action in a causal circumstance, or whether a circumstance con-tained some abnormal event. Nor is the seemingly causal question really a question having to do with any of our eight or nine categories. The talk of cause, which has these implications, is a kind of drapery.

The question expressed as whether a man caused a harm just *is* the question of whether he is legally responsible for the harm. It just *is* a question about no more than what legally ought to happen. Judges may see that the bad thing Y would not have happened if various things including the prerequisite X hadn't happened. They want no replicas of Y, and think that it is by punishing the doer of X that they can prevent replicas of that prerequisite. They would have called something else the cause if they could prevent replicas of Y that way. They should make a clean breast of this. They should confess that all they can really have in their heads, if their heads are clear, by declaring X to have been the cause of Y, is that this serves their end.

The salutary example of *Confessions of a Philosopher*, the later book by the philosophical lad Bryan Magee, has been on my mind, its having been pulped by a judge's order on account of what it said of Russell's secretary Ralph Schoenman. There were large damages to pay too. The judge, we are to take it, should confess that in taking the philosophical lad to have caused a harm, he was really announcing what legally ought to happen.

What of the rest of life, outside of law courts? If we think over the eight or nine categories of causes, it is clear that our practical interests and purposes also get into the story here – whether or not our explanations-by-cause are deceptive in the way they seem to be in the law. Why do we attend to abnormal or unusual events? Sometimes curiosity or intellectual interest, but often because what we *want* is a repetition of the effect, which was something good, or no repetition of the effect, which was something bad. The abnormal event beforehand, as against the ordinary state of affairs that will go on existing, is exactly what we need to concentrate on in order to get repetitions or no repetitions. I do not have to spend time directing attention to today's presence of oxygen to make it more likely that oxygen will be present tomorrow.

Similiar reflections apply to the other categories of causes. We may attend to the particular condition of an effect that was the one human action partly because we think this is the easiest or cheapest way of increasing production in our shoe factory. Better tools would be more expensive. So too, often, with the very last item in the causal sequence before the effect. That is what we can most efficiently attend to in order to try to get or prevent what we want. The fact of practical aim may be the same with unknown conditions, such as the cause of cancer.

Where does all this leave us with respect to explanation-by-cause? It is important to keep the right subject in mind. Explanation-by-cause is not explanation-by-condition – say the finding of a new and further condition for some effect, finding something that is required for and requires the effect. Explanation-by-cause, rather, is picking out one of the known conditions for an effect, maybe a just-discovered condition and maybe not, giving it the name of cause, and thus crediting it with explaining more than the other conditions.

It is easy to take a tough line about explanation-by-cause as so far understood. The tough line is that a chosen cause, as so far understood, gives us *no more knowledge at all of why something happened*, but is indeed only a matter of our interest and our practical interests. My interest or purpose is a fact about me. My choice of a cause, no matter how conventional or common, is something owed at bottom to my desiring nature rather than truth about the world and we who are in it. When I say 'X caused Y' I should be saying instead 'X is a surprise to me as a condition of Y' or 'Let us concentrate on condition X because that serves my purposes.' Explanation-by-cause is misleadingly named, disgracefully named. It is really not explanation at all. Picking out a cause sheds no further light on why something happened or is the way it is, whatever light is shed on he or she who does the picking out.

As for the problem of the praising of causes, it may have seemed to be the problem not only of explaining why we elevate a certain condition, but also the problem of showing why and how that condition is in fact more explanatory. In so far as the problem is taken to be the second thing, it is spurious. We get and give no further knowledge at all as to why something happened when we upgrade a condition to being what caused something.

I am inclined to the tough line. But might it be that it is a mistake, that it can be resisted or escaped? Well, there is one last thing, something more reassuring about our causes that really needs looking at before we press on. It has occurred to me since those earlier thoughts about the end of my early manhood, as things will after a tutorial. There is a second sort of activity we go in for having to do with a part of a causal circumstance, a second thing that can be called explanation-by-cause, rather different. There is one other sort of condition that can be called the cause, and surely it is more reputable.

What this amounts to is that in a causal circumstance we may find something that *makes a difference*. That is to say that with two different effects, the two causal circumstances in so far as we know them may be identical in all of their contained conditions except one. That condition in the first circumstance makes a difference from the second circumstance – makes for a different effect. What we find out is not that the condition is required for and requires the first effect, or is part of the guarantee, but that it is what makes for the difference in effect from the second circumstance.

This in itself is no matter of our interest or interests, nothing about our desires. It is a fact about the outside world. If we consider the two circumstances for two different lines of sexual conduct, the presence of oxygen and a lot else will be common to both of them. Very likely the two persons involved will be subject to a degree of self-interest, a similar degree. But that a naive desire turns up in the first of the two circumstances, and makes the difference, can perfectly well be a fact. It can be a kind of explanatory fact. It answers the question of why the first circumstance, as against the second, gave rise to the first line of sexual conduct. We have here, at least, a *more* reputable cause, whatever else is to be said.

It remains such, by the way, despite a couple of complications. One is that what makes the difference between two circumstances may also be a cause of one of our eight or nine earlier sorts – or it may be none of those things. Should you be inclined to suppose, by the way, that what makes a difference is always an abnormal or unusual condition in a causal circumstance, you can cure yourself of the idea easily. If an abnormal condition does make a difference in one compared circumstance, then presumably it will be precisely a normal or usual condition that makes a difference in the other circumstance. A second complication is that with a given causal circumstance, there is not just one thing that makes a difference. In fact, when you think of it, there are as many things as the number of other circumstances you can usefully compare it with, including imaginary ones.

These reflections can properly be fitted into something else that has exercised some speculative and higher-flying philosophers with no great interest in explanation-by-cause or indeed causation. Their interest is in *narrative*, this being something other than what we have so far had in mind in using the word. It is a less stiffly philosophical subject, more immediately invigorating, of greater interest to literary persons. We can best approach it pedestrianly.

My life through those years to this new millennium, according to the determinism of which you have heard a lot, was a sequence of events that were causal circumstances and their effects. Each effect was also an element or condition in the next causal circumstance. We can contemplate a model of a fragment of the sequence – a tiny bit of the progress, if that is what it was, towards some large thing in my life, say this book. The model is of only two circumstances and the effect of the second.

A

B

C

D

E

The first circumstance contained elements or conditions *A* and *B*, and the later effect of the circumstance was *C*. It along with *D* made up the second circumstance, for the still later *E*.

However, it is not essential to what is now to be said that you accept or contemplate determinism here. You need not suppose that the events *A* to *E* were parts of a deterministic story. Suppose, if you want, that these events went into a story with origination or freewill in it, and that the connections between the items were such that none was a standard effect but only something made probable by its past. I will continue to talk in terms of the deterministic assumption only because it makes things plainer.

To our contemplation of the model, we can add our reflections on explanation-by-cause. There is the possibility of taking *A* as cause in the first circumstance, for whatever reason or to whatever purpose, and leaving *B* as mere condition. But, if the situation is a fairly ordinary one, there is also the possibility of just the opposite – giving *B* an explanatory ascendancy over *A*. So with the two elements *C* and *D* of the second circumstance. What interests us differs, as what is in our interests does too. Thus there are two choices as to causes and, as a result, four choices of what we can call causal lines finishing in an effect. These causal lines are *A–C–E*, *A–D–E*, *B–C–E*, and *B–D–E*. Each reflects an interest, maybe practical. The second one reflects an interest in *A* and *D*.

This can be fitted into and also help with the thinking of the good and characterful philosopher Alasdair MacIntyre in his audacious and maybe true book *After Virtue*. In it he asks what gives unity to a human life. He says that it is the unity of a narrative embodied in that life, which narrative has a goal that calls for certain virtues. Indeed, he goes a lot further, and says differently. We are to take it that a human life itself, mine or yours, just *is* such a narrative. Presumably a life itself is something whose parts are things related in the ways of parts of a narrative, of which the most obvious are a story-teller's choice of beginning, middle and end. A life itself, as distinct from a telling of it, has the properties of a story.

So a human being's just existing over time, maybe the stuff that might be captured by a fixed overhead camera, is not itself a life. It is not something with the unity of a life without there being a narrator on the scene, at least the narrator telling himself the narrative while living it. It is not as if a life itself consisted in a run of independently existing events or facts, out of which a narrative can be drawn or onto which a narrative can be imposed. A life exists only as the narrative, and not before. There is an analogy with ordinary human actions. It is not as if our actions were bodily movements, already there and in view before our intentions were had and grasped. Rather, to put it simply, perhaps too simply, actions are things owed to intentions. Intentions being of the essence, there are no actions to be contemplated independently of or without reference to intentions.

This kind of philosophy claims my attention more than it used to, but still resists my understanding. How can it be that a life *is* a narrative? If only a metaphor is intended, which is less than certain and would be sad, what are we to take as the literal content of saying a life is a narrative? Just that a life is a sequence of which someone is conscious? That would be small beer. Exactly how are we helped by the analogy, if it is such, with human actions? Certainly we would not have a life in just a series of events at the level of mere bodily movements, with consciousness and everything in it left out. That leaves it still puzzling how a life itself *is* a story, or is to be taken as one. For present purposes, indeed, exactly what is a narrative? But I stop. This querulousness is not my aim.

Despite difficulties there is at least a temptation to think about a life and about each of its considerable parts in terms of a narrative somehow understood. Is it the case, whatever others find in *After Virtue*, that out of our thoughts on explanation-by-cause, and our little model of a fragment of my life, something unpuzzling can be made of the idea of narrative in connection with a life? So it certainly seems. The model offers us the possibility of *four narratives* – in our own new and precise sense. The first narrative reports the causal line $A–C–E$, the others report the other three causal lines. We can suppose that the life itself, in the time in question, consists in all of A, B, C, D, and E. But there are the four explanatory stories to be told of it.

Does this attract you? Do you now want to go against that tough line in the last section about explanations-by-cause giving us no more knowledge at all of why something happened? Do you feel that we *do* get a grip on a human life, or more likely a part of it, by way of certain explanations-by-cause and thus a certain narrative as we now understand one? That we make sense of a part of a life by choosing a cause from each causal circumstance in a sequence and thus producing a particular narrative? Do you propose to do so with respect to large things in my life – the restrained philosophy, the women, the adversaries, the very character of the protagonist, his sort of success? Will you also make sense of a plethora of lesser but still sizeable things? The white wine, for a start, and my drinking less of it now?

To go back once more to the tutorial at the end of my account of my early manhood, do you now want to resist something else said in it, indeed the burden of it?* That was that it is no good elevating some childhood fact into a cause, supposing that it does more than some condition in early manhood to explain something else later on. Are you unwilling to be deprived of some proposition of yours that things later in my life were particularly owed to a cause in my experience of Baden, Ontario, Canada? Do you remark that while I gave up a certain epithet in description of the village of my birth, the fact that the epithet used to be on my lips is a good indication of *something* explanatory in the way now being contemplated? Do you insist that a compelling narrative begins with your chosen cause?

There is another question, not about your inclinations but mine. What you have heard from me of events, passages and parts of my life has in fact been full of tentative explanations, answers to the question of why something happened or was as it was. In good part they were exactly explanations-by-cause. They often came together into explicit or implicit narratives as we are now understanding them.

It seemed to me, for example, that *some* light was shed on my later person by the diffidence, rectitude and classlessness of Toronto. It seemed that there were useful stories told about my returning to university, my first marrying, my being awakened and alarmed into philosophical activity by Freddie's seminar, my getting back together with Pauline when she was going to have a child. Also useful stories about straying into affairs with undergraduates in Sussex, my nadir in morale, the battles about the Freud chair and promotion, my two chairs, the arrivals and departures of Helen, Janet and Jane. My getting into *Honderich v. Green Shoes* and out of *Honderich v. Flutter*, the writing of books, the tendency of my philosophy. The arrival of Ingrid sent by Plato. Can I not be slightly pleased with my efforts at explanation?

* See pp. 86–87

It is true that if you look back you will notice my confidence seemed to decline. There are fewer small essays in explanation and more guesses in the later part of my chronicle. To come up to date, I am not sure today why it has been taking so long to negotiate the details of sharing the freehold with our neighbours downstairs. It was back at the beginning of my chronicle that Kierkegaard was put in his place for saying that life has to be understood backwards, and it can't be, since it has to be lived forwards. It was also at the beginning that Nietzsche was put in his place for saying that memory always yields to present pride. Maybe I was anticipating our present reflections about explanation-by-cause. But even if my confidence declined, surely I *did* shed some light on myself by my explanations-by-cause and my narratives?

We are on the way to a conclusion, but let us proceed there clear-headedly. Remember that you do not get an explanation-by-cause by seeing for the first time that an item is in fact required for something and also is a requiring condition. *That* is explanation-by-condition and it does certainly shed light of a kind, despite the oxygen thought. Indeed there can be advances in knowledge and dramatic discoveries here. Explanations-by-cause are different, despite the optimism into which we have just been tempted.

To come to part of the conclusion, the optimism includes forgetfulness. We still have good reason to take the tough line against explanation-by-cause when we add in the clarification or elaboration that we can choose a particular string of causes as the stuff of a particular narrative. It may seem that things get worse. A narrative, after all, is precisely a product of interest and of interests. We tell stories because they appeal to us or captivate us, and in order to be heard or make points or apologies, and to defend ourselves or go on the attack. It *does* remain inescapable that in any singling out of causes, anyway of our first nine sorts, we are led by inclination and interests, however much they may be shared by others. Here, it seems, is a source of rational uncertainty about a life. You and I, it seems, need to abandon our explanations-by-cause and our narratives. We need to abandon the conventional and indeed rooted idea that a chosen condition in a causal circumstance explains more than any other condition. It seems we need to become post-modern, if that means unsure about explanatory facts.

That seems clear enough. But, to come to the crux of all this, indeed

411

the crux of this coda, there is that other side to the whole thing. That other side does exist, and it needs no help to claim attention. We weren't being *silly* in being cheered up by remembering our particular explanations-by-cause and narratives about my life. Think of them again, mine and yours, perhaps the one about Baden. It seems to me, as it should seem to you, that some explanations-by-cause *do rightly claim attention*. They are useful or even essential answers to the question of why something happened. Some seem very good. Some seem to hit the nail on the head.

In this apparent contradiction, this conflict of impulses and argument about the explanation of our lives, this apparent contradiction, we have a philosophical problem, in particular a philosophical problem about our lives. To separate it out from what we have called the praising of causes, it is the problem of the worth of explanation-by-cause. It is that we seem to have good reason to doubt explanations-by-cause having to do with our lives, and also seem to have immediate reason to affirm some of these explanations.

Can we escape the problem by returning our attention to our tenth and last category of causes as against conditions, our causes of a reputable kind? Remember that after first falling into doubt about the respectability of explanations-by-cause in nine categories and being tempted to the tough line about their being a disgrace, we found a reason for hope, a tenth category of causes. Causes of this category are *items that make a difference* – such a cause is an element in a first causal circumstance that makes for the difference between its effect and the effect of a second causal circumstance being compared with the first. Certainly, as we concluded, there are facts in the comparison, not just our interest and our interests. It seemed promising – but in philosophy, sometimes, things do not stand still. I have been doing a bit more thinking this morning about those items that make a difference.

What it comes to is that our interest and our interests get into this story too. As in our explanations involving the first nine sorts of cause, we explainers turn out to be human, all too human. Here this is a matter of the chosen comparison – of choosing a comparison. In choosing a real or imagined circumstance to compare with a first one, you are not forced or constrained by any facts about a life. In choosing a run or sequence of circumstances to compare with a first run, you are not forced or constrained by any facts about a life. You can discover a truth by a certain comparison, but your preferred comparison is not a truth. It is something you like.

You may, by a good choice of a circumstance of comparison, enable yourself to see my life in terms of my starting out with my membership problem in my filthy peasant village and my not feeling myself a member of things thereafter. All you need to do in order to get these explanations-by-cause and the resulting narrative is to compare me with the right person. Say a secure young Mennonite lad in Baden who had no sad experiences in starting out and was lucky thereafter. By this chosen comparison, you get what you want, a certain view of my life.

By the choice of another comparison, you may leave the membership matter behind and kindly make more of my native disposition to inquiry and reflection, my struggles towards clarity and truth. Another account will have in it my disposition first noticed by way of the pleasant sensation produced by leaning against the drinking fountain at school, and then the rising inclination of a bodily kind at 18, more clearly connected with girls. Here you may compare me with a figure in the species noticed some time ago – mates early and once, stays out of trouble, thinks there's something in Wittgenstein, Senior Lecturer. Or you can imagine an account that gives a large place to my Anabaptist heredity. You may abandon those themes of membership, intellect, carnality and heredity, and go over to self-deception, or perhaps the state of being out of touch with one's feelings. Dr Hart, I remember, could discern the latter sad condition at quite a distance.

Truth, it seems, does not select one of these accounts. Objectivity, it seems, does not decree that one stands above the others. And yet, as before, something else is also the case. You are likely to want to persist in thinking that you *do* shed light on my adventures and me by the facts that emerge from a particular comparison. One or perhaps several, you may think, are crucial. I share your inclination. Thus we have come round to the same point and crux again – a philosophical problem about explaining our lives. Perhaps this problem of the worth of explanation-by-cause is ultimately about a connection between truth and desire.

That is not quite the end. It now seems necessary to return to our dismissal of what were called understandings of my life, summaries, of which a number were tried out. Can we really conclude with so much confidence as we did that all are attitudes, owed at bottom to desires, and hence that none stands above the others? Look back. Think of your own preferred understanding. Maybe one about my being impeded by myself rather than others, or one about empathy. Does your preferred understanding not stand out because of something like its *truth*? We took the view, in short, that about all that can be said of an understanding is that somebody likes it. Can that really be so? That our philosophical problem turns up in this locale as well is not surprising. The distinction between explanations-by-cause of both kinds, and the earlier understandings, is not sharp. The understandings themselves have a certain amount of causal content – have explanations-by-cause in them – as another look at them will reveal.

It would be a mistake to make our central philosophical problem about explanation-by-cause, this rational uncertainty, into a state of encompassing darkness. It would be a mistake to say that we *make up* lives, or just choose any explanations we want. It was not reassuring when Paul Feyerabend, my valued contributor to *The Oxford Companion to Philosophy*, reported that science was voodoo. It would be as wrong to take our lives somehow to be fictions, the large things in them as relativistic or even personal constructions.

In this connection it also needs to be kept firmly in mind that the actual explanations given by me in the course of my story, and no doubt your own preferred explanations, are only in good part explanations-by-cause and the related narratives. It is only in good part that my explanations and yours are attempts to praise or dignify one or some conditions in a causal circumstance above others. They are also in good part discoveries, identifications and specifications of needed conditions for an effect – explanations-by-condition. With luck we bring into focus conditions that others have missed or misconceived. These are respectable endeavours to establish what is true or false – that a particular item understood in a certain way was actually required for a given effect and required its occurrence. There is also the separable enterprise, respectable if unsatisfying, of rough and large descriptions of causal circumstances, and of moving closer to full explanations of things, explanations-by-causal-circumstance.

In all three enterprises, incidentally, the problem of truth may be not so much bringing oneself to tell it as seeing what it is. It seems so with me. It is not so much the problem of resisting the temptation to conceal the truth as the problem of arriving at it. Not the problem of bringing oneself to reveal facts but the problem of selecting them. Arriving at the truth is so hard. One needs not only to be Thrasymachean in one's scepticism but also charitable or generous in understanding. The latter is needed not only in decency but as a means to truth itself. As any good Thrasymachean knows, charity and generosity are needed because given an eighth of a chance one will favour oneself.

I find myself less certain about my life than I began, but not about to abandon my life to anyone's devising. Nothing is clearer, of course, than that others see my life differently, as I see theirs differently. Some will take what has been said by me to be one side of the story, or self-deceived, or a monstrous travesty. That was certain from the start. There is something more interesting, the philosophical problem that has emerged. The problem of the worth of explanation-by-cause awaits further attention. Those of us who seek truth with the best will in the world, including some of my adversaries, maybe even all, cannot be confident. In our explanations and narratives we run into a kind of contradiction and conflict.

Despite earlier discouragement, do you murmur, even stand up and declare, that this reflection on a life could be improved by reflection on an unconscious mind? That if we cannot solve our new problem, we can at least make it clearer? Your idea is that there are certain deep sources of our activities, unconscious ones – unconscious desires, beliefs, fears, motives, intentions, impulses and so on – and you may be in the class of reflective readers who need to be paid attention by me. You may be a philosopher in excellent standing. You may be my friend Gabriel Segal, and you may be Richard. You may even be Pauline or Kiarney, if not John. So a word or two more is in order. Freud will be in view, but less for himself than as an example . My aim is a small substitute for a survey of a great deal of freer and deeper thinking than my own about a life.

You suppose, say, that a groan is owed to something much more hidden than a plastic sheep in front of a green palisade. Or you suppose that a man's pompous behaviour is owed to an unconscious desire or belief. Maybe the desire to act in such a way as really to conceal that as a reasoner he is always on weak ground. Or you suppose that when he says that the wider world is sceptical of the members of something, maybe a particular club, this comes out of a belief that he is not up to being a member himself. If you are what we may call an ordinary or standard Hampstead believer in the unconscious mind, from the cradle or by conversion, you in fact have a paradoxical idea of any such desire or belief. It is that despite its name, despite its very definite description, an unconscious desire or unconscious belief *is* somehow conscious. You have the idea that it has *some* existence in the subjectivity that is the consciousness of the person in question. That the thing is called a desire or belief already leads inexorably in this direction. So too does the plain fact that the thing is said to be somehow in the mind, indeed in an important part of the mind, and is capable of being brought to its surface under the right conditions, traditionally involving a couch.

How the desire or belief is in consciousness, to the extent it is, is certainly unclear. Does the owner have a flicker of it at apposite moments, and then carry on forgetfully with business at usual, walking the dog? Is the desire or belief with him often, but so ghostly or insubstantial that it is an unremarked presence? I leave to others the answering of the question of how the desire or belief is within consciousness to the extent that it is. In the Freudian doctrine of the unconscious mind, we hear of feelings being altered, transformed into fantasy, projected onto new people, and so on. These explanations have been pretty much the stuff of psycho-analytic theory since the heady days of the Rat Man. It was he, on account of a desire for his mum, of whom it is delicately said that he was given to imagining his father being eaten into from behind by hungry rats.

All that I myself wish to suppose can be put in the following way: for the ordinary or standard Hampstead supporter of the unconscious mind, *more* is true of a so-called unconscious desire or belief than that it was had or felt as an infant or child, and then never experienced again or remembered. Roughly speaking, the situation is rather that while the desire or belief is enough out of the mind to be called unconscious, it also makes something of an entry at certain moments or is a ghostly presence more of the time.

If this *is* what we are to be understanding, there is a certain consequence. It is that the owner of the desire or belief is in a better position than anyone else in the world to know about the existence of the desire or belief – and its possible use in explanation of his activities. The essential point in that he does not have to *infer* the desire or belief, get to it by the relatively uncertain route of argument or speculation from other premises. Rare or elusive as the thing is, he *has* it.

No doubt a bit of qualification is in order, but not much. Let me say just that the owner is in a better position to know of the desire or belief than anyone else if he is ordinarily *compos mentis*, supplied with the usual concepts, self-recollective to the usual degree, has had some experience of life, and has read a few novels. There is certainly no need for another qualification. There is no need to say that the person with occasional or veiled access to his own desire or belief is not in a better position to know about it than someone else who is possessed of some theory or doctrine. That other person is not in a better position to know about my very own desire or belief than I am, I being without the help of his theory. However rich his speculations, I am one up on him. I *have* the thing about which he can only theorize.

You will anticipate my first conclusion here. It is that if the supposition as to my unconscious mind is this first one – that it is something *somehow* open to me – then definitely it has not been left out of my reflections in trying to understand or explain my adventures. In fact, I have spent a lot of early mornings wondering about ideas, temptations and motivations that from time to time might have been in my mind and moving me, or were somehow there all the time influencing me. I know more about these possibilities than anyone else. This is the fact of what philosophers call a person's privileged access to his or her own conscious life. It raises questions of analysis, but has never been open to serious dispute.

My second and lesser conclusion on our current assumption is one you will also anticipate. It is that I have not had and not been moved by such particular desires and beliefs as Freud supposes are the lot of all of us. I did not desire Rae Laura, I did not contemplate a terrible fate for my dad, I did not fall into related attitudes to other significant persons, and I did not later have feelings that took their conscious character from such beginnings. Will it now be said, in that way that was once mildly inflam-matory, that I am *resisting* what I know to be truth? I reply with greater authority than my interpreter that it is he or she who is doing the resisting. *I* have something of it from inside.

The very fact of privileged access may be part of what leads a second and more consistent supporter of the unconscious mind to a different position. As I am freed to say by imputations of self-deception from the other side, he or she may be subject to a wish as a result of having invested money, emotion and time in a practitioner of psychoanalysis. This more consistent supporter of the unconscious may wish to make it really possible that a subject's grip on their own desires or beliefs is less good than that of an outside theoretician, the Freudian, Kleinian or other practitioner. So the second supporter of the unconscious mind makes that thing in a way absolutely and totally unconscious. It is not dimly lit but pitch-black. A certain desire or belief was conscious in infanthood or childhood. But since then it has never been experienced and never remembered. In a way, its owner is no better placed with respect to knowledge of it than anyone else. In a way, the practitioner at the head of the couch has as much authority. It's not *in* either of their minds.

We need to ask what this really non-conscious thing is. We ought to have asked the question of our previous supporter of the unconscious mind. What is the thing of which the previous supporter casually says that *it* sometimes comes into consciousness or that *it* is there in a veil? There seems to be only one answer, of which you have heard before. There seem to be only two categories into which to put the things with which we are concerned in thinking of our own existence. There are minds, as ordinarily and properly understood, and there are brains. More particularly, there are conscious things and there are neural things.

So – unconscious desires and beliefs, things properly so-called, must be facts of the brain, electrochemical facts. As they were earlier, they can be called neural structures. Our previous or Hampstead supporter of the unconscious mind might have improved on his usages. Instead of saying, mysteriously, that one and the same belief is usually unconscious but becomes conscious occasionally, he ought to have said that an unconscious belief, a neural structure, occasionally gives rise to what is somehow related but in another category, an ordinary or conscious belief.

Or that an unconscious belief is a neural structure but has an ongoing ghostly counterpart in consciousness.

But leave that. Our present idea, that of the second supporter of the unconscious mind, is the firm one that in setting out to explain someone's activities by unconscious desires and beliefs, one is setting out to explain them by nothing more than neural or electrochemical properties of that person. Certainly these facts *can* be spoken of as desires and beliefs of a sort. They can be beliefs in the sense that the guidance system of an American missile may believe it is over Baghdad. To mention a better class of fact, they may be desires in the sense that a pot plant on Ingrid's balcony, being phototropic, wants to face the sun, and, as can be added, is trying to do so.

Putting aside for a minute Freud's special views as to what they include, I do for the purposes of argument accept the existence of unconscious desires and beliefs as we are now conceiving them. They are related, if distantly, to what were earlier called dispositions, in connection with my Sussex adventures and before then.* Those are ongoing facts, in an extended sense mental, that sometimes give rise to conscious states or events. Among such dispositions, commonly accepted and thought about long before Freud, is what can be called my dispositional knowledge that the name on my birth certificate is 'Edgar Dawn Ross Honderich'. The difference in kind between such personal dispositions, as understood, and the things we are now contemplating, is as follows. The dispositions issue, sometimes, in conscious desires, beliefs and so on, as well as in resulting behaviour. The things we are now contemplating issue in behaviour *without* issuing in consciousness.

Why shouldn't there be such items? After all, there are myriad things that contribute to my activities without going via my mind. There are things about my right knee that do so, cartilege being one. In each of us there is a whole system, the Autonomic Nervous System, which by first giving rise to perspiration, digestion and the like, also gives rise to subsequent actions and activities. Still, there are difficulties about unconscious states as we are now contemplating them, three for a start.

* See pp. 32, 127

One is that these neural things cannot be explanatory in any way that is peculiar to conscious events and states. Conscious states and events they are not. They cannot be explanatory in any way that involves holding their owners responsible for the actions or activities to which they give rise. They cannot be explanatory in any way that involves them being good reasons that the person has, in the ordinary sense, or for that matter bad reasons. Secondly, these neural things are among the various conditions that together give rise to a piece of conduct – some of the other conditions being conscious ones such as a plan or desire, and of course an intention. The common attempt to elevate the unconscious thing from being a mere condition, and to turn it into 'the cause' of the piece of conduct, something more explanatory than other conditions, faces the new problem of which we know.

Thirdly, consider the possibility of coming near to excluding *conscious* antecedents from the explanation of a piece of conduct. There is an exceedingly strong inclination on the part of supporters of the unconscious mind to do so. Conscious antecedents cannot be absolutely excluded, of course, or there will be no piece of conduct to consider, as distinct from bodily movements. A conscious intention is needed for an action. But suppose there is exclusion of much of the agent's conscious belief about his situation, even if arrived at by careful inquiry, and also exclusion of his pressing conscious desire with respect to the situation.

What is left is a bare little conscious intention – and the large unconscious desire or whatever, the neural thing. Here we have a story akin to the remnant of nineteenth-century physiology remarked on several times already – Epiphenomenalism, the absurdity that absolutely excludes our thoughts and feelings from the explanation of our actions. It is certainly a story fallen into by some enthusiastic supporters of the second idea of the unconscious mind, supporters of certain wholly neural conditions of our conduct.

On this present assumption as to the nature of unconscious states, what of the particular ones assigned to us by Freud, having a lot to do with earlier sex, mothers, and the stages of oral, anal and genital gratification, not to mention the ego, id and super-ego? I do indeed allow that in one way, an analyst of mine, if I succumbed in the end to having one, would be on a level with me in detecting Freudian unconscious states. By definition, I would not *have* these things called desires and beliefs. I would be like him, theorizing about them. But that is to forget some other things.

The general idea is that such unconscious states have to be postulated in order to explain behaviour, usually funny behaviour. But this behaviour, as we know, is not mere bodily movements. It consists in an action or activity, or a string of these. Actions and activities are very conscious indeed. An action, for a start, is typically bound up with an ongoing conscious intention, not just a prior one. The conscious intention is of a certain content, character and flavour. Who knows best about that content, character and flavour? In my case, I do. And so, to come to a further conclusion, it is I who am best placed to guess what sort of *unconscious* state would explain it, if any, and indeed which one. In fact, if we keep in mind the application of the truth of privileged access to one's consciousness-in-action, it can become clear there is no great help to Freud's philosophers in making the preceding unconscious desires and beliefs into things that really deserve the name.

Suppose that as a boy I had a bad experience in my village, a hurt entirely different from any episode now consciously remembered, such as the one involving my tricycle. Suppose that this forgotten hurt, owed to a man, and the persistence of it in an unconscious and neural form, are in fact an explaining condition of my predilection for the company of women. I don't think there is such a thing, entirely out of my conscious life, but suppose there is. In competition with the practitioners of psychoanalysis, I do indeed fancy my chances of being first to uncover the old village hurt. It is *I* who has the conscious predilection for women as against men that informs my activities. I'm the one who knows the feeling of those activities. I know the inside nature of this effect, and therefore am best placed to speculate about an ancient and continuing cause.

So it seems to me, admittedly on the grounds of a certain confidence that properly can be shared only by most people, not quite all. If I were a man who moved house four times, and thereafter explained that he did it the first time to save money, the second time for the trees, then for quiet, and then to be near the 24 bus route, and it was only coincidence that each house was beside a brothel, you would have better ground to doubt my supposition about my being well-placed to find things out about myself. I am more ordinary than such a fellow. My point is that an analyst of mine might be better at seeing my really unconscious states if I were pretty batty, but I am not.

In short, the *Routledge Encyclopedia of Philosophy* seems dead right in the entry that says that the central methodological question about psychoanalysis is whether there now is or ever has been any evidence supporting its truth. The answer is close to being that psychoanalysis, whatever explains local enthusiasms for it, and whatever help it may be to the sad, maybe a lot, was an illusory discovery. This is also the tenor of the entry on Freud in *The Oxford Companion to Philosophy*. No surprise? As editor I was true to John Stuart Mill on free speech, and first asked Richard to write it. He declined, and in choosing another contributor I made good use of my free hand.

One last item. We noticed that it is ordinary to take the unconscious mind as somehow conscious, that this raises a great difficulty for its Freudian supporters, and that they may then seek to preserve the authority and dignity of Freudian practitioners and interpretations by making the unconscious mind, whatever infant or childhood events may be in its past, absolutely and totally unconscious. This in turn raised difficulties. In addition to those already looked at, there is one more, a difficulty that is as much a matter of an attitude as anything else. There is also a brave and philosophical strategy for dealing with the difficulty.

If the unconscious mind is made wholly neural, it is demoted. It is hard to escape the attitude that it is dull stuff as against the wonderfully rich subject of the conscious mind, partly as a result of comparisons mentioned above. That is, the conscious mind has in it things for which we are responsible, and reasons as ordinarily understood, and, so to speak, is the stuff of our lives. What is wholly neural is more appealing to neuroscientists than the rest of us, but not such as to preoccupy even them outside working hours. Among philosophically minded enthusiasts of the unconscious mind, there is now a strategy for dealing with this, seemingly simple. What you do is take advantage of some loose talk of Freud's about brain and mind, and marry his doctrine taken as wholly neural to something else.

Officially, in expounding him, you give him membership in a declining but still audible movement in the contemporary Philosophy of Mind. This is the one that eliminates its subject-matter, doesn't notice, and ploughs on regardless. Its doctrine and platform is that the mind, by which is ordinarily meant the conscious mind, *is* the brain – where that identity-claim is taken to mean that the mind has only electro-chemical properties. This is the insight associated with places of strong sunlight, notably Australia and California, of which you have heard several times. Eliminative Materialism, sometimes coated with Functionalism.

The joy of making Freud a member of the movement, to philosophers of Freud, is that the unconscious mind, taken as only neural, is now on a level with the conscious mind. Both are tides of brain events, just electrochemical. So there is no demotion of the unconscious mind – that is the official story of these philosophical enthusiasts. In being just cells, it is not a lesser thing. Thus, to save one, both of Freud's minds are dished for him. With friends like this, what need has Freud of me?

So much for the official position of the philosophers of Freud. Their real position, as it seems to me, is different but not happier. I offer you an interpretation of it, free of charge. Eliminative Materialism, however the pill is coated, is not actually believed by many people. It is not believed by many Freudian philosophers. What they really do, after officially embracing Eliminative Materialism or the like, and thus putting the conscious mind and the unconscious mind on the same level, is somehow to get consciousness back into both minds, maybe privately. That is a kind of reversion to the thinking of your ordinary or standard Hampstead supporter of the unconscious mind, which we considered earlier. It is not good thinking.

I leave you unsatisfied, my friends of the unconscious. My overall verdict is that no important thing has been avoided and left out of our inquiry into why my life so far has gone as it has. Nor do we get help with the new problem of explaining our lives.

Has part of my life, now 67 years of it, been well conducted? Has it been well conducted in terms of the seeking of my ends or goals, my life-hopes? That is, has it been rational in what is sometimes said to be the only useful sense of the word? Rationality of this kind is not about choosing or justifying ends, or justifying means in an ordinary sense. It consists only in adopting efficient and economical means to whatever ends one has. Efficient means are those that actually produce the end. Economical means are a matter of much more than money, even as a measure. Economical means have to do with costs in time, feeling, dignity, sleeping well, and so on, and are not so costly as to make the end not worth it.

Has my life so far been rational in this sense? You have heard reflections on that. The question is complicated by the new philosophical problem on my plate, but on most days I say my life has gone pretty well, and could have gone a lot worse, maybe tragically. Might I, if I had gone to Cambridge, become a Wittgensteinian? Certainly I have not done all that I wanted. There is a good deal left to occupy me in my philosophical maturity, my years of emancipation. But some books have been written, including the one you are reading. Sometimes I like it. In general, the reasons that have moved me in the past now seem to have been pretty efficient and economical means to my ends, even if it might have been better to have been less trenchant in expressing truth and more careful to make more friends.

Good things have happened. I remind you of my watching brother Robert paint his shields for the restaurants, and the intrinsic interest of my travels with Elvis. Of First Love and all who came after her, of excitements and happinesses with every one. The fineness of my son's being born, the size of the audience for my inaugural lecture, the satisfaction of being the Grote, and of my mightily solving the consequences-of-determinism problem, as in moments of self-toleration I know I did. Gladness in wine, and, as Helen used to call it, the buzz of a fag. Getting straight about the subjectivity of consciousness, anyway for the time being, and an election that lightened my dismay about England. Affections lasting out of the past that will last as long as I do. Contentment with a fine partnership, the last attachment.

Both my means and my ends, of course, are open to a very different kind of question, of a moral kind. It is the question of whether they were right. In the form that it always comes to me, a bit embarrassingly, it is the question of whether I have been decent. It too is complicated by the new philosophical problem, but it persists. Have my reasons for my conduct been good in the sense of being decent? Above all, have they made the conduct decent? Some of you, having been rightly persuaded of the rectitude of my careerism, will take the women to be the problem, including getting into bed with undergraduates.

Happy truth to tell, I am more inclined to celebrate all that than to judge it. There was hurt in it, maybe more for others than for me, but there was much more. It will be some time before I bow my head to judgemental persons who see in sexual relations between teachers and students something very different, and considerably more disturbing, than in relations between men and women in other walks and ways of life. There is an innocence in this judging. I would still not subtract one connection from my past. Would the women? I wonder about that, optimistically. First Love, about whom I was apprehensive, had a daughter, and now manages an immense budget of which she is proud, in a good cause. It still seems to me that the morality of sexual relations has in it no truth of anything like the weight of the Principle of Equality.

The mention of that principle brings to mind what embarrasses me more. That is the conjunction of my moral and political principles and, as they now are, three and a half items of residential property, the last being down the hill towards Bloomsbury at Mornington Crescent. Also some liquid assets in the Nationwide, the building society joined by me because it did not privatize itself into a bank. If I did not have children, my situation would be a lesser one but might also be more decent, because less might be owned by me. I said what I can in defence of myself and my situation earlier on. It was not quite enough. Writing this book has shamed me, and so two causes have lately had my support. £5,000 for Amnesty International, and £5,000 for Ken Livingstone to encourage him early on to run for Mayor of London on behalf of something like my official principle rather than New Labour – anyway New Labour before its half-decent budget. Not enough money got rid of, but maybe a start.

It seems pretty certain that another start is also to be made. A place where things happened is surely about to be left behind. It seems that the freeholders downstairs, maybe rationally, want to hang onto their small advantage in neighbourly relations. Anyway, they will not be selling half of it. And you can tire of Arcadia. I've had enough of The Studio, haven't I? There was that struggle, too, to stop the chopping-down of the lime trees across the street. Shall we move over the Heath to the agreeable detached villa in Dartmouth Park, with freehold? Shall we decamp further? Ireland certainly comes to mind. *Country Life* has pictures of smashing Georgian houses for sale in County Cork. One of those might suit very nicely.

Is there more for me to tidy up here at the end? Well, as for that early theme about our being person-stages, and maybe not responsible for what was done by our earlier selves, I suspect the truth is simple. If it *were* true that the man I am now had in him nothing relevant of the man I was, I would be off the hook. But it is hard to believe that any of us makes an entire escape from our earlier selves, a clean break.

Here I end, unwilling on this sunny afternoon to think about any remaining matters, restless to get on with the rest of my life. Ingrid and I will be meeting this evening, as we do every evening now. We'll be reading aloud some more of *Narziss and Goldmund*, very likely about playing the joyous secret game of lips and limbs. There is more philosophy to be started, once again, very early tomorrow morning.

INDEX